Sexual underworlds
of the Enlightenment

Sexual underworlds of the Enlightenment

edited by
G.S. ROUSSEAU
and
ROY PORTER

University of North Carolina Press
Chapel Hill

First published in the United States 1988

by The University of North Carolina Press

Library of Congress Cataloging-in-Publication Data

Sexual underworlds of the Enlightenment / edited by G.S. Rousseau and Roy Porter
  p. cm.
Includes index.
Contents: From lascivious erudition to the history of mentalities / Théodore Tarczylo – The discourse on sex, or sex as discourse / Peter Wagner – Modern prostitution and gender in Fanny Hill / Randolph Trumbach – Imagination, pregnant women, and monsters in eighteenth-century England and France / Paul-Gabriel Boucé – The sorrows of Priapus / G.S. Rousseau – The culture of travesty / Terry Castle – Vulnerability and the age of female consent / Antony E. Simpson – A touch of danger / Roy Porter – Passing women / Lynne Friedli – Sex and shamanism in the eighteenth century / Gloria Flaherty.

ISBN 0-8078-1782-1

1. Sex customs—Europe—History—18th century. 2. Prostitution—Europe—History—18th century. 3. Pornography—Europe—History—18th century. I. Rousseau, G. S. (George Sebastian) II. Porter, Roy, 1946–
HQ18.G7S47 1988
306.7'094–dc19   87-27893
                                                                      CIP

Printed in Great Britain
by Billings & Son Ltd, Worcester

Contents

Preface — vii

G.S. Rousseau and Roy Porter Introduction — 1

Part 1 Sex and discourse

1 *Théodore Tarczylo* — 26
From lascivious erudition to the history of mentalities

2 *Peter Wagner* — 46
The discourse on sex – or sex as discourse: eighteenth-century medical and paramedical erotica

3 *Randolph Trumbach* — 69
Modern prostitution and gender in *Fanny Hill*: libertine and domesticated fantasy

4 *Paul-Gabriel Boucé* — 86
Imagination, pregnant women, and monsters, in eighteenth-century England and France

5 *G.S. Rousseau* — 101
The sorrows of Priapus: anticlericalism, homosocial desire, and Richard Payne Knight

Part 2 Sex and society

6 *Terry Castle*   156
The culture of travesty: sexuality and masquerade in eighteenth-century England

7 *Antony E. Simpson*   181
Vulnerability and the age of female consent: legal innovation and its effect on prosecutions for rape in eighteenth-century London

8 *Roy Porter*   206
A touch of danger: the man-midwife as sexual predator

Part 3 Sex at the margins

9 *Lynne Friedli*   234
'Passing women': a study of gender boundaries in the eighteenth century

10 *Gloria Flaherty*   261
Sex and Shamanism in the eighteenth century

Index   281

Preface

This volume originated in discussions between its two editors in the immediate aftermath of its predecessor, *Sexuality in Eighteenth-Century Britain*, edited by P. G. Boucé and published in 1982 by Manchester University Press. Both of us had contributed to Boucé's volume and while we were assessing its niche in 1983 it became evident that much more work remained to be done. Boucé's anthology pioneered the subject and began to ask the right questions, and these in turn provoked further questions. It was this need for ever greater eclecticism, more than any other feature, which concerned us in the conception of the present book and we were disappointed that a scholar as knowledgeable and cosmopolitan as Lawrence Stone would dismiss Boucé's volume as 'almost entirely unhelpful' and as dealing 'mostly in pornographic trivia', apparently because its authors were merely 'scholars of English literature'.[1]

Towards this eclectic goal, we drew up a list of desiderata for the future. Paramount among these items was an elusive but nevertheless defensive attitude among some of Boucé's authors — ourselves included — whose near-prudery had been dictated in part by the amenities of Academia. We believe the time has arrived to shed this attitude of reticence; if its vestiges endured in the polite pockets of our profession, we might be pardoned, we hoped, for daring to ask questions that could not be addressed just a decade earlier.

Furthermore, it soon became clear that Boucé's volume had tapped only a few of the crucial areas for further research; many books, actually a library, was needed for elucidation of the subject. Hence we thought it premature to set about searching for a new model of sexuality in the Enlightenment, let alone announce that we had found one. More reprehensible in our view would be any autocratic imposition of a model, especially a new model, on researchers when so much field-work remained to be accomplished. If such a model were to suggest itself in the couse of research (just as certain feminist scholars of the 1970s discovered a new model of the eighteenth-century woman – literate, educated, intelligent, sensitive, sexually aware and sexually intense, artistic, scientific and making monumental contributions to a culture then still largely patriarchal), this was all to the good. However, the external imposition of a model, whether for the genders or the sexual activities practised by these genders, seemed premature before further research which constituted the very *raison d'être* of our continuing activity. For the simple fact was that not enough research into Enlightenment sexuality – of any variety – had been conducted, and even our (the editors) present plan for a trilogy may be inadequate to obtain the much desired new model.

Finally the temper of the early 1980s. The impact of the late Michel Foucault, whose influence was then at a peak, was widely felt: Volume One of A *History of Sexuality* had appeared in French in 1976, in English translation in 1978–9, and was everywhere being reviewed and assimilated. Volumes Two and Three were promised soon in a six-part history. It was evident that Foucault's series would radically transform the field, as everything he wrote had that eventual effect on so many who pondered the subject afterwards. In this specific area – sexuality during the Enlightenment – his impact was pervasive with a difference, for here no thinker had been original for decades. Female and male historians, even such influential historians as Lawrence Stone in *Family, Sex and Marriage in England, 1500–1800* – a brilliant if controversial book – had of course accumulated vast stockades of facts and constructed interpretations based on these data, but no scholar had transformed the map, or blueprint, as Foucault had and the first volume of his *History* portended magisterial changes to come. As one of us (G. S. Rousseau) had then written in the *Journal of Modern History*: 'It ought not to be overlooked, or forgotten, that Foucault is no longer writing histories of madness but now histories of sexuality. They too will eventually bear fruit'.[2]

Against this backdrop, we began to conceptualise several books that would build on Foucault's map without discarding the older dyad of liberation versus repression. In truth, we were not abashed by this or any other dyadic scheme inasmuch as it had shed much light on gender and sexuality before the advent of Foucault, nor were we embarrassed by the presentation of fresh research that might as yet be lacking a context and ideological framework, as in the case of Enlightenment pornography where the bibliographical record remains to be retrieved and where all too little of this chaotic but vast archive is known. If, in 1982 or thereabouts, the dyad of liberation versus repression was an ideological shackle, it was nevertheless a protective one which continued to stimulate the imagination of researchers. As scholars and future collaborators we agreed on what we did *not* want in subsequent volumes, i.e. an arbitrarily imposed interpretation merely to avoid the old dyads of liberty versus repression, freedom versus enslavement, licence versus tyranny, male versus female, heterosexual versus homosexual, and so forth. Recognising that future volumes would not be exhaustive, we instead sought for an open investigation, an honest exploration, free of the extremes of prudery and prurience, based on data that kept speculation at a minimum (even if a quantum of speculation is always inevitable in matters dealing with the bedroom) and written without prejudice or polemic. We hope that in this Era of Theory information has not sunk into such disrepute that fresh material can only be presented if it displays a *new* conceptual blueprint.

Yet, even if we had wished to, we as editors could not have compelled our authors to rid themselves of assumptions they hold dear: assumptions about the roles and relations of the sexes, about the formation of gender identity and the etiology of sexual roles, about the gender-biases of language and – especially in a book studying 'Sexual Enlightenment' – about beliefs regarding sexual progress or its lack during the last three centuries. We could no more impose on our contributors our own deeply held beliefs about sex than we could artificially compel them to demarcate scientific and non-scientific discourse when no such neat divisions were made in the European Enlightenment.

The best alternative then seemed to be two subsequent volumes planned along these lines: one dealing with sex, discourse and society in Western Europe, and a second dealing with sex – especially the sexually exotic customs and practices – in the Orient. So much work has already been accomplished in the so-called respectable domain of European sex (we think of Iwan Bloch, G. Rattray Taylor, Alex Comfort and Lawrence Stone) that we intend here to emphasise 'sexual underworlds' and we shall focus, in the company of distinguished Orientalists, on images of the Orient and on exotic Oriental sexual practices in the third volume of the trilogy. By 'underworld' we include those underground domains that lie on the margins of respectability and that necessarily overlap with conventional institutions, but we do not construe this category monolithically or claim any exclusivity or particularity for it. Indeed, many of the sexual underworlds we describe here can be turned around, as it were, and shown to be 'overworlds', or conventional zones, of sexual behaviour and thought. We merely hope to open up in this volume discussion about topics that have been understudied relative to the rest of contemporary scholarship: areas such as female and male prostitution, lesbianism and transvestism, the vast world of pornography – its schemers as well as practitioners, the perennial vexing matter of sodomy and homosexuality, and, of course, the life of fantasy about these subjects held by common people and captured in such institutions as carnivals and masquerades. If our authors, like Boucé's contributors in the first volume, collectively remain somewhat defensive about any of these subjects, we implore our readers to ponder how it could have been otherwise, living as we do in an age when these subjects are politically explosive everywhere. Our ultimate aim is frank debate about topics too infrequently discussed; we ask for nothing more.

In these last three years our project has acquired many friends on several continents. We hope that all these associates, whose many acts of kindness we cherish, will understand why we cannot list their many names here, and this book could not have come into being without the continuing support of our editor in Manchester, John Banks, who unrelentingly encouraged us from the day when we first proposed the project to him. G. S. Rousseau is especially grateful to Mrs Leila Brownfield, his research assistant, who has continued to ferret in arcane archives and obscure libraries, and to check quotations and sources when everyone else was persuaded that nothing more remained to be found. We should also like to thank George St Andrews for translating Dr Tarczylo's article from the French.

G. S. Rousseau
University of California
Los Angeles
August 1986

Roy Porter
The Wellcome Institute
for the History of Medicine

Notes
1 *New York Review of Books*, 31 (29, March 1984): pp. 46–8.
2 G. S. Rousseau, *Journal of Modern History*, 55, 1983, p. 530, a review essay dealing with the historiography of madness.

Introduction

G. S. ROUSSEAU
and
ROY PORTER

It is tempting to write the history of sex as if all in darkness lay till God said 'Let Freud be' and all was light. However, a similar temptation obviously lures the eighteenth-century scholar too, for if we slip into the labels and stereotypes so tempting in the history of ideas, we can easily conjure up a vision in which, after the stern asceticism of the age of the Reformation and Counter-Reformation, after the celebration of the triumph of Reason over the passions to be found in the Classical tradition from the early Renaissance onwards, and particularly in seventeenth-century Stoicism, the Age of Enlightenment presents itself as an age of sexual enlightenment as well.

Not least through Linnaeus's highly influential taxonomy, eighteenth-century biology came to recognise the fundamental sexuality of all living beings,[1] and in Erasmus Darwin's evolutionary theories a vision of cosmic organic progress found expression which enshrined sexuality as the fundamental agent of progress, order and happiness in the universe (nature's 'chef d'oeuvre' as Darwin phrased it).[2] New currents of philosophical hedonism, led by Lamettrie, d'Holbach and Diderot,[3] and of utilitarianism, systematised by Jeremy Bentham, gained ground, advancing the view – popularised in novels such as John Cleland's *Memoirs of a Woman of Pleasure* – that sex was a basic mode of human enjoyment,[4] and that whatever forms of sexual expression created more pleasure than pain – be they modes traditionally labelled as vicious, sinful or unnatural – were *ipso facto* desirable and good. Such currents, powerful for example in

Jeremy Bentham,[5] linked up with a new libertarianism about sexual activities. Drawing on discoveries such as the innocent promiscuous sexual conduct of the Tahitians,[6] writers as diverse as Swift and Diderot came to regard the sexual prohibitions of the Europeans as merely arbitrary, imposed upon man in his ignorance by a scheming priesthood.[7]

Such taboos, it was alleged, fundamentally contradicted human nature. Attempts to enforce artificial values such as chastity contrary to human nature would only result (argued Diderot in his *La religieuse*) in the scandals and perversions of the life of the cloister – a favourite hobby-horse of anti-clericals. It is easy to find works of eighteenth-century eroticism and pornography – in real life, albeit imaginatively embroidered, Casanova's *Memoirs* form the classic example – which regard sexual expression as perhaps the supreme instance of an activity which is healthy, happiness-producing and creative of social harmony.[8] And if the ultimate message of the Enlightenment was that of cultivating one's garden – in other words, putting one's theories into practice – all the evidence which biographers and social historians have brought to bear suggests an unusually prominent and public sexual culture, ranging from the most notorious libertines, such as Casanova, to the swarms of prostitutes, brothels, sexual prints and titillating publications that made up the increasingly commercialised culture of the emerging consumer society.[9]

Things are of course – as Tarczylo explores in his essay in this volume – far from being as simple as this epitome might suggest. Nowadays, only members of the Freudian world church believe that Freud achieved a paradigm switch into sexual understanding and emancipation. On the one hand, many have shown how Freud's sexual insights were 'anticipated' by a whole range of nineteenth-century developments and, on the other hand, radicals and sceptics, above all, perhaps, the late Michel Foucault, have put a powerful counter-case, arguing that what masqueraded as sexual liberationism in Freud was actually yet another twist of a repressive sexological screw, another extension of those kinds of intrusive *savoir pouvoir* which co-opt individuals into the policing and standardisation of their lives.[10]

Similarly, a parallel kind of revisionism is obviously highly applicable to the eighteenth century as well, for it would not be difficult to regard it, too, less as an age of erotic pleasure than as a new era of sexual anxiety, its strident liberationists actually proving what Alex Comfort has dubbed 'anxiety makers'.[11] It was during the Enlightenment that the moral scare over the evil consequences of masturbation grew to panic proportions, associated with new fears of personal and national decay arising from the debilitating effects of waste of semen in what Barker-Benfield has called the 'spermatic economy'.[12] It was then, recent historians have argued, that official attitudes towards homoeroticism hardened, turning the occasional sin of buggery into the more terrifying stereotype of the sodomite – after all, even Cleland's attitudes towards homosexuality, as expressed in *Fanny Hill,* are hardly approving.[13] It was also then that the dread figure of the nymphomaniac began to loom large in the proto-psychiatric imagination.[14] If remote Tahiti seemed to show innocent sex among the savages, the moral might well be an anticipation of the Freudian dilemma that sexual happiness and the order of civilised society were utterly incompatible. After all, and partly as a result of a new physiological sexology of the nervous system, sex regarded as a mere physical appetite seemed to chime ill with the strivings towards a more ethereal sensibility during the second half of the eighteenth century.[15] *La nouvelle Héloïse* had as its fashionable message the view that a higher form of love, passion and fulfilment could and should exist than the merely sexual, and in the cult of the 'Jacobin novel' in England, it was the decadent aristocratic debauchees who stood for the principle of sensuality, whereas the new order of nobler bourgeois minds had its eyes on higher things.[16] For all his commitment to happiness and utter anarchic libertarianism, William Godwin looked forward to a world in which sexual desires would just wither away;[17] as people grew more absorbed with matters of the mind and disregarded gross corporeal concerns, they would live ever longer, thus obviating the need for procreation.

Moreover, scholars have been showing the darker, indeed seamier, side of the Enlightenment embracing of sexuality. As Lester Crocker argued many years ago,[18] the more sexual desire was installed as the hub and primum mobile of the 'moral order', the more that order became amoral or immoral. Sexual liberalisation led to libertinism, and libertinism culminated in the despairing, destructive erotic nihilism of the Marquis de Sade, for whom the pursuit of sex was itself eventually unmasked, being revealed as the pursuit of evil.[19] Romantics such as Stendhal long ago argued that the libertinism of a Don Giovanni comprised a Sisyphean wheel of his own creating. Conquest after conquest was at best hopeless, doomed escape from boredom, a compulsion to endless repetition which a modern Freudian would see as neurotic or infantile. And whether or not we agree, there is certainly something painful, pathetic or even appalling about the rods which a typical eighteenth-century philandering *homme moyen sensual* such as James Boswell was forever creating for his own back, hating himself for his inability to resist drunken bouts of low sexual debauchery which would leave him despising himself, in vile odour with his wife, whom he loved dearly, and not infrequently clapped as well.[20]

Above all, perhaps, recent academic feminism has demanded a reconsideration of the vision of the eighteenth century as a kind of erotic golden age.[21] Golden age for whom? they briskly ask: evidently, for men. Insofar as the sexual enlightenment liberated the libido – to use an anachronistic concept that the eighteenth century would have well understood – stressed the health-giving qualities of the spermatic principle, and urged a permissiveness and diversification in sexual partners; didn't this all essentially create an image of sexuality utterly modelled on the norms, the fantasies even, of male sexuality; wasn't it – like the 'all you need is love' permissiveness of the pill generation of the '60s – basically a charter for the emancipation of the male of the species from traditional sexual restraints? Wasn't liberation for men a new way of controlling women?

There is clearly much truth in this insight. And if freedom meant freedom chiefly for men, in many other respects, too, eighteenth-century attitudes towards gender served only to heighten the differentiation of the sexual division of labour and to generate that idealisation, that angelification, of woman which found its apotheosis in the frail, feeble, but blameless Victorian wife. After all, the psycho-physiological underpinnings of (the then crucial) sensibility stressed the mental and physical fragility of women,[22] while the new social glorification of family life and natural motherhood – so powerfully represented, if also resented, in J. J. Rousseau – spelt out domesticity as the true woman's calling and the home as her shrine. Moreover, it is important to stress how such stereotypings of woman as merely private (in contrast to man's public role) and as a product of nature (as distinct from man's role within culture) were not excrescences of the *ancien régime,* against which the paladins of the Enlightenment were committed to do battle, but were to a large degree the *creation* of the Enlightenment and its fellow-travellers from Addison and Steele onwards.

Fiction especially helped spread and support such values. Above all, Richardson was influential in inventing the patterns of female virtue (as victim in *Clarissa Harlowe,* as triumphant heroine in *Pamela*) which would set the standard for the following century. More than that, Richardson helped establish the novel as a seductively feminine art form, thus creating (as it were) a protected, hothouse literary environment for the further production of images of female delicacy.[23] But in real life too, a gender-based division of sexual labour continued to reign supreme, based upon the 'double-standard'. Samuel Johnson argued that sensible wives would turn a blind eye to their husbands' infidelities;[24] after all, no harm was done (the husband did not foist bastards onto his wife). In a similar way, Boswell assumed his right to take sexual liberties. However, when his Dutch sweetheart, Zélide, required the equivalent for herself, he was deeply shocked and denounced her as a 'frantic libertine'.[25] Feminist readings of the emergent fictional tradition of 'virtue in distress' have argued that this brave new world of sexual liberation may have represented almost an all-time *crisis* in women's own sense of the construction and control of their sexuality. Hence it is crucial that we do not conflate images of women as entertained by Enlightenment men with the real experiences of women themselves.

Other groups have also suffered from the so-called 'emancipationism' of eighteenth-century eroticism. Perhaps no better example can be found than that of homosexual men who then, no doubt, became the targets of greater abuse and even stricter legal punishment at this time. Indeed, the stigma-bearing category of the homosexual type began to harden, as Randolph Trumbach and G. S. Rousseau have recently demonstrated, in the public demonological imagination.[26] Anthony Simpson in particular has claimed (in chapter 7, as well as elsewhere) that this was merely a spin-off of a new typing of the heterosexual male.[27] In the competitive market-place world of the eighteenth century, in which all that many young men had to offer was their physical strength, a more 'macho' image of the heterosexual male came to define 'normal' male culture; its obverse was the new stereotyping of the 'abnormal' male.

All this may seem a lengthy preamble to an obvious point: that sexual attitudes and activities during the Enlightenment were no simple matter, unidimensional, all black or white, good or bad. Yet it is a point worth emphasising, not least because popular stereotypes and widely-read books still promote such oversimplifications.[28] Fortunately, however, the last twenty years have seen a remarkable turn-about in scholarly assessments of the eighteenth century. In place of the sedate politenesses of traditional history of ideas and literary history, matched by polished coffee-table books showing off the elegances of Rococo civilisation, the Enlightenment has now become a battleground once more.[29] Witness the intense controversy created by Foucault's interpretations in the history of eighteenth-century ideas and by 'deconstructionist' and other French-inspired readings of Richardson and others in literary history.[30] And notions of Enlightenment as the time when humanity came of age ('the recovery of nerve', as Peter Gay phrased it in his great, generous liberal synthesis born of the age of John F. Kennedy)[31] have been severely challenged from all sides, above all by that interpretation developed by Foucault via Adorno, which is not less suspicious of the claims of reason to serve the purposes of liberation than it is of the powers of sexuality to achieve them.[32]

Recent studies of the Enlightenment in many European states – in Austria, Bavaria, Sweden, Russia and the Italian duchies for example – have argued how far the Enlightenment lay in the service of the *ancien régime*, rather than acting as its chief enemy; radical words may have pre-empted radical action as often as they precipitated it. And, as a challenging survey of the case of eighteenth-century England by J. C. D. Clark amply shows, eighteenth-century political and social historians are fundamentally split as to how far to regard the century as the end of the *ancien régime* or the harbinger of the modern world,[33] and similar problems beset the way we construe the Enlightenment and its sexual outlooks.[34] As we lurch today from the fashionable permissiveness of ten or fifteen years ago into the promised land of the moral majority and feminist sectarianism, our interpretations of sex and sensuality in the age of the Enlightenment are in danger of becoming equally politicised, polarised and polemical.

The sharpening of scholarly debate is no bad thing, so long as what sharpens it is not a clarifying ignorance. But here lies the danger, for the simple fact of the matter is that while certain aspects of the eighteenth century have come fully into the glare of empirical knowledge and informed analysis (for instance, thanks to Ariès, Plumb and others, we now know quite a lot about eighteenth-century childhood and child-rearing theories), so many other areas remain black holes of ignorance and misinformation.[35] When Lawrence Stone came to write his section dealing with individual sexual lives in his monumental *The Family, Sex and Marriage in England 1500–1800*, he found a handful of sexually loquacious males – men such as Boswell and Pepys – about whose sexual escapades and etiquettes it was possible to write with some confidence. But, as Stone recognised, these were, by definition, highly exceptional men – fantasists even – and their stories could tell us little about men in general, and still less about female sexual attitudes and experiences (no full non-fictional female diary recording sexual experiences seems to survive at all). When he came to write about sexual behaviour amongst the lower orders, Stone had to build up an interpretation from hearsay, folklorish evidence, moral condemnations from their superiors, and pure guesswork. The result was not satisfactory (one eminent reviewer said it formed a section of the book which could safely be pulped).[36]

Of course, historiography has become aware of these problems of the recovery of experience, and many leading currents of thought over the last generation have helped rectify these deficiencies, not least the *Annales* school in France with its attempts – through quantification and the investigation of popular culture – to recover the *mentalités* of the past. But this is easier said than done, for the difficulties facing the scholar researching eighteenth-century sexuality exist on several different levels. First, there is the simple problem of ignorance. A few great names have been extensively researched – in real life, the sex lives of men like Boswell have been thoroughly examined (although we know next to nothing about such contemporaries as Akenside, Gray and Gibbon) and, in fiction, the writings of Richardson, Rousseau and Goethe have been subjected to all the latest ways of interrogating texts (though it should be noted that for all the close reading of Richardson's novels, his life remains largely a closed book, not least because two-thirds of his letters remain unpublished).[37] However, what most people – people of *all* social classes – said, thought or did lies inevitably beyond our reach. This is of course true for most sectors of history, yet the problem is greatest with sex because, even then, sex was a delicate matter, hardly fit to be recorded, because of pressures of censorship, both from outside and from the superego within. Read many eighteenth-century diaries and it is possible to know what the diarist had for dinner almost every day of his life, but impossible to tell what he did in bed. It is even easier to know what he dreamed than to speak with confidence about his pelvic thrust. As David Vincent has shrewdly noted, most 'improving' working-class autobiographies proudly set out the author's reading life but not his love life.[38] Some things we will never know, nor can we expect to.

But problems exist on other levels as well. During the eighteenth century, the quantity of advice and information printed on sexual matters increased very considerably, ranging from fairly expensive guides to eroticism such as Nicolas Venette's *Tableau de l'amour conjugal* to cheap publications such as *Aristotle's master-piece*.[39] There must have been some relationship between the contents of these books and the development of popular attitudes and practices, but because we have only the scantiest of documentary evidence recording people's actual responses to reading them (as distinct from bantering comments in plays and the like), it is almost impossible to say how far such literature reflected or actually shaped what people thought and did. For example, *Aristotle's master-piece* told young people that it was good for their sexual general health to marry. What was the deeper significance of this viewpoint?[40] Was this an argument mainly directed against those who would have been content otherwise to copulate with no lawful union? Was it an attempt to overcome the quite common late seventeenth-century feminist objection that 'wedlock' was just a 'lock' to fix otherwise free women within an inferior social role? Was it a further attempt to whip up a moral panic against unnatural acts such as sodomy, or did it actually prove useful ammunition to young people themselves against the stern advice of worldly-wise parents who urged prudence and delay? At this stage at least we can only speculate. Such problems of course should not hinder us from making full studies of history of sexual advice literature, but it will remain a floating enterprise, hardly anchored to real life, unless we can know more about the dynamic dialectics of reading, learning and doing,

The same difficulty applies to fiction and the visual arts. There are, of course, rich and rewarding techniques of literary criticism and art history and criticism, concerned with the interpretation of such works simply as works of art, but the temptation inevitably arises to try to extrapolate from works of the imagination the mind or spirit of the age. This can be done crudely, using snippets from novels or prints from Hogarth as if they were snapshots from the past, accurate views of what the eighteenth-century prostitute looked like or of the mentality of the seducer. It can also be attempted in a rather more sophisticated way, reading the message of such works as *The Harlot's Progress* or *Pamela* as engaging in ideological dialogue with cross-currents and counter-currents of sexual thought, here naturalising a gender stereotype, there challenging a commonplace about the relations between lust and love, sex and sin. Yet both these approaches which hope to look through the mirror of art at life are fraught with grave difficulties.[41]

In respect of visual messages, Ronald Paulson has sounded a timely warning.[42] Both in his interpretations of Hogarth and in his more recent investigation of the psycho-sexual dimension of visual images of the French Revolution, he has stressed the dangers of simplistic one-to-one readings, of seeing art straightforwardly as a mirror of life or as the embodiment of mass ideology or, indeed, as an X-ray of the artist's mind. Art – indeed, the arts in general – has its own language, traditions and conventions, and the anxiety of influence must be held in mind whenever we are tempted to seize upon a Boucher nude or a Hogarthian priapic orgy as snapshot evidence of *wie es eigentlich gewesen war*. Often what we are really seeing is not real life through the artist's documentary eye, but an elaborate, ironical and self-referential play upon art itself, crammed with quotation and visual puns.

The same applies to verbal fiction too. Fiction didn't reflect fact. The world of the eighteenth-century prostitute – as Randolph Trumbach argues in this volume – certainly wasn't that evoked by Cleland's *Fanny Hill*, which was not merely a man's fantasy of the life of a harlot but – more complexly still – a very peculiar fantasy of prostitution as a quasi-domestic, bourgeois institution. But neither can we simply read off ideological messages. It is easy to read such works as *Clarissa Harlowe* or the collected *oeuvres* of de Sade as anti-feminist, yet – as recent interpretations by Terry Eagleton, Angela Carter and others have stressed – such works are open to a variety of readings, both in their authors' intentions and in their wider effects.[43] When approaching Hogarth's sexual prints, his 'Harlot's Progress' and 'Rake's Progress' above all, we are confronted with messages subverted by messages, as Ronald Paulson has taught us to see.

Problems such as these admit of no easy solution. Yet one indispensable requirement for the advancement of our understanding is that we should go about filling in some of the grosser gaps in our knowledge. At present our ready repertoire of eighteenth-century sexuality seems a bit like a Christmas party to which MacHeath, Moll Flanders, Lovelace, Tom Jones, Casanova, James Boswell, some of Boucher's models, Emma Hamilton (née Lyons), the occasional Tahitian and supporting cast have been invited. This must be changed because it is essentially a fantasy, both of historians of some mythic erotic golden age, and of the phobic imagination of a long tradition of moral puritans, from Dr Bowdler at the beginning of the nineteenth century onwards, for whom the need to expose past vice and clean up history was integral to their contemporary moral mission.[44]

In conceiving and executing this book, we have tried to rectify this simplification in two ways in particular. On the one hand, we have very seriously tried to avoid the 'big names', the notorious rakes, the standard texts, the major authors, without worrying that, because we study the second rank or lower, we, the authors, will be adjudged to be second-rank.

When it comes to sexual advice literature, the discussion to be found here will not principally be about *Aristotle's Master-piece, Onania* or the works (widely disseminated in the eighteenth century) of Bienville and Tissot on nymphomania and masturbation respectively. Rather (as Paul-Gabriel Boucé's essay demonstrates), it is rewarding to look slightly more obliquely at gynaecological works and books of childbirth, especially to see how the powers of the mother's sexual imagination continued to be construed throughout the eighteenth century.[45] This proves an important and fresh way of understanding the continuing misogynistic fear of the female imagination, as well as offering the scientific and medical background to ideas about monstrosities and heredity, as they underpin such works as *Tristram Shandy*.[46] The standing of the male imagination, and its powers to produce moral and physical monsters, remains an important issue for further research. Towards the close of the eighteenth century, Erasmus Darwin, in his evolutionary theories, was formulating a medical theory of the role played by a father's imagination in shaping future generations, an idea which may have influenced Mary Shelley's conception of Dr Frankenstein and his monster. But despite recent scholarly work, the full range of notions of the imagination in the eighteenth century is still to be teased out, and there is still a pressing need, as G. S. Rousseau suggested almost twenty years ago, for a scientific and medical study of imagination before, and during, the Enlightenment.[47]

If, in areas such as sexual advice literature, this book aims to probe beneath the surface and avoid the most obvious instances, the same policy is followed in its investigations of the relations between the sexual and the exotic. For too long scholars have taken the Tahitians as the paradigm case of the European discovery of 'primitive' sexual practices during the eighteenth century.[48] However, this amounts to a grave distortion, which Gloria Flaherty sets out to put right in her examination of the wider field of Enlightenment sexual anthropology. Her accounts, for example, of the rites of initiation and of healing performed by shamans amongst the eskimos shows how complicated and puzzling a set of problems exotic sexual practices could present to the European eye: rituals neither obviously primitive nor civilised; ones, in certain respects, barbaric to the Western mind yet highly intelligible in terms of an at least latent grasp of the crucial integrative role of patriarchal sexuality (one feels the leap to *Totem and taboo* was but a short one).[49]

Indeed, we get a very distorted picture of the eighteenth-century 'exotic' if we concentrate unduly on classic texts such as Diderot's

Supplément au Voyage de Bougainville. For one thing, the typical 'exotic' in the eyes of the eighteenth-century European imagination was not the savage Polynesian (noble or ignoble) but a highly civilised being, the 'oriental'. The stigma of orientalism has been explored, of course, by Edward Said and others, but it must be stressed that, for the Enlightenment mind, orientalism was at least as much of a shibboleth as a stigma.[50] If the Chinese were becoming object lessons in the depotism of custom, their aesthetics and eroticism were held in high regard, just as though, as Mozart so well exemplifies, the figure of the Turk was almost synonymous with arbitrary power, being Turkish had far different and (for many) more estimable erotic connotations.[51] Whenever Boswell hoped to legitimate his polygamous leanings, the bashaw with his seraglio seemed as good a model as the Biblical Patriarchs.

So this book deliberately eschews the great names and texts, looking for writings and figures which may prove more representative or (if that is an elusive ideal) will at least offer a different perspective from the familiar books and faces. However, it also tries to explore the sexual 'underworld' – a vast underground when measured by any yardstick – in a further respect, by giving pride of place to kinds and expressions of sexuality other than the standard Heterosexual's Progress of romance, seduction, matrimony, prostitution and adultery. Emblematic of this approach is Terry Castle's contribution on the masquerade, for, as she demonstrates, masquerade was the sexual world-turned-upside-down of the eighteenth century, in which, within the limits of a metropolitan commercial entertainment (this was not a wood just outside Athens with a handy Puck), the rule was that anything heterosexually erotic went, as long as it didn't go by its own proper name. The resultant erotic mix – with men and women *en travestie*, with servants and masters mingling, respectable ladies being permitted indulgences (male indulgences) usually withheld them, with the confusion of the harlot and the harlots' customers, often reversing roles – gives at least some sign that the kinds of explorations of the sexual boundaries pursued, say, in some of Diderot's fantasies or – more by way of double entendre – in *Tristram Shandy* would have had familiar enough real-life resonances for at least a slice of the Enlightenment's fashionable society. The links between masquerade and the ambiguous standing of women thus become clear: society made women go masked and it was only by exchanging regular for radical masks that women could step out of their ordained roles. The implications of ' masking' and 'unmasking' for other sexual groups at this time – not least the homosexual community[52] –

would repay further study, as would also the political implications of the masquerade (how far was there a congruence, suggested above all by the example of Wilkes, between political libertarianism and sexual libertinism?).

The theme of travesty – literally, of course cross-dressing – is followed more specifically by Lynne Friedli. Examining eighteenth-century women who 'passed as men', she shows that such occurrences must be decoded on numerous different levels. There was a simple cross-dressing, as in the by-now-notorous cases of Mary Hamilton (whose career intrigued Henry Fielding, as shown by Terry Castle in chapter 6) and Charlotte Charke, Colley Cibber's daughter. But there was also the question of anatomical aberration: did nature actually produce sexual monsters, equipped with a bizarre mixture of male and female genitals? Here the question of the imagination, so prominent in Boucé's paper, again raises itself, for one eighteenth-century solution to this problem of sexual monstrosity – a problem which seemed to impugn the harmony, order and design of nature – was to assert that no such thing as hermaphroditism existed, or rather it existed, but only in the mind, as the influential works of James Parsons, the Fellow of the Royal Society, suggested.[53] The implication of such a view was that hermaphroditism was not a real aberration of nature, but was a phantom of the human imagination foisted upon nature by some process of psychopathology, perhaps paralleling contemporary analysis of how nymphomania or priapism were not so much truly anatomical or physiological defects, but rather products of the lurid imagination. Here, as elsewhere, the vast mind/body problem, which the legacy of Descartes had bequeathed to Europe and which was to dominate philosophical discussion throughout the whole of the Enlightenment, took specific sexual expression.[54] Slowly, questions of sexuality underwent a long sea-change, from being essentially organic and physiological in their location (as in advice literature such as that by Venette) to becoming part of abnormal psychology.

A crucial dimension of such 'underworlds' – then as today – is inevitably the question of homosexual subcultures. These were highly codified underworlds in the eighteenth century, but they have suffered special 'ghettoisation' amongst modern scholarly communities who, till very recently at least, have been afraid to tackle such contentious subjects head-on.[55] However, this must stop, G. S. Rousseau suggests in his exploration of literary Englishmen travelling abroad in the first half of the century. Yet we must tread carefully too. It was one of the blunders of nineteenth-century sexology to invent the pantechnicon category, the 'homosexual', and no scholarly service is done (as Rousseau has cautioned elsewhere) by simply strait-jacketing the past with such lumbering terminology. Just as from the point of view of 'lesbian' history, Lilian Faderman has insisted that scholars must preserve clear distinctions between different kinds and levels of friendship, emotional involvement and love between women, some involving specific sexual/genital acts and some not,[56] so the same must also apply to studies of what were obviously highly differentiated expressions of male/male emotional or sexual pairing in the past. Friendship, and its spill-over into intellectual and avocational pursuits, remains one crux of the matter, as Rousseau's essay about homosexual desire and Englishmen abroad suggests. The problem here is not merely that friendship in relation to gender remains an impossibly elusive object to grasp, but also that what Rousseau is calling 'homosocial desire' is almost as intangible, if nevertheless palpably felt by those who experience it. This point remains the thrust of his essay about the altogether neglected priest of high neo-classical retrieval, Richard Payne Knight, who has been seen – when he is viewed at all – as a one-dimensional figure by art historians. As such, Rousseau's discussion of travel in relation to desire forms a concrete case-study of the more general problematic developed by such students of sexual desire as Gilles Deleuze and Felix Guattari in *Anti-Oedipus*, Guy Hocquenghem in *Homosexual Desire* and Françoise D'Eaubonne in *Eros Minoritaire*.[57] Categories and labels, emphasis and distinction, practice and discourse, remain at the heart of the riddle and permeate the whole contemporary historiography of the Enlightenment, not merely the one reserved for sex and sexuality. It has been tempting over the last generation for scholars to 'discover' that all seventeenth-century scientists were really magicians or that all the *philosophes* were really freemasons.[58] This will not do, and no purpose will be served either by sectarian scholarship attempting to capture the past for particular modalities of sexuality. Yet, in its various forms, homoeroticism has been, as Hans Mayer's magisterial work has stressed[59] and as G. S. Rousseau has been demonstrating, absolutely central to both mainstream and underground European traditions of the standing of 'culture', e.g. through its affinities with melancholy or the development of the concept of the hero. And its cultural embodiment within Enlightenment sexuality, hitherto much neglected, is underlined in the expansive but exploratory essay by G. S. Rousseau.

But this collection does not explore stereotypes, ideologies and literary subgroups alone. It also attempts to focus attention on some of the aspects of material culture through which sexuality found complex adumbration during the eighteenth century. Erotic-cum-pornographical writings form the key theme of Peter Wagner's essay. The study of pornography has typically been cleft between the genre of popular, voyeuristic history and the work of bibliographical *aficionados*. This means that its general cultural place and significance are both far too little understood. In the present essay, as well as in his large-scale monograph,[60] Wagner attempts to survey the range of pornographic publications available, stressing their diversity, the range they occupy from 'soft' to 'hard', and their rich variety of legitimations and rationalisations. Such studies provide an indispensable basis for helping to solve the fundamental questions about the nature of sexual *mentalité* in the early modern period.[61] How far were traditional popular attitudes towards sex (a kind of collective traditional unconscious) manifested in the tales, rhymes, jokes and prints of popular bawdy and pornography? Or how far, by contrast, did printed pornography represent the dissemination of an obscene 'high culture' of pornography developed in Renaissance Italy and France and largely introduced in England in the reign of Charles II? As yet, we desperately lack adequate scholarly studies of sexuality as implied by the ballad literature, in folklore, in chapbooks and in popular prints – studies of course made peculiarly difficult by the screen of Grundyism through which they have generally been passed down to us. The relation between the 'little tradition' of 'oral eroticism' and the dilution of a 'high tradition' seems a promising field of future study.

What makes the study of sexuality so important, yet so difficult, is its protean quality; its ability to be everywhere and nowhere at the same time – an element emphasised by recent studies of Sterne's deployment of a humour of constant sexual innuendo.[62] To grasp the sexual underworlds of the Enlightenment requires that we should also look where and how sex turned up when it was not particularly expected, or at least not expected to be explicitly present. This is the question underlying Porter's examination of the scandalous history of the new profession of man-midwife. The male obstetrician could easily be represented as a new mode of predator, a kind of licensed rapist, available without guilt to any woman who chose to use his services. But who was it who was turning the man-midwife into a *double entendre* for a seducer? Was it the operator himself? Or his client? Or those crusty moralists who deplored the rise of such a licentious tradition? Crucial to any notion of sexual (or other) underworlds and under-cultures is the question of their relative and selective 'visibility' and 'speakability'. Could the man-midwife, like the friseur or the dancing master, operate without a blush as a kind of licensed adulterer, the English equivalent of the Italian gallant, because – with the roles reversed – the presence of female servants in wealthy households had already licensed similar liberties for men time out of mind? This might be quite suggestive of shifting sexual dynamics during the eighteenth century. Doubtless there were many ways in which trends in eighteenth-century ideology were eroding the independence (sexual and otherwise) of the lady and identifying her more closely with marriage, the home, domesticity and the role of mother. But such may not have been the whole process, and the lady's sexual opportunities and licence may have been more impressive than recent feminist historians – all too ready to impose the role of victim upon women in the past – have credited.

The bottom line for sexuality remains the law. The sexual underworlds of the Enlightenment often enough ended up in court, sometimes even at the scaffold.[63] The law and the noose were not accurate registers of sexual transgression and criminality, but they do provide some kind of index of society's signals of its own boundaries of tolerance and its sense of moral identity. Simpson's essay explores one aspect of sexuality in the eighteenth-century dock, an all-too-often-neglected area. How far did the Georgian lawcourts punish rape? How much can one tell from the explicit and implicit messages which come across from the currents and cross-currents of pleas and excuses, judges' summings-up and royal pardons? Do such conclusions tell one more about the labyrinthine workings of the law itself or about living social attitudes? The issues are difficult. It is clear from the proceedings of trials that undoubted rapists were at least as likely to be exonerated by the law as punished by it. This seems to suggest – as a number of other papers do – that there was some isomorphism between sexual underworlds and overt norms during this period. The male chauvinism of the implicit attitudes of the workplace or the farmyard found their complex vindication before the tribunals of the law of the land. One of the major debates amongst eighteenth-century historians today regards the relationship between 'high' and 'low' cultures, and the increased 'laundering' of common attitudes allegedly being carried out from above during the century.[64] Yet in the matter of the basic inequalities of gender roles and power, there may be little sign of that. Fine studies of nineteenth-century prostitution such as that by Judith Walkowitz,[65] have stressed that the history of sexuality is meaningless unless seen in the context of class structure and class struggle. It is a lesson which historians of the Enlightenment could do well to learn.

A short volume can only plough a few furrows in depth, but can hope to suggest many new directions for the plough. The visual arts remain little discussed in this work (as a result of chance rather than positive decision) and the goal of genuinely cross-cultural and cross-national comparative studies still remains far off. But we believe this volume does break new ground in exploring many of the interstices between the common pillars of scholarship, and suggesting that many of the traditional beacons of orientation for understanding sexuality in the Enlightenment – the great texts and the notorious libertines – may be as misleading as they are prominent. There is no virtue in 'nooks and crannies' history, and that is not what we have attempted, however 'academic' or bookish our approach may be. This book has examined 'underworlds', but it rejects the notion that such underworlds, or undergrounds, were less important or influential than the sexual attitudes and actions more commonly on public display, more easily subject to scholarly study. In so doing, it attempts to place discourse and practice – in the sense that they reflect these attitudes and actions respectively – on equal footings, without privileging the one over the other. By opening up these underworlds, this volume seeks to show that so much more terrain requires to be explored before we can begin to get our real bearings on the history of Enlightenment sexuality.

Notes

1 See Michel Foucault, *Les Mots et les Choses*, Paris, Gallimard, 1966; English translation as *The Order of Things*, London, Tavistock, 1970; James L. Larson, *Reason and Experience. The Representation of Natural Order in the World of Carl von Linné*, Berkeley, Cal., University of California Press, 1971; J. Roger, *Les Sciences de la Vie dans la Pensée française au XVIIIe Siècle*, 2nd ed., Paris, A. Colin, 1971, and F. Delaporte, *Le Second Règne de la Nature*, Paris, Flammarion, 1979. The links between botany and human eroticism are established in Paul-Gabriel Boucé, 'Chthonic and pelagic metaphorization in eighteenth-century English erotica', in R. Maccubbin (ed.), *Unauthorized Sexual Behaviour During the Enlightenment*, special issue of *Eighteenth Century Life*, ix, 1985, pp. 202–16.

2 Erasmus Darwin, *Zoonomia*, 2 vols, 1794–6, i, pp. 146–7. Sex was so important in Erasmus Darwin's theorising because it linked cosmic utilitarianism with a theory of evolutionary descent. See Desmond King-Hele, *The Essential Writings of Erasmus Darwin*, London, MacGibbon and Kee, 1968, Chs. 5 and 6, and idem, *Erasmus Darwin and the Romantic Poets*, New York, St Martin's Press, 1986, pp. 29–36.

3 The links between sexuality and materialism are explored in *Dix-Huitième*

Siecle, No. 12, Paris, 1980, special issue: *Représentations de la Vie Sexuelle*; G. S. Rousseau, 'Nymphomania, Bienville, and the rise of erotic sensibility', in P.-G. Boucé (ed.), *Sexuality in Eighteenth Century Britain*, Manchester, Manchester University Press, 1982, pp. 95–119, and Leo Braudy, 'Fanny Hill and Materialism', *Eighteenth Century Studies*, iv, 1970–1, pp. 21–40.

4 Thus see Erasmus Darwin's opinion that 'animal attraction' is 'the purest source of human felicity; the cordial drop in the otherwise vapid cup of life', *Zoonomia*, 2 vols., London, J. Johnson, 1794–6, i, p. 147, or Boswell, who thought there was 'no higher felicity in Earth enjoyed by man than the participation of genuine reciprocal amorous affection with an amiable woman'. F. Pottle (ed.), *Boswell's London Journal, 1762–1763*, London, Yale University Press, 1950, p. 84. For Cleland, see the helpful introduction by Peter Wagner to the Penguin edition of *Fanny Hill*, Harmondsworth, Penguin, 1985. For the healthiness of seminal release, see N. Robinson, *A New Theory of Physick and Diseases*, London, Rivington, 1725, p. 40.

5 Bentham argued against sexual slavery: 'to be constrained to receive [an unwanted husband's] embraces, is a misery too great to be tolerated even in slavery itself'. Quoted in M. Williford, 'Bentham on the Rights of Women', *Journal of the History of Ideas*, xxxvi, 1975, pp. 167–76 and p. 171.

6 For 'anthropology', relativism and their sexual implications, see Bernard W. Smith, *European Vision and the South Pacific* (2nd ed.), New Haven, Yale University Press, 1985; G. S. Rousseau, 'Threshold and Explanation: The social anthropologist and the critic of eighteenth century literature', *The Eighteenth Century: Theory and Interpretation*, XXII, 1981, pp. 127–52, and M. Duchet, *Anthropologie et Histoire au Siècle des Lumières*, Paris, Maspero, 1971.

7 D. Diderot, *Supplément au Voyage de Bougainville*, ed. G. Chinard, Paris, 1935. For discussion see L. G. Crocker, *The Embattled Philosopher*, revised edition, New York, The Free Press, 1966; A. Wilson, *Diderot. The Testing Years*, New York, Oxford University Press, 1957, and A. Vartanian, *Diderot and Descartes. A Study of Scientific Naturalism in the Enlightenment*, Princeton, University Press, 1953. For Swift, see his comment abut homosexuality in Book Four of *Gulliver's Travels* ('A Voyage to the Houyhnhnms', ch. 7): 'I expected at every moment that my master would accuse the yahoos of those unnatural appetites in both sexes, so common among us. But Nature, it seems, hath not been so expert a schoolmistress; and these politer pleasures are entirely the productions of art and reason on our side of the globe'.

8 For Casanova, see A. Machen (trans.), *The Memoirs of Jacques Casanova de Seingalt*, 8 vols., New York, G. P. Putnam's Sons, 1894; and J. R. Childs, *Casanova*, London, 1961. Helpful studies of the values implicit and explicit in Enlightenment erotica include John Valdimir Price, 'Patterns of sexual behaviour in some eighteenth century novels', in Boucé (ed.), *op. cit.* (note 3), pp. 159–75.

9 The relations between eroticism and an emergent consumer and print society are fully documented in Peter Wagner, *Eros Revived*, London, 1987. An older, pioneering study is Iwan Bloch, *A History of English Sexual Morals*, trans. by W. H. Fostern, London, Francis Aldon, 1938. For a general approach to 'commercialisation' and modernisation, see N. MacKendrick, J. Brewer and J.

H. Plumb, *The Birth of a Consumer Society*, London, Europa, 1982. For a highly theoretical overview, see Herbert Marcuse, *Eros and Civilization*, London, Routledge and Kegan Paul, 1956.
10 M. Foucault, *The History of Sexuality*, Vol. 1. *Introduction*, London, Allen Lane, 1978.
11 Alex Comfort, *The Anxiety Makers*, London, Nelson, 1967.
12 The phrase is used by F. J. Barker-Benfield, *The Horrors of the Half-Known Life*, New York, 1976; see also E. H. Hare, 'Masturbatory Insanity: the history of an idea', *Journal of Mental Science*, Vol. 108, 1962, pp. 1–25; P.-G. Boucé, 'Aspects of sexual tolerance and intolerance in eighteenth century England', *British Journal for Eighteenth Century Studies*, Vol. 3, 1980, pp. 173–89; Peter Wagner, 'The veil of science and mortality: some pornographic aspects of the ONANIA', *The British Journal for Eighteenth Century Studies*, iv, 1983, pp. 179–84; J. Stengers and A. Van Neck, *Histoire d'une grande peur: la masturbation*, Brussels, Université de Bruxelles, 1984; M. Tissot, *Onanism or a Treatise upon the Disorders produced by Masturbation*, tr. A. Hume, London, for the translator, 1766; *Onania, or the heinous sin of self pollution*, London, P. Varenne, c. 1710. See also P.-G. Boucé, 'Les jeux interdits de l'imaginaire: Onanisme et cupabilisations sexuelles en XVIIIe siècle', in J. Céard (ed.), *La Folie et le Corps*, Paris, 1985, pp. 223–43.
13 A. Bray, *Homosexuality in Renaissance England*, London, 1982. Randolph Trumbach, 'London's sodomites: homosexual behaviour and western culture in the eighteenth century', *Journal of Social History*, XI, 1977, pp. 1–33; 'Sodomitical subcultures, sodomitical roles, and the gender revolution of the eighteenth century: the recent historiography', *Eighteenth-Century Life*, IX, 1985, pp. 109–21, and 'Sodomitical assaults, gender identity and individual development in eighteenth-century London', *The Pursuit of Sodomy in Early Modern Europe*, ed. Kent Gerard and Gert Hekma, New York, 1987. See also the following articles published in R. Maccubbin (ed.), *Unauthorized Sexual Behaviour During the Enlightenment*, a special issue of *Eighteenth Century Life*, ix, 1985; Michel Delon, translated by Nelly Stephane, 'The Priest, the philosopher, and homosexuality in Enlightenment France', *ibid.*, pp. 122–3; Arend H. Huussen, Jr., 'Sodomy in the Dutch Republic during the eighteenth century', *ibid.*, pp. 169–78; Michael Rey, translated by Robert A. Day and Robert Welch, 'Parisian homosexuals create a lifestyle, 1700–1750: the police archives', *ibid.*, pp. 179–91; G. S. Rousseau, 'The pursuit of homosexuality in the eighteenth century: "utterly confused category" and/or rich repository?', *ibid.*, pp. 132–68.
14 See G. S. Rousseau, *op. cit.* (Note 3) and M. Foucault, *op. cit.* (Note 10).
15 G. S. Rousseau, 'Nerves, spirits and fibres: towards defining the origins of sensibility – with a postscript 1976', *The Blue Guitar*, Rome, 1976, ii, pp. 125–53, and J. Hagstrum, *Sex and sensibility: erotic ideal and erotic love from Milton to Mozart*, London, University of Chicago Press, 1980.
16 See Gary Kelly, *The English Jacobin Novel 1780–1805*, Oxford, Clarendon Press, 1976.
17 For Godwin, see *Enquiry Concerning Political Justice*, London, 1793, ii, p. 511; Don Locke, *A Fantasy of Reason: The Life and Thoughts of*

William Godwin, London, Routledge and Kegan Paul, 1980, esp. pp. 108–9 and 159–60. More generally on these tendencies of the English Enlightenment, see Roy Porter, 'Mixed feelings; the Enlightenment and sexuality in eighteenth century Britain', in Boucé (ed.), *op. cit.* (Note 3), pp. 1–27.

18 L. Crocker, *An Age of Crisis. Man and World in Eighteenth Century French Thought*, Baltimore, The Johns Hopkins University Press, 1959.

19 Marquis de Sade, *Oeuvres Complètes*, 15 vols., Paris, Cercle du Livre Précieux, 1963–4. See also R. Barthes, *Sade, Fourier, Loyola*, Paris, Seuil, 1971.

20 W. B. Ober, *Boswell's Clap and other Essays*, Carbondale, Ill., Southern Illinois University Press, 1979, and Lawrence Stone, *The Family, Sex and Marriage in England 1500–1800*, London, Weidenfeld and Nicolson, 1976, esp. pp. 572–93.

21 For the development of feminist points of view, see the important anthology ed. by Elaine Showalter, *The New Feminist Criticism*, London, Virago, 1986. For some of its philosophical roots, see Elaine Marks and Isabelle de Courtivron (eds.), *New French Feminism*, Brighton, Harvester, 1981. For more detailed accounts, see Ruth Perry, *Women, Letters and the Novel*, New York, AMS Studies in the 18th century, No. 4, 1980. For eighteenth-century representations of women, see P. Hoffman, *La Femme dans la Pensée de Lumières*, Paris, 1977, and the major revisionist article, Sylvana Tomaselli, 'The Enlightenment debate on women', *History Workshop*, xx, 1985, pp. 101–24.

22 Rousseau, *op. cit.* (Note 3); idem, *op. cit.* (Note 15); see Carroll Smith-Rosenberg and Charles Rosenberg, 'The Female Animal; Medical and Biological Views of Woman and Her Role in Nineteenth-Century America', in J. W. Leavitt (ed.), *Women and Health in America*, Madison, 1984, pp. 12–27; N. F. Cott, 'Passionlessness: an interpretation of Victorian sexual ideology, 1790–1850' in *ibid.*, pp. 57–69; C. N. Degler, 'What ought to be and what was; women's sexuality in the nineteenth century', in *ibid.*, pp. 40–56; Elaine Showalter, *The Female Malady*, New York, 1986, and G. Rattray Taylor, *The Angel Makers*, London, Heinemann, 1958.

23 See for example Rita Goldberg, *Sex and Enlightenment: Women in Richardson and Diderot*, Cambridge, Cambridge University Press, 1984; Terry Castle, *Clarissa's Ciphers*, Ithaca and London, Cornell University Press, 1982; Terry Eagleton, *The Rape of Clarissa*, Oxford, Basil Blackwell, 1982, and Nina Auerbach, *Romantic imprisonment: women and other glorified outcasts*, New York, Columbia University Press, 1985.

24 G. B. Hill (ed.), *Boswell's Life of Johnson*, 6 vols. Oxford, The Clarendon Press, 1950, vol. 5, p. 209. On this 'double standard', see K. V. Thomas, 'The double standard', *Journal of the History of Ideas*, xx, 1959, pp. 195–216, and Roy Porter, 'Libertinism and promiscuity' in Jonathan Miller (ed.), *Don Giovanni*, London, Faber, 1987.

25 F. A. Pottle (ed.), *Boswell in Holland*, London, Heinemann, 1952.

26 Rousseau, *op. cit.* (Note 13), and Trumbach, *op. cit.* (Note 13).

27 A. Simpson, *Masculinity and Control: the prosecution of sex offences in eighteenth century London*, Ph.D. thesis, New York University, 1984.

28 For example, in his admirable *The Enlightenment, An Interpretation*, Vol. 2, *The*

Science of Freedom, London, Weidenfeld and Nicolson, 1969, Peter Gay offers a wholly optimistic picture of Enlightenment views on sex, arguing 'the philosophes' 'rescue' of sexuality was, if anything, more daring than their rescue of pride' (p. 194). The period appears all rollicking bawdry in such popularising works as A. Lloyd, *The Wickedest Age*, Newton Abbot, David and Charles, 1971.

29 Seminal in such revisions were Betty Behrens' review of Gay's *Enlightenment*, *Historical Journal*, XI, 1968, pp. 190–5; Franklin Ford, 'The Enlightenment: towards a useful redefinition' in R. F. Brissenden (ed.), *Studies in the Eighteenth Century*, Canberra, 1968, pp. 17–29; George Boas, 'In search of the Age of Reason' in E. R. Wasserman (ed.), *Aspects of the Eighteenth Century*, Baltimore, 1965, pp. 1–19, and R. Darnton, 'In search of the Enlightenment: recent attempts to create a social history of ideas', *Journal of Modern History*, XVIII, 1971, pp. 113–32.

30 For the eighteenth century as an age in which Reason lined up with Absolutism to impose a mental prison of conformity, see M. Foucault, *Folie et Déraison. Histoire de la Folie à l'Age Classique*, Paris, Plon, 1961, translated as *Madness and Civilization: a History of Insanity in the Age of Reason*, London, 1967. Underlying such readings is M. Horkheimer and T. Adorno, *The Dialectic of Enlightenment*, trans. J. Cumming, London, Allen Lane, 1973. For literary 'deconstructionism' towards the Enlightenment, see, for example, Terry Eagleton, *The Function of Criticism*, London, Verso, 1984, Ch. 1.

31 See Peter Gay, *The Enlightenment. An Interpretation*, Vol. 1, *Rise of Modern Paganism*, London, Weidenfeld and Nicolson, 1967, and Vol. 2, *The Science of Freedom*, London, Weidenfeld and Nicolson, 1969.

32 See Adorno, *op. cit.* (Note 30); Foucault, *op. cit.* (Note 14) and, above all, T. Tarczylo, *Sexe et Liberté au Siècle des Lumières*, Paris, Presses de la Renaissance, 1983.

33 J. C. D. Clark, *English Society 1688–1832*, Cambridge, Cambridge University Press, 1985, and its sequel, *Revolution and Rebellion*, Cambridge, Cambridge University Press, 1986.

34 For attempts to 'place' the Enlightenment, see A. N. Wilson, 'The philosophes in the light of the present-day theories of modernization', *Studies on Voltaire and the Eighteenth Century*, LVIII, 1967, 1893–1913, and H. B. Applewhite and D. G. Levy, 'The Concept of Modernization and the French Enlightenment', *Studies on Voltaire and the Eighteenth Century*, LXXXIV, 1971, pp. 53–96. Several of the articles in Roy Porter and Mikuláš Teich, *The Enlightenment in National Context*, Cambridge, Cambridge University Press, 1981, are relevant.

35 See, for example, Alan Bold (ed.), *The Sexual Dimension in Literature*, London, Vision Press, 1982, and R. Maccubbin (ed.), *Unauthorized Sexual Behaviour During the Enlightenment* (Note 13).

36 Lawrence Stone, *The Family, Sex and Marriage in England 1500–1800*, London, Weidenfeld and Nicolson, 1976. Stone's stimulating work has been widely criticised. For a recent example, see Alan Macfarlane, *Marriage and Love in England 1300–1840*, Oxford, Basil Blackwell, 1985.

37 For insights into plebeian sexuality, see John R. Gillis, 'Married but not

churched: plebeian sexual relations and marital nonconformity in eighteenth century Britain' in R. Maccubbin (ed.), *Unauthorized Sexual Behaviour During the Enlightenment* (Note 13).
38 David Vincent, 'Love and death and the nineteenth century working class', *Social History*, 5, 1980: pp. 223–47.
39 [Anon.] *Aristotle's Master-Piece*, London, How, 1960. There were scores of subsequent editions. N. Venette, *Le Tableau de l'Amour Conjugal*, Amsterdam, 1696, translated as N. De Venette, *The Mysteries of Conjugal Love Reveal'd*, English translation, 3rd edition, London, 1712; this work remained in print almost to the present day. For discussion, see D'Arcy Power, *The Foundations of Medical History*, Baltimore, Maryland, 1931, Lecture VI, 'Aristotle's Masterpiece'; J. Blackman, 'Popular theories of generation; the evolution of *Aristotle's Works*, The study of an anachronism', in J. Woodward and D. Richards (eds.), *Health Care and Popular Medicine in Nineteenth Century England*, London, Croom Helm, 1977, pp. 56–88; O. T. Beall, Jr., 'Aristotle's Masterpiece in America: a landmark in the folklore of medicine', *William and Mary Quarterly*, 3rd Ser., Vol. 20, 1963, pp. 207–22; Roy Porter, '"The Secrets of Generation Display'd": *Aristotle's Master-piece* in Eighteenth Century England', in R. Maccubbin (ed.), *Unauthorized Sexual Behavior During the Enlightenment*, special issue of *Eighteenth Century Life*, ix, 1985, pp. 1–21; J. Torlais, 'Un médecin rochelais au XVIIe siècle, précurseur de l'Eugenisme: Nicholas Venette', *Journal de Médecine de Bordeaux*, Nos. 47–8, 1940, pp. 610–23; Dr J. Torlais, *Medecine du Passé en Aunis et Saintonge*, La Rochelle, 1931, pp. 51–72; the admirable recent contribution by André Pecker, 'Nicholas Venette (1633–1698); Est-il le fils de Guy Patin?', *Bulletin des Sciences Médicales*, Vol. xvi, 1983, pp. 167–74, and Roy Porter, 'Spreading carnal knowledge or selling dirt cheap? Nicolas Venette's *Tableau De L'Amour Conjugal* in eighteenth-century England', *Journal of European Studies*, xiv, 1984, pp. 233-55.
40 See *Aristotle's Master-Piece*, 1690 ed., Ch. 6, 'Of the benefit of marriage to both sexes'.
41 For studies of sexuality and the visual arts sensitive to these problems, see N. Bryson, *Word and Image*, Cambridge, Cambridge University Press, 1981; P. Webb, *The Erotic Arts*, London, Secker and Warburg, 1975, esp. Ch. 4 (b); D. Posner, *Watteau's Lady at Her Toilet*, London, Allen Lane, 1973; B. Gip, *The Passions and Lechery of Catherine the Great*, Geneva, Nagel, and London, Skilton, 1971. For assessment of erotic aesthetics, see N. Bryson, *Vision and Painting*, London, Macmillan, 1983, Ch. 6, and *Word and Image*, Chs. 6 and 7. For discussion of these trends, see G. S. Rousseau, 'Traditional and heuristic categories: a criticism of contemporary art history', *Studies in Burke and his Time*, xv, 1973, pp. 51–96.
42 R. Paulson, *Book and Painting*, Knoxville, University of Tennessee Press, 1982, and idem, *Representations of Revolution (1789–1820)*, New Haven, Yale University Press, 1983.
43 Eagleton, *op. cit.* (Note 23), and Angela Carter, *The Sadeian Woman*, London, Virago, 1979.
44 Dr. Thomas Bowdler (ed.), *The Family Shakespeare*, London, 1807; P. Fryer,

Mrs. Grundy. *Studies in English Prudery*, London, Dennis Dobson, 1963; E. Trudgill, *Madonnas and Magdalens* (London, 1966), and N. Perrin, *Dr. Bowdler's Legacy – A History of Expurgated Books in England and America*, London, Macmillan, 1970.

45 G. S. Rousseau, 'Smollett's Wit and the Traditions of Learning in Medicine', in *Tobias Smollett. Essays of Two Decades*, Edinburgh, T. & T. Clark, 1982, pp. 160–83. See also J. A. Blondel, *The strength of imagination in pregnant women examined; and the opinion that marks and deformities arise from thence demonstrated to be a vulgar error*, London, J. Peele, 1727; a book that spurred debate for decades and gave rise to fierce controversy.

46 See Louis A. Landa, 'Shandean Homunculus: The background of Sterne's "Little Gentleman"', in Carroll Camden (ed.), *Restoration and Eighteenth Century Literature*, Chicago, University of Chicago Press, 1963, pp. 49–68, and V. Grosvenor-Myer, 'Tristram and the animal spirits', in *idem* (ed.), *Laurence Sterne. Riddles and Mysteries*, London, Vision, 1984, pp. 99–114.

47 See G. S. Rousseau, 'Science and the discovery of the imagination in Enlightenment England', *Eighteenth Century Studies*, iii, 1969, pp. 108–35. Rousseau's caveat was developed in his 'Psychology', in G. S. Rousseau and Roy Porter (eds.), *The Ferment of Knowledge*, Cambridge, Cambridge University Press, 1980. For the literary and philosophical dimensions, see J. Engell, *The Creative Imagination*, Cambridge, Mass., Harvard University Press, 1981; E. L. Tuveson, *The imagination as a means of grace*, Berkeley, University of California Press, 1960. The scientific, intellectual and ideological histories of the imagination remain desperately in need of further study.

48 See Note 6.

49 For patriarchal sexuality, see Eva Figes, *Patriarchal Attitudes*, London, Faber, 1970. There is a historical assessment of feminist use of ideas of patriarchy in Roy Porter, 'Rape – Does it have a historical meaning?', in Sylvana Tomaselli and Roy Porter (eds.), *Rape*, Oxford, Basil Blackwell, 1986, pp. 216–36.

50 E. Said, *Orientalism*, London, Routledge and Kegan Paul, 1978. A good overall survey of changing attitudes to exotic civilisations is P. Marshall and G. Williams, *The Great Map of Mankind*, Cambridge, Harvard University Press, 1982, See also Basil Guy, *The French Image of China*, Geneva, Institut et Musée Voltaire, 1963, *Studies on Voltaire*, 21.

51 'I am too changeable where women are concerned,' confessed Boswell, allured by 'Asiatic ideas', 'I ought to be a Turk'. F. A. Pottle (ed.), *Boswell's London Journal*, London, Heinemann, 1950, pp. 164 and 54.

52 See Note 13 above.

53 James Parsons, *A Mechanical and Critical Enquiry into the Nature of Hermaphrodites*, London, J. Walthoe, 1741. A physician and antiquary, Parsons (1705–70) specialised in the physiology of the muscles. For background on Parsons and hermaphrodites, see G. S. Rousseau (Note 45), p. 172, especially the discussion there of the physiology of hermaphroditism.

54 On the Cartesian legacy to the eighteenth century, see (within a vast literature) A. Vartanian, *op. cit.* (Note 7); J. Yolton, *Perpetual Acquaintance from Descartes to Reid*, Oxford, Basil Blackwell, 1984; A. O. Rorty (ed.), *Essays on Descartes' Meditations*, Berkeley and Los Angeles, University of

California Press, 1986; T. Brown, 'Descartes, dualism and psycho-somatic medicine', in W. F. Bynum, Roy Porter and Michael Shepherd (eds.), *The Anatomy of Madness*, 2 vols., London, Tavistock, 1985, ii, pp. 40–62; R. B. Carter, *Descartes' medical philosophy*, Baltimore, The Johns Hopkins University Press, 1983; L. J. Rather, *Mind and Body in Eighteenth Century Medicine*, London, Wellcome Institute for the History of Medicine, 1965; G. S. Rousseau (ed.), *Mind and Body in the European Enlightenment: The Clark Library Series for 1985–86*, Berkeley and Los Angeles, forthcoming.
55 There is a useful discussion of modern attitudes towards homosexuality in Jeffrey Weeks, *Sex, Politics and Society*, London, Longman, 1981, and Dennis Altman, *The Homosexualization of America*, Boston, Beacon, 1982.
56 Lillian Faderman, *Surpassing the Love of Men*, New York, Morrow, 1981.
57 See Gilles Deleuze and F. Guattari, *Anti-Oedipus: Capitalism and Schizophrenia*, with a preface by Michel Foucault, Minneapolis, University of Minnesota, 1983; Guy Hocquenghem, *Homosexual Desire*, trans. D. Dangoor, London, Allison and Busby, 1978, and F. D'Eaubonne, *Eros Minoritaire*, Paris, André Balland, 1970.
58 I. Couliano, *Eros et Magie dans la Renaissance*, Paris, 1984. For a sober assessment of occultism in early modern science, see Robert S. Westman, 'Magical reform and astronomical reform: the Yates thesis reconsidered' in *Hermeticism and the Scientific Revolution*, Los Angeles, University of California Press, 1977. For Freemasonry, see M. C. Jacob, *The Radical Enlightenment* London, George Allen and Unwin, 1981.
59 H. Mayer, *Outsiders. A Study in Life and Letters*, Cambridge, Mass., The MIT Press, 1982.
60 Peter Wagner, *Eros Revived: Erotica of the Enlightenment in England and America*, London, Secker and Warburg, 1987.
61 For illuminations of the 'low' tradition, see Margaret Spufford, *Small Books and Pleasant Histories*, London, Methuen, 1981. See also Gillis, *op. cit.* (Note 37).
62 M. New, 'At the backside of the door of purgatory', in V. Grosvenor-Myer (ed.), *Laurence Sterne. Riddles and Mysteries*, London, Vision, 1984, pp. 15–23; J. Berthoud, 'Shandeism and sexuality', in *ibid.*, pp. 24–38; E. A. Bloom and L. D. Bloom, '"This fragment of life": from process to mortality', in *ibid.*, pp. 84–98; and D. Furst, 'Sterne and physick: images of health and disease in *Tristram Shandy*', Ph.D. Thesis, Columbia University, 1974.
63 Bawds and prostitutes were frequently sentenced to whippings. The few rapists who were actually tried and found guilty were not uncommonly hanged, though that fate was more frequently reserved for male homosexuals. See John Forrester, 'Rape, seduction and psychoanalysis', and Roy Porter, 'Rape – does it have a historical meaning?', both in Sylvana Tomaselli and Roy Porter (eds.), *Rape*, Oxford, Basil Blackwell, 1986, pp. 57–83, 216–36.
64 R. Malcolmson, *Popular Recreations in English Society 1700–1850*, Cambridge, Cambridge University Press, 1975; P. Burke, *Popular Culture in Early Modern Europe*, London, Temple Smith, 1978, and J. M. Golby and A. W. Purdue, *The Civilization of the Crowd. Popular Culture in England 1750-1900*, London, Batsford, 1984.
65 J. R. Walkowitz, *Prostitution and Victorian Society*, Cambridge, Cambridge

University Press, 1980; P. McHugh, *Prostitution and Victorian Social Reform*, London, Croom Helm, 1980, and Alain Corbin, *Les Filles des Noces*, Paris, Aubier Montaigne, 1978. For eighteenth-century images, see *Satan's Harvest Home, or the Present State of Whorecraft* [etc], London, 1749; Saunders Welch, *A Proposal to render effectual a plan to remove the nuisance of Common Prostitutes*, London, 1758; R. Dingley, *Proposals for Establishing a Place of Reception for Penitent Prostitutes*, London, 1758; Vern L. Bullough, 'Prostitution and reform in eighteenth-century England', in R. Maccubbin (ed.), *Unauthorized Sexual Behaviour During the Enlightenment* (Note 13), pp. 61–74; Stanley D. Nash, 'Social attitudes towards Prostitution in London from 1752 to 1829', Ph.D. thesis, New York University, 1980, and 'Prostitution and charity: the Magdalen Hospital, a case study', *Journal of Social History*, XVI, 1984, pp. 617–28.

Part 1
Sex and discourse

1

From lascivious erudition to the history of mentalities

THÉODORE TARCZYLO
(*Translated by George St Andrews*)

'Love is more difficult to explain than hunger...(Diderot, *Elements of Physiology*)

In France, and even beyond, the conventional image of the French eighteenth century is still, for a great number of people, that of a fierce struggle against all the obscurantisms and all the oppressions, ending in the apotheosis of 14 July 1789. Rousseau and Voltaire always, Montesquieu sometimes, and Diderot increasingly, figure as the heroes of this epoch, whose framework was solidly tied together under the Third Republic, henceforth constituting what, by a happy expression, has been called 'the memory of the Republic'. This memory is periodically kept up with a flourish of official commemorations.[1]

In parallel, but more discreetly, at times almost in secret, the equally prestigious image has been put forward of a singular liberty of manners and of an art given over to eroticism (I use the term in its widest sense). The first to furnish us with this image were, as one might expect, the painters and engravers. Through multiple reproduction, all the nuances of sentiment and of the flesh are laid bare, from the delicacies of a Watteau to the perverse mawkishness of a Greuze, not forgetting the slightly provocative nudes of a Boucher and a Fragonard.

The writers are not outdone, and the literature of the century offers an extensive palette from the pastels of Marivaux and the subtle tonalities of Crébillon *fils* to the purer colours of Nerciat and the violent ones, dark as

FROM LASCIVIOUS ERUDITION TO THE HISTORY OF MENTALITIES

a 'black sun', of the Marquis de Sade. Some personalities seem to have come straight out of a novel – indeed have left us the novel of their life: a Casanova, a Prince de Ligne, a Duc de Richelieu, whom one knows (at least the first of them) without even having read them, and of whom one forgets that they are not even necessarily French – these round off the familiar gallery of one of the most tender of ages.

Then comes the 'new history'. It pulls down the picture rails, tears up and tramples on the canvases, and hangs the walls with an immense funeral veil, in the name of austere Truth. The 'royal buttock', as this iconoclast spitefully calls it, is a piece of trickery, a lying mythology which hides from us the lived reality of the century of so-called 'Enlightenment' – the clerical and bourgeois repression of sexuality, a repression which was general since it went beyond an aristocratic élite to touch the greatest number, that is, the people.[2] A simple episode, in fact, of a generalised repression extending to all forms of deviance, and primarily those of poverty (vagabondage, madness, etc.), since it concerns all social relations (table manners, speech, modesty, etc.).[3]

On the methodological level, this reaction appears justified. What I shall call 'lascivious erudition' is reproached with having recourse to artistic and literary sources where reality is already filtered and deformed by aesthetic and ideological conventions. As for the documents which purport to provide a more direct witness, intimate journals and memoirs, one knows how much they can be prone to the weaknesses of subjectivity. To consider only the most favourable of these cases, the favourite evidence of 'lascivious erudition' still sins against the demands of truth – by omission. The image of the practices that it claims to reconstitute concerns only an élite, leaving the rest of the population (eighty per cent!) in the oubliettes of history. Although limited, this would still be a history, but, given the nature of the evidence, there is every reason to fear that it would be only the representation which an élite has chosen to give of its own practices. Thus 'lascivious erudition' would be only one literary genre among others . . . more pernicious, however, in that it lays claim to scientific objectivity.[4]

There is no such thing as innocent history. Behind its pretensions to science, because of its very methodological weaknesses, 'lascivious erudition' would conceal other weaknesses, unavowed because unavowable. Its complacency in serving the delights of a defunct élite would betray its own class nature. It would merely be the pleasant pastime of an élite – bourgeois in this instance – accommodating itself to the sacrifices imposed on the people. Not a science, or so little so, 'lascivious erudition' would not even be a real pleasure. Under the alibi of art, an unassuaged desire would be concealed, which the bourgeoisie, not content with denying it to others, would deny to itself; would not even dare to admit to itself. In sum, 'lascivious erudition' would be the worthy daughter of that Third Republic in which freedom was only for notables. Under a form more odious for being hypocritical, the repression of the workers and that of bodies are linked, avatars of the centuries-long Judaeo-Christian repression of desire and the immemorial domination of the master over the slave. We get the history we deserve.

The new history, calling both on Marx and Freud, claims, then, to contribute towards the true liberation of bodies.[5] It attempts in the domain of sexuality the same operation with which it was so successful in the political order, drawing on the role of the masses in the French Revolution. Its objective, therefore, will be to recover, through the thickness of a double lie – that of 'lascivious erudition' and of the fashionable gallantry of the Enlightenment – the practices and the representations of the majority. One could not reproach it with the cynicism of the one or still less with the hypocrisy of the other. The new history has, for its part, generosity of intention and transparency of enterprise. It displays its values. That is why it can equip itself with the means of true science – in any case, with a more effective knowledge: henceforth, statistical rigour, the neutrality of figures, the distance and the coldness of the scientific gaze replace anecdotal impression and disturbing description: in a word, voyeurism.[6] One will not contest the reality of the evidence obtained thus. Techniques, as the critique of 'lascivious erudition' amply demonstrates, are of the same worth (if applied correctly) as the principles they serve. One will, then, wonder about the significance of this recourse to statistics for the history of sexual practices in the eighteenth century.

'Lascivious erudition' claimed to find in the erotic splendours of the ancien régime a freedom unknown to contemporaries. Guillaume Apollinaire will serve as spokesman for the whole tradition: '. . .physical love appeared everywhere . . . It was not, as today, a statue of a little, naked and sick god . . .'[7] The historian (we refer here only to the Marxo-Freudian) finds in the past that repression lived each day in the present. This is a truth so well anchored – at least in France – that the debate is often limited to determining the degree of intensity of this repression, to condemning it or praising its virtues.[8] It is, however, its reality that is in question. If the freedom proclaimed by 'lascivious erudition' has been denounced by the historian as the mere mask of real suffering, this is necessarily with reference to a truer conception of freedom which, beyond value judgments, cannot be denied. This fixed point for the historian, rarely made explicit, is the notion of need, an irrefutable and measurable biological reality. One can certainly calculate, for example, the calorific needs of an organism, but the biologist cannot claim to dictate to society the limits, and especially not the form, of its diet. Marx, in any case, did not forget the cultural dimensions of need: 'It is a matter of absolute indifference whether or not some product, for example tobacco, is or is not a means of consumption dispensable from the physiological point of view; it is enough for us that habit should have rendered it indispensable'.[9] As for Freud, he, it seems, never quantified the notion of need, leaving to pathology the task of revealing dissatisfaction. Who indeed will say with what quantity and in what ways sex can be satisfied? The demographer? The biologist? The psychologist? . . . they talk about something else. In seeking in these terms the degree of sexual freedom of past generations, the historian indeed runs the risk of only finding himself.

The sociologist has at his disposal first-hand evidence, since he can have recourse to a survey. The famous report of Dr Kinsey in the USA, the *Sorensen Report* on adolescent sexuality, or again that of Dr Simon on *The Sexual Behaviour of the French* (*Le comportement sexuel des Français*) are well-known examples. The historian has no such tools at his disposal; he makes up for them by reconstituting reality from sources which are more or less indirect, more or less incomplete.

Judicial archives allow him a first approach to sexual behaviour in its criminal form: bestiality, homosexuality, rape, etc. Obviously they do not give an exact statistical picture of actual deviance, but of that recorded by the police and judiciary. It will generally be necessary to raise the figures, but by what proportion? It will sometimes be necessary to lower them – for example, not every rape case implies an actual rape, but can turn out to be a specious manoeuvre of the plaintiff who is looking for a way of getting married . . . again, in what proportion? Do these statistics permit us, at least in comparison with those of other periods, to measure the variation in these kinds of behaviour? This is open to question, as in trials for sodomy. Frequent in the sixteenth century, they seem to have disappeared, or almost so, in eighteenth-century France.[10] In the absence of a change in the penal legislation, does this clear drop in numbers reveal the increasing rarity of the practice? The concomitant example of witchcraft trials leads one to think that it is rather a matter of the authorities' laxity under the influence of new moral values.[11] The present French legislation on rape provides another, but contrary, example. The increase in penal rigour (rape has passed from the category of offence to that of crime) in no way signifies a disturbing increase in the number of cases, but evidently an evolution of cultural values. If there is no longer a place for bestiality or incest in the mind of a French judge of today, can one imagine indecent behaviour or rape within marriage in that of an eighteenth-century judge? If judicial statistics give us only limited information on the reality of criminal practices, they do, nevertheless, allow us to measure with more certitude the intensity of repression in a society with regard to what it holds as deviance or, at least, as an intolerable manifestation of sexual desire. From facts, they lead us to values.

Only the comparison of penal systems, supplemented by observation of their application, can legitimately lend itself to judgement. This latter, besides, would go beyond the historian to become the affair of every man responsible for his destiny. Further, for a legitimate comparison one would need to add the extra-judicial means of coercion. The priest and the neighbourhood (think of the charivari) could in the eighteenth century exert gentler but quite as effective pressure. Such a synthesis is still to come. Were it available, one would have to answer this other question: was what we conceive of as an intolerable attack on individual liberty (for example, the punishment of homosexuality) so perceived by the offender? Nothing could be less certain. The majority of witches believed themselves genuinely possessed. How many sodomites did?

Historical demography offers the advantage of providing us with raw facts. Its boom in the last few years has been such that it has been possible to go beyond the stage of monographs. There are now sufficiently broad and reliable syntheses for the historian to be tempted to advance general hypotheses, sometimes extending to the *'longue durée'* – Jean-Louis Flandrin studied *Les Amours paysannes* from the sixteenth century to the nineteenth century, Solé writes on *L'Amour en Occident* during the modern era, and J. van Ussel tells us the *History of Sexual Repression* from the middle ages to the nineteenth century. With regard to France in the eighteenth century, there are two essential facts: the age of marriage gets later and later (an average 28.5 years for men and 26.5 for women) and fertility declines sharply, and very early in the century.[12] A godsend for the Marxo-Freudian historian! Here is a population who were young (so necessarily goaded by sexual desire) and who could not be satisfied in marriage for a long time. The extra-conjugal solutions remain to be evaluated; we will finally know whether or not repression was effective. Those which involve criminality (and have already been mentioned) concerned only a tiny minority. As for prostitution, the archives tell us that, harshly repressed (by hospitalisation, banishment and deportation), it was in sharp decline. Besides, it concerned only city dwellers. Demography completes the picture: illegitimate births, which generally befell the daughters of the lower classes, were clearly on the rise in the course of the century.[13] Looked at over the whole of France, the phenomenon would not be decisive, as it essentially concerns the towns. The same would be true for prenuptial conceptions, which also multiplied.[14] However, an inversely proportional relation between these two variables has been noted, which has been interpreted as a 'success for the pressures in favour of marriages of reparation'.[15] From this, the historian has gone on to suggest that a whole population could certainly have been the object of massive and victorious sexual repression. By the priest, of course, and his morality of renunciation, but also – and such is presented as the characteristic of that epoch – by a newcomer, a product of the then rapidly rising bourgeoisie: the doctor, whose knowledge permitted a form of repression better adapted because desacralised. That he did not always get on with the former becomes a secondary matter, since they agreed on the repression of desire. For the historian, the anti-onanist campaign, begun by doctors in capitalist England and pursued on the continent from 1760 by other doctors, is the striking illustration of this.[16]

In the noticeable absence of other outlets, there is a great temptation to link this campaign with the increasingly late age of marriage. Masturbation, then, would be the solution to forced abstinence. One has certainly to admit that the later the age of marriage became, the more the anti-onanist campaign, at least the written campaign, developed. It is a matter of near certainty. It is enough, however, to prolong the two curves into the nineteenth century to notice that soon, as the age of marriage began to fall (which it did more and more), the anti-onanist campaign continued nonetheless, and to an extent never attained before. What seemed obvious goes up in smoke.[17]

For historians such as J.-L. Flandrin, this failure modifies only part of the picture; on the whole, the hypothesis of a generalised repression remains valid. Such an idea seems to me to be characteristic of the abuse of statistics. A demographic synthesis on the scale of France is perfectly legitimate and extremely useful: it permits significant comparisons in space and time. This procedure voluntarily ignores local differences in order to keep to the masses; it is valid at the continental or global level. Thus it has been possible to bring to the fore the opposition in the eighteenth century between a 'full' world – by and large, northern Europe – where people married late and where the birth-rate stagnated or decreased, and an 'empty' world – that of the margins, the Americas, the east of Europe – given over to colonisation, favourable to demographic explosion.[18] Can one infer from the data of Weltpolitik an overall picture of the sexual behaviour of the French eighteenth century? We do not think so, because this population, in its social reality, in its mentality and its forms of behaviour, was not a homogeneous whole.

Let us take the age of marriage. We know for sure that in the élite people marry young – see, for example, dukes and peers.[19] If one examines nuptial behaviour in the countryside, one sees that the result varies noticeably according to the social group and its relation to property.[20] From one region to the next, according to the laws of succession, the age of marriage can vary to a considerable extent; a fact that the national average obviously masks. Thus, fifty per cent of the young married before the age of twenty-one in the Limousin and Poitou-Charentes (in 1978, the average age was 24.9 for men and 22.8 for women); late marriage was above all a Parisian phenomenon (26.6 and 24.5 on the Île de France) and an urban one (Reims: 27.7 and 25.2, Lyons: 29 and 27.5 and Caen: 30.6 and 28).[21]

With regard to behaviour, the disparity is just as great from one region to the next. What is the value of the picture of a constraining ritual governing relations between the sexes in the French countryside? Doubtless, it bolsters up the idea of an absence of freedom. What are we to make, then, of the extremely advanced familiarity of the Poitevin maraîchinage, or of a trial marriage in the Basque country, or of prenuptial concubinage in Corsica?[22] In the eighteenth century, the image of French sexuality is, as is true in many other respects, one of the most extreme and sometimes the most surprising variety; certainly not of the uniformity characteristic of our mass civilisation, which the use here of the crude instrument of the national average would suggest.

Let us take another look at the figures complacently interpreted in terms of repression. Moral deviance seems to be an essentially urban phenomenon: precisely where celibacy is more widespread, where marriage is latest. Note, besides, that a number of the illegitimate births recorded in towns could involve village women who had fled the reprobation of their native place. As for 'amendment' marriages (i.e., ones in which the marriage is celebrated after sexual relations are begun), which are presented as a proof of the successful pressure of the clergy, they can equally well be interpreted as a sign of the weakening of the most constant teachings of the Church – which would besides be more in conformity with what we know of dechristianisation, whose extent has been measured (in other ways) well before its acceleration during the revolutionary period.[23] Finally, note the increasing importance of the practice of concubinage among the urban proletariat. Social realities indicate that marriage was above all an economic question.[24] Of no use in destitution, it could be a factor of impoverishment for the intermediate classes: they married late to give themselves time to get established, not from moral (or immoral) necessity. It is just what such a judicious commentator as Chamfort suggested: 'Modern philosophy used to be blamed for multiplying the number of bachelors; M says of this: "So long as it is not proved to me that it was the philosophers who clubbed together to raise money for Mlle Bertin and to set up her shop, I shall believe that celibacy could well have a different cause"'.[25] At the level of behaviour and of sexual morality, the age of marriage appears a very questionable indicator; it certainly cannot signify *ipso facto* the victory of a repressive morality. One could even ask whether morality ever was a significant and direct influence on the age of marriage and on the birth rate. One should, rather, privilege age as the prime factor. Although it is difficult to establish the statistics for this in the eighteenth century, some of the work done leads one to think that not all married couples waited until their belated wedding night.[26]

In the absence of a true synthesis, we can of course only leave the conclusion hanging. But if it were necessary to put forward a hypothesis on the basis of the bundle of elements already gathered, I would be inclined to say that the massive repression that many historians flatter themselves that they show is highly improbable. Taken in relation to the discourses of that time, the hypothesis of repression appears even less credible. It is this which needs to be examined next.

The dichotomy of freedom and repression produces the same reductive effect when applied to the reading of normative systems. The landscape appears even more sombre here: on one side the massive presence of the repressive discourses, those of the Church, the State, medicine, the moralists à la Rousseau; on the other, the voice of freedom, almost solitary and quasi-clandestine, that of Diderot being the best-known. On one side the complicity of the official, or quasi-official, institutions, perpetuating the long tradition of asceticism; on the other, our values, announced by a few pioneers. While political history, by restoring *sans-culottisme* to its true place, has damaged the legend of a democratic bourgeoisie,[27] in the ideological order the historian is bringing to light the scandal that the Enlightenment, as soon as it was concerned with sexuality, fell back into the most narrow obscurantism. What is its rationalist prestige worth, faced with the fantastic theory which makes masturbation a pathological activity? From the beginning, one may say, the two repressive faces of the bourgeoisie appear: political and sexual. It was foreseeable. One author goes as far as to assert that the birth of the anti-masturbatory campaign in England was due to 'English ideological advancement'.[28] All it was was the pamphlet of a quack. Oh Marx![29]

In practice, this tendency to standardisation does not go so far as to deny all tension between the systems, but it does tend to minimise its import. For the historian, even if intentions diverge, there is a *de facto* collusion. Let us concede him this with regard to the struggle against 'the popular mentality'.[30] The Church, in conjunction with medicine, proposed to push back 'supersitition'.[31] Can one see in this the repression of an original freedom and of a spontaneous expression of the body, represented by peasant customs? Such an idea, more or less, haunts the discourse of the historian. It is, however, the very reality of the notion of 'popular mentality' which is problematic, its own originality which is in question. Thus, prenuptial pregnancies in the countryside are often only the conformity of the ignorant, for whom engagement itself is already true marriage. For his part, the doctor worked to extirpate all belief in the powers of magic upon the body: for example that which sees impotence as the effect of a curse – the 'tying of the knot' (*nouement de l'aiguillette*).[32] Both were conscious of bringing true freedom along with true knowledge.

Agreement was far from perfect between these two 'accomplices'. Church and medicine were in permanent conflict, especially on the terrain of sexuality, the latter going so far as to deny the former any competence in this domain.[33] Conflict was not limited to these two protagonists. Church and State were in competition over the age of marriage and on the subject of parental consent. The State did not favour early marriage, and insisted on parental authorisation up to an advanced age. The Church, by protecting the freedom of children (for example, in secret marriage), meant also to protect the freedom of vocations and to preserve the sacramental value of marriage. Connivance between the doctors and the State was not always evident. Tissot, for instance, complained about the banning of L'Onanisme.[34] In fact, we are in the presence of a multiplicity of intersecting relations, of momentary and limited connivances, of mutual exclusions. The State, as temporal power, was courted as much by the Church as by the doctors. Among the latter, some (increasingly rare, it is true) lent their support to moral theology, thus perpetuating a long-standing role as servant. Hecquet, for instance, demonstrated the innocuousness and even the beneficence of abstinence.[35] While the Church combated superstition, there were limits to this (as the doctor obligingly underlined) in that she could not totally dissociate herself from the magical mentality. This is clearly seen in her definition of a miracle.[36] The Church, the doctors and the State, it seems, favoured populousness; all three agreed in denouncing contraception, but each one for its own reasons, incompatible with those of the others. Finally, in order to balance out the complicities and the exclusions, and clearly delimit the sides in this imbroglio, we need first of all to determine the criteria of division. This clarification can only come after the opposing values have been defined.

If the historian detects *de facto* collusion between Church and doctors, it is because he is forgetting the nature and relations of the moral concepts he is employing. Freedom and repression are not two autonomous concepts, but the two opposing sides – or rather the two contradictory interpretations – of a single principle: the good. To define the good supposes a choice, and therefore a rejection, that is, a constraint. To do good is to constrain oneself to reject evil. A mild constraint (though sometimes difficult), since freely consented to; a legitimate constraint, hence freedom. But the good does not impose itself as self-evident upon everybody; if one inverts the contents of good and evil, freedom changes into repression, into a constraint which is imposed and illegitimate.

This is an elementary truth strangely neglected by the historian, who makes an absolute out of *his* conception of the good, and does not permit himself to notice that one man's liberty may be another man's repression. Thus, for the theologian, to renounce carnal desire at God's call is obviously to constrain oneself, but to constrain oneself freely, to affirm one's will to be saved. It is true freedom because it is the rejection of evil and the choice of the good. The doctor[37] sees in this an attack on human freedom: he places the criterion of the good in nature (at least, his conception of nature) and not in a super-nature which he regards as chimerical. Chastity is a bad choice in the eyes of nature (it can be fatal!) and to wish to impose it in the name of an illusory reality would inevitably be repression. On the other hand, the affirmation of freedom as a response to the call of nature also supposes choices, and a rejection of what is not natural: masturbation, homosexuality, bestiality, etc. To reject these practices is not, for the doctor, repression, but rejection of what is bad. From the height of his conceptions as a man of the twentieth century, for whom God is dead, and whose sexual morality separates pleasure and reproduction, the historian claims to reject these two conceptions of freedom. That is his privilege, but can he, as a historian, confuse them and make them two varieties of one repressive attitude? Such a confusion might be admissible in a theoretical treatise of morality, but cannot account for the lived historical reality of the doctrines in question. It involves postulating that the doctor and the theologian, though in different terms, were denouncing the same thing, speaking of the same reality. They were doing nothing of the sort.

Here again we find ourselves in the presence of the prejudice which consists of implicitly introducing evidence of naïve realism in the treatment of cultural facts. Sexual practices are treated by the historian as brute facts, always and everywhere the same, as facts of nature, as needs, which, as such, do not even need definition. Doubtless he sees that where the doctor speaks of masturbation, the theologian never uses the term (which, however, he could have known, for example from Martial).[38] So the historian sets out to translate! He relates different facts, unknown to our taxonomy, to our own mental universe. He reduces the unknown and the strange to the known and the familiar. It is easy then for him to look for – and to find! – *his* liberty and *his* repression. Now, if one pursues the example of masturbation, one can say that it exists only for the doctor. Not that the theologian is ignorant of ejaculation provoked by touch, but this activity is included by him in a much larger group of practices comprised under the generic term of 'voluntary pollution'.[39] For him, there is practice as soon as there is active volition (one can sin in thought!) and not only when there is willed bodily movement. Quibbles, extravagance of precision, lexicological byzantinism, it will be said. Not at all: he who, after eating too well, is subject to pollution (and knows its cause) sins. For the doctor, what is involved here is a morally neutral and physiologically beneficial mechanism, which has nothing to do with masturbation because it is nature which activates the body (the doctor calls this phenomenon 'involuntary pollution' or 'nocturnal pollution') and not the subject who does violence to nature. One can see that the taxonomy is already a function of the criterion chosen to define what is good and what is bad. There is no universally valid and morally neutral scheme of taxonomy. This is a piece of evidence that the historian splendidly ignores in his practice. For him,[40] the scholastic universe of the theologian and the mechanistic universe of the doctor are equivalent on the theoretical level and in their moral consequences.

Whatever element of taxonomy one chooses, however, it has no reality in itself; it exists only in relation to the other elements and is purely dynamic. It is an 'axiological vector'. Thus, when the theologian condemns voluntary pollution, he is affirming the superiority of absolute chastity, while conceding the legitimacy of coitus when kept within strict limits and sanctioned by a sacrament. Conversely, when the doctor rejects masturbation as an activity contrary to nature, he is affirming the primacy of coitus and the harmfulness of chastity. If it is allowed, finally, that there was some difference in conception between the theologian and the doctor, it will be claimed that at least the latter, when he speaks of masturbation, is speaking the same language as us. The only divergence would be in moral judgment. Gross illusion! Our conception of masturbation (which is no more purely biological than his) proceeds from a sexology of Freudian inspiration. Under the same term there are two different realities. If the hypothesis of masturbation making up for the prolonged celibacy of youth already of reproductive maturity comes to the historian's mind, it is because our conception of masturbation makes it a replacement for coitus, a substitute for pleasure between two people. This is why a new term tends to compete with the old in works of sexology: auto-eroticism. The doctor of the Enlightenment was attacking precocious marriage, seeing in it the sign of a society prey to artificial excitation, not the cry of nature. The almost total absence of women from the anti-onanist literature, when they constituted the most abundant group of celibates, is explicable by the same logic. If the notion of the repression of masturbation by the Enlightenment doctor has been talked of, it is owing to a confusion between his conception of this activity and ours.

If we take the taxonomy of coital positions, we will notice the same divergences which forbid all assimilation, all translation. The Church recognises as legitimate only the so-called 'missionary position' (the man on the woman). However, it allows some dispensations in exceptional cases (obesity, illness, etc.) in order to permit the accomplishment of conjugal duty. A doctor such as Venette may recommend the rear entry position (condemned by the theologian) because it allows a better penetration of the semen (according to him). As for the modern sexologists, such as Masters and Johnson, who take only pleasure into account, they will advise such or such a position as a function of the action of the organs on the nervous centres of pleasure. Anatomy, for the sexologist, is orientated by the concern for pleasure (for example in the works of W. H. Masters and V. E. Johnson); for the doctor of the Enlightenment, the pursuit of impregnation, but in close connection with pleasure, conceived as the auxiliary of the former; for the theologian, the body is a place of perdition which it is better to have nothing to do with or, if this is too much to ask, as little as possible. Hence, too, there are certain attitudes on the question of modesty that can appear strange. The theologian cannot be suspected of favouring the spectacle of nudity. However, he allowed the 'congress' in which a man was summoned to give public proof of his virility. This practice was to be denounced by the doctor as morally indecorous and physiologically aberrant. He would also advocate recourse to the obstetrician instead of the midwife – something the theologian would not permit.

Let us take the advocacy of populousness, thought to be the point of convergence of doctors, Church and State. In fact, the Church (Catholic, of course) was not an advocate of populousness; to claim the contrary is to succumb to the Quebec syndrome. For the Church, celibacy remained the essential virtue. Procreation was only a pretext for the limitation of pleasure, an obstacle on the rake's path. Christian strictness would have spouses live as brother and sister once posterity had been assured. Besides, it never called into question sterile unions. The historian is so firmly persuaded that he is dealing with a doctrine of 'multiply and be fruitful' that he analyses moral theology as moral legislation or book-keeping (which it is in part, but not essentially). He forgets that it is only the codification of conjugal chastity and that, even if many content themselves with this second-rate holiness, it is the demand for absolute chastity which presides at the choice of such or such a prohibition. As for the doctor, his taxonomy of the carnal acts couldn't overlap with the theologian's since only the ('natural') criterion of fecundity through pleasure guides his apprehension of reality. The world of the doctor is irremediably foreign to the world of the theologian, as both are to ours.

Further, the deviations noted by one of these points of view were blamed on the errors of the other. Lay celibacy or late marriage were

ROYER'S
flowers & gifts

Camp Hill	3015 Old Gettysburg Rd	730-4090	Palmyra	131 N. Railroad St	838-5728
Columbia	902 Lancaster Ave	684-2081	Reading	640 N. 5th St	(610)372-7861
Ephrata	165 S. Reading Rd	733-6588	Shillington	407 W. Lancaster Ave	(610)777-7937
Harrisburg	4907 Orchard St	545-3220	Wernersville	366 E. Penn St	(610)678-7370
Hershey	304 W. Chocolate Ave	534-2834	York	2555 Eastern Blvd	755-7673
Lancaster	201 Rohrerstown Rd	397-0376		805 Loucks Rd	854-7733
	873 N. Queen St	394-6339			
Lebanon	810 S. 12th St	273-2683			
Leola	232-A W. Main St	656-2911			

After hours, call toll-free:

1-888-2-ROYERS

on-line: www.royers.com

~~$20.25~~
with discount
$17.21!

~~$13.50~~
with discount
$11.48!

~~$16.50~~
with discount
$14.03!

Place your corsage or boutonniere order by

Wednesday

of your Homecoming/Prom week and receive

15% OFF!

Stop in or call for our full selection!
Phone orders, ask for operator #75.

denounced by the Church as a debauched attitude influenced by the 'philosophes' (as Chamfort reports). Conversely, doctors denounced the advocacy of sterility, and saw the practice of masturbation or precocious union as the price of a devaluation of marriage. We can see another example in the mythical sociology of the Enlightenment, as it figures in *Émile*. The denunciation of excess, in accordance with the mechanistic schema of the doctors, takes on a double face there and is incarnated in the priest and the aristocrat. The artisan, who represents the nobility of the people, realises in his behaviour the happy medium, which alone is in conformity with nature. As for the servant, who represents the people debased, he is the synthesis of lack of culture and of refined perversity. Far from signifying a concrete rationalisation of the exploitation of the masses, the sexual morality of the Enlightenment leads to a fantastic reading of social reality. There is a paradise on earth, and it is the innocence of the people. There is a hell, and it is the work of the priest and the debauchee: the epidemic of masturbation, the degeneration of the race, etc. The need, then, here as elsewhere, is to replace an order incapable of keeping to what it promises (since chastity leads to adultery and homosexuality, since it takes up arms against nature, witness the *castrati*); to replace an illusory order, itself productive of disorder, by a true order, truly moral because it is respectful of nature.[41]

If each side threw in the other's face the responsibility for such or such a practice, it was because contemporaries were well aware of the values that were at stake. Is it for the historian to ignore these values in order retrospectively to impose his? It is not his task to write a new version of the *Critique of Practical Reason*.

We find the same blindness at work in the analysis of the 'positive' discourse of the Enlightenment. The work in question is Diderot's *Suite de l'Entretien*, generally held to be a model of boldness in this century so decidedly hostile to sex. Besides, Diderot was a materalist, whereas Rousseau . . ., besides, Diderot was a sensualist, whereas Rousseau, unfortunately for this conception, was forgetting! The setting of the *Suite* is bourgeois, and Diderot (almost) a sadist – the cutlery! Let us re-read Diderot's text with its contradictions. Bestiality? An amusing fable (that of the satyrs), but a fable. Homosexuality? Masturbation? On one side there are the rights of nature, pleasure, and on the other, a confidential morality (no servants!), the products of deranged minds, of exhausted organisms. These are contradictions because there are two different levels in the work: on one side a regular demolition of moral theology – this is the polemical level, and, on the other, the affirmation of a positive morality conforming in all respects to that of enlightened doctors – that of double excess. Such is the ambivalent nature – the reality and the legend – of this famous text.[42]

The place of masturbation in this debate seems essential to me. That it is always invoked by the historian to justify his pessimistic version of Enlightenment sexuality is symptomatic, even if he is astonished that the anti-onanist campaign appeared jointly with a will to inform, with an actual project of sexual education, and even in a writer such as Rousseau. As if it were not a matter, in educating according to nature, of rejecting artifice in its double form. It is essential, in that this notion had necessarily to appear in a system which rested on the idea that nature – and, in nature, procreation – provides the ideal and universal criterion for sexual morality. It could not be present in theological discourse with the same vigour and the same distinctness, because the criterion of truth lay in a nature subordinated to supernature, in a sexuality dominated by the supremacy of chastity. In such a system, the ultimate in disorder could only be the height of submission to the carnal, namely bestiality. It was this, precisely, that Diderot put at the heart of his polemic in the *Suite*. On the penal level, ecclesiastical 'barbarism' was understood as a violation of the sacred order of nature, for which purificatory atonement must be made. With the doctor, the rejection of the punishment of the stake is explained by his seeing the phenomenon as a malfunction of nature; the zoophile and the homosexual are madmen in need of cure, victims (like the masturbator) who need to be protected from themselves – hence the relative laxity of the doctor and of the magistrates who increasingly follow his view.

But masturbation is something else as well: not the response to a physical lack in a century of oppression, but the solution to a theoretical lacuna in the struggle of the doctor against the oppressive sexual morality of the Church. It occupies a strategic place in the new taxonomy of the doctor, in place of the nebulous 'voluntary pollution'. In this sense, I have been able to speak of invention and of liberation. There is no question of an invention *ex nihilo* (that would be to get back to the most narrow realism), but of a presence new to a new consciousness of what was before merely an unnoticed objective presence. There is no other explanation of this 'invention' but in the struggle between doctor and theologian, this struggle being only an episode in the more general struggle of the *philosophes* against the Church, a struggle itself revelatory of other conflicts. That that freedom does not suit us is another matter.

It is a domain distinctly unstable in its moral and cultural (and even biological!) reality, so much as to appear hardly recognisable from one group to another, from one time to another; ceaselessly rearranged, reshaped, resurveyed, reinvented according to principles which are external to it. Sexuality, finally, is only a pretext. Is there no permanence in this perpetual slippage? Yes, sexuality remains one of the places where the battle of castes, of classes and of ranks is played out indefinitely.

In the guise of science, in place of 'lascivious erudition', what new mythology does the historian serve up to us? His 'invention' is the general repression of sex in the eighteenth century. It rests, as did its medical ancestor, on the illusion of possessing absolute politico-moral truth, and hence of feeling the absolute of pleasure (*jouissance*). The historian, like the militant – and, before, the priest, the doctor, the aristocrat or the bourgeois – is at the heart of truth, politically and sexually. He is free because he has been able to recognise and abandon error.

These mythologists, however, are no more interchangeable than their mythologies. Each one bears a specific relation to the object which he has invented for himself, according to his own situation on the moral, political and sexual level. To confine ourselves to the 'lascivious erudite' and Marxo-Freudian historians such as Solé and Ussel, let us recall that the first revels in a documentary material which has already been codified and is already arrayed with literary and aesthetic properties. Quite normal, say the latter, he is 'repressed'. His unhealthy pleasure is but the result of a 'poorly assumed' sexuality. It should be noted that Rousseau, in *Émile*, had already cast in doubt the reality of the pleasure of the *coquette* or, more precisely, placed it in her vanity. To this pleasure 'of the head' he opposed true pleasure according to nature. Without demanding the talent of a poet, one might reasonably expect a certain lyricism from the historian; his style is the most distant there could be. Scientific neutrality? The doctors of the eighteenth century, even Tissot, nonetheless always used to offer up some dithyrambic lines on the altar of sexual pleasure. How to affirm one's delight in pleasure if not through jubilation? The coldness of the historian is but a necessary effect of his mythology; is he, like the erudite, going to let himself personally be suspected of some pathetic repression by lending too complacent a pen to the description of past caperings? The historian must retail the most salacious adventures without batting an eyelid, he must assume an attitude of indifference. It is a point of honour and of method. I even suspect him of taking a certain coquettish pleasure in voluntarily confronting himself with the sexual activities held to be the most 'shocking'. The competition in this field is such that under the most austere ceilings remarks are declaimed which one would hardly dare murmur in a brothel. Good form requires that one yawns while reading the libertine authors of the eighteenth century. With Sade, one is bored stiff. If, through art, the erudite marks his distance from the vulgarity of popular instincts, the historian marks his in relation to the murky emotion of the 'bourgeois' by displaying a conspicuous disdain for the proprieties. He thus offers himself the ideological comfort of the sect – the contemporary equivalent of the caste and the class, where one is unique along with others. He gives himself and others the spectacle of his own liberation.

Every mythologist has his methods, according to his historical situation. The erudite is but an artisan, a weekend archaeologist. The erotic past is for him only a heritage of which he has taken up guard – by right, since he has won. But first the safeguard, since the French revolution, against the 'vandalism' of the populace. Was the word not invented by the revolutionary bourgeoisie to denounce the exactions of the *sans-culottes*? The erudite, then, is also a collector. The historian, himself, cannot offer himself a borrowed lustre: he is duty bound to conquer 'his' past, as he wishes to conquer his future. The historian, then, must bring to light, reveal, fabricate the past reality he needs. What the erudite is content to heap up, he must invent; only he could create the history of sexuality. In this enterprise, statistics are not a more neutral technique than the accumulative curiosity of the scholar, they are not more effective in themselves, but in relation to the project of the historian. They are one mode of existence of sex. Witness their absence for the doctor of the eighteenth century, witness for the historian their presence in place of every known fact. Masturbation exists only through the table of titles of works devoted to it (no more need to read them! Hence the confusions); the repressive efficacy of confessors is to be checked through the absence or presence of such or such a sin from one edition to the next.

This *'savoir-dire'* is in the image of the relations between the sexes. Proprietor of his mistress, his dancing girls, his servants, his whores and, of course, his wife, benefiting from a *de facto* monopoly inherited from the ancien régime, the bourgeois can, at minimal expense, arrogate to himself the honorific signs of the proprietor. In the eyes of those around him, his virility is affirmed as an obvious fact through his lascivious erudition. The historian cannot hope for immediate recognition because of the levelling effect of contemporary democracy (and in conformity with his own mythology). On the henceforth free market of erotic conquest – a market finally in conformity with the true nature of the bourgeois economy – he will affirm his virility by the roundabout means of his stylistic indifference; he will impose himself on the suffrages of woman, his equal in principle, while asserting his lack of prejudice. His intellectual liberty will be a token of his acrobatic capacities; it will attest his mastery of the technologies of happines. 'Savoir-dire' is also savoir-faire.

Is this to say that nothing remains of his enterprise? Assuredly not. The materials are there, though scattered, to attest the impossibility of achieving the history of a chimera: sexuality.

Notes

1 Cf. the speech of Maurice Barrès in Parliament against commemoration of Rousseau (11 June 1912) and his hostility against the national celebration of Diderot (15 November 1913), in Les Maîtres, Paris, 1927, pp. 165–70 and pp. 173–82. See also the celebration of Voltaire and Rousseau's bicentenarian in Revue d'histoire littéraire de la France, March–June 1979, Nos. 2–3: Dix-huitième siècle, 1979, No. 11 and Annales historiques de la Révolution française, 1979. Recently, 1984 was for Diderot an official apotheosis (see 1984, l'année Diderot, supplement to Dix-huitième siècle, 1985, No. 17).
2 See Solé's introduction to his L'Amour en Occident à l'époque moderne, 1976, p. 11.
3 Two examples of this conception: J. Van Ussel, Histoire de la répression sexuelle, Paris, 1972, and J. Solé, L'Amour en Occident à l'époque moderne, Paris, 1976.
4 That is the main reason for suspicion against the historical works of the Goncourt brothers.
5 See for instance Sexualités occidentales (1979–80), published in Communications, 1982, 35.
6 Comparison between the titles is illuminating: on the one hand, evocative titles, such as La Galanterie parisienne (1905), Le Régence galante (1909), Jean Hervez, Les Demoiselles d'amour du Palais-Royal (1911) Fleischmann, Cythère XVIIIe siècle (1952), Chaumadin, or, more recently, the popular Histoires d'amour de l'Histoire de France by A. Castelot and A. Decaux; on the other hand, 'cold' titles for 'hard' subjects, such as Amour illégitime et société à Nantes au XVIIIe siècle, Mariage tardif et vie sexuelle . . ., La Sodomie à l'époque moderne en Suisse Romande, . . .
7 Cited by Michel Décaudin in his preface to the posthumous work of Guillaume Apollinaire, Les Diables amoureux, Gallimard, Paris, 1964, p. 13. Apollinaire

became famous in the two ways of that tradition: as an *érudit* he wrote (with F. Fleuret and L. Perceau) the *Enfer de la Bibliotèque nationale* (1919) and as a novelist his *Onze mille verges*.
8 For instance, P. Chaunu in *La Civilisation de l'Europe des Lumières*, Paris, 1971, reprint 1982, pp. 99–100.
9 *Le Capital*, ed. Sociales, Paris, 1953, L. II, t. II, Ch. XX, p. 56.
10 Cf. E. W. Monter, 'La Sodomie à l'époque moderne en Suisse romande', *Annales (ESC)*, July–August 1974, ed. A. Colin, pp. 1023–33 and Maurice Lever, *Les Bûchers de Sodome*, ed. Fayard, Paris, 1985.
11 Cf. Boucher d'Argis's 'Sodomie' in *Encyclopédie*, Diderot's *Suite de l'entretien* or Voltaire's 'Amour nommé socratique' in *Dictionnaire philosophique* (note of 1769).
12 Cf. J. Dupâquier, *La Population française aux XVIIe et XVIIIe siècles*, P.U.F., Paris, 1979.
13 Cf. J. Depaw, 'Amour illégitime et société à Nantes au XVIIIe siècle, *Annales (ESC)*, VII–X, 1972, pp. 1155–82. A. Lottin, 'Naissances illégitimes et filles mères à Lille au XVIIIe siècle', *Revue d'histoire moderne et contemporaire*, IV–VI, 1970, pp. 278–322; A. Molinier, 'Enfants trouvés, enfants abandonnés et enfants illégitimes en Languedoc aux XVIIe et XVIIIe siècles', *Mélanges Reinhard*, 1973, pp. 445–73.
14 Cf. J. L. Flandrin, *Les Amours paysannes (XVIe–XIXe siècle)*, Paris, 1975, p. 239.
15 J. L. Flandrin, *ibid.* p. 241.
16 Cf. Solé, *op. cit.*.
17 Cf. Théodore Tarczylo, *Sexe et liberté au siècle des Lumières*, Paris, 1983, p. 151. The intention behind this work has been misunderstood, since people have wished to see in it a contribution to the history of sexual repression!
18 P. Chaunu, *op. cit.*, pp. 35–70.
19 Cf. C. Lévy and L. Henry, 'Ducs et pairs sous l'Ancien Régime', *Population*, No. 5, 1960.
20 Cf. B. Derouet, 'Une démographie différentielle', *Annales (ESC)*, January–February 1980, pp. 3–41 and P. Chaunu, *op. cit.*, pp. 71–92.
21 Cf. J. Dupâquier, *op. cit.*
22 Cf. J.-L. Flandrin, *op. cit.*, pp. 184–200.
23 *Cf.* M. Vovelle, *Piété baroque et déchristianisation*, Paris, 1973.
24 Cf. Edward Shorter, *Naissance de la famille moderne* (French translation, 1977).
25 Chamfort, *Maximes, pensées, caractères et anecdotes*, ed. J. Dagen, Paris, 1968, 1014, p. 274
26 Cf. J.-P. Bardet and J. Dupâquier: 'Vierges sages ou vierges folles, nos ancêtres étaient-elles vertueuses?' in the collective work *La Première fois, ou le roman de la virginité perdue . . .* , Paris, 1981.
27 See Albert Mathiez, *La Vie chère et le mouvement social sous la Terreur*, 1927, reprint 1973, 2 vols., and Albert Soboul, *Les Sans-culottes parisiens en l'an II. Mouvement populaire et gouvernement révolutionnaire, 2 juin 1793–9 thermidor an II*, 1958, reprint 1962.
28 Solé, *op. cit.*, p. 110.
29 Cf. T. Tarczylo, *op. cit.*., pp. 108–14.

30 See R. Muchembled, *Culture populaire et culture des élites dans la France moderne, 15ᵉ–16ᵉ siecles*, 1978.
31 Cf. Jean-Baptiste Thiers, *Traité des superstitions*..., 1679, reprint, 1697–1703, 4 vols.; Pierre Lebrun, *Histoire critique des pratiques superstitieuses*..., 1702, reprint. 1732–7, 4 vols.; Dom Calmet, *Dissertation sur les apparitions*..., 1746; abbé Nicolas Lenglet Dufresnoy, *Recueil de dissertations (...) sur les apparitions*..., 1751.
32 Cf. Nicolas Venette, *Tableau de l'amour conjugal*, 1741, II, p. 378 et seq.
33 Cf. N. Venette, *op. cit.*; Ménuret de Chambaud, 'Observateur' in *Encyclopédie*; S. A. A. D. Tissot, *Discours préliminaire* to his translation of Haller's *Dissertation sur les parties irritables et sensibles des animaux*, Lausanne, 1755, etc.
34 In his letter to Rousseau, 8 July 1762, cf. Rousseau, *Correspondance complète*, ed. R. A. Leigh, 1979.
35 Philippe Hecquet, *Traité des dispenses du carême*, Paris, 1709.
36 See Note 31.
37 See for instance Nicolas Venette, *Tableau de l'amour conjugal* or Ménuret de Chambaud's essays for the *Encyclopédie*.
38 Cf. A. de Liguori, *Theologia moralis*, 1753–5.
39 Cf. T. Tarczylo, *op. cit.*, pp. 99–106.
40 Jean-Louis Flandrin claims to 'translate' the vocabulary of theologians into the language of modern sexology.
41 Cf. J.-J Rousseau's *Emile*.
42 I refer to my analysis of this text in *Eighteenth-Century Life*, Williamsburg, Virginia, USA, May 1985, Vol. ix, n.s., 3, pp. 43–60.

2

The discourse on sex – or sex as discourse: eighteenth-century medical and paramedical erotica

PETER WAGNER

The eighteenth century adored both science and sex. When science was applied to sex, the result was a plethora of highly equivocal writings on a great variety of apects of sexuality and sexual behaviour. To some extent, this was the consequence of the changes the medical field underwent after 1700. A phalanx of learned medical authorities absorbed Enlightenment ideas and applied them in their treatises. But although medicine forcefully stepped out of the shadows of the Middle Ages, the medical profession as such could improve its status only very slowly. For, in addition to the established experts, whose constant squabbles and feuds further lowered the doctors in the esteem of the public, hacks, quacks, and charlatans declared themselves physicans overnight and, often at the cost of their patients, began practising and publishing.[1] The achievements of the medical fringe have been unjustly disregarded and it is only recently that we have come to realise that the Enlightenment, as far as medicine is concerned, did not come exclusively from above, from the intellectuals, and that there may well have been an upward diffusion of ideas.[2] To be sure, the high element of speculation and, more often than not, of fabrication has stood in the way of a fringe-centred account of the history of medicine. Especially for the medical fringe, the combinations of sex and sensation, sex and taboo, and sex and conjecture, proved extremely tempting because they promised fame and money. In many cases, science served as a veil or pretext for the discussion of issue that were otherwise considered obscene or taboo. But the literature on sex that was circulated to the public from medical, paramedical, and religious quarters proves highly rewarding ground for research, not least for the testing of how Enlightenment ideas were propagated or disregarded at the popular level, if one abandons the idea that medical and paramedical writings from the fringe of eighteenth-century medicine are of little import for the rise of medicine.

This chapter focuses on the erotic and entertaining dimensions of this literature, on its discourse, which was either intrinsically erotic or toyed with the readers' prurience. To some extent, the erotic attraction of the popular writings on sex made up for the lacking reputation of the authors and served as a come-on for readers who, along with titillating descriptions, were exposed to medical information that reached from the highly advanced to the deeply prejudiced and excessively repressive.[3]

The salacious aspects of eighteenth-century sex guides, such as *Aristotle's Master-piece* and Venette's *Tableau de l'amour conjugal*, have been discussed by a number of scholars and need not concern us here.[4] Among the writers who relied rather heavily on the lure of the sexually equivocal, John Marten came to be known as a self-appointed expert in the cure of venereal disease. He was for some time employed by the ubiquitous pornographer Edmund Curll, for whom he published a few treatises under the pseudonym of T. C. Surgeon. Marten's rather hilarious literary battles with John Spinke who, unlike Marten, advocated mercury as a cure for VD, have been adequately described by Philip Pinkus.[5] Spinke not only attacked Marten's refusal to accept the traditional use of mercury but also reproached him with salacity. 'Your book', he wrote about Marten's *Treatise of all the degrees and symptoms of the Venereal Disease* (London, 1708), 'shews your great Esteem for old Songs and Ribaldry', while in general he accused him of 'Rhetorical Flourishes . . . ill Language, Smut, Obscenity'.[6] In 1709 Marten was prosecuted for the publication of an appendix to the sixth edition of his treatise on VD. This appendix, entitled *Gonosologium novum, or a new System of all the Secret Infirmities and Diseases natural accidental and venereal in Men and Women* (London, 1708), was a sort of sex guide which treated 'of the fallacy of some opinions to extinguish Amorous Thoughts . . . as also how to incite to lawful Love'. The index of seven pages made it very easy for readers bent on a little sexual titillation to pick out passages on 'the Venereal Desire in Women' and 'Desire of Venery in Women superabounding'.[7] The indictment, which was finally dismissed, charged that 'seduced by cupidity', Marten intended to 'corrupt the subjects of the Lady the

Queene'.⁸ It is very likely that the prosecution was a result of the animosity between Marten and other quacks. To begin with, the *Gonosologium* is rather harmless and has about the same number of spicy passages as other works of the same period. Immediately after the affair, a publication appeared which undertook to defend Marten's allegedly pornographic *Gonosologium*. Although *An Apology for a Latin Verse in Commendation of Mr. Marten's Gonosologium Novum* (London, 1709) was probably commissioned or written by Marten himself, the work discloses that the chief instigators of the prosecution were 'Spinck and Sinclaer' (sic), two former workers turned quacks.⁹ The author of the *Apology*, 'a Physician in the Country', defends Marten's description of the genitals and their functions by trying to prove 'that the same liberty of describing the . . . diseases of the secret parts of both sexes, and their cure (which . . . is said by some to be obscene) has been . . . us'd both by ancient and modern authors'.¹⁰ Needless to say, the whole work turns out to be an anthology of erotic and pornographic passages culled from a series of medical and paramedical works. Apart from some spicy sections from Latin authors, an English work is cited containing a report 'of a young Man of 22 years of Age, who without any trouble, for half an Hour together, carried a Pewter Flagon, containing five Measures of Ale, upon his standing Yard'. This is followed by extensive quotations of paragraphs dealing with women's genitals and hermaphrodites. 'Ambrose Parey' (i.e., Ambroise Paré), surgeon to 'two or three Kings of France', provides further material:

> When the husband cometh into his Wife's Chamber, he must entertain her with all kind of dalliance, wanton Behaviour and Allurements to Venery; but if he perceive her to be slow, and more cold, he must cherish, embrace and tickle her, and shall not abruptly . . . break into the Field of Nature, but rather shall creep in by little and little, intermixing more wanton Kisses with wanton Words and Speeches, handling her Secret Parts and Dugs, that she may take Fire, and be enflam'd to Venery . . . But if all these will not suffice to enflame the Woman . . . it shall be necessary first to foment her Secret Parts with the decoction of hot Herbs, made with Muscadine . . . and to put a little Musk or Civet into the Neck or Mouth of the womb.¹¹

If Paré's example did not exculpate Marten, then the influential Venette certainly did. Indeed, the author of the *Apology* cites a few bawdy paragraphs from Venette and mentions that pornography like the *Memoirs of the Court of England* or *The Virgin Unmask'd* had not been censored.¹²

Ironically enough, the *Apology* was more salacious than the allegedly pornographic work of Marten, thus proving that the actual prosecution of the *Gonosologium* was initiated either by hypocrites or, more likely, by 'the Malice of some Quacks that are exposed to it'.[13] Titillating stories and detailed descriptions of the nature and functions of female genitals were the erotic lures in 'physical directories' for ladies.[14]

A delightful if peculiar genre of sex guide is that written verse. Poetry served as a vehicle for many purposes in the eighteenth century, from social criticism and lampoons to love letters and epitaphs. Nobody objected to its employment in the description of sexual relations. One of the more successful works of this kind was Claude Quillet's *Callipédie ou Art d'avoir de beaux enfants* of 1655. This was first translated as *Callipaedia* and a little later as *The Art of getting beautiful Children* (London, 1712 and 1727). A free adaptation of this poem was then published as *The Joys of Hymen, or, The Conjugal Directory: a poem* (London, 1768). Reputable doctors like John Armstrong used verse to express their medical opinions. His *The Art of Preserving Health: a poem* (London 1744), although not particularly erotic, was rather successful and saw a second edition in 1745 which was followed by many reprints. Armstrong also wrote a poetical treatment of sex which found as much interest as his health guide. *The Oeconomy of Love. A Poetical Essay* (London, 1736) first describes the time and signs of puberty in both sexes and pronounces warnings against early love affairs. Making love, after choosing and marrying a 'soft nymph', is the focal point of the following passage:

> Now with your happy Arms her Waist surround,
> Fond-grasping; on her swelling Bosom now
> Recline your Cheek, with eager Kiss press
> Her balmy Lips, and drinking from her Eyes
> . . . .
> Stretch'd on the flow'ry turf, while joyful glows
> Thy manly Pride, and throbbing with Desire
> Pants earnest, felt thro' all the obstacles
> . . . .
> Then when her lovely Limbs,
> Oft lovely deem'd, far lovelier now beheld,
> Thro' all your trembling Joints increase the Flame;
> Forthwith discover to her dazzled sight
> The stately Novelty, and to her Hand

> Usher the new Acquaintance. She perhaps
> Averse will coldly chide, and half afraid,
> Blushing, half pleas'd, the tumid Wonder view
> With Neck retorted and oblique Regard;
>
> . . . .
>
> Perhaps when you attempt
> The sweet Admission, toyful she resists
> With shy reluctance; natheless you pursue
> The soft Attack, and push the gentle War,
> Fervent, till quite o'erpower'd the melting Maid
> Faintly opposes. On the Brink at last
> Arriv'd of giddy Rapture, plunge not in
> Precipitant, but spare a Virgin's Pain . . .

A true follower of Enlightenment ideas, Armstrong then warns against dedicating too much time and attention to love, advises 'those that pursue Amours . . . to be discreet and secret', and is in accordance with other writers in his rejection of homosexuality and perversion:

> For Man with Man,
> And Man with Woman (monstr'ous to relate!)
> Leaving the natural Road, themselves debase
> With Deeds unseemly, and Dishonour found.
> *Britons*, for shame! Be Male and Female still.
> Banish this foreign Vice; it grows not here,
> It dies, neglected; and in Clime so chaste
> Cannot but by forc'd Cultivation thrive.

The view that buggery and sodomy were 'unnatural' and of foreign origin, especially Italian or Eastern European, was quite common among English writers until well into the nineteenth century. Armstrong's poem is designed to facilitate the finding of special, titillating passages, as line references and contents are given on a page entitled 'The Argument' which precedes the actual text.[15]

Apart from masturbation, on which the eighteenth century developed a massive literature that thrived on the pornographic potential of the subject,[16] unconventional sexual behaviour received ample attention. While the literature on flagellation as a means of sexual stimulation reached its heyday only in the nineteenth century, public appetite was quite obviously being whetted in the age of Enlightenment. Inspired by Jacques Boileau's *Histoire des flagellants* (Amsterdam, 1701) and the many sequels and mock attacks it spawned, but also by Ned Ward's satirical comments on the use of the rod in his *London Spy*,[17] Edmund Curll, in 1718, thought the time had come to exploit, and make money from, the more salacious features of erotic flagellation. Adding an explicit frontispiece and a *Treatise of hermaphrodites* to an English translation of John Henry Meibomius's *De usu flagrorum* (Leyden, 1639; 2nd edn. Frankfurt, 1670), he published A *Treatise of the Use of Flogging in Venereal Affairs* for which he was later prosecuted.[18] This treatise was republished in 1761 with a cover, before the title, reading, 'The use of Flogging, as provocative to the pleasures of love. With some Remarks on the Office of the Loins and reins.' In the preface, Curll defended himself against accusations of pornography, arguing that 'the Fault is not in the Subject Matter, but the Inclination of the Reader, that makes these Pieces offensive'. The opening section of Curll's book consists of 'A Letter from Thomas Bartholin, On the Medical Use of RODS, To Henry Meibomius' [the son of the author] which praises flogging as a cure for several diseases, mentions its popularity throughout the ages and also deals with sexual stimulation achieved by flogging the loins. The actual Meibomius treatise starts off with quotations from classical literture and medical works on men and women incapable of reaching sexual satisfaction without flagellation. Further sources are then cited proving that 'there are Persons who are stimulated to *Venery by Strokes of Rods, and worked up into a Flame of Lust by Blows;* and that the Part, which distinguishes us to be Men, should be raised by the Charm of invigorating Lashes'. Arguing that the reins and sides influence the genitals, Meibomius concludes, '*Strokes* and *Stripes*, indicated on the Loins, are Incentives to Lust'. He supports his argument with classical quotations and the observation that old lechers use flogging to 're-inflame the cold parts'. The work concludes with another letter from 'Henry Meibomius, the Son, To the most Excellent Thomas Bartholin' on the latter's intention to reprint *Of the Use of Flogging*. The son does not agree with his father's theory about the importance of the reins but concedes that the loins as well as heat are relevant if sexual stimulation is to be attained.[19]

Flagellation, though not always in a sexual context, continued to interest publishers and readers. Discussions and letters dealing with the art of flogging can be found in the erotic periodicals throughout the century, from the *Gentleman's Magazine* (which carried the occasional, slightly erotic article) in the 1730s to the *Bon Ton Magazine* in the 1790s.[20] In 1782 the subject gained a legal dimension when a judge by the name of

John Buller declared that a man could legally chastise his wife, provided he used a stick no thicker than his thumb. Several cartoons immediately satirised the words of this learned man. Iwan Bloch provides sources proving the existence of specialised flagellation brothels and clubs of flagellant women in eighteenth-century London. In the light of the evidence, it might be possible that Volumes I and II of J. C. Hotten's *Library illustrative of social progress*, (7 vols., London, 1872) were really first published in 1777 and 1785, respectively. H. S. Ashbee does not doubt the publication date of the two books entitled, *Exhibition of Female Flagellants in the modest and incontinent world. Proving from Indubitable Facts, That a Number of Ladies take a Secret Pleasure in Whipping their own, and Children committed to their Care...*[21] The first volume is a collection of anecdotes describing whippings of men by women, but especially of boys and girls. Volume II includes letters to the editor on the first book of 1777 and another series of anecdotes on parents flogging their children. The two books smack slightly of nineteenth-century flagellomania and, in their display of masochistic and sadistic features, are unique and quite uncharacteristic of eighteenth-century pornography. Like flagellation, 'amorous strangulation' found much interest with those seeking extraordinary ways of sexual stimulation. Strangulation for erotic purposes united both pornographers and medical quacks of late eighteenth-century London. Their relationship is highlighted by the peculiar case of Franz Kotzwara, a composer whose music was rather popular in England and America until well into the twentieth century. Kotzwara's penchant for wine, women and kinky sex led to his accidental death in 1791, which in turn was the cause of a trial in the Old Bailey and much satire and speculation in Grub Street.[22]

Those lovers of the joys of Venus who found flagellation and strangulation too dangerous or perverse but wanted additional stimulation could always have recourse to less spectacular sexual aids. One of them is described by Georges-Louis Lesage (1676–1759) who visited England in 1713–14. According to this French traveller, who is not identical with the author of *Gil Blas*, there were always some women in St James's Park, London, carrying baskets full of dolls which seemed to be in great demand with the younger ladies. Instead of legs, the dolls sported a cylinder, covered with cloth, which was about six inches long and one inch wide. Lesage reports in an anecdote that a young women found her purchase too big and ordered a smaller one. But the saleswoman insisted on being paid in advance, arguing that she would not be able to sell it, if ever the young lady changed her mind, since only big ones were being asked for.[23]

'Signor Dildo', as Rochester called this 'cylinder' in his poem of 1678, was apparently not only known but also in demand and, consequently, a subject of literary comment. Samuel Butler may have written *Dildoides. A burlesque poem* (London, 1706) and the same topic is also treated in *The Bauble, a tale* (London, 1721). It may be of some interest to have a closer look at *Monsieur Thing's Origin: or Seignor D——o's Adventures in Britain* (London, 1722),[24] a rather badly-rhymed poem which, despite its mediocre quality, provides some eighteenth-century opinions about the dildo, its alleged origin and uses. It was an eighteenth-century English myth that everything perverse or 'unnatural' could only have had its origin in such immoral and sexually corrupt countries as Bulgaria, France, Italy and other Mediterranean localities. Not surprisingly, the poem inquires into the birthplace of the dildo and ascribes it to France.[25] The anonymous author accompanies the dildo after its arrival in London, from Covent-Garden to Fleet Street and on to the houses of several ladies in dire need of the extraordinary device which is thus described:

> The Engine does come up so near to Nature,
> Can spout so pleasing, betwixt Wind and Water,
> Warm mild, or any other Liquid softer,
> Slow as they please, or, if they please, much faster.

'Monsieur Thing' afterwards meets a merchant's wife who is immediately very fond of him:

> She boldly work'd him up into an Oil,
> So did she make the Creature slave and toil;
> She wrought him till he was just out of breath,
> And harrast Seignior almost unto Death.

His tribulations are not finished with this episode, however. He must satisfy an old maid and encounters two lesbians. One of the girls ties him to her middle:

> She acted Man, being in a merry Mood,
> Striving to please her Partner as she cou'd;
> And thus they took it in their turns to please
> Their Lustful Inclinations to appease.

The dildo also goes to the court before ending up with some old maids who enjoy his company in secrecy. The poem's tone is playful and occasionally lapses into satire, but the author succumbed to one of the main obsessions of his age, the fear of depopulation. For this very reason, the alien instrument was not to be accepted in Britain, as the last four lines make clear:

> Now [sic] doubt but this Uncouth contri'd New Fashion
> Was to destroy the End of Creation;
> Like that foul Sin which is as bad in Men,
> For which God did the Eastern World condemn.

Sold at sixpence a piece, *Monsieur Thing's Origin* did not meet everyone's taste. *The Daily Journal* of 9 June 1722 reports that a female bookseller sent constables to stop some hawkers selling the poem.[26] Given its scabrous reputation, it is obvious that the dildo became a 'must' for erotica such as *The History of Signor Del Dildo* (London, 1732). In *A Voyage to Lethe. By Captain Samuel Cock, sometime Commander of the Good Ship Charming Polly. Dedicated to the Right Worshipful Adam Cock, Esq., of Black Mary's Hole, Coney Skin Merchant* (London, 1741), the hero pays a visit to the goddess Dildona, 'worshipp'd by the *Sterilians*, Inhabitants of a very unfruitful Country . . . Women of all Ranks and Ages; young and old maids; Widows and Wives; all sacrificing with great Zeal to the Goddess, whose Image was at the Altar adorn'd with the Branches of the *Dildo* Tree, with silken Girdles, and with the Tongues of Lapdogs'. The instrument makes further appearances in Charles Borde's *Parapilla, Poème en Cinq Chants. Traduit de l'Italien* (1776), which was well known in England, and in Henry Fielding's *The Female Husband: or, the Surprising History of Mrs. Mary, alias Mr. George Hamilton* (London, 1746) in which a transvestite or cross-dresser successfully employs the dildo while posing as a man.[27]

If the evidence contained in a poem published in 1748 is correct, we can assume that eighteenth-century males with sufficient financial means could order life-size dolls for their private amusement. The preface of *Adollizing: or, a lively picture of a doll-worship. A poem in five cantos* (London, 1748) justifies the introduction into the English language of a new word and assures the reader 'that the ground-work, from whence the term of adollizing was taken, is a real fact . . . A person of high distinction failing in his attempt on the virtue of a young lady . . . , resolves to enjoy her at any rate, and thereupon has recourse to the extraordinary method here attempted to be described'. The poem relates the story of Clodius, a young gentleman used to easy conquests, who falls in love with the icy-cold and indifferent Clarabella. His fruitless efforts render him furious:

> Woman, cries he, when man's neglect denies,
> With mimic art the real thing supplies:
> When of dear copulation she despairs,
> At once a dildo softens all her cares.

Clodius decides to do alike and has a doll made for himself, 'as big as life'. Again, it is indicative of eighteenth-century English opinions on the origins of sexual perversity that 'a Latian artist' does the job, and not a morally upright English workman:

> On the arch'd mount, just o'er the cloven part,
> A tufft of hair he fixes with nice art,
> . . . .
> A seven-inch bore, proportion'd to his mind,
> With oval entrance, all with spunge he lin'd,
> Which warmly mollify'd, is fit for use,
> And will the sought-for consequence produce.

Clodius is very eager to try the invention forthwith:

> Stretch'd on a couch he *Claradolla* lay'd,
> (For so he call'd the figure newly made.)
> Her cloaths uplifted, bare her legs and thighs,
> And all expos'd, he feasts his ravish'd eyes:
> Prostrate before the secret seat of bliss,
> The room resounds with ev'ry ardent kiss
> . . . .
> With this, fierce back the supple joints he flings,
> And his proud matters to a level brings
> . . . .
> Then breathing quick, lust rushes thro' each vein,
> And for that time concludes the filthy scene.

Despite its bawdy irony, the poem is opposed to the 'unnatural' practice of 'adollizing'. Indeed, the hero, after some further experimenting with his doll which includes the changing of heads, grows tired of his peculiar hobby-horse. Clarabella's ice melts away with his ardent declarations of love and they decide to marry. The author thus showed the 'person of high distinction' how to get rid of his strange passion, also informing him in the preface that he would be exposed if he did not 'return to Venus'.[28]

The eighteenth century produced a considerable body of literature on the freaks of sexually abnormal people. Eunuchs, hermaphrodites, homosexuals, lesbians and transvestites were the objects of treatises, satirical attacks, moral diatribes and erotic fiction which, despite their different literary origins, had one common denominator. This was the calculated effort on the part of the publishers to meet and exploit the prurient interest of the readers in a notoriously scabrous subject matter whose mysterious and occasionally frightening aspects literally invited comments, reaching from enlightened speculation to satire and deliberate fabrication.

The castrated male or eunuch received ample literary attention. Continuing a tradition going back to Roman and Greek times, eighteenth-century scholars, notably in Germany, wrote dissertations and college essays which were restricted to an educated audience as they were written in Latin, although frequently laced with the vernacular. *Eunuchi Conjugium. Die Kapaunen-Heyrath* (Halle, 1697?), to give just one example, seems to have been rather successful in academe since it was reprinted in Jena in 1730 and 1737. This theological treatise focuses on the actual case of a marriage in 1666 between a eunuch and a woman. The marriage was eventually annulled. Latin being the lingua franca of eighteenth-century academic Europe, it is imaginable that such works were read in England too.[29] The circulation of these books from one country to another is borne out by the appearance in England of the standard work on eunuchs. Originally published as *Traité des Eunuques* (1707), Charles Ancillon's treatise was translated and printed for the sly Mr Edmund Curll. His name on the title-page of *Eunuchism Display'd, Describing all the Different Sorts of Eunuchs etc.* (London, 1718) bespeaks the pornographic potential of the 240 pages of text sold at 3/-. In the true spirit of eighteenth-century thinking, 'eunuchism' is analysed in relation to procreation. After an inquiry in Part I into the nature and social rank of eunuchs, Ancillon tries to find out 'what right Eunuchs have to marry'. Part III refutes possible objections that might be put forward against the arguments discussed in the treatise. A whole chapter (iv) of Part II is dedicated to the 'inconveniences generally attending Eunuchs marriages'. 'It may happen', warns the author, 'that . . . if a Woman, that does not find at Home, wherewithall to satisfy a provok'd Passion, should receive elsewhere, what may be necessary to lay and becalm . . . Rage and Fury'. While Ancillon is not totally opposed to the idea of marriage between fertile women and castrated men, 'since there are some capable to satisfy the Desires of a Woman', he pronounces certain reservations:

> However it is certain that an Eunuch can only satisfy the Desires of the Flesh, Sensuality, Impurity, and Debauchery; and as they are not capable of Procreation, they are more proper for such criminal Commerce than perfect Men, and more esteem'd for that Reason by lewd Women, because they can give them all the Satisfaction without running any Risk of Danger.[30]

The idea that sexually promiscuous women relied on eunuchs to enjoy fornication without any danger became attached to castrated men for the rest of the century. It is perhaps most evident in fiction. In *New Attalantis for the Year 1762; Being a select Portion of Secret History Containing Many Facts Strange! But True* (London, 1762), a collection of five 'histories', the first episode describes the 'Amours of Lady Lucian' who is neglected by her husband. A good friend advises her ladyship to take a *castrato* for a lover since 'these creatures are very tractable; it gratifies their pride to be taken notice of by a woman; and . . . they toil like horses'. Lady Lucian decides to try Signor Squalini, a singer, who turns out to her entire satisfaction and is employed as her music master. One day, however, the happy musicians were interrupted by the lady's husband who passed at her door and:

> heard his lady cry out in an extatic tone of voice, 'Give what thou can'st, and let me dream the rest.' His lordship was too well read in Pope, not to know where that line was, and the occasion of speaking it; he laid his hand immediately upon the lock of the door, and giving it a push open, for the lady had omitted to bolt it, he beheld my lady and her master – not playing the harpsichord, but playing upon it; her ladyship couchant on the instrument, which served her for a sopha, and the master recumbant on the lady, while every now and then he touched the keys of the harpsichord with his feet.

Three days afterwards, husband and wife part by mutual consent, which allows Lady Lucian 'opportunity to enjoy the society of her dear castrato without molestation'. When Squalini leaves her, she consoles herself in the arms of another eunuch singer.[31] Similar episodes can be found in the *Rambler's Magazine* of 1783.[32]

The claim of *New Attalantis* to veracity of the facts related in the stories may not be very far from the truth. The 1720s and 1730s saw a wave of bawdy and ribald satirical attacks on the famous castrato singers Carino, Farinelli and Senesino. Carino was held up to ridicule in *An Epistle from the platonick Madam Bier* [i.e., Barbier] *to the celebrated Signor Carino* (London, 1734). Carlo Broschi, alias Farinelli, arrived in London in 1734 and spent three years there as the rival of Senesino. Both singers kept the satirists busy. Farinelli served as their butt in *An Epistle to John James H–dd–g–r* [Heidegger], *esq, on the report of Signor F–r–n–lli's being with child* (London, 1736). *The happy courtezan: or, the prude demolish'd* (London, 1735) is a bawdy epistle from Constantia Phillips to Farinelli mocking his feminine looks and praising him as being more beautiful than 'tough' men. The advantages of castratos are thus pointed out:

> Eunuchs can give uninterrupted Joys,
> Without the shameful Curse of Girls or Boys:
> The violated Prude her Shape retains
> A Vestal in the publick Eye remains
> . . . .
> With eager Fondness yet can yield her Charms,
> When raptur'd in her darling Eunuch's Arms.

The lacking manhood of Senesino received satirical comment in *Mocking is catching, or, a pastoral lamentation for the loss of a man and no man* (London, 1726) and in *An epistle to the most learned Doctor W–d–d* [John Woodward], *from a prude, that was unfortunately metamorphos'd on Saturday Dec. 29, 1722* (London, 1723) which was probably prompted by Dr John Arbuthnot's *Annus Mirabilis*, a pamplet predicting that everybody was going to change sex, and that the catalyst of this change would be the sight of a *castrato* making an 'unusual motion'. The first bewails his departure from England, while in the epistle a 'prude' changes her sex while seeing Senesino at the opera.[33] It should also be remembered that Curll's *Eunuchism Display'd* claimed on the title-page that the treatise was 'Occasion'd by a young Lady's falling in Love with Nicolini, who sung in the Opera at the Hay-Market, and to whom she had like to have been married'.

Being incapable of producing children for a country which feared depopulation in the face of wars, castrated men could not be tolerated and were hence punished with ridicule. A serious sympathetic consideration of the eunuch's situation was out of the question, unless it took place in the erotic-satirical framework of periodicals like *The Bon Ton Magazine* which in 1791 presented to its readers a tongue-in-cheek series of 'historical' essays on the eunuch.[34]

Cases of physical and psychic hybrids fascinated the eighteenth century reading public. Many of the hermaphrodites, as the bisexuals, transsexuals and transvestites were indiscriminately referred to, were simply poseurs or 'cross-dressers' while others were male homosexuals. For centuries, the problem of hermaphrodites had provoked strong reactions. Real hermaphrodites, extremely rare cases, were often put to death in antiquity. The Middle Ages knew a tradition of transvestite female saints, and the eighteenth century, which was deeply interested in monsters, continued to be attracted by the ambiguity of the subject, not least because a number of men and women declared themselves 'hermaphrodites'.[35] The eighteenth-century writings on hermaphrodites as well as the mostly venomous publications on the dreaded 'mollies' (homosexuals) have been sufficiently covered.[36]

It is obvious that good money could be made by describing the seemingly lurid practices of allegedly unnatural people. What is interesting in this context, however, is that lesbians found more leniency with the writers. *Satan's Harvest Home*, for instance, merely contains a mild rebuke for sapphic ladies. The weaker sex, argues the author of the pamphlet, 'not content with our Sex, begins *Amours* with her own, and teaches the Female World a new Sort of Sin, call'd the *Flats* . . . practis'd. . . at Twickenham at this Day'. While homosexual men were exposed, ridiculed and ostracised, lesbians received occasional poetic praise. Possibly influenced by such French productions as *Poésises de Sapho* . . . (London, 1781), English lesbians were celebrated in *A Sapphic epistle from Jack Cavendish to the honourable and most beautiful Mrs. D.* (London, c. 1782), a bawdy satire on an unnamed 'Mrs D' and her lesbian adventures in Italy. A 'history' of lesbianism with reference to a 'Queen of England' is contained in *The Sappho-An. An Heroic Poem, of three Cantos. In the Ovidian Stile, Describing the Pleasures which the Fair Sex Enjoy with Each Other. According to the Modern and most Polite Taste. Found amongst the Papers of a Lady of Quality, a great Promoter of Jaconitism* (London, 17–?). These literary examples would seem to corroborate the remarks of the German traveller, Johann Wilhelm von Archenholtz, who recorded the existence of 'Anandrinic Societies' and the prevalence of lesbianism among actresses in late eighteenth-century London.[37]

To the writers at least, the behaviour of homosexual women seems to have been less objectionable since they remained female in their manners and did not adopt features of the opposite sex like the dreaded mollies. Clearly, the strongest sexual taboo of eighteenth-century England concerned male homosexuals whose behaviour seemed to threaten the independence and aggression that were traditionally associated with the male.[38]

Artificial insemination, conception without intercourse, and the 'cabbage theory' of human procreation were especially popular fields for dabbling quacks and speculating charlatans but also for trained doctors. Downright lies went down very well, for the Age of Reason was apparently gullible enough to believe in such impostors as Richard Hathaway, an apprentice who, in 1700, vomited nails and pins claiming he had been bewitched by an old woman. John Maubray's report in 1724 of the alleged birth of a monster he termed 'sucker' was outdone two years later by the sly and clever St André's sensational pamphlet describing the delivery by Mary Tofts of two rabbits and another litter of seventeen 'coneys'. This case kept the medical and especially the satirical presses going for a while, and as late as 1762 Hogarth incorporated the cases of Hathaway and Tofts in his attack on credulity and superstition.[39]

The many comparisons that were made in the scientific world between the sexual life of men and plants gave a new impetus to the discussion of, and the frantic speculation on, artificial insemination. Philip Miller's *Catalogus Plantarum* (1730) and the books of Linnaeus prodded the satirists into writing numerous bawdy and obscene skits. Toward the end of the century, the scientific analysis culminated in Erasmus Darwin's *The Loves of the Plants* (1789) and *The Economy of Vegetation* (1791) and R. J. Thornton's *A New Illustration of the Sexual System of Linnaeus* (1797–1807) which contained poetical descriptions and relied on the earlier work of Linnaeus.[40] In the wake of these works in the field of botany, some quacks and charlatans lined their pockets with the receipts of semi-pornographic treatises that skilfully mixed fact, fiction and mystery. Sir John Hill, who became known as the author of some remarkably well-written works on botany and medicine but was never admitted to the Royal Society, attacked that venerable institution in a satire entitled *Lucina sine Concubitu . . . in which proved . . . that a Woman may conceive . . . without any Commerce with Man* (London, 1750). Hill reports in this work that he successfully conducted an experiment in which a chambermaid became pregnant after he had given her a drink containing semen. He was duly answered by a writer who assumed the apt name of Richard Roe in *A Letter to Dr. Abraham Johnson* [i.e., Sir John Hill] *on the subject of his new scheme for the propagation of the human species: in which another method of obtaining that great End, more adequate to the Sentiments of the Ladies, is proposed; And, The Reflections that Author has cast upon the Royal Society of London, are answered* (London, 1750). Instead of Hill's potion, Roe proposed to the ladies his 'Tree of Life, the Arbor Vitae of the World' (i.e., the penis), obviously an allusion to Thomas Stretser's ribald poem of 1741 which was apparently still very popular. Roe's letter makes fun of Hill's experiment and parodies him in another experiment – wine bottles installed in the dung of his garden received the embryos of numerous ladies who happily lay their eggs, as it were – to show the absurdity of Hill's claim. These bawdy answers to scientific speculation found a strong echo, the reverberations reaching as far as France where Roe's answer and Hill's letter appeared as *Concubitus sine Lucina, ou le plaisir sans peine. Réponse à lettre intitulée: Lucina sine concubitu* (London, 1776). In 1752, Vincent Miller, 'M.A. and Professor of Philosophy' according to the title-page of his treatise, came out with *The Man-Plant: or, Scheme for increasing and improving the British Breed*. Miller announced that he had experimented with some poultry and had managed to extract fertilised eggs from 'within the dark-Holds and Fastness of the Womb'. Eventually, he found the 'critical Instant for proceeding to the Extraction of the Egg, or Human-foetus' and selected the conservatory as the best location for the foetus of 'Man-vegetable, in its State of Germination'. After solving the problem of nutrition, he made particular arrangements to accommodate upper-class eggs. 'I propose,' he writes, 'to employ Down, Atherdown, Silk-cotton, Porcelain-earth, and Rose-Water for Eggs of high Degree, and laid by Ladies, Duchesses, Princesses, or Money-jobbers Wives'. His next problem was to find a suitable human guinea-pig. As his wife 'had been long past the Season of Fecundation', he was 'obliged, as they say, to go farther a Field'. Luckily, the eighteenth-century household offered servants for this kind of situation:

> I pitched them upon my Gardener's Daughter, for an Essay of this infinite Importance. Her name was *Sally*. And I could not have found a properer Subject. She was very pretty, healthy, ruddy-complexioned, and between eighteen and nineteen Years old. I examin'd her attentively for some Days, and, I saw distinctly, by her Eyes, her Looks, and occasional Flushes, that she was in that critical Season, when the Integrity of a Girl hangs upon a single Hair, and

> her Virgin-flower sits so loose, that it drops with the least Shake, or warm Breath . . . There happened then to be a Wedding in our Neighbourhood, to which I knew this Girl was invited; and which I honoured with my Presence, purely that I might not lose Sight of this future Subject of my Experiment. The Country-dances went briskly forward, and produced their usual predisposing Ferment of the Blood. I remarked that *Sally* was provided with a Partner, a Sweet-heart of hers: This was a young Country Lad . . . flush of Health and Vigour. After dancing together till they were tired and enflamed, I observed them get into a snug Corner, and following them with my Eyes, I saw the young Fellow courting her, with such an Expression of Passion, as shewed he was as urgent, and as dangerous as I could have wished him for my Purpose; he kept for some Time her Hands locked up in his, and spoke so softly to her, that I could not overhear what he said. She seemed in a strange taking. Her Agitation was visible. Stifled Sighs, amorous Breathings, interrupted or altered the Tone of her Voice. Her Cheeks were flushed with the Picturesque Glow of Modesty, fainting with its Wounds, and breathing its last under the Violence of its sweet Enemy. Her Eyes appeared languishing, and suffused with an Humidity, through which all the Fires of Desire sparkled, and made them glisten like a watery Sun. The Rise and Fall of her Breast were more quick and laborious; every thing, in short, on both Sides, seemed to threaten imminent Extremities: Concluding then from all Symptoms, that the Girl's Hour was come, and that she was fairly on the edge of being qualified for the Experiment I had fore-laid, and which was to depend upon her True Love's laying the Foundation of a future *Foetus*, I judged sagaciously, that my Absence would spoil nothing, and withdrew, well satisfied with leaving them to Nature and themselves.

A poet could hardly have provided a better erotic description of his scheme which, in the literal sense of the word, bears fruit after a short time. The pregnant Sally wants to hide her shame and declares herself willing to obey his directions. After thirty-nine days he conducts her into the conservatory:

> There I placed her a straddles on a *Bidet* or Machine, such as the French Ladies use when they perform their Ablutions. There the Situation of her Body being vertical to the Cavity of my Hand, well and duly warmed for this Function, she had not been six Minutes, and eighteen Seconds in this Posture, when, without any Pain, she cried out, 'That she felt plainly something dripping from her but what it was she could not tell.' Nothing could be truer; for I, on that Instant, received it in my Hand; upon the withdrawing of which I had the Pleasure of seeing distinctly a human Egg, in which, with the Help of a magnifying Glass, I could easily discern a vernicular Motion, and the rubid Speck, or *Punctum Saliens*; which satisfied me, that I had got a well conditioned *Embryo*, endued

with the necessary Principles of Vitality. I immediately then put it gently into the prepared Bladder, of which I closed up and sealed the Opening, with a proper Mark and Label, affixed it, after an Affusion Chimico-lacteal Liquid, destinated to the Sustenance of the Foetus, thus committed to my Charge from the Date of its Expulsion; and which, I instantly planted in a Basket of Earth, in Readiness for that Purpose.

His efforts are rewarded in the eighth month with a 'fine full-formed Man-plant, a Male-infant, and vivacious'. Once his successful experiment had become known, he was 'beset with an infinite number of nominal Maids, Wives or Absentees, and wise Widows personally offering me their Service towards multiplying my Experiments'. In the final part of the treatise he speculates on the consequences of his experiment. Apart from peopling north America and the Indies with true Britishers, he explains another advantage: 'The Women delivered from the dreadful Apprehensions of the Pangs of their Labour, of which the Men are the Causes, without the least Share of the Burden falling upon them, will drink the Draught of Pleasure as pure as we do. We shall have no longer to encounter with their opposition or Repugnance founded on the Fears of the Consequences'.[41] In the wake of Hill's bawdy skit, Miller was obviously more interested in the satirical aspects of the cabbage theory which he thus exploited in an amusing parody of Hill's satirical letter.

In addition to these charlatans and satirists, several self-styled doctors specialised in sexual therapy. In Bath and London, the quacks developed treatments that came close to magic and religious practices. Again, sex proved an extremely rewarding subject for a group of sly medical priests who exploited the sexual dimensions of the new health cult. The field was large enough to allow specialisation. Martin Vanbutchell (1735–1814) catered to those who needed 'special' sexual stimulation, and the Italian alchemist and impostor Giuseppe Balsamo (1743–95), alias Count Cagliostro, derived large profits from the sale of aphrodisiacs in London and Paris in the 1770s. Animal magnetism arrived with Franz Mesmer's book, published in London and Geneva in 1779, and James Graham (1745–94), the British master of sexual therapy, incorporated Mesmer's theories into his own sexology.[42] In many respects, the role of the sexologists in late eighteenth-century England is comparable to that of Oswalt Kolle and Alex Comfort in Germany and Britain in the 1960s (and early 1970s). They claimed, and rightfully so, that enlightenment was needed in an area of human behaviour that was haunted by taboos and prejudices and, when they finally set to work, they catered for obviously existing needs but knew prefectly well that the very ambiguity of their subject guaranteed excellent sales for their publications.

Surveying the genre of medical and paramedical erotica, which constitutes merely a small segment of the larger field of the literature on sex in the Age of Enlightenment,[43] one is of course tempted to adopt Michael Foucault's convenient theory that the discourse on sex gained in volume after 1600.[44] However, a number of caveats must be entered against such an interpretation. To begin with, Foucault never cared very much for the nitty-gritty of historical research and preferred the bird's-eye view which allowed him majestic strides from BC to AD in a single paragraph. In the last decade or so, the empirical dimensions of his work have come under some criticsim, while acknowledgement has been made of his original mind.[45]

As far as the eighteenth century is concerned, Foucault's thesis of a growing discourse on sex holds true only for literature – and, even in this area, a closer analysis reveals a complicated picture that still needs to be examined, especially if one looks at the much neglected level of popular reading – but not for the oral tradition. We have sufficient evidence suggesting a causal relation between the rise of pornography in the two centuries before the French Revolution and an increasing privacy in social relations,[46] though this is only one of several factors. More privacy, however, apparently meant a higher consumption of erotica. After literature and, significantly, allegedly medical and moral works like *Onania* had successfully applied the originally religious confessional technique to erotic fiction, sex and sexual desire were transformed into discourse – sex became erotic discourse.[47]

By the eighteenth century, this discourse clearly began to assume psychologically alleviating roles for both writers and readers. Psychologists are familiar with a phenomenon called 'Pseudolismus' in German, which denotes the urge to talk about or record sexual fantasies, erotographomania being one of its variations.[48] Some psychologists see erotica as a sort of mental masturbation and, even if one does not agree with the theory that there seems to exist something like a need to talk or write about sex, the relations between an increasing privacy and the growing demand for erotica are of great interest. Medical and paramedical erotica, like the related field of erotic fiction, can thus be seen as a multifunctional discourse providing some sexual relief, erotic entertainment, a mixture of correct and false information, and leading to the demand that the discourse be continued.

Notes

1 On the development of the medical profession, see Peter Gay, *The Enlightenment: an interpretation*, (London, 1973), vol. II; Bernice Hamilton, 'The medical professions in the eighteenth century', *Economic History Review*, IV, 1951, pp. 141–69; Roy Porter, 'Medicine and the Enlightenment in eighteenth-century England', *Bulletin of the Society for the Social History of Medicine*, XXV, 1979, pp. 27–40; Guy Williams, *The Age of Agony: the art of healing*, London, 1975, and Jean Donnison, *Midwives and medical men*, London, 1977.
2 On the role and importance of quacks, see Derek Jarrett, *England in the Age of Hogarth*, London, 1974, pp. 193–5; Eric Jameson, *The Natural History of Quackery*, London, 1961; Charles John Samuel Thompson, *The Quacks of Old London*, New York, 1928; Donnison, *Midwives*, passim, and Iwan Bloch, *Sexual Life in England Past and Present*, London, 1958, pp. 301–19. In addition, see Roy Porter, '"Under the Influence": Mesmerism in England', *History Today*, 1985, pp. 22–9.
3 For studies discussing aspects of 'medical' erotica see Paul–Gabriel Boucé, 'Quelques aspects de la sexualité au xviiie siècle', in Michaèle Plaisant, ed., *L'Eccentricité en Grande Bretagne au xviiie siècle*, Lille, 1976, 139–58; Michel Delon, 'Le prétexte anatomique', *Dix-Huitième Siècle*, XII, 1980, pp. 35–48, and Roy Porter, 'Mixed feelings: the Enlightenment and sexuality in eighteenth-century Britain', in Paul-Gabriel Boucé, ed., *Sexuality in eighteenth-century Britain*, Manchester, 1982, pp. 1–28. A more detailed discussion with a wider scope can be found in my *Eros Revived: erotica of the Enlightenment in England and America*, London, 1987, I.
4 See, for instance, Otho T. Beall, Jr., 'Aristotle's Master-Piece in America: a landmark in the folklore of medicine', *The William & Mary Quarterly*, XX, 1963, pp. 207–22; Roger Thompson, *Unfit for Modest Ears*, London, 1979, pp. 161–7; Thomas H. Johnson, 'Jonathan Edwards and the "Young Folks' Bible"', *The New England Quarterly*, V, 1932, pp. 37–54; Lawrence Stone, *The Family, Sex and Marriage in England 1500–1800*, London, 1977, pp. 493–4; Vern L. Bullough, *Sex, Society and History*, New York, 1976, pp. 93–104; Alex Comfort, *The Anxiety Makers*, London, 1967, pp. 20–7; and Roy Porter, 'Spreading carnal knowledge or selling dirt cheap? Nicolas Venette's *Tableau de l'amour conjugal* in eighteenth-century England', *Journal of European Studies*, XIV, 1984, pp. 233–55.
5 On Marten, see Philip Pinkus, *Grub Street*, London, 1968, pp. 51–66.
6 John Spinke, *Venus's Botcher*, London, 1711, p. 7, and *Quackery unmask'd*, London, 1709, p. 70.
7 Marten, *Gonosologium*, pp. 51–4, 102–3.
8 See David Foxon, *Libertine Literature in England, 1660–1745*, New York, 1966, p. 13.
9 See *An Apology*, pp. 53–4. On pp. 29ff. Marten's ideas and nostrums are so well defended as to suggest that he wrote the treatise himself.
10 *Ibid.*, title-page and p. 5.
11 *Ibid.*, pp. 16 and 27–8.
12 *Ibid.*, pp. 41–5.
13 *Ibid.*, p. 46.
14 See, for instance, such guides as *A rational account of the natural weaknesses of Woman*, London, second ed., 1716, later published as *The ladies physical directory*,

London, eighth ed. 1742; John Maubray, *The female physician*, London, 1724; the anonymous *The ladies dispensatory, or, every woman her own physician*, London, 1770?, and the handbooks for midwives, such as Nicholas Culpeper's *Directory for Midwives* and John Pechey's *The compleat midwife's practice enlarged*, which both date from the seventeenth century and continued to sell after 1700. In addition, see Robert A. Erickson, '"The books of generation": some observations on the style of the English midwife books, 1671–1764', in P.-G Boucé, ed., *Sexuality*, pp. 74–95.
15 Armstrong, *The Oeconomy of Love*, pp. 13–18 and 42.
16 See my article 'The veil of science and morality: some pornographic aspects of the *Onania*', *The British Journal for Eighteenth–Century Studies*, VI, 1983, pp. 179–84; George S. Rousseau, 'Nymphomania, Bienville and the rise of erotic sensibility', P.-G. Boucé, ed., *Sexuality*, 95–120; and P.-G. Boucé's essay on masturbation and fantasy in this book.
17 See J. L. Delolme, *The history of the flagellants . . . being a paraphrase and commentary on the Historia Flagellantium of the Abbé Boileau*, London, 1783, and *Memorials of human superstition, imitated from the Historia Flagellantium of the Abbé Boileau*, and Edward Ward, *The London Spy*, London, 1704, pp. 32–3.
18 See Thompson, *Unfit*, pp. 164–6. The prosecution was, however, more concerned with Curll's publication of *Venus in the Cloister*.
19 *A treatise of the use of flogging*. London, 1719, pp. 33 and 58.
20 See the *Gentleman's Magazine*, January/February 1735, October 1780, and *The Bon Ton Magazine*, November 1791, March–July 1792, August 1793, February/March 1794, November/December 1795 and January/February 1796.
21 See Bloch, *Sexual life in England*, pp. 320–86, and Henry Spencer Ashbee, *Index librorum prohibitorum*, London, 1877, reprint New York, 1962, pp. 238–49.
22 On the Kotzwara case and the publications it spawned, see Richard J. Wolfe, 'The hang-up of Franz Kotzwara and its relationship to sexual quackery in late eighteenth-century London', in my *Sex and Eighteenth-century English Culture*, *Studies on Voltaire and the Eighteenth Century*, CCXXVIII, 1984, ed. H. T. Mason, pp. 47–67.
23 Georges-Louis Lesage, *Remarques sur l'état de l'Angleterre*, Amsterdam, 1715, quoted in Boucé, 'Quelques aspects', *loc. cit.*, p. 151.
24 The poems are listed in David Foxon, *English Verse 1701–1750*, 2 vols., Cambridge, 1975, Vol. I. A copy of *Dildoides* is held by Trinity College, Dublin, *The Bauble* in the Bodleian Library, and *Monsieur Thing's Origin* can be found in the British Library.
25 See *Monsieur Thing's Origin*, pp. 7–8, and Paul-Gabriel Boucé, 'Aspects of sexual tolerance and intolerance in eighteenth-century England', *The British Journal for Eighteenth-Century Studies*, III, 1980, p. 180.
26 See *Monsieur Thing's Origin*, pp. 12, 16, 19, 23, and Foxon, *English Verse*, 413.
27 See *A Voyage to Lethe*, pp. 34–5, and *The Female Husband*, pp. 37–49.
28 *Adollizing*, pp. iv and 17–19.
29 See Henry Spencer Ashbee, *Catena Librorum prohibitorum*, London, 1885, reprint New York, 1962, pp. xviii and 15–20.

30 *Eunuchism Display'd*, pp. 168–9, 206–7.
31 See Ashbee, *Catena*, pp. 270–1.
32 See 'Adventures of an Eunuch', in *The Rambler's Magazine*, I, London, 1783.
33 On Carino and Farinelli, see Philip H. Highfill, Jr. et al., eds. *A Biographical Dictionary of Actors, Actresses, Musicians, Dancers, Managers, and Other Stage Personnel in London, 1660–1800*, III, 1975, and V, 1978, and David Foxon, *English Verse*, I, where the satirical attacks are listed. In addition, see *The happy courtezan*, p. 6.
34 See *The Bon Ton Magazine*, I, London, 1791.
35 For studies of the literature on hermaphrodites, see Marie Delcourt, *Hermaphrodite, Mythes et rites de la bisexualité dans l'antiquité classique*, Paris, 1958; Jean-Pierre Guicciardi, 'Hermaphrodite et le prolétaire', *Dix-Huitième Siècle*, XII, 1980, pp. 49–79; John Ashton, *Eighteenth-Century Waifs*, London, 1887, pp. 177-203; Iwan Bloch, *Sexual life in England*, 427–30. In addition, see Lynne Friedli's essay, 'Passing women: a study of a gender boundaries in the eighteenth century', in this book, and Chapter I of my *Eros Revived*.

Two eighteenth-century treatises on the subject are *Tractatus de hermaphroditis: or, a Treatise of Hermaphrodites*, published by Curll in 1718, and James Parsons' less sensational and more sober *A mechanical and critical enquiry into the nature of hermaphrodites*, London, 1741.
36 On homosexuals in eighteenth-century England and the erotica dealing with the 'mollies', see Chapter I of my *Eros Revived*; Chapter 3 of this book; Bloch, *Sexual Life*, pp. 394–426; Vern L. Bullough et al., *An Annotated Bibliography of Homosexuality*, 2 vols., New York, 1975; *ibid.*, *Homosexuality: a history*, New York and London, 1979; Montgomery Hyde, *The Other Love*, London, 1970; Randolph Trumbach, 'London's sodomites: homosexual behaviour and western culture in the eighteenth century', *Journal of Social History*, II, 1977, pp. 1–33; *ibid.*, *The Rise of the Egalitarian Family*, London, 1978, and Lawrence Stone, *The Family, Sex and Marriage in England 1500–1800*, London, 1977, pp. 541–2.
37 See *Satan's Harvest Home*, London, 1749, *passim*. Archenholtz's travel report is cited in Bloch, *Sexual Life*, p. 425. See also *ibid.* for other aspects of lesbianism in eighteenth-century England.
38 See Trumbach, *The Rise of the Egalitarian Family, p. 283*.
39 See John Maubray, *The Female Physician*, London, 1724. A more detailed discussion of such frauds, including the case of Mary Tofts, can be found in Guy Williams, *The Age of Agony*, pp. 35–8, and in Chapter I of my *Eros Revived*. The British Library has a collection of tracts relating to Mary Tofts in a volume available under the pressmark 1178 h 4 which includes the reports of St André and Manningham, as well as satirical works and cartoons.
40 See David Foxon, *Libertine Literature*, p. 17 n. 30, and Clive Bush, 'Erasmus Darwin, Robert John Thornton, and Linnaeus' Sexual System', *Eighteenth-Century Studies*, VII, 1974, pp. 295–320.
41 On the history, before the eighteenth century, of the discussion of breeding embryos in bell-jars, see R. C. Punnett, 'Ovist and Animalculists', *The American Naturalist*, 62, 1928, pp. 481–507. Even today, this is still a very good introduction to Enlightenment theories on reproduction. On Hill, see

the introduction in G. S. Rousseau, ed., *The Letters and Papers of Sir John Hill*, New York, 1982. In addition, see *The Man-Plant*, pp. 19–36.

42 On Graham's sexology and similar theories see Chapter I of my *Eros Revived*; Roy Porter, 'Under the influence', *loc. cit.*, Jameson, *The Natural History of Quackery*, Chapter VI; Williams, *The Age of Agony*, pp. 187–8, and Thompson, *The Quacks of Old London*, pp. 317–20.

43 We have barely begun to scratch the surface of vast and untilled fields in the area of erotica of the Enlightenment; see the bibliographies by Patrick J. Kearney, comp., *The Private Case, An annotated bibliography of the Private Case Erotica Collection in the British (Museum) Library*, London, 1981, and by Pascal Pia, *Les Livres de L'Enfer*, 2 Vols., Paris, 1978. My *Eros Revived* is an interdisciplinary and introductory study which also outlines what remains to be done. In addition, see my article 'Researching the taboo: sexuality and eighteenth-century English erotica', *Eighteenth-Century Life*, III, 1983, pp. 108–15, and my introduction to John Cleland, *Fanny Hill*, Harmondsworth, 1985.

44 See Michel Foucault, *The History of Sexuality*, New York, 1978, *passim*.

45 See, for instance, George S. Rousseau, 'Whose Enlightenment? Not Man's: The case of Michael Foucault', *Eighteenth-Century Studies*, VI, 1972, pp. 238–56; *ibid.*, 'Foucault's Death', *London Literary Review*, September 1984.

46 See, for example, Stone, *The Family, Sex and Marriage*, *passim*; Roger Thompson, *Unfit for Modest Ears*; Jean-Louis Flandrin, *Un Temps Pour Embrasser. Aux origines de la morale sexuelle occidentale*, Paris, 1983, and Ronald Paulson, *Representations of Revolution*, London, 1983, pp. 111–248.

47 See Foucault, *The History of Sexuality*, pp. 23 and 57–8.

48 See Hans Giese and Eberhard Schorsch, *Zur Psychopathologie der Sexualität*, Stuttgart, 1973, pp. 37f. and 90–3.

3

Modern prostitution and gender in *Fanny Hill*: libertine and domesticated fantasy

RANDOLPH TRUMBACH

It has become a commonplace that John Cleland transformed erotic writing in the early eighteenth century by applying to it the new techniques of the novel. Criticism has also begun to point out that with those techniques came the ideology of romantic love and marriage. Cleland's book becomes one of the easier demonstrations of the new conjunction of eroticism and matrimony. He is part of the history of the romantic, companionate marriage which the recent history of the family has analysed. Cleland's romantic eroticism, unlike that of most of his fellow novelists, was not, however, tied to a traditional Christian morality. It was instead libertine, anti-Christian and materialist, and it is one of the intentions of this essay to emphasise this by showing the disjunction between the world of prostitution in the fantasy of the novel and in the actualities of the legal sources. The other intention of this essay is to place Cleland's prostitute in the context of the gender revolution that was an essential part of the modern culture that emerged in north-western Europe in the 1690s. Here it is less clear than in the case of the ideology of romance that Cleland was in self-conscious control of his material, but it nonetheless affected him as powerfully. This essay is accordingly divided into three parts: there is first a discussion of the organisation of prostitution in the novel, there is then a brief analysis of gender roles in the novel and in the actual world, and, finally, the prostitution of the legal sources is compared with that in the novel.

I

Cleland makes prostitution in *Fanny Hill* a rather private affair. It is true that at the beginning of the second half of the novel Fanny declares that she was passing 'from a private devotee to pleasure into a public one'(92).[1] But all she really means to say is that, while in the first half of the novel she was the kept mistress of first Charles and then Mr H, she is, in the second half, the paid companion of many men. Almost all of her sexual activity still occurs in the very controlled environment of Mrs Cole's house. It will therefore be useful at this point to conduct a tour of Fanny's sexual environments.

Fanny begins her career in Mrs Brown's house which is described as a private house, with a well-furnished back parlour, and bedchambers on a second floor. When Fanny attempts to describe this house from Charles's point of view, she says that he had taken her 'out of a common bawdy-house'. But from her own point of view, Mrs Brown is very often her mistress, and Fanny an upper servant and sometimes a child. Mrs Brown promises to do 'more than twenty mothers' would for her (8). There is also the animal imagery which plays upon the theme of the domesticated pet. Fanny describes herself as a bird in a cage, 'so tame to their whistle' that she would not fly away even if her cage doors were left opened; 'nothing in short,' she says, 'was wanting to domesticate me entirely and to prevent my going out anywhere to get better advice' (23). Fanny is also sometimes the domesticated horse. Mrs Phoebe Ayres, who is presented by Mrs Brown as her cousin, is really the 'notable manager of her house – whose business it was to prepare and break young fillies as I was to the mounting-block' (9). Phoebe herself had endured 'a long course of hacney-ship' (10) and is 'thorough-bred' (12). Mrs Brown also conducts a market in her house (10, 14) and when she displays Fanny for sale, 'she omitted no point of jockyship'. Mrs Brown's house is also a convent where she is the 'venerable mother Abbess' (24, 17), Fanny's 'pious governess' (26), 'the venerable president of the college' (9); the girls are the members of 'her flock' (22), and Fanny is prepared 'for the purposes of my reception into that hospitable house' (17).

When Fanny elopes with Charles, they go first to 'a public house in Chelsea, hospitably commodious for the reception of duet-parties of pleasure' (38). He then removes her to 'a private ready furnished lodging in D—— Street, St. James's, where he paid half a guinea a week for two rooms and a closet on the second floor' (50). This house is really as disreputable as the one in Chelsea since the landlady, Mrs Jones, was 'a kind of private procuress', who rented out as lodgings most of the house she lived in (52). Mrs Jones extends credit to Fanny when Charles is taken away, and with the threat of the debtor's prison, draws her in to accepting the arrangement with Mr H, which Mrs Jones had been commissioned to effect (56–7). Mr H, who is forty and the younger brother to an earl, does things in high style: Fanny is put into 'the first floor, very genteelly furnished, for two guineas a week, of which I was instated mistress, with a maid to attend me'. It is in the house of a plain tradesman who is a dependent of Mr H. Fanny had become 'the kept mistress, in form', with a circle of similar acquaintances who mimic the lives of women of quality (66–7).

When Mr H breaks with Fanny, she turns to Mrs Cole as her 'gouvernante'. Mrs Cole arranges private lodgings for Fanny. Fanny's apartment is at 'a brushmaker's in R. . . street, Covent Garden, the very next door to' Mrs Cole's house, where there was no room. Fanny's rooms had been tenanted by 'several successions' of 'ladies of pleasure', the landlord was 'familiarized to their ways' and, provided 'the rent was duly paid', all was 'easy and commodious' (88–9).

Mrs Cleo's own house is, in outward appearance, a millinery shop where, during the day, three beautiful young women of eighteen or nineteen sit demurely at their work. But behind the shop is a spacious drawing-room and private rooms for the girls, who at night receive their male visitors. This house of pleasure is boarding-school, convent and flock rolled into one. Mrs Cole is the governess, and the girls her 'small and domestick flock' (93). Mrs Cole presides at the head of her cluck (94). Fanny is the new boarder presented to the other pupils (93). The girls pass through a 'due noviciate' (93) and a chapter is held 'for the ceremony of my reception into the sisterhood' (94). Mrs Cole has formed 'a little family of love' (93). The band of young men who are the chief supporters of her 'secret institution' style themselves 'the restorers of the liberty of the golden age' who bring simplicity and innocence to sexual pleasure, and free it from guilt and shame (94). Inspired perhaps by this programme, and by the arcadian theme that pervades the entire second half of the novel, Cleland, for the first (and I think the only) time in his novel, looks at a common English bawdy-house, and calls it 'this little seraglio' (95).

Only once does Fanny break out of this private world. It is when she meets the young sailor in the street. Excited by the thought of 'being treated like a common street-plyer', she goes with him to 'the next convenient haven', where in 'a little room on one side of the passage', he has her on the 'rickety table' which, with 'two or three disabled chairs', furnished the room (140–2). Fanny also hears of and observes sexual acts in two other disreputable places. Her companion Emily, after she is mistaken for a boy by her masquerade, is taken to a bagnio by a 'gentleman of distinction' who is appalled to find that she is a woman (154–6). Fanny herself observes (through the movable partition between two rooms in a public-house) the scene in which a nineteen-year-old gentleman sodomises his seventeen-year-old country lad (156–60).

Sex in the remainder of the novel occurs in safe and enclosed places. There is a picnic at the 'little but agreeable house' on the Thames (166). After this 'trip to Cythera' they return to 'the old haven' (171). Mrs Cole's family disbands. Fanny rents her own small house at Marylebone (173), which she leaves to live with her old bachelor in his house (175), but in neither of these places are sexual scenes described. The last sexual scene does occur in a room in an inn. But by then Fanny is a woman of property, and no longer a whore. Her companion is Charles, and the act is the prelude to her marriage.

II

It is apparent from this that Cleland's fantasy is excited by sex that is safe, comfortable and accompanied by love. Two of his modern critics have even claimed that his eroticism can be distinguished from that of his French contemporaries by his preference for having sex accompanied by romantic love. The heroine and hero of his two first novels eventually marry the objects of their desire. Cleland is, in this regard, one of the possible demonstrations of the claim that eroticism and marriage come to be conjoined in the eighteenth century, with wives becoming mistresses to their husbands. Fanny, on the other hand, is first a mistress and only then a wife, so that Cleland's fantasy cannot be too neatly domesticated.[2]

But Fanny's life was also not much like the lives of most of the more than 3,000 prostitutes whom Saunders Welch estimated to be active in London at mid-century.[3] Cleland was fully aware of this. In his later writings, the brothel becomes progressively a less and less salubrious place.[4] But even in the year that he published the *Memoirs*, Cleland wrote, in his account of the sailors' riots against the whores, a description of the lives of the common women of the town that was as grim as anything in the legal sources.[5] My own view of the prostitute's life is no doubt jaundiced by the fact that most of my information comes from legal sources; from the lives of women who had not managed to ply their trade safely but had instead been arrested. But whether one uses legal records, or the libertine literature with its genial view of prostitution for the upper classes (as the older scholarship and the amateurs do),[6] or the literature of the reformers (of which Cleland's pamphlet is an instance),[7] one becomes aware that there was in London, from the 1690s onwards, a new kind of prostitution which it is necessary to define before proceeding.

It has been suggested (playfully, to a degree) that the new social role for the prostitute was partly a result of the rise in status that all the traditional professions experienced in the course of the eighteenth century. The century 'discovered the tart with the heart of gold' and decided to save her.[8] But it is far more to the point to see that this new role arose from a reorganisation in male and female gender roles. These roles were a result of the same forces that brought about the new patterns in marriage and child-rearing which recent scholarship has identified,[9] but they were also a consequence of the appearance in northern Europe of cities with populations of 500,000.

This reorganisation of gender roles was probably a phenomenon occurring in at least all of north-western Europe.[10] The new role for women might be described by saying that it was ceasing to be thought that all women were potentially whores (and that married women, especially, required watching) and that it was instead the case that some few unmarried girls would, because of the peculiarities of their environment, take to walking the streets as prostitutes. Johnson made the point in his *Dictionary*. He gave as the first meaning of whore: 'a woman who converses unlawfully with men; a fornicator; an adultress; a strumpet'. It was certainly what the married women understood the word to mean when they brought the great majority of cases for sexual defamation in the Consistory Court.[11] Johnson gave as his second meaning of whore: 'a prostitute; a woman who receives money from men'. These proportionately few girls nonetheless made a great and very shocking crowd when from the 1690s onwards, night and day, they patrolled the principal thoroughfares of the great cities, insulting respectable women, corrupting drunken husbands and unwary apprentices, twitching at men's sleeves, thrusting their hands into men's breeches, and making daring propositions. It was a problem that grew larger in the nineteenth century when there were more cities of half a million inhabitants, but it was neither original to that century nor a result of industrialisation.[12] It was a problem that had probably existed ever since some states had ceased to license prostitutes in the sixteenth century.[13] But cities of 500,000 were able to support a greater complexity than ever before of subcultures, alongside more stable conventional majorities.[14] Grub Street, for instance, came into existence about the same time,[15] and London's prostitutes coexisted with a majority of women in a city which had probably one of the lowest bastardy rates in England.[16]

London's prostitutes also coexisted with London's sodomites, who produced the most notorious of the new subcultures. The two groups were linked by reformers for their abuse of public decency. The Societies for the Reformation of Manners boasted in 1710 that by its 'means our streets have been very much cleansed from the lewd night-walkers and most detestable sodomites'.[17] Modern analysis should also link the two since the sodomite's role was for men what the prostitute's was for women. Sodomy had traditionally meant any of three things: sexual intercourse between males, anal intercourse between men and women, or intercourse with beasts. In the eighteenth century it came to refer increasingly to male homosexual relations alone. This sort of sodomite was presumed to have no interest in women. By contrast, his seventeenth-century counterpart would have been found with his whore on one arm and his catamite on the other. The new exclusive adult sodomite was also supposed to be effeminate, and effeminacy lost its seventeenth-century meaning of referring both to cross-dressing boys and to men enervated by too great a sexual interest in women. The majority of eighteenth-century men therefore constructed their masculinity around their avoidance of the sodomite's role and, instead, fervently pursued women and, of course, prostitutes.[18]

Cleland, however, puts a scene between two sodomites into the heart of the second half of his prostitute's story – into the ideologically radical half of his book with its libertine, anti-Christian and materialist message.[19] It is the very scene which modern criticism says caused the book's eighteenth-century prosecution, and it is claimed that it is also the book's structurally central scene.[20] It now turns out as well that in his old age Cleland was accused of being a sodomite and socially ostracised for it.[21] If this was true and Cleland was a homosexually exclusive sodomite of the new kind, rather than a bisexual sodomite of the old kind, it would further complicate the already difficult problem of what occurs in an eighteenth-century novel when a male author impersonates a woman.[22] But even if Cleland were no kind of sodomite at all, it becomes possible to understand the necessity of his sodomitical scene, and his own condemnation of it in the novel, when one knows that the prostitute and the sodomite are both new and interrelated gender roles; the male impersonation of the prostitute tests the limits of gender identity in a world where men were now men because they did not know what it was like to desire men, since only women now had such knowledge. This was a standard which did not yet apply to women. When Phoebe seduces Fanny, it is brushed aside as 'the gratification of one of those arbitrary tastes, for which there is no accounting' (12). But the sodomite was described as a man whose character was in all respects 'the most worthless and despicable that could be' (159). Cleland was, however, fascinated by the question (as was Fielding) of whether relations between women were not as criminal as those between men; in his commentary (1751) on the translation of an Italian case, he speculated whether homosexual behaviour in women was the result of 'some error in nature, or from some disorder or perversion in the imagination'. Like Fielding, he knew that society had not yet constructed a lesbian role, and so he claimed that his purpose was to inform others that the behaviour existed.[23]

Unlike Fielding, Cleland had no intention of baptising sex into a Christian world. He sang the praises of an affectionate and domesticated sexuality, but it was to be enjoyed in an earthly paradise: his lovers embark for Cythera (171). This is why it is unwise to regard the second letter as a description of Fanny's continued moral education.[24] The second letter is instead a deliberate reversal of the moral expectations of the first. Fanny, unlike Hogarth's whore, does not slide into destitution and death when her keeper deserts her. Under the aegis of Watteau's happier mind, she takes a trip to Cythera with her friends. Much of the remainder of the second letter is taken up with the various fetishistic forms of sexuality, which are justified on the traditional libertine ground that all pleasures were good, provided they 'blew nobody any harm' (144). As in the French libertine novels (from which some critics have tried to distance him), there can be little doubt that Cleland's intention was to propose a sexual morality based on goodness of the body and freedom of choice, rather than on the traditional Christian foundations of procreative purpose and a hierarchy of forbidden acts.[25] Sodomy between men was alone of all the acts condemned. It must therefore be that Cleland's sexual imagination operated not only within the bounds of the new ideal of a romantic, married sexuality, but also within the bounds of the new gender roles which set the limits of the acceptable by redeeming the prostitute and ostracising the sodomite.

III

The principal complaint against the prostitute throughout the eighteenth century was that she did not conduct her business in private. Cleland went to great pains to save Fanny from such a charge. He also protected her from most of the sleaziness that in many other writers was apparently an important part of the prostitute's power to excite. This decision was, no doubt, partly a result of his individual sexual disposition. But it was also necessary to his arcadian and libertine purpose. Hogarth's more realistic representation of prostitution could be tied too easily to the traditional Christian suspicion of sex. Cleland's fictional world does, however, have connections with the actual world in addition to the ideological presumptions that have already been discussed. He seems, for instance, to have obtained the germ of his story from an incident related to him by Charles Carmichael. It is also well known that Mrs Cole is based to some degree on a well-known procuress of that name, but it is unlikely that Mrs Cole's bagnio ever provided the fantasies of the novel. These would more probably have been found later in the seraglios that came into vogue after 1750.[26] A comparison of the details of the novel with those of the legal sources will therefore help to establish the extent of Cleland's fantasy.

We might start with the question of seduction into prostitution. It is the point at which Cleland allows the danger of the law's prosecution to enter the lives of his prostitutes. To ensure that Mrs Brown will not attempt to recover Fanny for her house, Charles has a lawyer friend go to speak to her of having 'decoy'd, under pretence of hiring as a servant, a young girl just come out of the country' and to threaten her with a 'Justice of peace, Newgate, old Bailey, indictments for keeping a disorderly house, pillory, carting, and the whole process of that nature' (49).

Young girls were decoyed, but not so happily as Fanny was. Isabella Cranston in 1724 applied for poor relief to the parish of St Margaret's, Westminster because she was pregnant by Colonel Charteris. She said that she had first had sex with him in the house of Mrs Jolly in Suffolk Street, where 'she was decoyed under pretence of being hired into service'. She had, however, not become part of Mrs Jolly's establishment, and after seeing the Colonel several times in other places, and him alone, she was pregnant and abandoned.[27]

But a servant girl who had been seduced could be reclaimed by determined action. There is the case of Hannah Smith in 1729. She was fourteen years old and apprenticed to James Gerrard of Moorfields and his wife Mary. At Easter her employers gave her leave to visit her sister who lived across town in Westminster. As she went through the Park, she met an old acquaintance named Winnifred Lloyd who invited her to come and visit her at her lodgings in John Street. After visiting her sister, Hannah went to Winnifred Lloyd's lodgings and found her with a man called Squire Janssen. Janssen told Hannah she was pretty, asked Mrs Lloyd to be kind to her and let her want for nothing, gave her half-a-crown himself, and said that she should come and see Mrs Lloyd often where she would be made much of. As Hannah apparently made no further move of her own, Mrs Lloyd three weeks later came to visit her at five in the evening when her employers were away. She took the girl to her lodgings, where Janssen joined them. He hugged and kissed Hannah. At ten o'clock all three went together in a coach to a tavern opposite the Mews, where Mrs Lloyd got out, but before she left them, she pulled Hannah from her seat opposite the Squire and put her next to him. The coach now drove to the bagnio in St James's Street at the end of Pall Mall. They were shown up a staircase to a room with a bed in it. The Squire told the waiter to knock before he came in. Janssen now gave the girl a few kisses and caresses, and then threw her upon the bed and had sex with her three times during the following hour or so until they left at midnight. They hired a coach and collected Mrs Lloyd. The Squire soon left them, and Hannah went to spend the night with Mrs Lloyd at her lodgings. Hannah gave to Lloyd the ten shillings that Janssen had paid her and told her all that had happened. Lloyd asked Hannah whether Janssen had not hurt her. Hannah replied that he had almost stifled and killed her. "'O," says Mrs Lloyd in answer ". . . when he first lay with me, I cried out murder, but if you was forty years old, it would not hurt you'". And so Lloyd encouraged the girl, saying that Janssen 'would make a woman of her forever'. Hannah, sometimes with another girl, continued to visit Lloyd and Janssen. But her mistress grew suspicious that Mrs Lloyd had 'seduced away her maid servant', forced a confession out of the girl, and took the matter to the magistrate.[28]

Hannah had a careful mistress and sister; Fanny of course was an orphan and new to town. Many of the girls taken out of the street by the magistrate were orphans. Unlike Fanny, however, they were not fresh from the country but the children of the London poor who had begun their sexual lives between the ages of twelve and fourteen.[29]

Many of these younger girls had families to be sent home to after their arrest, especially in the second half of the century. Rosetta Webbe was taken home by her mother, Elizabeth Rose and Sarah Powell were delivered to their fathers, Catherine Kendrich went to her godfather, and Martha Brown's brother promised to take her home.[30] Even the more hardened prostitute sometimes had a family who came to her rescue. Mary Geary was a nightwalker well known to the constables. Three times in little over a year in 1722–3 they arrested her: on the first two occasions, Edward Geary, a weaver, stood her bail, and on the third, James Geary, also a weaver, did so. Mary Wilkinson was bailed by another Mary Wilkinson. After Catherine Moore was taken in a private room above a public house, her husband bailed her, and John Buckmaster accompanied his wife when she went strolling to pick up men; he tried to rescue her from the arresting constable.[31]

Fanny, like the girl seduced by Colonel Charteris, does become pregnant. Fortunately, she miscarries, but the vulnerability of her illness lays her open to the exactions of Mrs Jones, and completes her seduction into prostitution. In this respect, Fanny's experience touches the life of another women in the legal sources. Mary David was born in Herefordshire. Her father died when she was a child, her mother remarried a poor man, and Mary was sent to London as a servant. She served for two years as a servant in a family in Berkeley Square. The footman, although he was already married, seduced her under promise of marriage. She lost her place when she became pregnant. The man helped her at first with the child, but then she took a place as a wet-nurse and put her own child out to nurse with a woman in Tottenham Court Road. The child she nursed was weaned, her milk dried up and she went to live in the house in Tottenham Court Road. The landlady was at first very civil and allowed her to get into debt. Then 'one night between eleven and twelve, she went upstairs to her, with manners totally changed, and swore with the grossest abuse, that she would turn her into the street, child and all, unless she brought her some pay'. When Mary asked how she could possibly do that, the landlady replied 'that girls with worse faces than she often picked up a great deal'. Mary now discovered that one other young lodger in the house was a kept mistress, and the house 'was, in fact, though in a very private way, a bad house'. Mary took to prostitution, 'driven out in bitter anguish', and eventually found poor friends who took her in. She swore her child to the parish and returned to her mother in the country, but she found to her 'inescapable grief' that she was pregnant again 'from the sad effects of the prostitution'. Her first child was now dead; the parish had refused to take it from the parish nurse and it had died with a black eye, a broken collarbone and sick from whooping-cough. Her second child she managed to persuade the Foundling Hospital to take, and from this we learn her story. Since that story was not known in the country, she planned to return there after she had sold her milk in London.[32] Mary's tale, unlike Fanny's, lacks glamour, yet she was, like Hannah Smith, able to escape from her seduction into prostitution because she had a family to take her in. Fanny Hill, however, never had to endure the painful experience of Mary David in having one child dead and battered and the other surrendered to an orphanage.

Mrs Brown and Mrs Jones – the pretended mistress and the unscrupulous landlady – have their analogues then in real life. But what of Mrs Cole the milliner? Campbell in *The London Tradesman* advised parents not to apprentice their daughters to milliners, because the poor wages and the constant resort of beaus and rakes to the millinary shops meant 'that nine out of ten of the young creatures who are obliged to serve in these shops are ruined and undone'. 'Take a survey,' Campbell wrote, 'of the common women of the town, who take their walks between Charing Cross and Fleet Ditch, and, I am persuaded, more than one half of them have been bred milliners'. Campbell especially warned against those 'who pretend to deal only with a few select customers, who scorn to keep open shop. . .these are decoys for the unwary; they are but places of assignation, and take the title of milliner, a more polite name for bawd'.[33] Mrs Cole's home was presumably such a place. But the essential point for this essay is Campbell's presumption that the seduced milliner would end up publicly walking the streets between Charing Cross and Fleet Street. She would probably, in the end, also become pregnant. This was what happened to Elinor Snawden. In 1721 she was an unmarried woman of nineteen who had served an apprenticeship of four years to a mantua-maker. (Campbell makes an equivalence in the lives of mantua-makers and milliners.) Three years later she was pregnant by Thomas Hayes, and three years later still, in 1727, she was pregnant again by Colonel Bing of the Foot Guards, who had had her twice in the St James's Guard Room.[34]

Fanny's world is a real world but it is a world with the pain left out. It is a world where the seduced servant and milliner did not become pregnant. It is also a world where they did not contract venereal diseases, unlike twenty-year-old Catherine Jones. After her seduction, she went on the town for her subsistence, was soon infected, and entered the Lock Hospital. The religious instruction she received there had its effect and she applied to enter the Lock Asylum for reformed prostitutes. However, she was not only sick, but also pregnant. Afraid that the pregnancy would keep her out of the Asylum, she concealed her condition until a few hours before her delivery. The Foundling Hospital took her child.[35] By contrast, Fanny's one brush with venereal disease comes when she fears that her encounter with the common sailor in the street may have left her infected (141–2).

But Fanny's world is most unlike the world of eighteenth-century prostitution that I know in five respects: it is free of drunkenness, it is not associated with crime, it is run entirely by women, it all takes place in safe, indoor environments, and it is a vice, more or less, of the middle and upper ranks of society. In contrast to the novel, the legal material presents prostitutes as frequently drunk. Three out of eight women arrested in the city on a night in 1786 were very much drunk. Two women brought in to the Guildhall in 1795 were accused of drunkenness as well as prostitution: Elizabeth William was drunk and picking up men in Fleet Street between twelve and one at night; Bathia Atkinson was drunk and with a man at ten o'clock in the morning.[36] This is no surprise since the most common kind of bawdy-house was in fact a tavern to which streetwalkers brought their customers, usually by agreement with the manager or owner of the house. Drink could be used to decoy a girl into prostitution, as Mary Bennet complained that Andrew Rider, a coffee-man in St James's, Westminster, had done to her.[37] Men not infrequently complained that they had been robbed by a prostitute because they had been too drunk to be aware of what was happening.

William Green complained in 1726 that Samuel Roper and his wife kept a house in St Sepulchre's full of lewd women, one of whom had picked his pocket of 45s. Timothy Tool said in 1792 that the landlady of a house and another woman had robbed him of a guinea after he was taken there by a third women, but he was unable to be very specific in his charges since he had been very drunk. The proceeds of these robberies often had to be disposed of, and this tied the women to the underground of thieves. There were indeed some houses notorious for being resorted to entirely by whores and thieves.[38]

Many of these houses were certainly run by women, but men were also charged with keeping bawdy houses, though perhaps not so frequently. In a single session roll, one finds the male and female bawds side by side. Elizabeth Langley of Drum Alley, Drury Lane, harboured and countenanced lewd women who deluded men into her house to commit notorious disorders. John Dantrey of Tavistock Street, Covent Garden, sent out for loose women for three customers and then fell to fighting with them.[39] In

1789 Susanna Elliott was clothed by a man who kept a house off Fleet Street and she gave him her earnings in return. In 1791 John Britt kept a house where the girls paid him 14s a week for board, and 2s for every gentleman they brought to their lodgings.[40]

Most prostitutes, however, did not have lodgings to take their customers to. They were street-plyers, as Fanny called them, who made for the nearest public house or, if they were very needy, made do with a dark place in the street. In 1720 Elizabeth Noble was found in a private place in the street with her strange man, Susannah Evans used a dark alley, as did Margaret James, whom the constable caught in the very act. George Mattocks and Christian Watts were taken late at night in one of the many private courts. Prostitutes, at least those who gave recognisances, were slightly more likely to be arrested in the street than in a public house; in the City in 1720 and early 1721, it came to forty-six in the street and thirty-seven in a house. Once the constable was inside a bawdy house, he could expect to find any number of sexual situations. Katherine Gerrard was taken with two men. Thomas Skeels was taken with two women, enacting lewd postures. Very often the couple had taken a private room in the house, and they might be found in bed together, or with signs of very recently having been there. George Leapidge was in bed with two women. John Dale's woman was stark naked. James Reyney and William Cane were with two women who had shown them lewd and indecent postures. And Joseph Farrant, a loom-maker from Shoreditch, was found with a women who, it was apparent, 'had whipped him naked with rods in a most scandalous lewd manner'.[41] The sexual invention of these low places equalled anything to be found in Mrs Cole's seraglio. However, Fanny whipped Mr Barville, and was whipped in her turn, with no apprehension that the constable might break in upon the exercise of what Mrs Cole called 'those arbitrary tastes that rule their appetites of pleasure with an unaccountable control' (44).

The other men in this last paragraph were, for the most part, of a social class similar to the loom-maker from Shoreditch who liked to be whipped. One was a basket-maker, another a bricklayer, a third a skimmer, and a fourth a plumber. And since the magistrates, in the City at least, still thought it a disreputable thing, as late as the 1720s, for a man to be found in a bawdy-house, they arrested the men as well as the prostitutes whom they found in these houses. In 1719, for instance, a wine-cooper, a turner, a joiner, a shoemaker, a cordwainer, a musician, a labourer, a yeoman, two blacksmiths, a victualler, a cornfactor and a brewer were each on separate occasions taken with a lewd woman in a bawdy-house. John Loftus, a carver, was taken with two, and Thomas Carr, a coachman, was found in a brandy shop with his whore, with his breeches down. Men were also taken for strolling in the streets with a whore: two tailors, a cordwainer, a yeoman and a gentleman. Augustine Parker pretended his whore was his wife, and John Dusson, a gentlewoman's servant, went strolling with two women rather than one. These men represent the standard working occupations of London – and the list of trades would grow if one added other years. Prostitution was pretty much a business between persons of the same class; gentlemen were no more over-represented here then they were among the seducers of servant girls.[42]

But what of the prostitute's end? Hogarth has her die of drink and disease. Cleland has her marry happily. The only thing that is certain is that most girls left the life of prostitution after the age of twenty-five; this was approximately the traditional age of marriage. They had usually begun to walk the streets at about fifteen, or the normal age of menarche.[43] In 1786 only about five or six per cent of the girls who had entered the Magdalen Hospital since 1758 had been married. On the other hand, more than half had either been taken in again by their families or had been placed as servants.[44] But the Hospital only took in the younger girls who showed no sign of venereal infection. It is likely, therefore, that a substantial proportion of those who had been on the town for some time died from drunkenness and disease, as the nineteenth-century statistics suggest. Some clearly did return to the world of work and family, but it is difficult to tell if prostitutes really did go back and forth between these two worlds, as it has also been suggested they did in the nineteenth century.[45] Fanny's happy marriage was probably a fate reserved for very few. The traditional wife had always been suspect because she could cuckold her husband and hide her whoredom in her marriage. It is less likely that the young, unmarried prostitute was ever able to reclaim respectability in the bonds of matrimony. This new style of prostitute was, however, a part of the price paid for an overall rise in the status of most women, who were no longer branded with the automatic suspicion of whoredom. Cleland's fantasy is therefore in that distant sense feminist, even though its effect is to enforce the bounds of masculine power.

Notes

1 Page references in the text refer to John Cleland, *Memoirs of a Woman of*

Pleasure, ed. Peter Sabor, New York, 1985.
2 Barry Ivker, 'John Cleland and the Marquis d'Argens: eroticism and natural morality in mid-eighteenth century English and French fiction', *Mosaic*, VIII, 1975, pp. 141–8; Raymond K. Whitley, 'The libertine hero and heroine in the novels of John Cleland', *Studies in Eighteenth-Century Culture*, ed. Roseann Runte, Madison, Wisconsin, 1979, IX, pp. 387–404; Lawrence Stone, *The Family, Sex and Marriage in England 1500–1800*, New York, 1977, Ch. 10.
3 Saunders Welch, *A Proposal to . . . Remove the Nuisance of Common Prostitutes from the Streets*, London, 1758, pp. 13–14, reprinted in *Prostitution Reform*, ed. Randolph Trumbach, New York, 1985.
4 Peter Sabor, 'The decline and fall of the brothel in the writings of John Cleland', American Society for 18th-Century Studies, Toronto, April 1985.
5 John Cleland, *The Case of the Unfortunate Bosavern Penlez*, London, 1749, esp. pp. 4 and 10–11. This was identified as Cleland's by Roger Lonsdale, 'New attributions to John Cleland', *Review of English Studies*, XXX, 1979, pp. 270–5. On these riots, see Peter Linebaugh in Douglas Hay et al., *Albion's Fatal Tree*, New York, 1975, pp. 89–101.
6 Iwan Bloch, *A History of English Sexual Morals*, London, 1936, pp. 122–61, 206–11; Fernando Henriques, *Prostitution in Europe and the Americas*, New York, 1965, Ch. 5 and E. J. Burford, *The Orrible Synne*, London, 1973.
7 Stanley D. Nash, 'Social attitudes towards prostitution in London from 1752 to 1829', PhD thesis, New York University, 1980; 'Prostitution and charity: the Magdalen Hospital, a case study', *Journal of Social History*, XVI, 1984, pp. 617–28.
8 W. A. Speck, 'The harlots' progress in eighteenth-century England', *British Journal for Eighteenth Century Studies*, III, 1980, pp. 127–39.
9 Stone, *Family, Sex and Marriage*; Randolph Trumbach, *The Rise of the Egalitarian Family*, New York, 1978, and Cissie Fairchilds, *Domestic Enemies*, Baltimore, 1984.
10 For France, see Colin Jones, 'Prostitution and the ruling class in eighteenth-century Montpellier', *History Workshop*, No. 6, 1978, pp. 7–28; D. A. Coward, 'Eighteenth-century attitudes to prostitution', *Studies on Voltaire*, CLXXXIX, 1980, pp. 363–99, and 'Restif de La Bretonne and the reform of prostitution', *ibid.*, CLXXVI, 1979, pp. 349–83.
11 In 1700–9, wives brought 205 cases, spinsters 58, and widows 40 (Greater London Record Office, hereafter GLRO).
12 Contrary to Richard J. Evans, 'Prostitution, state and society in imperial Germany', *Past and Present*, No. 70, 1976, pp. 106–29.
13 On licensed prostitution, see Jacques Rossiaud in *Deviants and the Abandoned in French Society*, eds. Robert Forster and Orest Ranum, Baltimore, 1978; Elisabeth Pavan, 'Police des moeurs, société et politique à Venise à la fin du Moyen Age', *Revue historique*, CCLXIV, 1980, pp. 241–88; Richard C. Trexler, 'La prostitution florentine au XVe siècle patronages et clientèles', *Annales: E.S.C.*, XXXVI, 1981, pp. 983–1015, and M. E. Perry, 'Deviant insiders: legalized prostitution and a consciousness of women in early modern Seville', *Comparative Studies in Society and History*, XXVII, 1985, pp. 138–58.
14 Claude S. Fischer, *To Dwell Among Friends*, Chicago, 1982.

15 Pat Rogers, *Grub Street*, London, 1972, p. 350.
16 It is very difficult to produce a bastardy rate for eighteenth-century London because of deficiencies in the sources. But when bastardy can be measured, in the early seventeenth and in the nineteenth centuries, London has one of the lowest rates. Peter Laslett suggests that such local traditions are enduring until the twentieth century when London has, of course, one of the highest rates. It is possible, though, that the eighteenth century saw a reversal of local tradition. (Roger Finlay, *Population and Metropolis*, Cambridge, 1981, and Peter Laslett et al. (ed.), *Bastardy and Its Comparative History*, Cambridge, Mass., 1980.)
17 *The Fifteenth Account of the Progress made toward suppressing profaneness and debauchery*, London, 1710.
18 Randolph Trumbach, 'London's sodomites: homosexual behavior and western culture in the eighteenth century', *Journal of Social History*, XI, 1977, pp. 1–33; 'Sodomitical subcultures, sodomitical roles, and the gender revolution of the eighteenth century: the recent historiography', *Eighteenth-Century Life*, IX, 1985, pp. 109–21, and 'Sodomitical assault, gender identity and individual development in eighteenth-century London', *The Pursuit of Sodomy in Early Modern Europe*, eds. Kent Gerard and Gert Hekma, New York, 1987, also published as the *Journal of Homosexuality*, XIV (1987).
19 Leo Braudy, 'Fanny Hill and materialism', *Eighteenth-Century Studies*, IV, 1970, pp. 21–40; cf. William H. Epstein, *John Cleland*, New York, 1974, p. 225 n. 52.
20 David Foxon, *Libertine Literature in England 1660-1745*, New Hyde Park, 1965, Ch. 4; Janet Todd, *Women's Friendship in Literature*, New York, 1980, pp. 96–7.
21 Henry Merritt, 'A biographical note on John Cleland', *Notes and Queries*, XXVIII, 1981, pp. 305–6; cf. Trumbach, 'London's sodomites', pp. 13–14.
22 Nancy K. Miller, '"I's" in drag: the sex of recollection', *The Eighteenth Century*, XXII, 1981, pp. 47–57.
23 Lonsdale, 'New attributions,' pp. 276–80; Henry Fielding, *The Female Husband*, London, 1746. A further example of this libertine attitude towards sexual relations between women is to be found in *The History of the Human Heart*, London, 1749, (Garland Reprint, New York, 1974), pp. 20–1. For the libertine, women were still allowed to be bisexual under the influence of prostitution or the longings of pregnancy. It did not decrease their feminine standing. There were, of course, women who passed as men in their dress, but it is not clear that, in most cases, this was done in order to have sexual relations with women. It was even possible for one of Mary Hamilton's wives to claim that she did not know her husband was a woman. (Sheridan Baker, 'Henry Fielding's *The Female Husband*: fact and fiction,' *PMLA*, LXXIV, 1959, pp. 213–24.) But, in other cases, the male transvestite role of one woman probably did facilitate a sexual relationship with another woman. See, for example, *The Annual Register*, IX, 1766, pp. 116, and 144.
24 As do Ivker, Whitley, Todd, and B. Slepian and L. J. Morrissey, 'What is *Fanny Hill?*', *Essays in Criticism*, XIV, 1964, pp. 65–75.
25 For the hierarchy of acts, see Thomas N. Tentler, *Sin and Confession on the Eve*

of the Reformation, Princeton, 1977, pp. 141–3. Cleland may have been influenced by the form of Defoe's novels (Michael Shinagel, 'Memoirs of a Woman of Pleasure: pornography and the mid-eighteenth-century novel', *Studies in Change and Revolution,* ed. Paul J. Korshin, Menston, Yorkshire, 1972, and Myron Taube, 'Moll Flanders and Fanny Hill: a comparison', *Ball State University Forum,* IX, 1968, pp. 76–80), but Defoe's morality in a work like *Conjugal Lewdness,* London, 1727, is quite traditional.

26 Cleland, *Memoirs,* ed. Sabor, pp. xiii–xiv; E. B. Chancellor, *The Annals of Covent Garden,* London, 1930, p. 65, and Bloch, *Sexual Morals,* pp. 123–32.
27 Westminster Public Library (hereafter WPL): e.2576, #103.
28 GLRO: WSP, 1725 July, Examinations 1, 2, 3.
29 British Library: Additional MS, 27825, f245; *Lloyd's Evening Post,* 3–5 May 1758.
30 Corporation of London Record Office (hereafter CLRO): Guildhall Justice Room, Minute Books, 1786–95.
31 CLRO: Sessions Rolls: September 1722, Recog. 32; December, recog. 41 and 34; May 1724, recog. 124; July 1724, recog. 34; April 1724, recog. 31.
32 GLRO: Foundling Hospital, Petitions, Vol. 22, 1798.
33 R. Campbell, *The London Tradesman,* London, 1747, pp. 208–9 and 227–8.
34 WPL: E.2575, #141a; E.2756, #106; E.2577, # 88.
35 GLRO: Foundling Hospital, Petitions, Vol. 17, 1791.
36 CLRO: Guildhall Justice Room, Minute Books, 1786–95.
37 GLRO: MJ/SR/2032 (July 1704) Recog. 91.
38 GLRO: Sessions Roll: January 1726, Recog. 9; Guildhall Justice Room, Minute Books, 1786–95; Jonathan Wild, *An Answer to a Late Insolent Libel,* London, 1718, reprinted in F. J. Lyons, *Jonathan Wild,* London, 1936, pp. 259–61.
39 GLRO: MJ/SR/2230, June 1714, Recog. 36, 16 and 15.
40 CLRO: Guildhall Justice Room, Minute Books, 1786–95.
41 CLRO: Sessions Rolls: April 1720, Recog. 27; April 1720, Recog. 21; April 1721, Recog. 4; February 1722, Recog. 61; January 1722, Recog. 5; December 1722, Recog. 32; January 1725, Recog. 13; August 1724, Recog. 3; April 1725, Recog. 29; January 1724, Recog. 11.
42 CLRO: Sessions Rolls: January 1720 *et seq.*
43 William Brodum, *A Guide to Old Age,* London, 1795. 2 vols., II, pp. 69–70.
44 *General State of the Magdalen Hospital,* London, 1786, p. 4.
45 Frances Finnegan, *Poverty and Prostitution,* Cambridge, 1979, and Judith R. Walkowitz, *Prostitution and Victorian Society,* Cambridge, 1980.

4

Imagination, pregnant women, and monsters, in eighteenth-century England and France

PAUL-GABRIEL BOUCÉ

In a popular manual of midwifery, *Instruction familiere et utile aux sages-femmes*, first published in 1677, Madame de la Marche, who practised at the Hôtel-Dieu in Paris, sums up, in catechetical fashion, beliefs and myths concerning the part played by imagination in false pregnancies and the procreation of monsters. To the question 'What is the cause of the monstrous false germ?', she provides a perfectly acceptable answer, according to the lights of theories currently held in the late seventeenth century and throughout the eighteenth century: 'The cause is both external and internal. The external one is the outside object on which the woman has cast her eyes; the internal one is the strength of the imagination, which, after receiving the impression from the outside object, communicates it to the informing faculty which then imprints it on the seed'.[1] On the next page, she defines a *mole* as a fleshy mass caused by either defects in the informing faculty, or in the seed, not to mention menstrual blood. A mole is characterised by its weighty immobility, its only way of moving within the womb being not of itself – as a male foetus should at three months, a female one at four, Madame de la Marche reminds her less enlightened colleagues – but by following the pregnant woman's body motions. She also notes that 'in a mole the woman's breasts swell without milk therein, and after the fourth month she feels no stirring in her womb, which should occur, were the woman quick with child', an impeccable conclusion.

Such beliefs were not confined to midwifery manuals, but were

IMAGINATION, PREGNANT WOMEN, AND MONSTERS

apparently so widespread that Smollett in *Peregrine Pickle* (1751) poked most enjoyable satirical fun at them in Chapters V to X, where he lovingly describes the eccentricities of both Mrs Pickle, the mother of the eponymous hero, and of Mrs Trunnion, the Commodore's wife, when the latter hopes against gynaecological hope that she is well and truly pregnant by the works of the ageing and somewhat battered retired sailor. Smollett was in fact exploiting for comic purposes the teachings of such immensely popular manuals as *A Directory of Midwives: Or, a Guide for Women in Their Conception, Bearing and Suckling Their Children* (1651) by the famous Nicholas Culpeper, or that anonymous book, *Aristotle's Compleat Experienc'd Midwife* (1700) which went through countless editions down to the 1930s. Thus her sister-in-law forbids Mrs Pickle to eat a peach, a fruit supposed to be injurious to pregnant women's health, but as she immediately remembers that if such a desire is thwarted 'the child might be affected with some disagreeable mark, or deplorable disease, she begged as earnestly that she would swallow the fruit, and in the meantime ran for some cordial of her own composing, which she forced upon her sister, as an antidote to the poison she had received'.[2] In a perversely wayward fashion, Mrs Pickle then decides to play on her longings and on the nerves of her family, variously demanding pineapples,[3] three black hairs from the poor harassed Commodore's chin – lest the child be born with a grey beard – and a fricassee of French frogs fetched from Boulogne. Most whimsically, she longs to pinch her husband's ear and takes a sudden capricious liking to a precious porcelain jordan belonging to a lady of quality living in the neighbourhood. Smollett's satire mixes pregnant women's picas and eccentric whims, but there is no doubt that it uses as a submerged referent a complex nexus of deeply rooted beliefs and myths, the very warp and woof of the mythical in everyday life for an eighteenth-century reader. Likewise, Mrs Trunnion plays on the Commodore's virile vanity and fond expectations, when, in spite of her (for the times) well-advanced years – she is over thirty when she marries – she fools herself and the Commodore into believing she is pregnant, displaying after four months of wedlock the following signs of pregnancy: 'she was seized with frequent qualms and reachings, her breasts began to harden, and her stomach to be remarkably prominent'.[4] Alas, after some feminine exploitation of the Commodore's hopes of paternity, such hopes wax smaller and smaller in proportion to Mrs Trunnion's deflating belly, so that the disappointed and somewhat shameful couple must at last admit it was but a nervous pregnancy, or 'false conception', as it was then called in manuals of midwifery.

Beyond the satirical anecdote skilfully handled by a novelist who was also a doctor of medicine and took an interest in obstetrics, one may detect the intertextual echoes harking back to a more than millenary tradition, such as Aristotle's theories in *De Generatione et Corruptione* on the strength of the imagination of pregnant women on the foetus. To such a tradition belong the prestigious names of Hippocrates, Empedocles, Galen, Pliny and, closer to us, Marsilio Ficino, Ambroise Paré and Malebranche. To this great tradition of 'official' medicine should definitely be added the diffuse but tenacious influence – some traces of which are still to be found in the popular beliefs which surround pregnancy and childbirth – of a vigorous para-medical literature. The most famous – or notorious – example of this perverse longevity is *Aristotle's Masterpiece*,[5] uninterruptedly reprinted from 1684 to the 1930s in both Great Britain and the United States, thus becoming the most widely circulated sex manual of all times.

Finally, it should be stressed that, in all those controversies and polemics bearing on the influence of the mother's imagination on the child *in utero*, the concept of *imagination* was never defined precisely. It covers such widely different phenomena as the sequels of an affective trauma (joy, terror, surprise), cravings for strange foodstuffs which are manifestations of a pica (for instance, the depraved longings some pregnant women experience for earth, chalk and coal, diagnosed by modern medicine as caused by deficiencies in vitamins or metals), wild fantasising, psychosomatic effects, and the imaginative faculty every (supposedly) rational being is endowed with. Hence, a pervasive epistemological haze blurs all those controversies and quarrels which have so violently at times disturbed the medical and scientific establishment throughout the eighteenth century, both in England and on the continent.

Briefly then, what is the theoretical background inseparable from such debates? My purpose is not to repeat here the findings of G. S. Rousseau (see Note 3) or Lester S. King,[6] but rather, with the help of a few works published in the first half of the eighteenth century, to place in their sociocultural context the antagonistic theories, bitterly and often acrimoniously warring with each other.

The notion that a mother's imagination was capable of stamping more or less monstrous marks on the foetus is not specifically English or European. Not only does it belong to the Greco-Latin history of mentalities but to the Judaeo-Christian tradition as well, as is instanced by the famous passage in Genesis Ch. 30:V.31–43, where the wily Jacob operates on Laban's flocks what must be considered as the first genetic manipulation in order to obtain 'ringstraked, speckled, and spotted' cattle. Ambroise Paré, whose works were translated into English as early as 1634, reserves the whole of Chapter IX of his illustrated *Des Monstres et Prodiges* (1573) to the 'Imagination-made Monsters', that 'ardent and obstinate fancy a woman may experience while she is conceiving, owing to some object or fantastic dream, or some nocturnal visions that a man or a woman may have at the time of conception'.[7] Paré quotes the usual cases to be found in the manuals of teratology, such as, to cite but a few, the girl as hairy as a bear, brought into the world by a mother who had gazed for too long at the picture of St John wearing a bearskin, or, that hoary chestnut of popular teratology,[8] the white princess delivered of a black child because of the portrait of a Moor by her bed. By the end of the sixteenth century, Paré heralds in both the epistemological break with ancient teratology – *teras* being also the premonitory sign sent by the gods – and the still modest beginnings of a scientific, medical semiology of the monster. Thus, Paré went back to the Aristotelian tradition which – as opposed to the Augustinian one – saw in monsters but *lusus naturae*, whereas St Augustine 'rejects divination but not all idea of prodigy'.[9] In seventeenth-century Italy the erudite professor of medicine, Giovanni Benedetto Sinibaldi (1594–1658) published an extraordinary *summa sexologica* of 1050 folio columns, *Geneanthropeiae sive de Hominis Generatione Decateuchon* (Rome, 1642), where he too affirms the capital influence of imagination during copulation and pregnancy.[10] In France, Malebranche in his treatise, *De la recherche de la vérité* (1674) attributes to 'sympathy' the faculty maternal imagination has of creating monstrous marks on the foetus, and he quotes the case – debated well into the eighteenth century – of a child born with broken limbs (probably a case of acute rickets) after his mother had watched a criminal being broken on the wheel.

During the third decade of the eighteenth century in England, two doctors both of them with diplomas from the Royal College of Physicians, Daniel Turner (1667–1741) and James Augustus Blondel (d. 1734), launched into a bitter controversy over the origins of birthmarks and the power of the mother's imagination over the foetus.[11] Turner, in the second edition (1723) of his dermatological treatise, *De Morbis Cutaneis* – the first to be published in English, in 1714, in spite of its Latin title – and then in his works published in 1729 and 1730 in reply to Blondel's attacks, maintains that the imagination in pregnant women acts on the foetus with a strange and almost incredible power. For Turner, who cites a formidable array of authorities, including Aristotle, St Jerome, Malebranche, Descartes and Willis, it cannot – and should not – be doubted that 'powerful emotional events during a woman's pregnancy gave rise to malformation of the offspring',[12] thus stamping marks, stains and stigmata on the foetus. The effects of imagination are not brought about directly 'but mediately by the Interposition of the Blood and nervous Fluid, set at work by the Appetite first excited, which occasions or brings about the same'.[13] Turner was such a believer in the psychosomatic force of imagination that he also held that 'by causing a Motion of the Humours and Spirits in the Body of Men [fancy] is capable of producing almost every Disease therein',[14] including squinting, stuttering by imitation and catching smallpox or the plague, and that not only by contagion but also by fear and the mere force of imagination. He never relinquished his convictions, even after the discovery of Mary Tofts's notorious fraud at Godalming in 1726–7, whereby she had managed to hoodwink some medical pundits into believing she had given birth to seventeen rabbits. Blondel, in his *The Strength of Imagination in Pregnant Women Examin'd* (1727), sets out to demolish Turner's theses, which he does with cold logic and sharp common-sense. Basically, Blondel is a sceptic who casts systematic doubt on the cases reported by ancient or modern authors, as well as on their theories and conclusions. Reputations fail to impress him, even that of a great philosopher such as Malebranche. Writing about his *Recherche de la vérité*, Blondel deplores Malebranche's credulity when dealing with two cases of monstrous marks on foetuses: 'there's nothing in all this, but meer Enthusiasm and Bigotry',[15] a bluff but not undeserved judgment. As L. S. King remarks about Blondel, 'his contribution to science was critical rather than substantive, but none the less important, for the question "what can be accepted as evidence" underlies all scientific endeavour'.[16] For Blondel, the infant *in utero* lives 'in a State of Neutrality',[17] completely isolated from all sensations or emotions experienced by the pregnant mother. His book reads like a curious mixture of sound logic and sharp scientific spirit of healthy doubt, but he is crippled by his lack of genuine physiological information, as he appears unaware of the circulation of blood between mother and foetus, although he knows the function of the umbilical cord and placenta. Finally, Blondel makes a brave attempt at explaining 'logically' the causes of the marks and monstrous deformities in children: first, 'the Variety of Particles and of their Combinations' (p. 96), second 'Distempers of Children in Utero' (p. 97) and third, 'The Increase of some Parts of the Foetus being interrupted', which includes malnutrition of the foetus by stopped vessels and, lastly, 'Force and Violence upon the Body of the Foetus' (p. 104), by which he means accidental falls of the mother, wounds, blows or even violent natural contractions, a position perilously close to Malebranche's views on the case of the child born with limbs broken as if on the wheel.

Blondel's ideas were further developed by a Bordeaux doctor, Isaac Bellet (d. 1788), in his very didactic and somewhat lengthy *Lettres sur le pouvoir de l'Imagination des femmes enceintes* (1745), translated into Italian in 1751 and into English in 1765. Bellet addressed a female public, whom he judges less than conversant with the technicalities of embryology and obstetrics. He repeatedly attacks Malebranche and, throughout his twenty-three letters (numbering 226 pages!), he attempts to produce a genuine epistemological demythification of the so-called force of imagination in pregnant women. He explains marks, pigmented naevi, malformations and other monstrous deformities by accidental differences in the fecundation of the germ: 'the parts which have not put up too much resistance will be fecundated; on the contrary, that which, through too much resistance, has failed to let the liquor in, will not be fecundated. The fecundated parts will receive nourishment and increment, whereas the unfecundated part will disappear totally'.[18] According to Bellet, the monstrous excrescences, looking like draperies of loose skin, mitres and royal head-bands, are due to an excessive nourishment of the foetus *in utero*, while marks resembling redcurrants, brambles, strawberries and raspberries are but hypertrophic dilatations of the vascular network, which freely let the red blood through when only the serosity should pass. Such marks have nothing to do, Bellet insists, with longings for those fruits, their falling on the body of pregnant women, a craving for wine or the spilling of it on the pregnant mother's body. Bellet repeatedly stresses that he buttresses his conclusions on *observations* made with the help of a good microscope, which at least demonstrates his resolution not to advance anything before it has been scientifically proved. All the same, Bellet is aware of what may be termed the psychosomatic influence of the pregnant mother on her child *in utero*, not through the force of imagination, but through the acceleration or momentary stasis of the flow of the blood under the influence of strong emotions liable to cause apoplectic fits, blood-spittings and haemorrhages, with abortion as a fatal result.

It would be idle to believe that throughout the eighteenth century there developed a linear progress toward the definitive eradication of the imaginationists' theses. In 1788 the French hygienist Louis-Nicolas Bablot (1754–1802) still published a *Dissertation sur le pouvoir de l'imagination des femmes enceintes*, upholding the views of Malebranche and Turner.[19] The obstinate resistance of myths, beliefs and orally transmitted para-cognitive lore concerning procreation and childbirth should never be underestimated, although it is doubtful that any *cliometricians*, even armed with computerised gadgetry, will ever manage to measure the gap between the Protean nexus of mentalities and the latest advances of official science. The sociocultural milieu in which scientific progress is taking place is neither neutral nor blank, it even tends to perdure and settle down to a self-complacent immobilism, which the dynamism of scientific discoveries can but irritate and perturb. It is also true that a sociocultural milieu is not isomorphic and that, according to its prior degree of acculturation, it will prove more or less quick to accept changes. Because childbirth was not only a vital matter, but also engrossed the care of a whole lifetime, because it took place before its institutionalisation in maternity centres almost exclusively at home, among female cronies, neighbours and midwives, any abnormal phenomenon,such as pigmented or vascular naevi (port-wine stains), uterine moles or deformed, missing or supplementary limbs, assumed such unnatural dimensions that the monstrous was deemed never far off. It is the monstrous, that readily-resorted-to and apparently satisfactory para-cognitive concept, which insidiously pervades those descriptions of unnatural longings, picas, nervous pregnancies and uterine moles, as set forth in John Pechey's popular manual of midwifery, *The Compleat Midwife's Practice Enlarged* (fifth revised edition, London, 1698). For instance, the uterine mole[20] is described as 'the *Moon-Calf*, which is a lump of flesh for the most part like the guisern of a bird, greater or lesser, according to the time of its being there, which is most commonly not above four or five months' (p. 58). The para-logical recourse to malefice as a ready 'explanation' is never far off either, not to mention the implicit transgression of traditional sexual interdicts such as coitus during the menses which, according to John Marten's sixth revised edition of *A Treatise of All the Degrees and Symptoms of the Venereal Disease in Both Sexes* (London, 1708?-9), produces puny and deformed offspring, and red-haired at that, a chromatic notion Marten rejects, but which may also be found in Nicolas Venette's extraordinary hodgepodge of sexual (mis)information, *De la génération de l'homme, ou tableau de l'amour conjugal* (Amsterdam, 1687),[21] translated into English in 1703 and often reprinted. If poor Mrs Trunnion had read the twenty-third edition of *Aristotle's Masterpiece* (London, 1749), she would quickly have realised that her fond hopes of maternity were unfounded and that her 'pregnancy' was but a monstrous delusion of her imagination. In Chapter IX, 'Of a mole or false conception. . .', she would have perused the symptoms of a uterine mole: 'the monthly courses are suppressed, the Belly is puffed up, and also waxed hard, the Breath smells, and the Appetite is depraved' (p. 86).

The teratological semiology of birthmarks and congenital malformation is ruled by a bipolarity which is as complex in its nuances and chronological hesitations as the erratic developments of the theoretical controversy over the force of imagination in pregnant women. A credulous author like Daniel Turner in his *De Morbis Cutaneis* (1723) gives a whole chapter (XII) to 'Spots and marks of a diverse resemblance, imprest upon the skin of the foetus, by the force of the mother's fancy: with some things premis'd of the strange and almost incredible power of imagination, more especially in pregnant women' (pp. 155–90), while Dr John Maubray in his manual, *The Female Physician* (London, 1724), returns to a quasi-Biblical notion of the genetic influence of the milieu on human and animal procreation. Thus, in order to obtain white peacocks, males and females must couple in places hanged 'with white *Linnen-Cloths, Papers*, etc.: As in Snowy Mountainous Countries we find always white *Peacocks, Quails, Wolves, Hares*, and other *Creatures*' (p.60). Likewise, in order to bring forth dappled horses or spotted dogs, it is enough for these animals to copulate in stables or kennels draped with speckled cloths, which, one suspects, would be both costly and hardly practicable. Maubray postulates a similar mimetic plasticity in pregnant women, thanks to the ever-present force of their imagination: 'Wherefore it is very wrong and highly impudent in *Women* that have conceived, to please themselves so much in playing with *Dogs, Squirrels, Apes*, etc. carrying them in their *Laps* or *Bosoms*, and feeding, kissing or hugging them' (p.62), an apotropaic warning not devoid of Biblical repulsion for a quasi-diabolical familiarity with unclean beasts. Maubray still thinks that if an animal happens to jump on a pregnant woman, either a cat, a dog or a weasel, or if a fruit falls on her body, it will immediately impress a corresponding mark on the child she is bearing, 'unless the Woman (in that very moment) wipe that *Part* or *Member*, and move her *Hand* to some more remote, private, or convenient *Place* of the *Body*' (p.63). Then the mark will obligingly remove itself from a left nostril to a right buttock, which probably presented a more obvious aesthetic interest in the early eighteenth century than in our late twentieth century of G-strings and aggressive nudity on the sun-worshipping beaches.

As for monsters, their semiology does not vary much, from Ambroise Paré to the late eighteenth century. It is as though human imagination or, rather, more or less scientific observation embellished by teratological fancies, were content with a few venerable stereotypes: the child with a cat's or frog's head, the black offspring of white parents, the hairy child and the infant born with broken or crucified limbs. To this should be added the whole erratic range of fabulous monsters, half-men and half-animals, such as centaurs, satyrs, aegipans, tritons and sirens with which Greco-Latin mythology is so rife. It is noticeable how the upper half, i.e. the nobler one, is always human, while the lower one, the realm of baser instincts, is always animal. From Ambroise Paré to the countless editions of *Aristotle's Masterpiece* and to the Regnaults' extremely fine iconography in *Les écarts de la nature ou recueil des principales monstruosités* (Paris, 1775),[22] may be found the habitual classification of monsters into three categories: monsters by excess (Siamese twins and bicephalous, macrocephalous, four-legged or multi-breasted human creatures), monsters by lack (cyclopses, monopodes and anapodes, and headless, armless or legless beings), and monster by inversion, i.e. with their left organs on the right and vice versa. The imagination of pregnant women is one of the causes advanced by the anonymous author of the twenty-third edition of *Aristotle's Masterpiece* (London, 1749): 'The imaginative power, at the Time of Conception, which is of so much Force, that it stamps a Character of the Thing imagined upon the Child: so that the Children of an Adulteress, by the Mother's imaginative Power, may have the nearest Resemblance to her own Husband, though begotten by another Man' (pp. 89–90). In view of such genetic camouflage due to a sinful mother's plastic imagination, 'It is a wise father that knows his own child'. But here monstrosity is psychological and ethical, not anatomical. Yet it is disturbing to discover that the same passage, with exactly the same illustrations of monsters, figures verbatim in an edition of *Aristotle's Masterpiece* published in about 1850, and yet again in an early twentieth-century edition in my possession. Myths are long-lived and time-resistant, especially when they thrive on a rich subsoil of superstitions, oral legends and religious interdicts which are more or less diffuse (for instance, intercourse with beasts, or during the menstrual period). Monsters then appear as the pitiful proof of the sin against nature, punished by divine wrath, which enables God to reassert forcefully and tangibly His omnipotence or, as Pope puts it in *An Essay on Man* (1733–4), the ontological and metaphysical interdependency of all creatures in the 'vast chain of being': 'From Nature's chain whatever link you strike/ Tenth or ten thousandth, breaks the chain alike' (Epistle I, II. 245–6). Among the thirteen causes of monstrous births, Ambroise Paré in *Des monstres et prodiges* (1573) begins his classification thus: 'The first is the Glory of God. The second, His Ire'.[23] A couple of centuries later, in the twenty-ninth edition of *Aristotle's Book of Problems* (London, 1775), to the question 'Doth nature make any monsters?' the following reply is made: 'She doth; for if she did not, she would then be deprived of her end' (p. 67), a classic use of the *plenum* hypothesis in optimistic theodicies, although the explanation of those *lusus naturae* remains in that popular manual at the less elevated level of some dire astrological influence which has momentarily defeated the universal teleology tending towards the good and the beautiful. Again, it should be noted that such an inadequate paralogical 'explanation' is to be found verbatim in several nineteenth and twentieth-century editions I have looked up. Myths die hard.

Since antiquity, monsters have aroused persistent questionings; whether they were apprehended as accidents of nature (Aristotle's view), or, according to St Augustine, as part and parcel of a divine teleology, a project Man cannot grasp spontaneously in its cosmic entirety, which Pope neatly sums up in one line of *An Essay of Man*: ''Tis but a part we see, and not a whole' (Epistle I, 1.60). Man is both repelled and fascinated by the spectacle of the monstrous, for monsters throughout the eighteenth and nineteenth centuries, and well into the twentieth, were actually exhibited to the public gaze in freak-shows. Monsters opportunely remind man *in vivo* of his original sin, his fall from grace and his semi-bestiality –certainly more than 'semi' in Swift's horrendous description of the Yahoos – of 'animal rationis capax'.

Finally, one may well wonder whether the strident controversies and polemics about the imagination of pregnant women in the eighteenth century signify a totally innocent discourse – medical, para-medical, ethical and psychological. All this lay preaching for or against the imagination of women, is, first and foremost, an all but exclusively *male* discourse, with the exception of a few midwifery manuals composed by females who obediently followed the theories of their male colleagues and adopted their axiology. Even though the proclaimed purpose of such anti-imaginationists as Blondel and Isaac Bellet was to combat beliefs injurious to women's health and hence detrimental to society, nevertheless the debate about the force of imagination in pregnant women was instrumental in creating, or strengthening, a nexus of stifling interdicts, imperatives and more or less pressing advice. Chapters V to X in *Peregrine Pickle* may (should?) also be read, beyond the enjoyable satirical slapstick of grotesque eccentricities, as a latent form of ontological *'Angst'* surrounding pregnancy and childbirth. The whole problem of the possible influence of mind over body preoccupied physicians, philosophers, poets and theologians throughout the eighteenth century, as it still does to a certain extent today. Even in a ridiculous and objectionable way, the imaginationists thought that they held the carnal proof – birthmarks or some more monstrous deformities – that Man is possessed of a tiny fraction of mysterious freedom and power over his own body; a force that could be exploited to positive and aesthetic ends in calligenesis. Such is the laudable purpose, to name but one work, of the neo-Latin poet and physician Claude Quillet's (1602–61) *Callipaedia, sive de Pulchrae Prolis Habendae Ratione* published in 1655, translated into English in 1710, and reprinted half a dozen times by 1761. Quillet's *Callipaedia* was also quite popular in France where it was translated and reprinted at least six times before 1832. It was also openly imitated, not to say pirated, in an anonymous work, *The Joys of Hymen, or, the Conjugal Directory: A Poem in Three Books* (1768), its author entirely omitting Quillet's fourth book, which deals more with practical and moral precepts of education than actual calligenesis. *The Joys of Hymen,* though so close to the 1761 reprint of Nicholas Rowe's translation of the *Callipaedia* that it verges perilously on paraphrastic piracy, even at times lifting whole lines or sequences of lines from it, is all the same composed in a different spirit, in which a British element is quite perceptible. There is certainly nothing offensive about *The Joys of Hymen,* which is honestly meant, as virtuously stressed in the preface as a poetic sex manual, rife with mythological allusions and lore, but not devoid of plain English common-sense as well. The translator of the *Callipaedia* is actually much more straightforward in his references to the sexual organs and intercourse. *The Joys of Hymen* abounds with unashamed eugenic advice, such as: 'Let the deform'd avoid the rites of love / And none but beauteous limbs the raptures prove'.[24] Therefore, the sick, suffering from gout, rheumatism or, even worse, venereal disease or mental illness should abstain from the bliss of connubial love. Furthermore, detailed procreative precepts are expounded, such as apotropaic warnings against any unseemly haste on the young couple's wedding night, lest the husband's semen should turn into but 'An unconcocted tepid, drizzling show'r' (p. 36) because 'All these (a rude and indigested heap) / Digestive pow'rs will ripen while you sleep, / Strain through unnumber'd tubes and flowing tide, / And blood from chyle and sperm from blood divide' (p. 37). Love-making then should be indulged in only after a good night's sleep: 'Prefer the morn to night's unwholsome shade; / For morning ever for the male is best, / The seed maturing in the time of rest' (p. 58). Future parents should beware of baneful astrological influence, Gemini being considered as a favourable sign of the zodiac under which to conceive, but not so Cancer, 'Author of monstrous shapes ! uneven set, / Of tumours, wens and members incomplete! / Hence apish forms, and ugly births began, / And gibbous dwarfs, beneath the strain of man' (p. 45). If Virgo and Libra are benevolent enough, Scorpio turns out to be an evil sight: 'His nauseous products through the world are seen; / Long legs, large feet, red hair and hideous mien' (p. 47), while 'CAPRICORN, to Saturn near ally'd, / Curs'd by the vig'rous fire and teeming bride, / Deforms the face, and blisters all the skin, / And fills the mind deprav'd with letchery and sin' (p. 48). Such astrological advice may sound ridiculous to late twentieth-century readers, who nonetheless will look up their horoscopes in the daily newspapers with surreptitious avidity. Sterne had already poked devious fun, mixed with probable double entendre, at such astrological balderdash, when he had Walter Shandy gravely explain to a bemused Uncle Toby his less than entirely successful procreation of Tristram: 'the trine and sextil aspects have jumped awry, – or the opposite of their ascendents have not hit it, as they should, – or the lords of the genitures (as they call them) have been at *bo-peep*, – or something has been wrong above, or below with us' (*Tristram Shandy*, Vol. V, Ch. 28). *The Joys of Hymen* carries the old Biblical interdict against coition during the menses: 'Or if an offspring rise, the infant's veins / Shall prove the poison which that stream contains' (p. 52). Likewise, in the *Callipaedia*, wedded couples are warned against sex during pregnancy, 'For if the Womb then glow with lustful Fire, / And, ev'n tho pregnant, rage with fresh Desire; / Some shapeless Creature will perhaps proceed / From the ill-tim'd Embrace, and mar the Breed'.[25] Finally, in *The Joys of Hymen* the positive influence of the pregnant mother's imagination is, for once, fully explained. The expectant mother should avoid all uncomely sights and, on the contrary, would be well advised to dwell on joyful scenes and to gaze at beautiful objects, which would duly impress their calligenetic effects on the foetus in the womb:

> For while the curious work unfinish'd lies
> The brain, to whose close cells each object flies,
> Conveys, by subtile atoms, to the womb
> All images which from the senses come.
> The passive foetus no resistance makes,
> But ev'ry form and light impression takes (p.67).

Both the *Callipaedia* and *The Joys of Hymen* aptly illustrate the ambivalent role played by the mother's pregnant body, which acts both as a kind of screen or filter, protecting the foetus against the potential aggressions of the outside world, yet at the same time, as was commonly held in eighteenth-century medical or para-medical handbooks, reacting as a highly sensitive conductor of impressions, sensations, shocks and emotions; truly a 'body electric' receptive to the mother's fears, joys, dreams and phantasms.[26] Examples of such freakish births abound, not only in eighteenth-century medical literature, but in such popular publications as *The Gentleman's Magazine*, where a mother is reported to have given birth to a leonine monster, 'with nose and eyes like a lyon, no palate to the mouth, hair on the shoulders, claws like a lion instead of fingers, no breast-bone, something surprising out of the navel as big as an egg, and one foot longer than the other' (XVI, 1746, p. 270), the monstrous sequel to a fright during a visit to the lions in the Tower.[27] Beyond the anecdotal, the implicit discourse of the Enlightenment might be analysed as one of the insidious assimilation of the pregnant woman with an abnormal creature, potentially sick both in her body and mind, and subject to uncontrollable picas, dreams and fantasies, so potent that they will, through her highly conductive body and essentially plastic mind, leave their monstrous impressions on the foetus. The pregnant mother appears as the great culprit, the evil scapegoat, much more so than the father. A physically and mentally crippled creature during pregnancy, she is finally made responsible for any marks or monstrous deformities of her offspring.[28] However, it might, conversely, be contended that the whole of Tristram Shandy's (apparently) melancholy tale of pre-and post-conception woes is but a fictive illustration of the father's imaginative powers (or abruptly thwarted potency by Mrs Shandy's untimely liminal question) at the crucial time of seminal ejaculation. Hence, Walter

Shandy's tearful complaint: 'My Tristram's misfortunes began nine months before ever he came into the world' (Vol. I, Ch. 3), or again: 'Unhappy *Tristram* ! child of wrath ! child of decrepitude! interruption ! mistake ! and discontent!', bitterly bemoaning the 'embryotic evils' (Vol. IV, Ch. 19) that have befallen his son because of the probable dispersion of the vital animal spirits at Tristram's interrupted conception. The fictive art of interrupted interruption really lies at the heart of *Tristram Shandy*. But beyond an undeniable taste for freakish childbirths and *lusus naturae* – a taste still evident today in the keen interest taken by the press and other media in test-tube babies and genetic manipulations – all the controversial eighteenth-century polemics about the force of pregnant women's imagination over the foetus may well be construed as a devious latent anti-feminist discourse. Whether to the imaginationists or the anti-imaginationists, woman appeared as the frail and wayward instrument of procreation, the consenting victim of her wild fancy, a creature in turn reified and deified by Man, himself 'Sole judge of Truth in endless Error hurl'd: / The glory, jest, and riddle of the world!'.[29]

Notes

1 Marguerite de la Marche, *Instruction familiere et tres utile pour les accouchemens*, Nouvelle edition, Paris, 1710, p. 29. My translation.
2 Tobias Smollett, *Peregrine Pickle*, World's Classics, Oxford, 1983, p. 21.
3 See G. S. Rousseau, 'Pineapples, pregnancy, pica, and *Peregrine Pickle*' in G. S. Rousseau and P.-G. Boucé (eds.), *Tobias Smollett*, New York, 1971, pp. 79–109.
4 *Peregrine Pickle*, p. 47.
5 On *Aristotle's Masterpiece* and on sexual myths in general, see my chapter 'Some sexual beliefs and myths in eighteenth-century Britain' in P.-G. Boucé (ed.), *Sexuality in Eighteenth-Century Britain*, Manchester, 1982, pp. 28–46. See also my essay, 'Les jeux interdits de l'imaginaire: onanisme et culpabilisation sexuelle au XVIIIe siècle" in J. Céard, (ed.), *La folie et le corps*, Paris, 1985, pp. 223–43; Roy Porter, '"The secrets of generation display'd": *Aristotle's Masterpiece* in eighteenth-century England', in R. F. Maccubbin, (ed.), *Unauthorized Sexual Behavior during the Enlightenment*, special issue of *Eighteenth-Century Life*, IX, n.s.3, 1985, pp. 1–21.
6 See his *The Philosophy of Medicine : The Early Eighteenth Century*, Cambridge, Mass., 1978, in particular Ch. VII, 'The power of the imagination', pp. 152–81.
7 Ambroise Paré, *Des monstres et prodiges*, ed. J. Céard, Geneva, 1973, p. 35. My translation.
8 It was still a current notion in Normandy – or at least a feeble mythical attempt at explaining miscegenation due to sexual promiscuity with black American soldiers – in 1945 after the landing of the Allied troops. In actual fact, no one actually *believed* in such a mythical 'explanation', but some blond Norman women held that they were delivered of a black child solely because they had been 'frightened' by the

first Negro soldiers they had ever seen. The Normans are possessed of a sense humour certainly close to the English one.
9 Jean Céard, *La nature et les prodiges: l'insolite au XVIe siècle*, Geneva 1977, p. x. My translation.
10 See Col.624 a.
11 For the chronology of their polemical publications, see G. S. Rousseau, *op. cit.*, Note 3, p. 89, Note 18.
12 See P. J. Hare, *Our Credulous Countryman*, University of Edinburgh Inaugural Lecture, No. 37, Edinburgh, 1968, p. 8. Hare calls the quarrel between Turner and Blondel a 'wordy vendetta, acrimonious on Turner's side, good-humoured and witty on the Frenchman's' (*ibid.*). In fact, whatever the difference in personalities, Blondel's books are just as strident as Turner's, but pack a much more logical and scientific punch.
13 Daniel Turner, *De Morbis Cutaneis*, London, 1723, p. 162.
14 *Ibid.*, p. 166.
15 James Augustus Blondel, *The Strength of Imagination in Pregnant Women Examin'd*, London, 1727, p. 22. Translated into French in 1737, and quoted by Isaac Bellet in the 'Advertisement' to his *Lettres sur le pouvoir de l'Imagination des femmes enceintes*, Paris, 1745, p. v, with qualified approbation, as Bellet held that Blondel was not methodical enough.
16 See *op.cit.* Note 6, p. 170.
17 Blondel, p. 55. All further references are included in the text.
18 Bellet, p. 133.
19 On Bablot, see Pierre Darmon, *Le mythe de la procréation à l'âge baroque*, Paris, 1977, pp. 182–3. On the controversy about the force of imagination, see his Ch. X, 'Le foetus', pp. 161–88.
20 On uterine moles, see Jacques Gélis's admirable *L'arbre et le fruit: la naissance dans l'Occident moderne (XVIe-XIXe siècles)*, Paris, 1984, pp. 356–7, and the whole of his chapter, 'Où commence l'homme, où finit la bête?' in Part II, pp. 352–70, *passim* on monstrous births.
21 On Venette, see Roy Porter, 'Spreading carnal knowledge or selling dirt cheap? Nicolas Venette's *Tableau de l'amour conjugal* in eighteenth-century England', *Journal of European Studies*, XIV, 1984, pp. 233–55.
22 See a few illustrations taken from this book in P. Darmon, *op. cit.* Note 19, pp. 109–13. See also his Ch. VI, 'Systèmes extravagants, grossesses masculines, erreurs de la nature', pp. 101–20.
23 *Op. cit.* Note 7, p. 4.
24 *The Joys of Hymen*, London, 1768, p. 17. All further references are included in the text.
25 *Callipaedia : A Poem in Four Books*, Written in Latin by Claudius Quillet. Made English by N. Rowe, Esq., London, 1761, p. 65.
26 See Gélis, *op. cit.* Note 20, pp. 118–24.
27 See Roy Porter, 'Lay medical knowledge in the eighteenth century: the evidence of the *Gentleman's Magazine*', *Medical History*, XXIX, 1985, p. 148.
28 See Daniel Teyssiere, *Pédiatrie des Lumières: maladie et soins des enfants dans l' 'Encyclopédie' et le 'Dictionnaire de Trévoux'*, Paris, Vrin, 1982, pp. 53–9.
29 Alexander Pope, *An Essay on Man*, Epistle II, ll. 17–18.

5

The Sorrows of Priapus: anticlericalism, homosocial desire, and Richard Payne Knight

G. S. ROUSSEAU

Knight was about a century and a half ahead of his time; and, indeed, so little in the interim has the field of phallic worship been systematically explored that Knight's work may still be used as a valuable and stimulating introduction to this interesting and illuminating aspect of men's behavior. (Ashley Montagu, *Sexual Symbolism: A History of Phallic Worship*, 1957, p. iii)

The *Discourse on the Worship of Priapus, and its Connexion with the Mystic Theology of the Ancients* (1786–7) by Richard Payne Knight (1751–1824) is a book of 217 quarto pages and two dozen sexually explicit black-and-white illustrations.[1] Containing no chapters or overarching plan, it seems to sprawl structurelessly, presenting its observations and accumulations of facts arbitrarily. Its ostensible form would seem to be that of the learned dissertation. As such it contains many footnotes, a small number of which are culled from the writings of the Baron d'Hancarville – about whom much more will be said later – as well as from primary sources of the Greeks and Romans. Knight's purpose, as he explains more than once in the *Discourse,* is to substantiate and amplify Sir William Hamilton's as yet unpublished 'Account of the Remains of the Worship of Priapus lately existing at Isernia, in the Kingdom of Naples', a brief essay which appears at the beginning of Knight's *Discourse* in the first edition of 1786–7. The aim in publication that lay furthest from Knight's conscious mind – now bearing in mind the title of the book in which my own essay appears – was the creation of a sexual underworld, or any 'sexual underground' even remotely resembling the promiscuous sexual inferno that was associated with certain quarters of Paris and virtually all the Italian cities by the mid-1780s. That Payne Knight's *Priapus* should have had an effect that could eventually give rise to such a myth (i.e. that the creation of any type of sexual underworld had been his covert intention all along) is one of the major ironies of the story I tell here. Pornographic publishers and their illustrators, as we shall see, increasingly made use of *Priapus*, but this development must not in itself sway us to conclude that pornography, or any activity remotely related to or connected with pornography, was Knight's intention. Enlightened paganism was his goal, to the extent that one can discuss his consciously articulated programme, while orthodox Christian morality, especially its teachings generated during the decades of the 1760s and 1770s in a mood that seemed increasingly rigid vis-à-vis sexuality, remained the ultimate, furtive perversion for him.

No reason exists to doubt Knight's stated intention to examine Hamilton's work, and close scrutiny of his text confirms how faithfully he adhered to his purpose; so faithfully that in the last two centuries many readers who have quickly scanned the book, oblivious to its illustrations, have never suspected that *Priapus* was anything but a dry eighteenth-century dissertation written long before archaeology and anthropology had become formal university subjects. And yet, lurking on almost every page is some form of scepticism about the institution of Christianity: not merely about the established Church of England but the whole development of the Church from its inception. The tone of these sceptical tropes varies: some are conveniently parenthetical asides which most readers overlook; others are substantial sub-texts that jump out of the page. A clue, however, can be found in the pronouncements of the opening paragraphs: a passage permeated with innuendoes and acid invectives against 'the zealous propagators of the Christian faith', who 'condemn the rites and doctrines of others, and the furious zeal and bigotry with which they maintain their own', and who excoriate 'devout persons of all religions'. The attentive reader of passages like these (of which there are many) soon realises that Christian morality is the pre-eminent target of this work, enlightened paganism, especially its toleration for homosocial desire, its primary endorsement.

From the outset, Knight's stated aim is to provide a comparison of ancient (pagan) and modern (Christian) religious rituals in the hope of demonstrating, in his own words, that 'both . . . have the same meaning, and only differ in the modes of conveying it'.[2] He adheres to his purpose, despite a subtext present throughout the discourse, and by the end of *Priapus* the careful reader has realised that Knight's comparison of ancient and modern religions has developed into an unequivocal polemic; to such an extent that only a literal-minded reader in 1786 or 1787 can have imagined that the concluding statement was limited to the Roman Catholic Church:

> It is curious, in looking back through the annals of superstition, so degrading to the pride of man, to trace the progress of the human mind in different ages, climates, and circumstances, uniformly acting upon the same principles, and to the same ends. The sketch here given of the corruptions of the religion of Greece, is *an exact counterpart of the history of the corruptions of Christianity*, which began in the pure theism of the eclectic Jews, and by the help of inspirations, emanations, and canonizations, expanded itself, by degrees, to the vast and unwieldy system which now fills the creed of what it commonly called the Catholic Church [my italics].³

Despite the presence of what I am calling Knight's pre-text (Hamilton's work) and sub-text (the attack on Christianity), no reason exists to surmise that these two discourses represent counter-impulses within Knight; no reason to think that they are anything but the superficial narrative signs of a deeper, and possibly irreconcilable, tension within the imagination of the author; no reason to attribute dark motives to Knight which one text alone – either the main one expanding Hamilton, or the submerged one attacking Christianity – will reveal. For the lessons of Knight's life, coupled to the larger political events of the times – biography and social history combined – help to explain why he selected this particular generic and rhetorical vehicle. They also lead us to this most difficult question: why was Knight attracted to Priapus (the god) and matters priapeic or priapic (that is: excessively masculine and phallic) in the first place?

These themes, particularly the blend of biography and social history, are my subject here, especially insofar as they permit me to answer the most difficult question just articulated. After all, it would be tedious to revive a minor ancient work by endowing it with a microscopic reading it probably does not deserve. In my view, it is sufficient to identify its two strains – text and sub-text – explain their relation, and notice the tropes that attach to each. For *Priapus* is a blended literary form, with the archaeological sections seamlessly cemented to the polemical ones attacking the Church. It is not my intention, therefore, either to credit Knight with contributing to the development of this blended genre (better examples exist long before his), or to verify his facts and sources. But he was original, even radically innovative, as the distinguished American anthropologist Ashley Montagu has commented in the epigraph of this chapter, in his grasp of the religious significance of fertility rites among ancient societies. In this sense, and in this sense primarily, it is ironic that the one domain – phallic fertility – in which his contribution is genuinely important, should have been the one for which his contemporaries excoriated him. In decoding the cultural contexts of this denunciation, Knight strikes one – within certain differences – as a figure comparable in the previous generation to Passeran, as the notorious Count Radicati di Passerano was known in England, when, in the 1730s, he scandalised opinion by claiming that all moral standards were relative.[4] That Passeran was ostracised as a pariah is to put the matter too politely; he was denounced throughout the Realm, and in this sense his case genuinely differs from that of Knight's, which was never so extreme. Passeran, as James Peller Malcolm assured his readers early in the nineteenth century in *Anecdotes of the Manners and Customs of London during the Eighteenth Century* (1808), quickly became associated with two of the worst taboos: homosexuality and suicide. Just as Passeran's contemporaries reviled him for his belief that homosexuality suited the ancient Greeks, and that under certain conditions suicide was a viable alternative for Englishmen (Passeran was actually blamed for a number of suicides in 1732–3, on the grounds that his doctrine had encouraged them, and one Englishman left a note stating that he had been reading Passeran at the time he slit his wrists); so, too, Knight's contemporaries held Knight in contempt, for his undermining of an anti-phallic Christianity, and for his view that the erotic loves of the ancients were but the 'symbolic languages' of a higher religion. And, through rumours of Knight's own suicide (about which space does not permit much more to be said), they came to see him as a proponent of suicide and attributed to him the belief that suicide was not a pernicious act. Knight's image, therefore, gave rise to a reputation, during and after his lifetime, that was in many ways at odds with the real man. The ironies that attach to this image of Knight and the formation of this reputation delineates some of the boundaries of my concern here, and this incongruity – between the domain (phallic fertility) where he made a lasting contribution and the interpretation his contemporaries gave to this phallic campaign – is the matter so difficult to comprehend from our perspective late in the twentieth century.

There is another matter crucial to our discussion. It is important to notice what Knight's notion of the god Priapus and the priapeic tradition was (I use priapeic rather than the equally acceptable, although somewhat different, priapic and priapean, and in my usage priapeic refers to excessive male sexuality as well as to all things phallic). The priapeic tradition was not – as we shall see – a tradition presided over by the grotesque little demon with a huge and almost mechanically erect phallus of the iconographic record, but by a very different figure: a less godly and rather more vitalistic kind of life force. Here Knight deviated, although not entirely, from the school of Scaliger and the Renaissance Ovidians who had compiled and commented on this material. What matters, then is not the bibliographical dimension of this Renaissance corpus of writings and beliefs, but the increasingly cool reception it was given. After 1600, its contents became increasingly less well received. If the English Restoration had been less receptive to it than was the Renaissance, the eighteenth century forcefully spurned it as lewd, and abjured it in the name of obscenity. By the end of the eighteenth century, when sexual morality had become much more restrictive than it had been only a few generations earlier, as Lawrence Stone and other social historians have demonstrated, the topic of pagan phallicism – whether construed literally or symbolically – could not be discussed within polite society. Like the subjects sodomy and suicide, it was altogether taboo.[5] It angered, among others, the refined and wealthy Horace Walpole, about whose feud with Knight more shall be said later.

Knight's claim to orginality notwithstanding, my study is exploratory and heuristic. I do not explore *Priapus* for conclusions about accuracy or originality – subjects, however, germane to the broadly conceived anthropology of this book. Instead, I discuss Knight's intentions and how his most basic ideas came to be conceptualised. One wonders why this man *in particular* adopted this subject *at a specific moment* in Enlightenment culture, and what ideological programme may have lain beneath his interest in this subject? The question naturally implies a philosophy of literary criticism and cultural history, especially the notion that authors are not merely actors randomly acting on an historical stage, but characters who appear for specific reasons and who ultimately, if given a chance to speak for themselves, account for the ideologies they espouse and the acts they commit. They are characters whose lives reveal the reasons why they behaved in specific ways, if we will only investigate the details of time, place, setting and – most importantly – motive.

I conclude that Knight's conceptualisation of the discourse *Priapus* was anything but arbitrary. Given his social class and politics, his opulent lifestyle and deep aesthetic appreciation and his craving for intimate homosocial friendships, as well as the monumental success of the Neoclassical Movement and the climate of personal morality in England during the latter part of the eighteenth century, it is understandable why Knight, rather than any number of his contemporaries, should have written *Priapus*. In fact, the story of his conceptualisation of the project has never been related to the sexual climate of that period, partly because until recently it was considered to be in poor taste to explore subjects such as these. It was impossible to do so without jeopardising one's credibility in the republic of scholars.

I

Those who have commented on Knight's life and the discourse *Priapus* have generally connected them superficially. Thus Frank Messmann, who has written the most detailed study of Knight's career to date, views them in isolation, especially diminishing Knight's wealth, politics and personal sexuality. And even of such a crucial influence on Knight's writings as his religion and politics, Messmann writes: 'except for its usefulness in helping later generations to understand the eighteenth-century Establishment, Knight's political career is of relatively little importance'.[5] It is a strange conclusion and, with that disposed of, Messmann plunges into a discussion of the *Priapus*. By contrast, Peter Funnell's account in *The Arrogant Connoisseur* (1982) is more detailed and is also extraordinarily sensitive to the influences of Sir William Hamilton, the wealthy patron of neoclassical art and sponsoring member of the Society of Dilettanti, and Charles Townley, the wealthy collector, with whom Knight was on close terms beginning in 1782. Funnell is correct to contexualise *Priapus* within this milieu:

> . . .the Society of Dilettanti, of which Hamilton was a prominent member and [Sir Joseph] Banks the Secretary, had voted to print [Hamilton's] account. It eventually appeared in 1786 with an engraving of the 'Great Toes' serving as its bizarre frontispiece, followed by a far larger *Discourse on the Worship of Priapus*. . . written by the member of the society who supervised the publication, Richard Payne Knight. Hamilton's 'communication' provided the pretext for Knight's *Discourse*, but the *Discourse* is far more than a mere commentary on the

ceremonies at Isernia, and in fact owes far more to the ideas of Hamilton's old friend and protégé, the eccentric French antiquarian and adventurer Pierre François Hugues, self-styled 'Baron' d'Hancarville.[7]

Yet Hamilton's treatise was an excuse; *un prétexte* for ideas Knight would have developed under some other programme if necessary. For Hamilton had little of Knight's insight into phallicism and Christianity, especially the degree to which Christianity had been anti-phallic, and none of the cultural resonances Knight would give to fertility as a broader subject. Funnell is also correct to attribute much of the content in *Priapus* to d'Hancarville. But even these assumptions, and the many more that can be compiled from Messmann and Funnell, do not come to terms with *Priapus* as a vehicle of communication and self-expression. Funnell tries to create a Knight whose whole life is of a piece. At the end of his essay he discusses Knight's last composition, an 1823 'Romance in Rhyme' called *Alfred* which contains an apology for *Priapus* in its preface. 'The preface to his [Knight's] verse romance *Alfred*', Funnell writes, 'fully confirms that Knight was no less keen a controversialist in his seventies than he had been in his thirties – here he expresses his detestation of the Christian conception of everlasting damnation'.[8] The question of whether Knight's polemics were as sustained in later life as they had been during middle age is relevant, but it is much less crucial than the development of his early hostility to Christianity. And given Knight's affluent background at Downton Castle in Herefordshire and his subsequent public presence as a prominent Whig, we must discover how and why Knight, far more than Hamilton or Townley, allowed himself to become the national spokesman for phallic worship and anticlericalism. Some answers are provided in the *Discourse* and, to only a slightly greater degree, in the activities of the Dilettanti. More crucially, a larger context for Knight must be constructed if we wish to understand how he came to adopt these ideas and why he staunchly continued to defend them in old age.

Knight's early life is surprisingly undocumented. What has been recounted amounts to bare facts: birth into luxury in Herefordshire as the grandson of a man who had amassed a large fortune and the eldest son of a Reverend, chronic sickliness from an early age, described as a hypochondriacal disorder, home tutoring as a consequence of this chronic malady, years of wandering through Italy on and off from the age of seventeen to thirty, the return to Herefordshire, the inheritance of his grandfather's estate and the building of Downton Castle, 'a tower into which he could retreat'.⁹ As Elisabeth Inglis-Jones has shown, not only was Knight never educated in a public school or university, but his family and tutors were members of the Church of England, and were, moreover, the kind of Tory West Country landowners who devalued book-learning precisely because it could become a dangerous weapon, interfering with traditional piety and local custom.¹⁰ Knight, recalling this barren period of his early life, describes it as a time when:

> . . . no preceptor's care, nor parent's love,
> To form and raise my infant genius strove.
> But abandon'd in the darksome way,
> Ungovern'd passions led my soul astray. . .¹¹

Whether this 'darksome way' and these 'ungovern'd passions' were the result of a youth devoid of loving parents and/or tutors, or the more exotic fantasies of a young man who would eventually write the revolutionary *Discourse*, it is now impossible to know. Regardless, his genius developed at home in an atmosphere where paganism was deplored and traditional Christianity upheld. Any notion that the doctrines of the Christian church, of whatever sect, were false would have been abhorrent to the Knights. Even more abhorrent were the radical deism and heretical pantheism which Knight later advocated in *The Progress of Civil Society*.¹² Indeed, Knight's father had gone further; he forbade his son from studying the language of those 'pagan ancient Greeks' while he was boarding with a tutor in Warwickshire and, when Knight crossed him, it was interpreted as an act of rebellion.¹³ The scar left on Knight was so deep that one wonders whether his father did not have a strong motive of his own, such as guilty memories of youthful homosexual excesses, that may have inflamed his own imagination. In any case, Knight's attacks on the Church of England in adulthood, his fierce anticlericalism and preference for the freedom of a pagan Grecian past, for that 'fountain-head whence Grecian genius pours',¹⁴ arose from personal preference and choice, not from any beliefs inculcated at home. If anything, he rebelled against his father's strictures and the generally rigid mores of the Knight family for reasons suggested in part by the 'homosocial' component of this chapter.

The resemblances in background and early adult experiences among Knight, Horace Walpole and William Beckford are remarkable. Although Knight was not as wealthy as Beckford, 'England's richest man', his early life strongly resembled Beckford's: birth into luxury; early illness which rendered university life impossible; escape to the Continent, on the Grand Tour, or allegedly in search of health cures with a younger male friend; the return home, accompanied by the construction of some magnificent architectural edifice – Fonthill, Strawberry Hill, Downton Castle, and – most interestingly – the rejection of a fundamentally anti-phallic Christianity that had been ingrained in them during early years at home in favour of a Greek paganism and Gothic barbarism. Knight parts company with Walpole in this last category: Walpole admired the Gothic – what is Strawberry Hill if not the architectural miracle of a Gothic antiquity? – but rejected a pagan Greek past, for reasons which I believe were intrinsically tied to his passive, repressed sexuality.[16] Like Walpole and Beckford, Knight also had his young men. When he set out for Italy a second time – most probably in 1776 after Downton had been completed – he took with him John Robert Cozens, the precocious painter, who was two years his junior. Discovering why the affluent Knight selected Cozens and subsidised him is crucial for understanding the direction of Knight's life, as he was to continue to cultivate young men into his old age.

II

Cozens was the only son of the Russian-born landscape painter Alexander Cozens, and the grandson of Peter the Great. His mother was the sister of Robert Edge Pine, the landscape artist. An only child, Cozens, like Knight, was also sickly; his illnesses were more pronouncedly mental than Knight's and would eventually cause premature death at the age of forty-six. Knight and Cozens travelled together as far as Naples, and then separated for reasons never discovered.[17] Knight returned to England alone late in 1779 or early in 1780. Cozens stayed on in Italy, where he linked up with Beckford.[18] Although very little is known about his relation to Beckford, it is true that, while travelling in Italy and for much of his later life, Cozens was sponsored and subsidised by Knight and Beckford.

A few years after Cozens had returned to England in 1783, he became deranged.[19] Whether the condition owed anything to his travels with Knight and Beckford is unknown, but the chronological proximity is suspect. Back on his native heath, Dr Thomas Monro, the psychiatrist at Bethlehem, treated him,[20] but Cozens' condition was apparently hopeless – an incurable psychosis – and he remained deranged and was intermittently confined from the early 1790s until in death in 1799. It would be helpful to know whether Cozens and Walpole discussed Knight when the painter visited Horace Walpole at Strawberry Hill in 1790; by then Walpole had become outraged at 'Priapus Knight' and – as we shall see – had publicly lashed out at him. Although it would be folly to speculate on the nature or course of Cozens' mental malady, it is possible that his relationship with Knight intensified the atmosphere on the Grand Tour beyond a level Cozens could sustain, just as the increasing intimacy of Walpole and Thomas Gray, the poet, while they travelled in Italy seems to have contributed to their sudden separation at Florence a few years earlier.[21] Knight's Sicilian journal, discovered in Weimar in 1980 by Claudia Stumpf,[22] provides no details of their relationship, but it must have been intimate, for two decades later, when Cozens was impoverished and deranged, Knight did not forget his companion and raised a subscription for Cozens' further psychiatric and medical care by the finest physicians.[23]

On his travels in the southern part of Italy, Knight was joined by Charles Gore, a wealthy dilettante and student, and Philip Hackert, the German landscape painter whose life intrigued Goethe.[24] The group, having left Rome and its colony of Britons behind, voyaged southward from Naples to Paestum by boat, continuing to the islands of Stromboli and Lipari still further to the south, and eventually landed on the north coast of Sicily. They left Sicily on 3 April 1777, four or five months after they arrived, but it is unknown for how long, or to where they travelled. One especially wonders what Knight did between the summer of 1777 and the spring of 1780, when he returned to England. During this interim, Downton Castle was under construction, and Knight probably designed his itinerary to remain away from the hustle and bustle of workmen. Moreover, he is known to have been in Paris during the winter of 1777, though for what reason is unknown.

Claudia Stumpf has summarised the Sicilian trip well, especially by calling attention to the deep anticlerical strains in Knight's diary: 'With this [anticlerical] declaration the theme is set for the ensuing pages: political, economical, sociological and juridical grievances, the decline of the arts and sciences, and even the corruption of language, is put at the charge of the "sour mythology of the Christians."'[25] Knight also remarks on the enslavement of the people to priestcraft in southern Italy, attributing much to ignorance and superstition, encouraged – even instilled – by the Church. But there is more to say about Knight the traveller during the three years he remained away from home.

Knight was now (1777–9) in his late twenties, that period when most upper-class men, especially eldest sons of his social standing, were thinking of marriage. Considering his vast inheritance in 1775, he had all the more reason to contemplate marriage. Yet Knight had few female friends during his life, and I surmise that he did not feel comfortable with women except for the explicit purpose of sexual gratification.[26] The trip to Sicily was made entirely in the company of males younger than himself, those types with whom Knight could discuss the sins of Christian priestcraft and – by contrast – the delectable joys of ancient Greek civilisation. There are no accounts of his attendance in the well-known salons of Paris while he resided there in 1777. Stumpf notices that 'it has been proposed that Knight planned to take J. R. Cozens to Sicily but quarrelled with him (and thus took Hackert instead), but there is no evidence for this'.[26] Although unproven, Knight's disinterest in women while on the journey remains unassailable truth, as does his homosocial camaraderie with Gore and Hackert. How different was this form of ascetic travel on the continent from the sexual pilgrimages by Boswell and Wilkes undertaken just a few years earlier. Few young men, admittedly, could vie with the amorous Boswell or the lecherous Wilkes, but my intent is not to speculate about Knight's private sex life during these years, but rather to explore the degree of homoeroticism that was inextricably intertwined in his pursuit of the retrieval of a pagan Grecian past. As I have written elsewhere, 'thus far . . . the neo-Hellenism of the eighteenth century has been discussed apart from its sociological contexts, apart from its homoerotic basis. . .'[28] and I am suggesting here that even the best scholars of this neo-classical retrieval have been too shy to note or comment upon it.

III

Here, in 1780, it is useful to take stock of the man who will soon compose *Priapus*. The year Knight finally returned home from two long trips to Italy where he had gone first on a Grand Tour and then explicitly in search of the Greek remains in Sicily, he was a thirty-year-old millionaire (the buying power of the fortune he had inherited would certainly qualify him for this description). He had already built himself a palatial gothic retreat, his private religion seems already to have been as pagan as his politics were staunchly Whiggish, he would soon be elected a Whig MP for his county, and he had not showed the least interest in women for marriage. In point of fact, he was never to marry, but the purpose of this overview is to determine if there were predisposing factors to make him a likely candidate to write *Priapus*.

Knight's relation to Sir William Hamilton, the English envoy in Naples, and to Hamilton's circle in London contributes little to an understanding of his degree of homoeroticism, but it does pave the way towards understanding the next *dramatis persona*, the Baron d'Hancarville. Hamilton had gone to Naples in 1764, where he at once combined the practice of foreign diplomacy with the collecting of ancient vases.[29] Hamilton was still envoy in Italy while Knight was making his two trips, but there is no evidence that they had met, although it is possible that Knight attempted to contact his envoy, or that Hamilton sought him out in view of Knight's antiquarian pursuits. The first record of their meeting occurs in London in 1781, by which time Hamilton had already communicated to the Society of Dilettanti his discovery of the remains of an ancient priapeic cult in Isernia outside Naples.[30] Here it is important to reiterate what must be obvious to students familiar with this period in the history of the Society: it was not Knight, but Hamilton, who discovered the remains of Priapus. The priority is revealing.

More crucial for Knight in the long run was Hamilton's association with Pierre François Hugues, the so-called Baron d'Hancarville, as he came to be known in his time.[31] Haskell links d'Hancarville to Hamilton through the envoy's vase collection, but even Haskell has observed something extraordinary in the relationship between the envoy and the decadent Frenchman:

> The incredible speed with which he [Hamilton] proceeded can be seen from the fact that within a year of his arrival he already owned a sufficient number – several hundred [vases] in fact – to warrant publishing a huge illustrated book on them. In some way, which is not yet clear, the job was entrusted to d'Hancarville.[32]

If the reason for the entrustment 'is not yet clear', Hamilton's interest in Hugues is even more abstruse, for d'Hancarville was a drifter, forever being expelled from one place and seeking another, always in debt, often in prison, and never able to achieve any respectability. In brief, he was the perpetual pariah who intrigues ninety-nine men in a hundred by a deft combination of the forbidden and the exotic. By this combination he attracted Winckelmann, with whom he became friendly during the tenure of Hamilton's envoyship (1764–8),[33] and with these qualities he apparently also charmed Hamilton. The temptation to recite the exotic life of this creature of perpetual flight is great, but must be resisted in view of the splendid, if all too brief, new essay by Professor Haskell with its incisive conclusion: '. . . there are fleeting moments . . . during which we can grasp what it was about d'Hancarville that was at all times in his life to intoxicate those who came in touch with him – and they included some of the most brilliant people in the world – and to win their reluctant admiration even when it became all too clear that he was not the gentleman that he claimed to be'.[34]

This assessment captures d'Hancarville in his smallest essence and is entirely accurate, but Haskell set out to place the Baron only within the context of Enlightenment art history, not in the context of sexual exoticism, although d'Hancarville belongs in the latter camp as much as in the former. A portion of this exoticism entails his activities as a pornographer of the erotic in antiquity. If the unpublished correspondence of Thomas Jenkins and Charles Townley can be trusted, then d'Hancarville was expelled from Naples for publishing pornographic illustrations only two years after Winckelmann had been murdered in 1768 by a hustler in Vienna.[35] D'Hancarville persuaded Hamilton to use these erotic illustrations to adorn future compilations of catalogues Hamilton might make. Then in 1769 or 1770, d'Hancarville contrived to make a financial killing by producing cheaper, more popular, pulp versions. This occurred just as Knight was entering Italy on his first continental tour, and it is not impossible, given his precocity and his penchant for information about foreigners abroad, that he had heard about the exotic Frenchman. The slender volumes containing these erotic poses were appropriately entitled *Monumens de la vie privée des douze Césars* and *Monumens du Culte Secrèt des Dames Romaines*, two books so rare today that scholars remain unable to sort out their knotty bibliographical problems or establish the year of their publication.

Before 1770, Hamilton continued to retain and subsidise d'Hancarville. His reasons are unknown, as is his personal estimate of the character and ability of the man. The pretext was, of course, illustration of the book Hamilton was writing about Greek antiquities, yet one wonders what Hamilton thought as he saw the years pass (1767–70) without any sign of d'Hancarville's contributions. Did his earlier esteem continue, or did some other consideration, such as charm or charisma, guide him? Eventually Hamilton pursued his patronee to jail, and here the plot thickens, for one would have thought that this dire state of affairs would have provoked a termination of Hamilton's patronage. Yet, as Haskell has commented, d'Hancarville turns up starving seven years later (in 1777) in London, 'and from this patron [Hamilton] he was able to scrounge just enough help until he was picked up by Charles Townley'.[36] Had Hamilton forgotten d'Hancarville's procrastination in Naples and London, or was d'Hancarville so charismatic that he could talk his way out of any situation, no matter what? Those questions remain unanswered, but what we do know of d'Hancarville's relation to other members of the Hamilton-Townley circle, within and without the Society of Dilettanti, will provide us with a sense of the milieu in which *Priapus* was conceived and executed.

Hamilton returned to England briefly in 1777 and stayed just long enough to introduce d'Hancarville to Townley. Knight remained on the continent, in Paris, and would not return to England for another two or three years. But Townley, like Winckelmann and Hamilton before him, was dazzled by d'Hancarville and swiftly took him into his home to catalogue antiquities. It is Francis Haskell, again, who provides the clearest epitome of the relationship between the two men:

> Townley, a Catholic gentleman [a bachelor] from Lancashire, had spent much of his life in Italy and had devoted a great deal of time and expense in assembling one of the finest collection of antiquities to be seen in England; a famous picture by Zoffany, painted in about 1781, gives a vivid though fanciful impression of the sculptures he had brought together in his house in Park Street, Westminster – and in that picture we can see d'Hancarville seated at the very centre, explaining, in an almost proprietary way, the antiquities which he had been called upon to catalogue.[37]

Haskell then describes how d'Hancarville had won over Townley, but without providing the details that would allow us to get a clearer picture of this milieu of collectors and antiquarians. Townley was indeed a Catholic gentleman from the North-West, but his Catholicism had long since lapsed; if not in pagan Rome, which remained his favourite city, then perhaps elsewhere in Italy where he had lingered on many occasions spread over many years. If his anticlericalism was not of the intensity of Knight's, it was nevertheless a staunch anti-Catholicism that permitted him to accept the neo-classical theories of his new protégé, the Baron d'Hancarville.

As consequential was Townley's lack of conjugal life. Unmarried during this period (1777–80), he had never been interested in women. Indeed, nowhere do women crop up in his long life of sixty-eight years, except for the amusing anecdote, so often told, about the frenzy with which he sought to recover the famous bust known as Clytie, whom he dared to call 'his wife', when his mansion house in Park Street Westminster was threatened by the outbreak of the Gordon Riots in 1780.[38] Here Townley lived alone, in this large and fashionable house in Westminster, sharing his domain only with his servants. However, by 1781 or 1782 d'Hancarville had moved in, and the two men shared the premises and discussed their favourite subject: the arts of the ancients. By 1782, Townley was complaining to Knight, who had now returned home from Italy, about the high cost of maintaining a profligate bohemian like d'Hancarville who consumed too many of his guineas, even if he compensated with 'more rational and more Satisfactory [disquisitions on ancient art] than all I had found in the absurd books of Antiquaries'.[39] Although the extant correspondence between Townley and Knight is fragmentary and brief, it suggests that Townley's complaints were directed to a highly sympathetic listener. For Knight was also a passionate lover of antiquities, was also uninterested in women, was even more anti-clerical, and was politically as staunch a new Whig as any. The two men had all this in common: politics, religion, a deep homosocial proclivity, and – most crucially – aesthetics. What better reason for them to compare notes on the dazzling, if bizarre, Frenchman who had charmed even the usually circumspect Winckelmann!

Townley eventually drew Knight into his orbit on Park Street. He was the older man by fifteen years, the richer and by far the more consummate connoisseur. With great regularity Knight began to frequent Townley's drawing room – the one painted by Zoffany – and, predictably, was shortly as enchanted by d'Hancarville as all Knight's predecessors had been. By 1782 Knight was persuaded, as Knight's and Townley's extant correspondence reveals, that d'Hancarville was a genius of the first order who should be subsidised at all costs. 'Dancarville's [sic] Work', a book about the religious customs of the pagan Greeks, Knight wrote to Townley that year, 'promises to be such an Acquisition to all lovers of Ancient Arts and History that he must at all events be enabled to complete it'.[40]

Were Townley and Knight so myopic in the full face of d'Hancarville's limitations? Or, if not actually blind, so entirely oblivious to the gossip being generated in London by this man who was known on the continent as a fraud that they could write in these superlatives? This question continues to haunt the student of the Townley-Knight circle during the 1780s, especially in the period leading up to the publication of *Priapus*. Viewed in another perspective: what were the drawing rooms of the great Whig connoisseurs and collectors of the late eighteenth century like? Indeed, what was patronage then if it could permit blind endorsement of this type of man? For surely Hamilton, Townley, Knight and many others knew of d'Hancarville's theory of ancient fertility rites; he had been espousing them ever since Hamilton had met him in 1764, almost twenty years earlier. Could the group in Park Street have misgauged the moral temper of the times to such a degree, or have we students been looking in the wrong place for the wrong phenomena? Can it be that, however conventional these connoisseurs may have appeared in terms of politics, religion, and social status, however unaffected by revolutionary ideas so prevalent on the Continent they may have seemed at this time, *au fond* they were rebels with a more or less radical programme? I cannot prove that the latter was the case, but all along I have been suggesting that the possibility is worthy of consideration because the evidence points to it rather than to miscalculation on their part. Theirs was, it seems to me, a deliberate crusade against Christianity and prudery through the convenient vehicle of neo-Hellenic retrieval.

At any rate, d'Hancarville continued to be handsomely subsidised and his book appeared in 1785 in French – he could not write English.[41] Haskell comments that it 'could not have been written even a few years earlier, for it took into account the first shock waves of a crucial and very recent intellectual discovery that was on the verge of transforming the consciousness of Europe: first hand knowledge of the religions and literature of India and the Far East'.[42] Such transformation in the consciousness of an entire European continent is impossible, of course, to pinpoint at a specific time and place, and it is probably going too far to allege, with Haskell, that d'Hancarville's *Recherches* 'could not have been written *even* a few years earlier' (my italics). However, the point about India and the Far East remains secure and has been developed at monographic length by Partha Mitter.[43] Dr Mitter has shown that this outburst of European interest in India in the 1780s coincided with a new interpretation of ancient religion in terms of sexual symbolism. The issue is not that India rather than China or another part of the Orient was special, or that the whole of the Orient was believed to possess superior wisdom, but rather that Oriental religion permitted Europeans to recognise that fertility rites, as seen in the symbolism of the phallus, functioned as the common denominator of *all* religions. And Mitter pierces straight to the heart of the matter when he observes that, whatever else this movement towards the discovery of a universal religion represented, it was first and foremost 'a manifestly *anticlerical* doctrine which enthusiastically extolled the virtues of paganism'.[44] Once we have grasped this fundamental point, it is not hard to piece together the rest of our story and notice how interwoven was the phallicism, as well as the anticlericalism, pantheism and republican Whiggism, of the Townley-Knight circle in Westminster.

Given our pursuit of *Priapus* and the widespread shock of its first readers, the reception of d'Hancarville's book cannot concern us in any detail. Besides, Professor Haskell has already said a good deal about it in his essay on d'Hancarville. However, we must pause briefly to consider Knight's movements during the publication and reception of this work in 1785, as turbulence and revolutionary fervour in France gathered momentum.

During 1785 Knight was elected MP from Leominster, all the while remaining hard at work on the *Priapus*. He rarely visited Downton and spent almost all his time in London. Here he heard and read about the reception of d'Hancarville's *Recherches sur l'Origine, l'Esprit et les Progrès des Arts de la Grece* . . . Having subsidised its composition and patronised its author, he was given a copy of the very expensive three volumes and especially pored over the nearly one hundred pages of introduction, where d'Hancarville replied to his critics at large.[45] The reply was a book itself, containing d'Hancarville's view of ancient and modern theology (pp. iii-v); a discussion of Sir Walter Raleigh's discovery of the treasures on Mount Arrarat (p. ix); a synopsis of Louis Duten's *Inquiry into the Discoveries attributed to the Moderns* (p. x);[46] an inserted dissertation on hermaphrodites (pp. 42–4),[47] and – most significantly – a verbatim reprint of Paul Henry Maty's review of d'Hancarville's earlier books (pp. 57–64), which had appeared in the January issue of the *New Review*;[48] concluding with d'Hancarville's extensive rebuttal of that piece (pp. 55–6 and 65–85).

Knight was amused by Maty's ferocious strictures. Maty – not to be confused with his father, the physician and librarian of the British Museum – was an odd creature. By turns friendly and inimical, he himself had never got anywhere in life; had merely rested on his father's laurels, even to the point of inheriting his father's job at the British Museum and, more perfidiously if germane to our story here, had been accused of Arianism. Yet he was filled with antipathy for those antiquarians who, like the Townley circle, preferred pagan to Christian religion, and who found Christian values among the Dionysiacs or Bacchantes of ancient ritual.[49] Maty especially despised d'Hancarville and his *Recherches*. His reasons are couched in conventional jabber about conception and execution:

> As a reviewer, I must confess I could have wished for less tautology, more order, more clearness, less mixture of old and known things with the new, and a smaller torrent of erudition. But perhaps this was inseparable from the subject, and I ought to be thankful that the book which, I think, might have been compressed into half a volume, was not lengthened out into four [i.e. instead of three].[50]

This was the ostensible explanation, but the genuine reasons lay deeper. However much Maty may have thought of himself as a neo-classicist – and it was an age when almost all educated men were classicists of some type with views about every classical subject *except Priapus* – he was of the group who felt threatened by the priapeic interests of a Hamilton or Knight. This is why the review even proceeds to doubt the existence of the Renaissance *Priapeia*, and why Maty claimed, a few months later, to be revolted by Knight's *Priapus*. Yet all this scepticism and hostility left Knight unfazed; if anything, it gave him more ammunition for his own, as yet unpublished, polemic.

IV

The history of the publication and appearance of *Priapus* has often been told, however inchoately for lack of complete documentation. It requires no narration here. The main topics have often been discussed: the extent to which the Society of Dilettanti sponsored it and then planned to limit its circulation; how it was financed; who received the approximately eighty copies circulated; how it fell into the wrong hands and, its reviews and reception in England. What has not been discussed, certainly not at any length, is the way the camps of those who favoured and disliked *Priapus* disagreed. Factions arose based upon Whiggism, anticlericalism, radical metaphysics and the unspeakable subject – phallic worship, to say nothing of the even more sodomitically unspeakable homosexuality; this last phenomenon not called by this name, of course, since homosexuality is a late-nineteenth-century term with no exact equivalent in the eighteenth century. Nevertheless, homosexuality, however anachronistic and then in whatever procrustean conceptual form, lies close to the heart of the matter, although it is difficult to articulate it with any precision since it was not discussed.[51]

In brief, the reception of *Priapus* was a very different matter from that of d'Hancarville's *Recherches*. Despite Knight's indebtedness to d'Hancarville's ideas, moreover, almost every aspect of publication was different, despite the similarity of the subject matter – the symbolic languages of antiquity. Unlike d'Hancarville, Knight was English, wrote in English, thought in English and conceptualised his subject – even the tropes of his anticlericalism – in terms that were typically English. Where d'Hancarville digressed on all types of subjects in addition to religion and sexual mores (expanding on symbolism of every type and wandering into the realms of daily life), Knight was, in comparison, relatively brief and to the point. And where d'Hancarville basked in erudition, Knight had other aims: to write a polemic against the Church and explore the androgynous – even bisexual – origins of ancient religion. And finally Knight, unlike d'Hancarville, wrote directly and frankly about ancient phallic fertility rituals, a subject which seems not to have particularly interested d'Hancarville. D'Hancarville had been intrigued by sexual symbolism, but not by phallic rites, and in this regard the two men parted company, for not only did Knight have a fixation for phallic ritual, he also make these phallic rites the basis of his fierce polemic. It is therefore insufficient to view the *Discourse* merely in a limited context – as a narrowly conceived work of historical archaeology or, alternatively, as a satiric barb thrown at the Church of England in the guise of a history of pagan sexual worship,[52] or, even less accurately, as another of many links in the long chain of neo-classical revivalist studies. *Priapus* must also be viewed within the contexts of English *religion* and *sexual custom* during the tumultuous decade of the 1780s – subjects about which almost nothing has been written and about which rather little sense has been made.[53]

Peter Funnell has put his finger on an aspect of the above context when commenting on the assurances Knight had been given by the Dilettanti that the circulation of his book would be limited. This would seem to contradict the assumption that Knight and Townley were crusading against Christianity and prudery. After all, why limit circulation if a crusade is the point? But this approach confuses the private and public realms, and misgauges the aims of these men. Knight's style in *Priapus* offers us a better clue. Funnell comments that 'breaking through the erudite scholarship we sense a somewhat raffish delight in the indecency of its subject'.[54] Even more perceptive is Funnell's sense of the rhetorical vehicle and special tone Knight had decided to use: 'The disjunction [in the *Discourse*] between symbolic meaning and actual appearance is a source of ironic effect which contributes greatly to the character of the *Discourse* and perhaps serves to forestall ridicule'. Irony is thus maximized – an irony enhancing an already deep-seated polemical intent in the writer.

Yet none of these observations, however meritorious and shrewd, comes to grips with the gulf between Knight the real man, living in a particular place at a certain time, and the remarkably ambiguous and ironic tone of the *Discourse*. Why does Knight – a wealthy bachelor from an old established family who, from all accounts, lacked interest in women and about whom there remains little gossip about bawds or prostitutes – argue so polemically for sexual toleration based on a symbolic understanding of the cultures of the ancients and the Orient? According to Knight, the salvation of humankind – seen from the perspective of the 1780s – lay in the retrieval of a state-endorsed, if reverent and ironical, phallicism capable of liberating modern oppressed man from the sombre gloom of an incrementally industrialised milieu. Such phallic liberation forms the basis of his manifesto in *Priapus* about the Judaeo-Christian tradition. But what has not been grasped, perhaps as a direct consequence of his having gone begging for a serious biographer,[55] is the personality of the man behind the polemical and ironic treatise: his outlook, his intellectual beliefs and his personal sexuality.

Had Knight been an unknown political figure or a Grub-Street hack, *Priapus* would have been rather ignored. Given his social prominence and political stature, and especially in view of his wealth and his role in London society, the treatise, instead of being merely neglected, was savaged. Only a few of the young and independently minded Dilettanti seemed to respond favourably. When Lionel Cust's list of those members who were presented with a copy is studied, it is evident that viewed as a collective group, the Dilettanti were not at all happy with the book.[56] This may be why Knight soon attempted to buy back all existing copies. However, a few readers, according to Farington – whose diary remains the best source for the book's reception – were appreciative. Most of these were Whigs and, while it is obvious idiocy to suppose that Tories were incapable of finding any value in it, I have not recorded a *single* Tory who commented favourably. Charles Greville (1749–1809), Sir William Hamilton's nephew and a staunch Whig who was also steeped in antiquity, professed to be liberated by its discoveries.[57] And Roger Wilbraham (?–1799), another young Whig supporter of Fox, also became embroiled in the controversy and was highly sympathetic to Knight. Farington claims that Wilbraham was 'a debauchee & much given to lose conversation on such subjects [as Priapus], to which he finds Knight equally inclined'.[58] Perhaps so, but Farington's comment reveals as much about the milieu in which phallic worship could be discussed – literally and symbolically – as it does about Wilbraham's character. The responses of such recipients as Dr Charles Combe, the physician and numismatist, and Thomas Astle, the antiquary, remain undocumented, as do those of Edward Thurlow, the Lord Chancellor who was also an antiquarian, and the Prince of Wales, the future George IV. But Horace Walpole, Gibbon, Boswell, Malone, Wilkes and the Duke of Portland – among others – also received copies. Some of their reactions are more predictable.

Of Walpole's complex response more will be said shortly, for it embodies an aspect of his character not often understood. Gibbon, then in his fifties and having settled comfortably in Lausanne three years earlier, definitely received his copy, as the sales catalogue of his library demonstrates.[59] But if his confession about his own distance from Christianity made a few years later to Holroyd (Lord Sheffield), with whom Gibbon was then on the closest of terms, counts for anything, the anticlerical Gibbon must have been sympathetic at the very least: 'The primitive Church, which I have treated with some freedom [in *The Decline and Fall*], was itself at that time an innovation, and I was attached to the old Pagan establishment'.[60] Boswell may or may not have received his copy of *Priapus*; given his entrenched promiscuity by this time and the guilt with which he regarded his deviations from chastity, perhaps he did not need to.[61] No recorded comments of Malone and the Duke of Portland survive, and an extensive search has failed to produce any evidence that Wilkes ever read his copy. But by 1787, a somewhat reformed Wilkes had given up the mob and retreated into perpetual sinecure as Chamberlain to the City of London, and may have been either too busy assembling future editions of ancient lyric poets, especially Catullus and Anacreon, or simply too uninterested in primitive religious rites to bother with *Priapus*. On the other hand, Wilkes's deep interest in some of the most notorious classical poets, coupled to his own open homoeroticism with Andrew Baxter (the Scottish philosopher and tutor) while he was a student at Leiden, may argue for his endorsement of classical phallicism, and it may have been the case for Wilkes, as for others, that what disturbed them in

Knight's campaign was not the programme itself (phallicism, whether symbolically or literally interpreted) but Knight's flouting of the conventions of polite, Christian, English society. Whichever the historical veracity, it is hard to conjecture with any confidence that Wilkes's response to *Priapus* may have been, a difficulty that brings into the light of day one of the most intriguing aspects of homoeroticism in the eighteenth century: the degree to which it could be openly expressed, so long as the right conventions were observed. In the end, if Wilkes could have approved of the way Knight carried on his campaign, then Knight's anticlericalism, no matter how obscurely disguised, must have attracted the freethinking, antinomian Wilkes, who equated liberty with licence, and freedom with libertine ethics.[62] Indeed, Knight's anticlerical polemics, embedded in a prose vehicle which appears to be nothing more than an archeological treatise, would have appealed to Wilkes who had taken especial pleasure in reading Thomas Gordon's antinomian tracts, in which no obscenity against the Church was too great, and where the Scriptures could be described 'as contrary to Christianity, as sodomy is to nature'.[63] Gordon's anticlericalism is useful because it identifies another crucial aspect of the relationship between anticlericalism and sodomy: for every radical Knight (or, earlier, Toland and Radicati) who obviously connected anticlericalism to homosocial desire or sodomy, there were inevitably dozens of anticlericalists, like Gordon, who continued to be revolted by the thought of sodomy. Sodomy contrary to nature indeed! This was the typical anticlerical agenda rather than Knight's enlightened pagan version.

For the first few years after publication, Sir Joseph Banks, acting in an official role within the society of Dilettanti, controlled the distribution of all copies by ensuring that only those entitled to receive *Priapus* would do so. Gradually, from 1788–90, just at the time that reports were crossing the Channel about heads rolling at the Bastille, a rumour spread throughout England that the authorities viewed this book as subversive to the national Church and government. Shortly thereafter, many who would have wished to read it, or at least see its illustrations, could not obtain copies. Banks sent out no review copies, thereby preventing Grub Street from expressing its customary views. From 1786, when the book was published, to the end of the decade, no review or commentary appeared. But in 1790, T. J. Mathias (1754–1835), without knowing who the author was, somehow obtained a copy. Mathias was an Italian scholar and polemical satirist who had been born into established connections with the Crown, his father having served the Queen in various posts (as his son was to do), rising to the position of librarian of Buckingham Palace.[64] Addicted to literary satire from his years spent at Eton and Trinity College, Cambridge, Mathias seized the ready target of the new 'Priapus' and cast Knight as a leading dunce in the first dialogue of his *Pursuits of Literature*.[65] The result was disastrous for Knight. For almost forty years *Priapus* was an albatross on his back almost everywhere he went.

Mathias found every aspect of the *Discourse* revolting. Calling it 'criminal obscenity' intent upon promoting lewdness and debauchery wherever it was read, he claimed that it had even inflamed his *own* appetite while reading it, and excited the nether regions of his body.[66] He pronounced the illustrations to be 'disgusting', containing 'all the ordure and filth, all the antique pictures and all the representations of generative organs in their most odious and degrading protrusion'.[67] Charging that *Priapus* was intended for the 'obscene revellings of Greek scholars in their private studies', Mathias claimed the book to be dangerously subversive, as subversive as was 'the [phallic] emblem modelled in wax . . . [and] laid upon the table at their [the Dilettanti's] solemn meetings'.[68] And he prophesied a millenarian end to England – an apocalypse of Sodom and Gomorrah – if *Priapus* were to find its way to young men in schools and colleges.

But this was no random criticism from an impartial judge. Mathias was especially appalled because the *Discourse* aroused passions in him that hitherto had lain dormant. From his earliest days he was a loner, in the sexual domain incapable of mixing with either heterosexual or homosocial society, and he was to remain so into his eighties. Even as a boy he had been attracted to Italy and the Italians as a place where decadence flourished, but he was so revolted by the carnal act – in any form – that he could not bring sex into the history of Italian literature he was writing. He knew the tradition of Juvenal and Petronius as well as anyone, and could read their works more fluently than others, but he could not admit to himself any merit in pagan ritual and licence, and he was blind to the possibility – as the Circle of Hamilton, Townley and d'Hancarville had not been – that beneath the apparent immorality lay the most *sacred* of rituals. An eccentric bachelor who never married and about whom no report of frequenting prostitutes survives,[69] all Mathias saw in *Priapus* was lewdness, debauchery and immorality – the very immorality, he gasped, to which Parliament and the Established Church should continue to be opposed. Knight replied to the massive attack six years later in the long

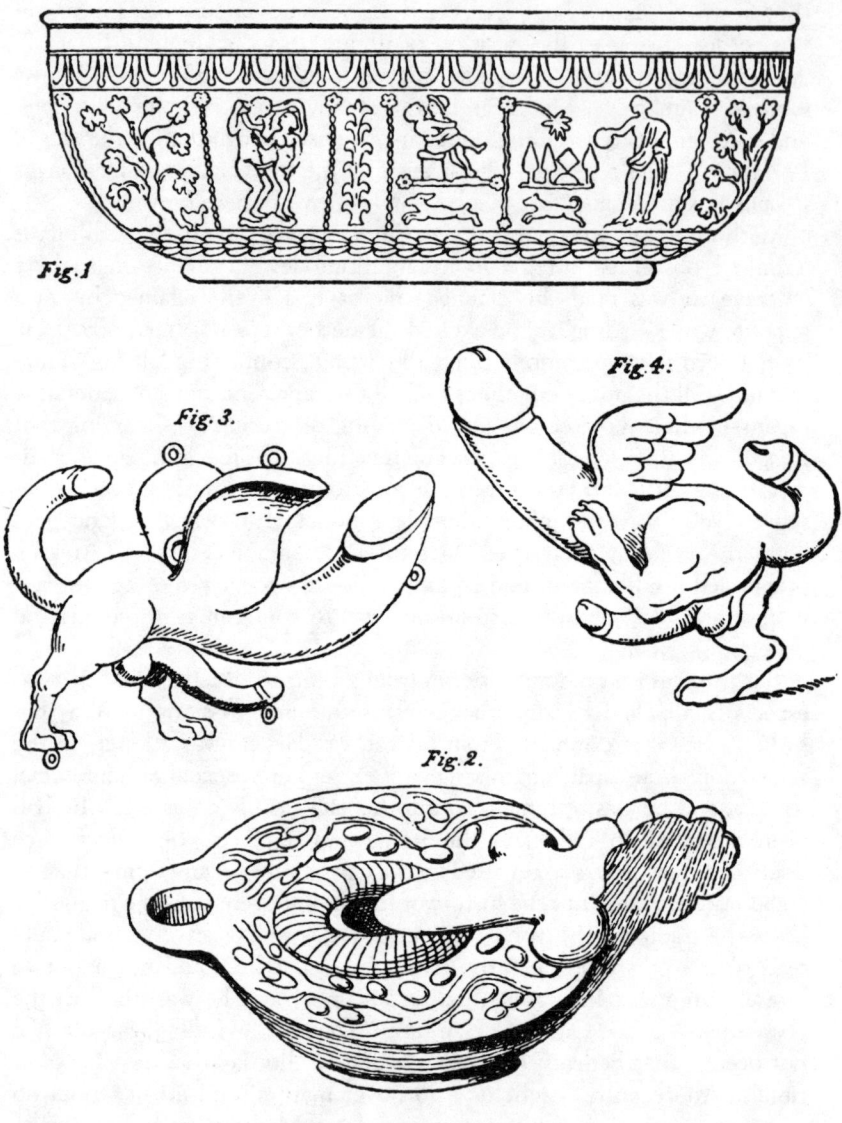

'Phallic Figures found in England', from Richard Payne Knight, *Discourse on the Worship of Priapus* (1786), facing p. 63

preface to *The Progress of Civil Society*.[70] But the matter is not whether Knight's vigorous riposte succeeded, nor whether it was justified, but rather his näiveté in failing to anticipate fierce criticism such as that from Mathias. It is Knight's utter astonishment at Mathias's critique that shocks us today; the total absence in the record of any statements by him to the effect that he expected *Priapus* to elicit such a reception; in brief Knight's incredible notion that his controversial book could have sailed through, given the rigid fibre of late eighteenth-century upper-class English society.

V

There is positively no doubt that Horace Walpole read his copy of *Priapus*, and he certainly knew who Knight was. He and Mathias shared a similar revulsion: no matter how genuinely interested in Italy Knight had been, and no matter whether or not he had graduated from a university (having never attended one, Knight claimed he was an independent scholar), he could not be forgiven for daring to bring sex into history in this blatant way. Walpole felt the urge to attack Knight publicly but claimed to be too constrained by his concern for Judith Damer, a close relation and friend, to declare 'open war'. As he confided to William Mason, the poet-editor of their late mutual friend Thomas Gray:

> Notwithstanding all I have said, I cannot engage in an open war with him and beg not to be named in it. He [Knight] is a great favourite of a very near relation of mine and intimate friend with whom I have already had a warm altercation [i.e. over Knight], and whom I should mortally disoblige, and through whom I have received several civilities from the person himself.[71]

The 'civilities' are not mysterious: Walpole allegedly indulged in frequent gossiping with elderly women, of whom Mrs Damer was one, and, if the talk of the town was true, she was also a lesbian, which Walpole may or may not have known.[72] When she sang Knight's praises during 1784–5, Walpole became sympathetic to Knight's research project and agreed to lend him an ancient bronze representing the goddess Ceres seated next to a bull, an emblem of just the type of sexual fertility Knight was studying. Knight personally fetched the bronze from Strawberry Hill but apparently did not encounter Walpole on that occasion. Later on, Knight forgot the favour and failed to ask the Dilettanti (especially Banks who distributed copies) to send Walpole a complimentary copy. Nevertheless, Banks,

'Bronze Statue of Ceres', Plate VIII of Richard Payne Knight, *Discourse on the Worship of Priapus* (1786), facing p. 68

without knowing about Knight's oversight, lent Walpole *Priapus* which Walpole speedily read and returned, not without expressing his irritation to Banks that Knight could forget his previous act of kindness. All this naturally predisposed Walpole to come out against Knight, but there were, as we shall see, other far more weighty, considerations.[73]

On 16 September 1790, John Cozens, the painter whom Knight had patronised in Italy, called upon Walpole at Strawberry Hill. Although Walpole's memoirs do not reveal the topics they discussed, it was widely known by this time that Knight had subsidised Cozens, and Knight's name may well have come up, especially in passing.[74] After 1790, Walpole's vexation with Knight continued, in part as a result of Ceres, but mainly as the inevitable consequence of the negative reception of *Priapus* by the select public, for Walpole yearned to conform to the rank and file of aristocratic mores and aesthetic taste, no matter how isolated and solitary he may have been at Strawberry Hill. But what was *Priapus* and the phallic campaign it implied – however symbolically or literally interpreted – to Walpole? By 1790 or thereabouts, the sequestered, septuagenarian bachelor, whose best biographer (Wilmarth Lewis) assures us that in old age Walpole enjoyed no 'senile salaciousness', had little to lose whether he came out for or against Knight in the debates over *Priapus*. Those who knew to what degree Walpole's sexuality – if sexuality was the issue – had always been a fragile commodity would not change their minds now, and the rest of the world viewed Walpole, more colourlessly as the wealthy, aristocratic son of a controversial Prime Minister and enjoyed no awarenes of his particular sexuality. Strawberry Hill had hardly acquired a reputation over the decades as a haunt for regular homerotic love-ins (as had the seats of other aristocrats) and even an irrefutable but casual association between Walpole and Knight would not automatically tarnish Walpole's reputation by suggesting that he, like Knight, had been consumed by homosocial desire. Gray, with whom Walpole had travelled on the Grand Tour and enjoyed powerful homoerotic intimacy, had been dead for over two decades, and Lord Lincoln – famous among the aristocracy for the length of his penis and the degree to which he used it with both women and men – was now (in the 1790s) just a memory for Walpole. Walpole had been madly infatuated with him while they were both in their twenties and – as Walpole's letters to him explicitly reveal – had not disguised the nature of his amorous passion. Walpole had also travelled in Italy with him (and his tutor Joseph Spence), had written love-letters to him and scurrilous verses about his physique and the size of his 'majestic vigour', had gossiped with his confidant Charles Hanbury Williams about Lincoln's phallic might and, on numerous occasions, anatomised the actual size of Lincoln's genitals. Walpole had even written short Persian tales and Oriental fables – such as 'Little Peggy' ('A Prophetic Eclogue, in imitation of Virgil's Pollio', an allusive narration of the growth of Lincoln's mighty cock, revealing 'How the majestic vigour it [Lincoln's cock] should rise') – casting Lord Lincoln as the protagonist. And long after their personal contact ceased (in the 1740s), Walpole continued to indulge a sentimental penchant for the masculine and handsome Lincoln. Why then should the author of all this explicitly Lincolnesque priapeia now suddenly claim to be shocked by Knight's *Priapus?* The question remains: what was Knight, or his *Priapus,* to a Walpole who could carry on as he had with Lord Lincoln?

Perhaps Walpole's sexual fragility is more complex than we have estimated and penetrates to the heart of the question through less direct channels. Can it be, one wonders, that nothing specific about either Knight or his *Priapus* aroused Walpole's wrath, but that (as the Freudians would have it) Walpole despised most in others those qualities he recognised as most potent, if also most ubiquitously latent, within himself? – more specifically, an ambivalent sexuality that was once powerful but that manifested itself over the years in outward neuter forms; a sexuality that continued to remain unresolved, one way or another, well into old age. If there is any validity in this explanation, then it may well be that, in Walpole's psyche, Knight represented betrayal at large but for no particular reason. Furthermore, we may be demanding too much from the evidence of a sexually fragile man if we expect to discover concrete answers to the question: betrayal for what explicit reason, betrayal to whom? Knight had committed no crime (except Ceres) against Walpole, but because of Knight's reputation by the 1790s the slightest event was required to ignite the flame that could spark a war. This, in fact, seems to have been what happened. In March 1794, Knight published *The Landscape,* the mere appearance of which threw Walpole into a rage that some Walpolians believe (excessively in my view) hastened his death two years later. Addressed to Uvedale Price, who had yet to publish his new celebrated essay on the picturesque, this was an ideological *tour de force* conceived in the heat of the French Revolution and comparable to Destutt de Tracy's works on primitive religion, as well as his pioneering study of the *Elements of Ideology,* written only a few years later in 1801.[75] The programme of *The Landscape* combines man's naturalness within his democratic aspirations and celebrates Rousseau's state of nature – nature and simplicity – while decrying the English aristocracy: their artificial parks and opulent country houses, their indolence and ostentation and their luxury and pretentious wastefulness.[76] In England it could be read as a declaration of ideological warfare against the ruling oligarchy, as Walpole and his friends immediately interpreted it, and it was bound to reinvigorate the old campaign against Knight that had diminished since the publication of *Priapus*, all the more urgently in view of the current political state of affairs in England and because Knight himself was rich and landed and had emerged from the same ruling class. Had Knight's *Landscape* not been published as a didactic poem but as a prose ideological treatise, it might have acquired more readers in the 1790s and created more antagonists. But blended genres were trademarks of Knight's writing; as in *Priapus*, where his anticlericalism was camouflaged in a work on primitive religion, here gardens and landscapes are the *raison d'être* for an ideological attack on the ruling oligarchy.[77] There is no need to hazard a guess at Walpole's response – the correspondence speaks thunderously for itself. If *Priapus* had disturbed him, *The Landscape* altogether enraged him. It attacked everything for which Walpole stood; it put his life on trial and stirred up ancient fears and anxieties, not least his ambivalent sexuality, because Knight was by now associated with repulsive phallic campaigns which betrayed the confidence of other homosocial bachelors (like Walpole). Although Knight was obviously not an aristocrat, he was, like Walpole, an independent scholar. He also owned a country house and seat, enjoyed a public career well-known to Walpole and travelled in some of the same all-male circles. For these reasons, the blow apparently seemed all the greater. Nothing in Knight's anticlericalism disgusted Walpole and his friends so much as Knight's exaltation of pagan religion through sexual enlightenment. This claim for sexual enlightenment through a 'symbolic language' which only the chosen could understand remained the crux of the matter.

'I am disgusted and offended', the venerable Walpole complained to Mason on 22 March 1796, 'by Mr Knight's new insolent and self-conceited poem; considering to what height he dares to carry his impious attack'.[78] And there followed a very long diatribe attempting to figure out how 'to dethrone this usurper'. Point by point, Walpole disagreed with Knight's egregious 'hog-wash' and professed to be most offended by 'the liberties' Knight had taken 'with our late great and respectable friend', Thomas Gray.[79] But Walpole, like Mason and all the others who quivered when they read the poem, saw behind its blank verse the contrary states of primitive pure religion and contemporary corrupt politics. Outraged at Knight's neo-Lucretianism – an undisguised atheism of which Knight was proud – Walpole compared Knight to the 'malignant Tom Paine and Joseph Priestley'. But Walpole was too cowardly to battle in public, offering old-age as his excuse. Old he was, though he did not know how close to death, and no one reasonably could say that his rage at everything Knight symbolised hastened that death, although the suggestion has been made. 'I acknowledge to you', Walpole pleaded with Mason, who desperately wished to enlist him as an ally in the paper war he (Mason) was plotting, 'that weak and broken as I am and tottering to the grave at some months past seventy-eight, I have not spirits or courage enough to tap a paper-war [with Knight]'. But the pusillanimous Walpole nudged Mason not to be diverted from 'dethroning this usurper'. Walpole continued by punning: 'I did ardently wish you had overturned this knight of the brazen milk-pot, and expelled out of gardens this new Priapus', and ranted on about Knight as if he were a leader of the French rabble 'who is only fit to be erected in the Palais de l'Egalite'. Sexuality (privately enacted or desired, sublimated or publicly discussed), homosocial desire paraded in public by all this priapism, staunch anticlericalism and radical politics: for Walpole they were of the same cloth. No wonder he mentally banished Knight to the *Palais de l'égalité*, a pariah he wished he could altogether expel from England.

Mason, also old and as cowardly as Walpole, could not be spurred to take action against Knight. 'Irony and ridicule', he pleaded in a reply to Walpole, 'are not weapons to be employed . . . on the wretch you have delineated'.[80] But Mason enlisted others, especially George Canning who wrote for the Tory *Anti-Jacobin*, to deride the new Priapus.[81] Others independently went about blackballing Knight. Farington records how Knight was ostracised in the London clubs, especially in the Literary Club,[82] and how Walpole's venom spread, through Mason, to others. After calling on Walpole himself, Farington wrote: 'he laughs at the systematizing plan of Knight and Townley etc., who attempt to prove the lascivious designs of antiquity to be merely emblematic of the creative power'.[83] The Farington memoir is crucial. It shows that, even in old age, Walpole and his cronies did not forget Knight's publication of a decade earlier. However offensive the new ideology of *The Landscape* may have seemed, Knight was still being derogated as 'the new Priapus'. The squire from Herefordshire who introduced sex into ancient history had committed a much worse offence, it seemed, than any Frenchman espousing 'liberty, fraternity, and equality'. It was already unforgivable that a member of their own class – a clubbable bachelor – should hold radical intellectual ideas. That he should combine these ideas with the rites of the pelvis (however symbolic he claimed the original rites to have been) and then validate them as a 'sacred, symbolic language', as if those rites could have been anything but 'the lascivious designs of Antiquity', was unthinkable.

It was also proof – the argument against Knight went – of feeble-minded aesthetic taste. Today, in part as a consequence of fragmented university subjects, we tend to think of neo-classical aesthetics as a system of pure beliefs devoid of political programmes, yet nothing could be further from the historical truth. Whatever the variety of aesthetic tastes may have been in the eighteenth century, it was something intrinsically tied to, indeed shaped by, political and class considerations. For example, one of the aspects of *The Landscape* that had most angered Walpole was Knight's intuition that Goldsmith could have been the rival of Pope. Farington reports that Walpole went on and on about this in conversation. 'His [Knight's] placing Goldsmith in the rank which he has done is a proof of want of judgment', Walpole contended.[84] 'Goldsmith in his *Deserted Village* had some good lines, but his argument "that commerce destroys villages," is ridiculous'. Here Goldsmith's high poetic talent becomes the servant of his doctrine of luxury and commerce. But what, we ask, and in the name of what, is the offence to Walpole? Clearly, that Goldsmith was so severely anti-luxurian in the face of an aristocratic Lord Orford who slept every night in peacock feathers and pink satin at Strawberry Hill.

VI

Taste and sex were thus commingled in the 1780s and 90s. A decade later, Farington wrote in his diary that a 'Committee of taste' had been formed in London, and he observed how various members, especially Sir Thomas Lawrence, the Royal Academician, opposed Knight:

> Lawrence observed to them that Mr. Knight's taste was just that which shd. not be adopted. It was founded on Sensual feeling. – The simplicity of Raphael, His Purity, & c afforded no gratification to Knight, – His pleasure was derived from the luxurious displays of Rubens. – Wm. Lock said he had noticed this at the Marquis of Stafford's where Knight was profuse in his admiration of a sensual

picture by Rubens but did not notice pictures by Titian to which Rubens would have bowed.[85]

Once it became widely known that Knight had written *Priapus*, it was impossible for him to live down his reputation as an erotic devotee worshipping in the Temple of Sensuality. With few exceptions, virtually every commentator in the first two decades of the nineteenth century referred to him as representative of hedonism and sensuality. The new Priapus was even caricatured as an ambulatory satyr – one whom husbands should fear for their wives. Lady Holland wrote in her diaries how he 'corrupted' several women of her acquaintance with his ideas (not his body, since in the carnal sense he was uninterested in women).[86] She recounted how he confused 'sensibility' with erotic nostalgia and ruined several of her other intimates. 'Ly. Hamilton [the wife of the Italian ambassador, Sir William Hamilton] was his Favourite; she absent, the admiration is transferred to Ly. O[xford]'. The crime? – 'he has corrupted her mind by filling her head with innumerable conceits, and teaching her to exclaim against institutions, especially that of marriage'.[87] These 'institutions' are all too clear: what began as field observations coupled with historical research into the phallic rites of the Greeks, ended with husbands practically boarding their doors to lock out the neo-Georgian satyr, the 'new Priapus' as Walpole dubbed Knight. And rumblings about Knight's interest in younger men did not help to diminish his priapeic image, although this aspect of the campaign against him is remarkably undocumented. If John Robert Cozens was now dead, there were others who replaced him, especially the youthful water-colour painter Richard Westall, with whom Knight spent much time after 1800. All these younger men had aesthetic interests similar to Knight's; none was merely a male companion of the type later cultivated by John Addington Symonds and Oscar Wilde. But gossip is merciless and knows no bounds. It haunted Knight to the end.

Even Coleridge, despite his own deep strain of pantheism, as Thomas Macfarland has demonstrated, could not be persuaded to see through the gossip and public cant. He obtained a copy of *Priapus* and 'opened the Book on this Page', he records in his marginalia on Wordsworth.[88] Which page is unknown. But as Coleridge scanned that page in *Priapus* he concluded that 'this single Period contains an absolute demonstration that Mr Knight is just as ignorant *in head* of Taste, and its Principles, as the Author of the Priapus &c must needs have been ignorant *in heart* of Virtue

& virtuous feelings'. Here again was the conflation, or confusion, of taste and sensibility – of aesthetic belief and an ideology of morals. No wonder that Nietzsche later exclaimed that he had built his own 'Gay Science' by conflating the two on a long tradition of forebears.[89] Peacock also seems to have admired Knight's courage in writing about a priapeic subject, but ultimately disapproved of such an anti-Christian enterprise. No Mathias, Peacock was unwilling to deprecate Knight as the modern anti-Christ, or attribute dark satanic motives to him. Peacock was still a babe in swaddling clothes when *Priapus* appeared and seems not to have read it in adulthood, but he was intrigued by Knight's radical views and advised his friends to shun them or be corrupted by them: 'I think silent contempt is in these cases the most effectual weapon'.[90]

By the 1820s, then, Knight's radical anticlericalism, pronounced in the name of a serious primitive phallic religion, had become legendary and notorious. Only Byron and Dr Samuel Parr (the classical scholar and unusually benevolent Christian despite ultra-liberal views who, like Knight, had also been the butt of Mathias's satiric bite) unequivocally defended Knight. Parr tempted friends to dinner by promising them conversation with 'Mr. K. – about the mysteries of oriental mythology, theology and theogony'.[91] It is a shame that no record of these nocturnal occasions exists for it might shed light on Knight in the aftermath of his notorious *Discourse*. *Quant à* Byron, there is (alas) no evidence that he ever read *Priapus*, but being the patrician advocate of things 'Grecian' that he was, and the pious devotee who worshipped in the Temple of Greek, as it were, rather than English, love, he probably would have sympathised with Knight's intentions.[92] The lacuna in extant evidence is much to be lamented.

Also to be lamented is the support of Thomas Hope, the patrician neo-classicist, if he could have read the book. Born in Holland into a millionaire family, like Byron he was passionate about everything 'Greek' and spent most of his youth wandering through Italy and the Levant.[93] A subject like the symbolic sexual language of the ancients and their fertility rites greatly interested him. In 1819 he published his adventures in a three-volume autobiographical novel called *Anastasius: or, Memoirs of a Greek; written at the close of the eighteenth century*. These gushing confessions of a sentimental youth he calls Anastasius, are the romantic memoirs of a rich Aegean boy stranded on deserted beaches and lonely Greek islands. Anastasius, although Greek is nevertheless the exotic Mediterranean projection of a Regency man about town and links up with an equally wealthy Greek merchant named Mavrocordato and his son Spiridion, for whom Anastasius develops a passionate attachment. The hero and Spiridion are lured by Greek women, but always manage to return to each other. At last, Spiridion is compelled to marry and lead a conventional life, but 'the youth [Spiridion] then resumed, never more to abandon it, the steady regular mode of life which only for my [Anastasius's] sake had been abandoned'. Many who read *Anastasius* in the 1820s were moved by its Grecian romanticism. Byron, who was often mistakenly identified as its author, was so moved that he is reported by Samuel Rogers and others to have wept as he read it. In a sense, the novel complements the aims of a book like *Priapus* in that each book is a metaphor for something else and is of a piece with the pagan-Greek neo-classicism of the early nineteenth century, so much of which rested on a sense of Mediterranean sun and rock, as well as being based on altogether different sexual mores from those of Christianity.

Before the advent of Knight, the view of Priapus had been sterile, grotesque and comic – anything but symbolic. The traditions of the priapeia as a body of lore about fertility, revived by Scaliger and others – to which reference has already been made – were largely suppressed in the eighteenth century. Priapus was almost always typified as a lascivious and primarily obscene little clown who used his huge and erect phallus for annoyingly trivial purposes. There was no sense, as I have suggested, of Priapus as the symbolic principle of fertility. He was merely personified as a pigmy with a huge cock. This pre-Knight profile was singularly roguish: a little demon, not even an adult rake, with a grotesque phallus – and this is the representation found in the pictorial art as well as in the imaginative literature of the period, especially in drama but also in the early satires, as well as in such later novels as *Tristram Shandy*.[94] The mythographers, historians and antiquarians of the seventeenth and eighteenth centuries also entertained a monolithic view that excluded symbolic fertility. Not aware, as late anthropologists would be, of the magisterial significance of the fertility rites of the ancients, writers before Knight had no inkling of the symbolic aspects of the little demon whose only function seemed to be diversion through his grotesque phallus. When John Pinkerton, an antiquarian whose real name was Robert Heron and who was also a correspondent of Horace Walpole's, invoked this proto-phallic god, he gave him a very different treatment from the one Knight would,[95] as did the anonymous author – an 'Englishman for many years resident at the Hague' – who conjured up this passage about 'the Dress of Priapus' while writing about the Italians:

> ...for two hundred and fifty years past, not only *Italy*, but the greatest Part of Europe, have been in a very gross Error concerning the *particular* Dress of *Priapus*; whereas now there is nothing clearer, than that the aforesaid God had several Dresses, which several eminent Men are now actually employed in making out.[96]

It is hard to know how to interpret the tone and contents of such passages which crop up in numbers, and in unexpected places, throughout the Enlightenment. It seems that even then there existed some understanding about this fecund deity that has since been lost. However obscure the secret code of passages like the one just cited, it thrived on a typology, or archetype, of fertility; one that then lent itself to constant comic relief. All this changed through the insight of Hamilton and Knight, but several prerequisites had to be met first: intimate knowledge of the place (Italy or the Mediterranean); erudition accompanied by curiosity, and the luck to have a mentor like d'Hancarville. Even more than these advantages, one needed the courage, as Knight eventually realised after the attacks made on him, to bring sex openly into the daylight of history and mythology. It was one thing for the Mediterranean d'Hancarville to bring sex into myth – the English could wash him away as a low-class scoundrel, as we know some did. It was quite another matter for a landed and wealthy Whig gentleman who was also a leading member of Parliament to address the question of sexuality in religion and myth. To compound all this temerity, Knight's anticlericalism was unsparing, and he lost no opportunity in *Priapus* to tell Christianity what he thought of it. 'The Christian religion being a reformation of the Jewish,' he affirmed, 'rather increased than diminished the austerity of its original',[97] and there are many other passages in *Priapus* with a similar complaint. For Knight, the whole of institutional Christianity was an intolerable church in whose temple he could never worship. Like Byron, he preferred the Greeks: their paganism, symbolism and priapism.

VII

Most Victorians spurned the anticlerical 'new Priapus' even more acrimoniously than Coleridge and the moral School of Taste had. It was not principally Knight the man they loathed but his view of the Greek myths. A religion whose deepest roots lay in phallic worship (as Knight had claimed) was nothing the non-priapeic Victorians wished to know about. There was a very different view of the Greeks promoted by Matthew Arnold and such nineteenth-century schoolish contemporaries as Connop Thirlwall, Thomas Keightley and Charles Kingsley, to name but three among many. Thirlwall managed to write an eight-volume history of Greece that was entirely silent about the figure of Priapus; he could not even bring himself to name him.[98] The Irish Keightley mechanically churned out textbook after textbook about the ancient Greeks, Romans and Asian Indians, 'for the use of students', but without having a clue about their mythology or religion, and certainly without mentioning the presence of lust, incest or phallic worship in its myths.[99] Thirlwall praised Keightley for making Greek history intelligible to students and fit for ladies.[100] But Kingsley wrote primarily for children, and told them that the Greek myths recounted stories 'too terrible to speak of here', yet that they might be told them when they grew up.[101] The tradition of censure, expurgation and silence continued well into this century, and there are still textbooks and schools where these subjects – certainly the name Priapus – remain taboo.

But Knight served a useful purpose. A small group of early nineteenth-century anthropologists could not have performed their work without his pioneering study. From the appearance of such works on Greek religion and mythology as those already mentioned by Dulaure, Dupuis and Destutt de Tracy (see page 136 above), to others written during and after the French Revolution, Knight's *Priapus* continued to be an inspiration.[102] From our vantage point late in the twentieth century, *Priapus* may not be an altogether accurate or rigorous account, yet it continued to sustain authors who would otherwise have been too timorous to tackle such a bold subject as phallic worship.

When Victorian rigidity somewhat diminished its stranglehold in the late nineteenth century and gave way to a less shackled milieu, it was Knight's *Priapus* which was read by students interested in early comparative religions, and read not merely in England but also on the Continent and in America.[103] No one has inquired why Thomas Wright, the prolific Victorian medieval scholar and author of – among many other works – a *Caricature History of the Four Georges*, sought to revive Knight and *Priapus* in 1866. He published an illustrated book entitled *The Worship of the Generative Powers During the Middle Ages of Western Europe* which opens with this sweeping remark:

Richard Payne Knight has written with great learning on the origin and history of the worship of Priapus among the ancients. This worship, which was but a part of the generative powers, appears to have been the most ancient of the superstitions of the human race, has prevailed more or less among all known peoples before the introduction of Christianity, and, singularly enough, so deeply it seems to have been implanted in human nature, that even the promulgation of the Gospel did not abolish it, for it continued to exist, accepted and often encouraged by the medieval clergy.

It would be informative to know what, if any, interest was aroused among Wright's contemporaries by this book in the decade after Darwin had rocked the boat of European civilisation (was fertility evolving in the way so many others institutions were?). Moreover, it may not be going too far to suggest a link between the burgeoning of mid and late nineteenth-century hypotheses about phallic worship and Freud's celebrated theory of penis envy, both of which originate in similar types of scientific enquiry.[104] Even Sir James G. Frazer had read *Priapus* before drafting the relevant section of *The Golden Bough* in the 1880s.[105] His account of the rites of fertility – particularly the homosexual and phallic aspects – is, as Frank Turner has noticed, 'veiled in polysyllabic descriptions',[106] and his treatment of Priapus and the priapic phenomenon in early religions actually seems less satisfactory than Knight's. Some late Victorians could not even bring themselves to Frazer's precipice. Sir Gilbert Murray, the great scholar at Oxford, and Jane Harrison, his most brilliant colleague at Cambridge and the author of a masterful *Prolegomenon to Greek Religion* (1903), never discussed Priapus at all – never brought sex into history as it were. However, many others were able to bring sex into history and, whether or not they explicitly say so, their gratitude to Knight continues to be shared by others in our own time.[107] The latter is the lineage that leads to such distinguished anthropologists of sex as the American Ashley Montagu, who lamented in 1957 that Knight's *Priapus* was unavailable in any modern edition and successfully rectified the situation by reprinting it.[108]

VIII

More recently, Eva Keuls maintains that:

> The story of phallic rule at the root of Western civilization has been suppressed, as a result of the near-monopoly that men have held in the field of Classics, by neglect of such rich pictorial evidence, by prudery and censorship, and by a misguided desire to protect an idealized image of Athens. As a Professor of Classics, I believe that an

acknowledgment of the nature of this phallocracy will have the effect, not of disparaging the achievements of Athenian culture but rather of enriching our sense of them, adding yet another level to their meaning. In any case, the evidence cannot any longer be ignored.[109]

It may or may not be true that the evidence can no longer be ignored, and in our time there will be a great debate about the very nature of the evidence itself, but every age has sought to forge out its identity by claiming that, in one way or another, the phallicism of the previous era was sorely misunderstood. Phallicism, however interpreted, would seem to be of central importance in any society, ancient or modern, eastern or western. Thus the Renaissance's exhilaration in discovery – or rediscovery – of the ancient priapeia; the Enlightenment's thrill in finding phallic remains in Isernia; the Victorians' calculated suppression of the loves of the Greek gods in the name of a higher, platonic morality; and now Professor Keuls' urgency to tell her (*pace!*) feminist tale about the development of phallocracy that men have labelled Western civilisation.

Yet by now it must be apparent that the issue at hand about matters priapeic, especially about fertility construed symbolically, has grown more complex as the natural consequence of accretion. As each century has added its contribution – archaeological and anthropological – a new dimension is provided. Precisely *what* the matter is, whether phallic worship, penis envy or now phallocracy, remains hard to identify and define; to pinpoint with a scientist's laser. But it is patent that a whole series of developments in our recent past has now made Knight and his *Priapus* seem more familiar, less remote, than he was in his own time. The familiarity has also been accompanied by a sense that in many ways the sexual Enlightenment was closer to our own contemporary situation – especially the pattern of gradual liberation followed by the retrenchment we experience today – than to the sexual milieu of the nineteenth century.[110] And towards an understanding of the A-B-A pattern of familiarity followed by remoteness now replaced by familiarity, it would be interesting to learn which of the dramatis personae in Steven Marcus's thorough study of *The Other Victorians* read Knight's work, scarce and expensive though copies were.[111]

Sexual research of different types lies at the heart of this affinity between our research and Knight's. For one thing, the science of anthropology has marched ahead just as it did in the eighteenth century – then it was called the 'sciences of man' – and we now know a great deal more about the symbolism of fertility than Frazer did, for example, in *The Golden Bough*. The more we learn, the more valuable Knight's observations – both his facts and fictions – become. For another, we have only recently begun to realise how variously – not merely symbolically – the phallus has been interpreted over the centuries.[112] Furthermore, Gilbert Herdt has now discovered and confirmed that pubescent males in Melanesia suck the phallus of their elders as part of their initiation into manhood.[113] The ritual occupies several days and includes ingestation of the older man's semen, as well as the oral stroking of his penis with the younger man's symbolic absorption of the strength and might of the elder man. Herdt calls this 'ritualized homosexuality', yet these *rites de passage* bear little resemblance to the structure of homosexuality in our Western sense. But they do resemble the ancient fertility rites that Knight pursued. Symbolically they designate entrance into manhood: the period of male generation, and they bear close kinship to the type of worship of the male generative principle Knight found in Italy in the 1770s. Finally, in our time the taboos on almost every form of sexual orientation and behaviour have been at least temporarily lifted, and it is now possible to discuss subjects such as homosexuality and the symbolism of male phallicism which were considered impolite just a few decades ago. Professor K. J. Dover, among the most respected of contemporary classicists, has not feared to inquire precisely what Greek homosexuality was; John Boswell, the medieval historian at Yale, has taken on the Church and its degree of toleration towards homosexuals in the Middle Ages,[114] and a large number of contemporary psychologists and psychiatrists have shown that, whatever bisexuality or homosexuality may be in psychodynamic terms, in some profound sense it consists of a symbolic transaction: the symbolic taking-in of the father to assuage the pain of the mother. This is an abstract idea which Knight would very much have understood, whether or not he himself was actively bisexual or homosexual.[115] It may be then, as Eric Neumann suggested almost thirty years ago, that at the heart of Western civilisation there lies a dilemma – a riddle – about the symbolic roles of the mother and the father, and that the great debates through the ages about the Greek myths – about the lewd romances and hedonistic pleasures of their gods – represents a continuing grand attempt to come to terms with this symbolic difference. As Neumann says: 'Greek mythology is largely the dragon-fight mythology of a consciousness struggling for independence from the mother image, and this struggle was decisive for the spiritual importance of Greece'.[116] It may also have been decisive for

Europe during the Enlightenment. In any case, it is evident that there is now a sympathetic climate of intelligence to come to grips with such an Enlightenment figure as Richard Payne Knight precisely *because* of his anticlericalism, his curious bachelorhood, his archaeology of sex, and possible suicide, and what I have called – for lack of a better term – his homosocial desire, which he assuaged in part by recreating the fertility cults of the ancient Priapus.

Knight's *Priapus* would seem, then, to have a magisterial implication for the historiography of the eighteenth-century Enlightenment, not merely for the *sexual* Enlightenment but for the Enlightenment at large. On the one hand, Foucault has led us to believe that the essence of Enlightenment thinking lay in a proliferating series of 'discourses' of social control.[117] These were not merely arcane tomes which produced no impact, but discourses whose programmes were in many cases officially adopted for the purposes of repression. On the other hand, a scholar with such insight as Jean Starobinski has claimed that, whatever else *lumière* was in the eighteenth century, it was first and foremost emancipation: the freedom of the individual to be himself or herself, whether woman or slave, labourer or servant.[118] And there can be no doubt that the liberating thought of the time did ultimately promote just such emancipation in concrete ways. These are both persuasive points of view, but their contrary states and complex implications are often lost in the thickets of contemporary controversy.

Moreover, it is gradually becoming evident that the eighteenth century was the crucial breakthrough – thinking now of Starobinski – for the liberation of *women* from social conditions that had hindered their freedom for generations. A whole library of feminist scholarship published in the last decade has argued (rightly in my view) for this point, despite the presence of an opposing camp of feminist scholars who continue to maintain that the seventeenth century, rather than the eighteenth, was the crucial breakthrough. However, when viewed from a *homosexual*, or homosocial, perspective; when gleaned in the light of Foucault's discourses of social control and repression, then the Enlightenment seems to have been a turning point *for the worse*, and the more that is written on this homosocial perspective, the worse the period appears. Had Knight published *Priapus* in 1986, or even 1886, he and his so-called dangerous book would have fared far better than either book or man did at the end of the eighteenth century. As Professor Keuls suggests (demonstrates is too strong a word in view of the elusive nature of phallocracy in general), the history of phallocracies and their versions of 'socially endorsed phallicism' are almost preternatural considerations for the history of repression and emancipation, and this extraordinary status of the phallocracy arises from its having been the norm for so long.

The implication here for the historiography of the Enlightenment is considerable. Whatever 'Enlightenment' connoted to people living on both sides of the Channel at the time of the French Revolution, concomitantly it necessitated a winter of discontent for those who, like Knight, had strayed outside the accepted and conventional homosocial pathways. It was a treacherous time for those men who thought they could reify a golden age of the phallus, whether as Dilettanti or members of the Hamilton-Townley Circle; as committed revolutionaries in France, like Dupuis, Destutt and Dulaure, or – to look again at the other side of the Channel and at the other end of the spectrum – as immensely rich, upper-class sodomites, like Beckford, who could be sentenced to death for their crime. A hundred years earlier, even two hundred, this degree of extremity would probably have been morally less repugnant and less severely enforced by the law. Within this context of sexuality, the author of our epigraph, the late distinguished American anthropologist Ashley Montagu, is then as accurate about Knight as he is lamentably incomplete, for if Knight 'was about a century and a half ahead of his time', in his thinking and his writing in *Priapus*, he was also a century or so too late. Perhaps – and it is perhaps with a capital P – Knight would have been happier living in Rochester's more libertine, and more androgynous, Restoration England or, at the other end of the spectrum in time, during the great wave of libertarian freedom in the middle of the twentieth century, but not in Britain during the eighteenth-century *fin-de-siècle*. This conclusion to a chapter within the history of phallicism should not suggest that Rochester and his libertine friends were any *happier* living in the Restoration than Wilkes and his radical associates were in the late eighteenth century, nor did Rochester, any more than Wilkes, regard his own phallic exploits, whether heterosexual or bisexual and homosexual (as in *Sodom*), as occasions for unmixed self-congratulation. All those figures discussed in this chapter who carried on phallic campaigns of a very disparate variety – Rochester and Wilkes, Radicati and d'Hancarville, Knight and his male friends, and even Byron – expected a certain amount of disapproval and received it in varying degrees and diverse ways. But Knight has never been associated with this radical, libertine tradition,[119] any more than the eighteenth-century Grand Tour has been viewed (either in the historical or historiographical sense) in its sexual contexts, or neo-classical retrieval as the modest vehicle of an enlightened paganism that permitted homosocial and homosexual desire to flourish. The significance of Knight, then, is not that he has continued to be misunderstood (this would endow him with a limited biographical importance), or that his priapeic treatise somehow represents a philosophically new version of homosocial desire,[120] but rather that his phallic campaigns reveal the presence of *another* eighteenth-century Sexual Enlightenment that has been overlooked, for whatever complex reasons, for too long. It is in this 'other Enlightenment' that Knight's *Discourse* has lasting significance.

Notes

1 My references throughout this essay are to this first edition which Ashley Montagu reprints in *Sexual Symbolism: A History of Phallic Worship*, New York, Julian Press, 1957, together with Thomas Wright's *The Worship of the Generative Powers During the Middle Ages of Western Europe* (625 copies privately printed in 1866 by the Dilettanti Society). Unless otherwise stated the place of publication of all cited works is London.
2 Knight, *Discourse on the Worship of Priapus*, p. 26. *Priapus*, as I shall now refer to the *Discourse* interchangeably with *Discourse*, has been *briefly* discussed by several commentators but has not elicited much analytic commentary. The most perceptive remarks I have found are in Michael Clarke and Nicholas Penny (eds.), *The Arrogant Connoisseur: Richard Payne Knight 1751–1824*, Manchester: Manchester University Press, 1982, especially ch. 4 written by Peter Funnell. See also (listed chronologically): Nikolaus Pevsner, "Richard Payne Knight", *Art Bulletin* 31, 1949, pp. 210–19, reprinted in his *Studies in Art, Architecture and Design*, 1968; Georges Bataille, *Death and Sensuality: A Study of Eroticism and the Taboo*, New York, Ballantine, 1962; Benjamin Walker, *Sex and the Supernatural: Sexuality in Religion and Magic*, Harrow, 1973; John Atkins, *Sex in Literature, Volume 2: The Classical Experience of the Sexual Impulse*, Calder and Boyars, 1973, pp. 306–20, 'Phallic Worship'; F. J. Messman, *Richard Payne Knight: The Twilight of Virtuosity*, The Hague, Mouton, 1974; John Boardman, *Eros in Greece*, J. Murray, 1978, and E. Chaney and N. Ritchie (eds.), *Oxford, China and Italy: Writings in Honour of Sir Harold Acton on his Eightieth Birthday*, Thames and Hudson, 1984.
3 *Ibid.*, pp. 207–8.
4 Radicati (1689–1737) fled to England from his native Piedmont to flee persecution for his heretical views where, he published, in 1731, *A Philosophical Dissertation upon Death. Composed for the Consolation of the Unhappy. By a Friend to Truth*, which was translated into English by Joseph Morgan and printed by William Mears. All three of them were apprehended

and tried for the doctrines set out in this book. After numerous unsuccessful attempts to remain in England undisturbed by the authorities, Radicati fled to the Netherlands, where he continued, in exile, to publish doctrines considered heretical to the traditions of Christian civilisation and died prematurely. His *Philosophical Dissertation* described the customs of Christian and non-Christian countries in vivid detail in an attempt to demonstrate that there was nothing sacred or absolute in the institutions of western civilisation that had been endorsed by the Church. Calling himself a 'pagan philosopher newly converted', and building on the ideas of Spinoza, Collins and Toland, Radicati openly advocated suicide and encouraged homosexual behaviour. These views, considered outrageous in England during the 1730s – as may be captured in an ironic passage about homosexuality in Swift's *Gulliver's Travels* (Book IV, Ch. 7, 1726) suggesting that it 'is entirely the production of art and reason' – elicited a flurry of attacks on Radicati by diverse writers, including Pope the poet who blasted him in a couplet in his *Epilogue to the Satires* (Dialogue I, lines 123–4). Radicati's life in England, as we shall see, bears certain resemblances to that of his countryman, the Baron d'Hancarville, a mentor to Knight who also fled to England from the Italian authorities at his own peril. Radicati's biography has been written by A. Alberti in *Alberto Radicati di Passerano*, Turin, 1931, and, most brilliantly, by Franco Venturi in *Saggi sull'Europa illuminista*, Turin, n. p., 1954. S. E. Sprott has evaluated Radicati's pre-Humean niche in *The English Debate on Suicide from Donne to Hume*, La Salle, Illinois, Open Court, 1961, pp. 106–9 and 130–2. M. C. Jacob has linked him to the Radical Enlightenment and endowed him with a prominent role in the eighteenth-century radical movement extending from Toland and Samuel Strutt (who may have known Radicati in England and may have been influenced by his works) to the radical John Wilkes later in the century; see her *Radical Enlightenment: Pantheists, Freemasons and Republicans*, London Allen & Unwin, 1981, pp. 172–6, 206 and 216.

5 For the tightening of English morality vis-à-vis all sexuality outside heterosexual marriage as the century wore on, see L. Stone, *The Family, Sex and Marriage in England 1500–1800*, Weidenfeld and Nicolson, 1977; R. Trumbach, *The Rise of the Egalitarian Family: Aristocratic, Kinship and Domestic Relations in Eighteenth-Century England*, New York, Academic Press, 1984, and R. P. Maccubbin (ed.), *Unauthorized Sexual Behavior during the Enlightenment: A Special Issue of Eighteenth-Century Life*, College of William and Mary, 1986.

6 Messmann, *Knight*, p. 40. Throughout this essay I suggest, contrary to Messmann, that Knight's radical Whig politics played a crucial role in the development of his image as an anticlerical, neo-pagan propagandist, consumed by pantheistic ideas and a homosocial ethic. Not all radicals or free thinkers of the late eighteenth century were, of course, homosocial or homosexual, but in the case of Knight these components – radical Whig politics, anticlericalism and homosocial desire expressed through a neo-pagan sexual enlightenment – coalesced into a single image and eventually became inseparable strains in the minds of his contemporaries. For a vivid

description of what radical Whig politics in the 1780s could mean for the public figure, see J. G. A. Pocock, *Virtue, Commerce, and History: Essays on Political Thought and History, Chiefly in the Eighteenth-Century*, Cambridge, Cambridge University Press, 1985, pp. 274–8.
7 Funnell, in *The Arrogant Connoisseur*, pp. 51–2.
8 *Ibid.*, p. 64.
9 Messman, *Knight*, p. 21.
10 E. Inglis-Jones, 'The Knights of Downton Castle, I and II', *National Library of Wales Journal*, 15, 1968, pp. 237-64 and 365–88. I am grateful to Miss Inglis-Jones for sharing her vast knowledge of Knight with me, and for making available her handwritten manuscript of an unfinished biography of Knight. Valuable information about Knight's life is also found in her book *Peacocks in Paradise*, London, Faber, 1950, pp. 104–28, 182–13 and 232–4.
11 Knight, *The Progress of Civil Society*, 1796.
12 This work enraged Horace Walpole, as we shall see. Walpole died only a few months later in March 1797.
13 See Messmann, *Knight*, pp. 14–15 for the biographical evidence.
14 *The Progress of Civil Society*, 1796, Bk. III, line 503.
15 See Boyd Alexander, *England's Wealthiest Son*, Centaur, 1962.
16 Brian Fothergill is perceptive on these matters in *The Strawberry Hill Set: Horace Walpole and his Circle*, Faber, 1983, pp. 138–43, but shies off from commenting on their relation to Walpole's sexuality, never addressing his homosocial involvement at all. Those who deny that Walpole was primarily homosexual fail to explain his sexuality, hiding instead under an explanation that arbitrarily calls him asexual.
17 See Messmann, *Knight*, p. 29.
18 See C. F. Bell and Thomas Girtin, *The Drawings and Sketches of John Robert Cozens: Walpole Society 1934–35*, Oxford, Walpole Society, 1935, pp. 4–5; A. P. Oppé, *Alexander and John Robert Cozens*, Cambridge, Mass., Harvard University Press, 1954, pp. 109–13; Brian Fothergill, *Beckford of Fonthill*, London, Faber, 1979, p. 134. Earlier, Beckford had told Cozens' father, Alexander, about his love for William Courtenay, the young boy whose family threatened to ruin Beckford.
19 See William Cosmo Monkhouse, 'John Robert Cozens', *Dictionary of National Biography*, 22 vols., Oxford, Oxford University Press, 1889, IV, p. 1350.
20 Manuscript Minutes of Bethlehem Hospital, 1793–4, patient lists. See also Rex Wright-St. Clair, *Thoroughly a man of the world: A biography of Sir David Monro*, M. D. London, Heinemann, 1971.
21 See R. W. Ketton-Cramer, *Horace Walpole: A Biography*, Faber, 1935, pp. 35–7.
22 This is the manuscript of Knight's English journal which was presumed to be lost until 1980. Scholars, however, have had access to it ever since Goethe inserted a German translation of it into his biography of Philip Hackert. See Messmann, *Knight*, p. 28, for further details.
23 *The Yale Edition of Horace Walpole's Correspondence*, W. S. Lewis (ed.), 48 vols, New Haven, Yale University Press, Vol. 12: p. 237.

24 See Bell and Girtin (ref. 18), pp. 8–9.
25 See Stumpf, *The Arrogant Connoisseur*, p. 29.
26 In her manuscript biography (see Note 10) E. Inglis-Jones comments that Samuel Rogers, the social commentator in London, noted that Knight had ruined his health by his 'amorous habits', and that he paid £3 per week to a Caroline Gregory to be his permanent standby and camouflage for his young male friends, but I have been unable to discover the source of the information despite a moderate search.
27 Stumpf, *The Arrogant Connoisseur*, p. 29.
28 In R. Maccubbin (ed.), *Unauthorized Sexual Behavior*, p. 160.
29 Brian Fothergill's *Sir William Hamilton – Envoy Extraordinary*, Faber, 1969, remains the most detailed life.
30 The letter appeared together with *Priapus* in 1786.
31 When I began to piece together this story in 1982 there was no available study of d'Hancarville's life. The appearance in 1984 of Francis Haskell's excellent, if all too brief, epitome considerably eased my task; see F. Haskell, 'd'Hancarville: an Adventurer and Art Historian in Eighteenth-Century Europe', in Edward Chaney and Neil Ritchie, *Oxford China and Italy; Writings in Honour of Sir Harold Acton on his Eightieth Birthday*, London, Thames and Hudson, 1984, pp. 177–91.
32 F. Haskell, 'd'Hancarville', in *Oxford, China and Italy*, p. 181.
33 For d'Hancarville and Winckelmann see Haskell, *ibid.*, p. 183 especially. Winckelmann was immensely intrigued by d'Hancarville but also suspicious, and poured out his fascination and doubt to his confidante Alexander Stosch over several years (1759–63); See Johann Joachim Winckelmann, *Briefe*, 2 vols., Berlin, Walter de Gruyter, 1954, II: pp. 6–7, 130–1, 350–1 and 373.
34 Haskell, *Oxford China Italy*, p. 184.
35 This is in the Townley family archive at Preston and is rich in materials dealing with d'Hancarville.
36 Haskell, *Oxford China, and Italy*, p. 186. For Townley, see M. L. Clarke, *Greek Studies in England*, Cambridge University Press, 1945, pp. 185–8, who notices Hope's novel called *Anastasius, or Memoirs of a Greek*, 1819, written much later, but who either overlooks or neglects to comment on its bisexual strain. 'This [novel] was attributed to Byron,' Clarke notes (p. 186), 'who, it is said, wept at not having in fact written it'. See Note 92.
37 *Ibid.*, p. 186.
38 As a nominal Roman Catholic, Townley and his house were vulnerable, but nothing actually happened. For Clytie, see Brian Fothergill, *Sir William Hamilton*, p. 123.
39 Undated letter from Townley to Richard Payne Knight, in the Townley family archives at Preston.
40 *Ibid.*, undated letter.
41 It is a rare work, with only a few copies known in North America and Britain. Haskell notes (*Ibid.*, p. 187, n. 37) that the Yale University Library owns a corrected manuscript draft of the work in six volumes. The notion that d'Hancarville wrote in French because English was too dangerous for

such a subject is silly. We shall see that one year later, in 1786, it was not too dangerous.
42 Ibid., p. 187.
43 See his *Much Maligned Monsters: The History of the European Reaction to Indian Art*, Oxford, Clarendon, 1977, especially pp. 85–104 and the crucial discussion of bisexuality on p. 98.
44 Mitter, *ibid.*, p. 86, italics mine.
45 See d'Hancarville, *Recherches*, 1785, III, pp.iii–xii and 1–65.
46 Originally published in Paris in 1766, the *Inquiry* was translated into English in 1769, and into other languages shortly thereafter. It claimed that ancient pagan religion was superior to modern Christianity on many grounds. Originally from a French Huguenot family, Dutens spent much of his life in England.
47 The philosophical reasons for hermaphroditism remained one of the most controversial subjects of the second half of the eighteenth century, and almost every writer on sex and sexuality had pronounced on it. For more background, see Pierre Darmon, *Le mythe de la procréation a l'âge baroque*, Paris, J. J. Pauvert, 1977, pp. 161–84 and *Le tribunal de l'impuissance*, Paris, Seuil, 1979, translated into English, 1981, as *Trial by Impotence*, pp. 53–6.
48 See *The New Review*, January 1785, Article III.
49 Three years before d'Hancarville's *Recherches* appeared, Maty had begun *A New Review*, a periodical whose main function was to epitomise foreign publications, which Maty read and reviewed almost single-handedly. But it was a failure almost from the start and lasted only four years, with Gibbon dispraising it as the prudish product of an 'angry son', and Horace Walpole rejecting its contents as generally 'pert and foolish'. John Gillies (1747–1836), a Scots Greek scholar resident in London, reviewed the book negatively for the *Monthly Review* 73, November, 1785, pp. 321–6. An unmarried itinerant tutor to the children of the Earl of Hopetoun (John and Alexander Hope), he had also written *A Grecian History* which omitted all comment about the amorous customs of the Greek gods.
50 Paul Henry Maty, *A Review, with Literary Curiosities*, 9 vols., 1786, Vol. VII, p. 23, which d'Hancarville quotes on p. 63 of Vol. III of the *Recherches*.
51 See R. P. Maccubbin (ed.), *Unauthorized Sexual Behavior during the Enlightenment*, Introduction and pp. 132–3 and 162, for discussion of the anachronism.
52 In the same year that Knight's *Discourse* appeared, Jacques Antoine Dulaure's *Pogonologia, or, a Philosophical and Historical Essay on Beards*, Exeter, R. Thorn, 1786, was translated into English by E. Drewe, possibly having appeared earlier in French. Writing while France was seething under the ancien régime, Dulaure selected the most mundane of objects – beards – to excoriate France's political fabric, and, as is evidenced by his many references to leading figures of the Church over the centuries, Dulaure singled out for blame the Church's condoning of the mores of the upper classes. Written in a genre similar to Knight's, Dulaure's long essay appears to be a work of historical archaeology, but is in fact a more complex satiric vehicle conjured

to expose France's supposed masculinity through the beards of her men. Later, in 1805, when Dulaure published his own treatise on phallic worship, *Des Divinités Génératrices, ou du Culte du Phallus chez les Anciens et les Modernes*, Paris, 1805, he made good use of Knight's *Discourse*, citing it frequently in his text.

53 Much has been written, of course, on the mood of the decade of the Eighties, beginning with the Gordon Riots and sustained by the radical intellectualism of such figures as Priestley, Price, Kippis, Godwin and all those who inherited the radical-libertine tradition of John Wilkes, but without considering the Dilettanti, for example, and all those Whig aesthetes, like Horace Walpole, Knight and the Circle of Townley, who were frequently anticlerical and anti-Establishment, and whose deepest sense of liberty thrived on a notion of the personal liberation of the individual.

54 *The Arrogant Connoisseur*, p. 58.

55 There has never been a proper or popular biography, despite vast amounts of printed and manuscript materials that would readily sustain one. The reason is not mysterious: until recently, works like the *Discourse* and their authors could not be discussed in public in polite society, and whereas Knight would have been the subject of many biographies had he been content to write poems like *The Landscape* and *Analytical Inquiry into the Principles of Taste*, the phallic *Discourse* tarnished his reputation for two centuries and placed him in a camp of figures whose work spread over many disciplines.

56 For the complete list, see L. Cust, *History of the Society of Dilettanti*, London 1914, p. 123.

57 See Lytton Strachey and Roger Fulford (eds.), *The Greville Memoirs 1814–1860*, 8 vols, Macmillan, 1938, IV, p. 182. Even his son Charles, the political diarist, appreciated Knight's efforts and, while visiting Downton Castle in 1839, commented that Knight was '. . . an Epicurean Philosopher, who after building the Castle went and lived in a lodge or cottage in the Park: there he died, not without suspicion of having put an end to himself, which would have been fully conformable with his notions. He was a sensualist in all ways and devoid of religion, but a great and self-educated scholar', see *ibid.*, p. 182.

58 See K. Garlick and Kathryn Cave (eds.), *The Diary of Joseph Farington*, 11 vols, New Haven, Yale University Press, 1982, Vol. III, p. 1035, for July 22 1798. Wilbraham befriended the Duke of Norfolk and frequently travelled to Arundel Castle, but Norfolk was also devoted to Knight, and is reported by Dyce and others to have been 'a gross sensualist'. He is said to have 'sat reading Payne Knight's *Essay on the Worship of Priapus*' while on a long journey to Arundel Castle with Thomas Taylor, the platonic philosopher; see R. J. Schrader (ed.), *The Reminiscences of Alexander Dyce*, Athens, Ohio University Press, 1972, p. 135.

59 Geoffrey Keynes (ed.), *The Catalogue of the Library of E. Gibbon*, St. Paul Bibliographies, Cape 1940, 1980 2nd ed., p. 291. *Priapus* was presented to Gibbon on 1 March 1789; there no marks or marginalia next to the entry.

60 J. E. Norton (ed.), *The Letters of Edward Gibbon*, 3 vols, New York, Macmillan, 1956, III. p. 216, Letter 771, 2 May 1791.

61 Frank Brady and F. A. Pottle never mention *Priapus* or Knight in *James Boswell: The Later Years*, New York, Macmillan, 1985.
62 None of Wilkes' many biographers discusses his receipt of the *Discourse* or his possible reading of it.
63 See R. Baron (ed.), *A Cordial for Low-Spirits*, 3 vols, 1763, I, Preface, p. x.
64 For his life, see W. P. Courtney, who despised Pope, in the *Dictionary of National Biography*. Mathias's unpublished letters are in the Wren Library at Trinity College, Cambridge. It is not known how he obtained a copy of the *Discourse*.
65 Five dialogues appeared in total, in 1790 (I), 1794 (II), 1796 (III), 1797 (IV) and 1805 (V); copious notes in the manner of Swift's *Tale of a Tub* or Pope's *Dunciad* adorned each page. Between the time he acquired the book and his review, Mathias learned that Knight was the author, and was able to name Knight in the copious footnotes.
66 See *The Pursuits of Literature, or what you will: Part One*, 1790, pp. 17ff, especially the long note accompanying line 128.
67 *Pursuits of Literature*, Dialogue II, 1795, Lines 144–56 and accompanying notes. The illustrations were not, of course, Knight's but d'Hancarville's.
68 *Ibid.*, Dialogue II, p. 19.
69 Eccentricity and extreme reclusiveness were accompanied later in life by illness, and in 1814 Mathias went south to his beloved Italy in search of health, where he lived until his death in 1835.
70 See pp. xix–xx. But Mathias did not let up. Attacking the obscenity of *Priapus*, and Knight as someone who 'wak'd to lust', Mathias threatened Knight's political position as well: 'If Mr. Knight's bed be a bed of tortures, he has made it for himself. . . . he has some sense of shame left, by endeavouring to *explain away* one of the most unbecoming and indecent treatises which ever disgraced the pen of a man, who would be thought a scholar and philosopher . . . I am as tired of him as he can be of me. As Mr. Knight is a Member of Parliament, I must fairly tell him, that if he is appointed Chairman of any polite poetical Committee, and any more "*reports* Progress [referring to the *Progress of Civil Society*], and asks leave to sit again," the motion will be *negatived by the whole house*'; see Part 2, 1796, Dialogue 2, pp. 60–1.
71 See W. S. Lewis, *The Yale Edition of Horace Walpole's Correspondence*, 48 vols, New Haven, Yale University Press, 1937–83, 29: 339.
72 See Percy Noble, *Anne Seymour Damer: A Woman of Art and Fashion 1748–1828*, London, Kegan Paul, 1908, p. 82. Damer's lesbianism even found its way into the satirical pages of *The Whig Club; or a sketch of modern patriotism*, 1794, often attributed to Charles Pigott, and is discussed briefly by B. Fothergill, Note 15, pp. 201–2.
73 Walpole's letters to Banks dated 31 March and 3 May, 1787 delineate the point. Couched in the urbanities and amenities which Walpole had long since mastered, he told Banks that, gouty and old though he was, he 'would wait on Mr Knight myself, if I were able'. See *Horace Walpole's Correspondence*, 42: 193–5.

74 *Ibid.*, Vol. 12; p. 237. The material in the rest of this paragraph derives from a number of sources: for the length of Lord Lincoln's penis, see Robert Halsband, *Lord Hervey: Eighteenth-Century Courtier*, Oxford, Clarendon Press, 1973, p. 91; for Walpole and Lord Lincoln on the Grand Tour, see R. W. Ketton-Cremer, *Horace Walpole: A Biography*, Faber, 1946; for the importance of Walpole's letter to Lincoln, see Wilmarth S. Lewis, *Horace Walpole: The A. W. Mellon Lectures*, New York, Pantheon, Bollingen Series 35, 1960, pp. 191–2. Lincoln's ability to dazzle women by his phallic charm is best captured in the correspondence between Lady Mary Wortley Montagu and Lady Pomfret, written during the 1740s while Lincoln was resident in Rome, and when he was often their guest; see R. Halsband, *The Correspondence of Lady Mary Wortley Montagu*, 3 vols, Oxford, Clarendon Press, 1965–7, II, pp. 210–55 *passim*. Volume 18 of the Yale Edition of the *Correspondence of Horace Walpole* prints Walpole's letter to Lincoln; on 13 February 1743, Walpole wrote one of several 'Persian letters' about Lincoln to his constant correspondent, Horace Mann, beginning 'We have heard prodigious things of these [Lincoln]: they say, thy vigour is nine times beyond that of our prophet; and that thou art more amorous than Solomon the son of David . . . May thy days be as long as thy manhood', *HW*, 18: 167. Walpole's erotic poem, 'Little Peggy', *HW*, 3, Appendix 2, allegedly named for Peggy Lee, one of Lincoln's whores, begins again on the note of Lincoln's long penis:

> Ye nymphs of Drury, pour a nobler strain!
> I like not rural themes, and scorn the plain:
> I sing of courts; and when of courts I sing,
> Notes worthy Lincoln flow, or Lincoln's King!
>   The hour is come, by ancient dames foretold,
> E're his small cock were yet a fortnight old,
> How with majestic vigour it should rise,
> Strong to the sense, and tow'ring to the skies!
> Women unfucked at sight of it should breed,
> And other virgins teem with heav'nly seed.

75 Originally it appeared in French, in several parts, published as *Elements d'idéologie* 1801–18. Destutt de Tracy is a vital link to Knight and the English Radical movement of the 1790s. A leader of the ideologues who had been staunch proponents of the revolution in France, Destutt, like Knight, was deeply interested in the meaning of pagan myths and the origins of the gods. In 1804 he published a one-volume synopsis of Charles Dupuis' book on phallic worship entitled *Analyse raisonée de l'origine de tous les cultes, ou religion universelle* . . . (Paris, an XII [1804]). Raymond Williams is accurate to note in *Marxism and Literature*, Oxford, Oxford University Press, 1977, p. 56, that ideology 'was coined as a term in the late eighteenth century, by the French philosopher, Desttut de Tracy'. But not even Frank Manuel has noticed that Destutt refers to *Priapus* and its author's Rousseauistic programme in *The Landscape*. See Frank Manuel, 'Charles Dupuis: The Phallus and the

Sun-God', in *The Eighteenth Century Confronts the Gods*, Cambridge, Harvard University Press, 1959, pp. 260 and 269–70.
76 Much of Knight's attack was political, and he knew there was no more effective way to savage the seemingly degenerate habits of the Conservatives and Tories who opposed his own radical politics than to attack their favourite pastime, gardening.
77 Marilyn Butler comments on target when she notices, in *Peacock Displayed*, Routledge and Kegan Paul, 1979, p. 31, that in the *Landscape* 'Knight offered his original Critique as a contribution not to aesthetics but to ideology', and this stricture should stand as a corrective to all those who have considered it *merely* in the tradition of landscape gardening, without consideration of the relationship between Knight's politics and sexuality.
78 *Horace Walpole's Correspondence* 29: 338. All quotations in this paragraph are from this letter.
79 Gray, a homosexual bachelor poet who buried himself in a sinecure in Cambridge University, had died in 1768; a friend never to be forgotten by either Walpole or Mason, although the latter two lived on for another three decades. No reason exists to believe that 'the offence' against Gray given here by Knight was in any way sexual. In *The Landscape* Knight claimed that Gray suffered from the very upper-class vices – luxury and waste – denigrated in his poem.
80 *Horace Walpole's Correspondence*, 29: 341–2.
81 See L. Rice-Oxley (ed.), *Poetry of the Anti-Jacobin*, Oxford, Oxford University Press, 1924, pp. 58–66.
82 *The Diary of Joseph Farington*, p. 327, 17 April 1795.
83 'Farington Anecdotes 1794', in *Horace Walpole's Correspondence*, 15: 319.
84 'Farington's Anecdotes of Walpole', in *Horace Walpole's Correspondence*, 15: 329.
85 *The Diary of Joseph Farington*, 7: 2606, 24 August 1805.
86 See the Earl of Ilchester, *The Journal of Elizabeth Lady Holland (1791–1811)*, 2 vols, Longman's, 1908, II; pp. 8–9 and 136–7. Edward Moor, the British student of Hindu mythology, went out to India in the early 1790s carrying a copy of *Priapus* with him. After fighting in the war for the Indian subcontinent, he published an account of his experiences, entitled *A narrative of the Operations of Captain Little's Detachment, and of the Mahratta Army*, 1794, verifying that what Knight had said about priapeic cults in Isernia was also be found in Hindustan; see pp. 54–61.
87 *Ibid.*, p. 136–7.
88 Quoted by E. A. Shearer, 'Wordsworth and Coleridge Marginalia in a Copy of Richard Payne Knight's *Analytical Inquiry into the Principles of Taste*', *Huntington Library Quarterly*, 1, 1937, p. 75. For Coleridge's pantheism, see Thomas Mcfarland, *Coleridge and the Pantheist Tradition*, Oxford, Oxford University Press, 1969.
89 Walter Kaufmann (ed.), *Friedrich Nietzsche. The Gay Science*, New York, Random House, 1974, pp. 76–7.
90 Thomas Love Peacock to E. T. Hookham, 18 August 1810, in H. F. B. Brett Smith *et al.* (ed.), *Works of Thomas Peacock*, 12 vols, Constable, 1934, 8:

188. Peacock was particularly interested in Knight's ability to enter into paper wars with others.
91 See W. Field (ed.), *Memoirs of the Life, Writing and Opinions of the Rev. Samuel Parr*, 2 vols, 1828, II. p. 137.
92 See L. Crompton, *Byron and Greek Love: Homophobia in 19th-Century England*, Berkeley and Los Angeles, University of California Press, 1985, who makes a strong case for Byron's bisexuality, and Bernard Grebanier, *The Uninhibited Byron: An Account of his Sexual Confusion*, New York, Crown, 1972, p. 33.
93 For Hope see D. Watkin, *Thomas Hope 1769–1831 and the Neoclassical Ideal*, John Murray, 1968. The most intimate romantic encounters between Anastasius and Spiridion are found in Vol. 2, pp. 132–8, 145–50 and 156–68. For Byron and the composition of Hope's *Anastasius*, see *Conversations of Lord Byron with the Countess of Blessington*, John Murray, 1893, 2 vols, 1891, II, pp. 74–6.
94 While meditating on death (*Tristram Shandy*, VII, p. 14) Tristram dreams of carnal times 'with *Priapus* at your tails – what jovial times! . . . and into what a delicious riot of things am I rushing?' Earlier Swift had wittily referred 'not only to the *Egyptian Osyris*, but to the *Grecian Bacchus*' yet not to Priapus; see A. C. Guthkelch et al. (eds.), *A Tale of a Tub . . . and the Mechanical Operation of the Spirit*, Oxford, 1958, (2nd ed.), p. 284. One of the most ridiculous, if bathetic, descriptions of Priapus is found in an anonymous mock-epic entitled *The Prophetic Physician; an heroi-comic poem address'd to the physicians*, 1737, p. 11.
95 John Pinkerton, *An Essay on Medals*, 2 vols, 1779, 2nd ed. 1808.
96 See the anonymous *Description of Holland: or, The Present State of the United Provinces*, 1743, p. 201.
97 Richard Payne Knight, *Priapus*, p. 205.
98 Connop Thirwall, *A History of Greece*, 8 vols, Longman, Rees et al., 1835.
99 Thomas Keightley, *The Mythology of Ancient Greece and Italy for the Use of Schools*, Longmans, Rees et al, 1835. It was reprinted many times by 1900 and over a dozen times in America by 1930.
100 Thirwall, *A History of Greece*, 1: 192.
101 Charles Kingsley, *The Heroes; or, Greek Fairy Tales*, Cambridge, Macmillan, 1856, p. 151.
102 See, for example, Cornelius de Pauw, *Philosophische Untersuchungen über die Griechen*, 2 vols, Berlin, Rottman, 1789, who makes use of *Priapus*.
103 Hodder M. Westropp, *Primitive Symbolism as Illustrated in Phallic Worship or the Reproductive Principle*, George Redway, 1885, pp. 18 and 42. Jean C. M. Boudin, a French physician much interested in the cults of Priapus, also made extensive use of *Priapus* in his *Etudes anthropologiques . . . culte du priape*, Paris, 1864.
104 The comparison is crude, of course, without consideration of the development of the biological sciences in the aftermath of the Darwinian revolution of the 1860s, and the outcome of the *fin de siècle*, of decadence *à la* Pater and Wilde.
105 R. A. Downie, Frazer's biographer in the only biography to date, *James*

George Frazer: The Portrait of a Scholar, Watts, 1940, does not comment on Frazer's reading.
106 Frank M. Turner, *The Greek Heritage in Victorian Britain*, New Haven, Yale University Press, 1981, p. 81.
107 See James Hannay, *Sex Symbolism in Religion*, Religious Evolution Research Society, 1922, pp. 27–8 and 220–9; W. M. Spink, *The Axis of Eros*, New York, Schocken, 1933, pp. 92–3; Stanley Coleman, *Sex Symbols and Phallic Phantasies*, Douglas, Folklore Academy, 1962, and Thorkil Vangaard, *Phallos: A Symbol and its History in the Male World*, translated from the Danish by the author, Jonathan Cape, 1972.
108 See A. Montagu, *Sexual Symbolism: A History of Phallic Worship*, New York, Julian Press, 1957, p. vii. The edition has continued to be reprinted since 1957.
109 Eva C. Keuls, *The Reign of the Phallus: Sexual Politics in Ancient Athens*, New York, Harper and Row, 1985, p. 1.
110 This is a point not often made about the eighteenth century, which is presented in most Anglo-American colleges and universities as if it were *much* more remote than the last century. The issue is ultimately not temporal but environmental and intellectual, and for this reason the degree of remoteness remains a relative quantum depending upon the view of these persons held by those who teach them. The further irony is that the nineteenth century believed itself to have innovated in practically every field where its predecessor – the eighteenth – had become derivative or moribund, whereas the fact remains that the palm for novelty should be awarded to the eighteenth as much as to the nineteenth century.
111 In *The Other Victorians: A Study of Sexuality and Pornography in Mid-Nineteenth-Century England*, New York, New American Library, 1974, Steven Marcus discusses the bookseller John Hotten's 1865 reprint of *Priapus*, a pornographer's printing that was limited to 125 copies and so expensive that only the wealthy could afford to purchase it. Marcus comments (p. 70): 'the market at which Hotten was aiming . . . was very small and very rich'.
112 See Vangaard, *Phallos*. The endemic folklore discussed in Vangaard's book needs more ventilation than it has received.
113 See Gilbert Herdt (ed.), *Ritualized Homosexuality in Melanesia*, Berkeley, University of California Press, 1984 and *Guardians of the Flute: Idioms of Masculinity*, New York, McGraw-Hill, 1981.
114 K. J. Dover, *Greek Homosexuality*, Cambridge, Harvard University Press, 1978; John Boswell, *Christianity, Social Tolerance, and Homosexuality*, Chicago, University of Chicago Press, 1980; J. M. Saslow, *Ganymede in the Renaissance: Homsexuality in Art and Society*, New Haven, Yale University Press, 1986, and – more generally – Reay Tannahill, *Sex in History*, Slough, Berkshire, Hollen, 1980, and Maurice Lever, *Les bûchers de Sodome: histoire des 'infames'*, Paris, Fayard, 1985.
115 Throughout this essay I have suggested that, based on all the available evidence, there is no reason to believe that Knight was *exclusively* heterosexual. There are ample grounds to surmise that, even when judged within the standards of his own age, he was more than usually homosocial

and homocentric, as were many of those (the Townley Circle, Knight's younger male friends, and their counterparts in Italy) with whom Knight was on intimate terms. But nowhere have I claimed that Knight was unequivocally homosexual, nor could I prove it if I had been foolish enough to claim it.

116 See Eric Neumann, *The Great Mother: An Analysis of the Archetype*, trans. Ralph Manheim, Princeton, Princeton University Press, 1956, p. 14.
117 Michael Foucault, *The Archeology of Knowledge*, trans. A. Sheridan, Tavistock, 1972.
118 Jean Starobinski, *The Invention of Liberty*, trans. B. C. Swift, Geneva, Albert Skira, 1964. Peter Gay also adopts this position in *The Enlightenment: An Interpretation – The Science of Freedom*, New York, Alfred A. Knopf, 1969.
119 For example, Knight is nowhere mentioned in Margaret C. Jacob's groundbreaking study of *The Radical Enlightenment* (Note 4).
120 In the sense that Roger Scruton considers sexual desire a complex philosophical subject and homosocial desire one of its components; see R. Scruton, *Sexual Desire*, Weidenfeld and Nicolson, 1985.

Part 2
Sex and society

6

The culture of travesty: sexuality and masquerade in eighteenth-century England

TERRY CASTLE

When the eighteenth-century moralist wished to decry the cheating and whorishness of contemporary life, he found a potent image close at hand. So ubiquitous were chicanery and vice, wrote Fielding in 1743 in his 'Essay on the Knowledge of the Characters of Men', the world was nothing more than 'a vast Masquerade', where 'the greatest Part appear disguised under false Vizors and Habits'. Owen Sedgewick, in the same decade, entitled a lascivious compendium of modern evils *The Universal Masquerade; or, The World Turn'd Inside Out*, and later, in a *Rambler* essay describing the corruptions of wealth (No. 75), Samuel Johnson asserted that the rich and powerful 'live in a perpetual masquerade, in which all about them wear borrowed characters'. 'The world's a masquerade!' wrote Goldsmith in his epilogue to Charlotte Lennox's *The Sister* (1762), and 'the masquers, you, you, you'.[1]

The rebarbative tone is ageless. The metaphor, however, places us at once in the hallucinatory lost world of eighteenth-century urban culture. For, moralism aside, each man was right in the literal sense: eighteenth-century English society was indeed a world of masqueraders and artificers, self-alienation and phantasmagoria. We are familiar of course with the many shape-shifters who inhabit the fiction and folklore of the period; Moll Flanders, Jonathan Wild, the female soldiers and masked highwaymen of contemporary balladry – these are among the archetypes of an age. But eighteenth-century culture as a whole might also be termed, without exaggeration, a culture of travesty. Especially in London, the manipulation of appearances was both a private strategy and a social institution. Readers of Boswell's journals will doubtless remember the occasions on which the future biographer adopted the guise of soldier or ruffian in order to search for clandestine sexual adventure in the London streets. But travesties took place on a larger, more public scale too. Whether practised in assembly-rooms, theatres, brothels, public gardens, or at the masquerade itself (which flourished in London from the 1720s on), collective sartorial transformation offered a cathartic escape from the self and a suggestive revision of ordinary experience. The Protean life of the city found expression in a persistent popular urge toward disguise and metamorphosis.[2]

The historian of sexuality will find much to ponder in the exemplary diversions of the eighteenth century. For travesty, of course, is never innocent; it is often a peculiarly expressive, if paradoxical, revelation of hidden needs. In *The Masquerade* (1728), Fielding observed that to 'masque the face' was 't'unmasque the mind'. Likewise, Addison, in *The Spectator*, noted that contemporary masqueraders invariably dressed as what they 'had a Mind to be'.[3] For Boswell and others, one might argue, disguise provided a much-desired emotional access to new sensual and ethical realms.

Yet travesty had an even more subversive function in eighteenth-century life. It posed an intimate challenge to the ordering patterns of culture itself. Michel Foucault has spoken of the haunting power of the transvestite in the eighteenth-century imagination.[4] In fashionable *équivoque* figures like the fop and amazon, moralising contemporaries were quick to see a profound affront to 'Nature' and the order of things. 'In every country', a writer in the *Universal Spectator* observed in 1728, 'Decency requires that the Sexes should be differenc'd by *Dress*, in order to prevent Multitudes of Irregularities which otherwise would continually be occasion'd'.[5] Nonetheless, sexual impersonation remained one of the subtle obsessions of the age. From the notorious actress Charlotte Charke, who recorded her many 'mad pranks' in male garb in a famous autobiography in 1755, to the hapless Chevalier d'Éon, with his sensational attempts at transvestite espionage in the 1770s and 1780s, a host of sexual shape-shifters throughout the century parodied and charmed away the hieratic fixities of gender. Even as the eighteenth century condemned such artifices, it also found in them an intimation of a quintessential modern truth: that culture itself was an affront to 'nature' – non-transcendental in origin, shaped by convention, the ultimate product of fashion. In the carnivalesque figure of the transvestite, eightenth-century society began to explore something of its own eminently secular and artifactual nature.

In examining the role of travesty in eighteenth-century life, I shall focus here on the public masquerade – the most expansive and controversial vehicle for the shape-shifting impulse in the period. I will touch, as a matter of course, on the masquerade's contemporary association with libertinism, and its place in the history of actual sexual practices such as homosexuality. But my main object is to present the masquerade as a representative institution – a magic lantern, as it were, in which we may see illuminated the new erotic self-consciousness of the age. For the masquerade indeed provided the eighteenth century with a novel imagery of sexual possibility. Its manifold displacements and enigmas were also heuristic – registering for the first time that ironic resistance to the purely instinctual which has increasingly come to characterise the erotic life of the West since the eighteenth century. In particular, through its stylised assault on gender boundaries, the masquerade played an interesting part in the creation of the modern 'polymorphous' subject – perverse by definition, sexually ambidextrous, and potentially unlimited in the range of its desires.

The charismatic institution known as the 'Midnight Masquerade' originated in England in the second decade of the eighteenth century. Similar events, to be sure, had taken place earlier; the impulse toward travesty had its historic roots in English culture. Popular religious rituals and seasonal festivities of the Middle Ages and Renaissance had often required the donning of costumes; the hobby-horse games and morris dances of rural England, in which men disguised themselves as women and animals, survived into the eighteenth century and beyond.[6] The court also had its early versions of the masquerade. Masked parties and entertainments, at times directly modelled on traditional festivals, had played an important part in the life of the English aristocracy at least since the time of Henry VIII. In the seventeenth century the masque was a lavish variation in the travesty theme: here nobility disguised themselves as gods and goddesses and acted out fantastic allegories of court life. During the Restoration period, as the Earl of Rochester's psychologically complex impersonations suggest, the court of Charles II offered a rich domain for sartorial play and self-estrangement.[7]

But only in the first decades of the century did the masquerade in the modern sense arise – as a form of large-scale commercial public entertainment, urban and non-exclusive in nature, cutting across historic lines of rank and privilege. Masquerades owed their sudden popularity in part to foreign influences; more travel abroad meant that more and more English people witnessed the traditional carnivals and fêtes of the Continent. The Venetian carnival in particular attracted large numbers of English tourists in the eighteenth century.[8] Foreign entrepreneurs, including the famous masquerade impresario John James Heidegger (the self-described 'Swiss Count') and the Venetian-born Theresa Cornelys, settled in London in the first half of the century and introduced the middle-class English public to the sophisticated masked balls and ridottos of the Continent. Walpole reports that the jubilee masquerade at Ranelagh in 1749 was advertised as being 'in the Venetian manner'. Masquerades throughout the century were described as 'mock-carnivals'.[9] Beneath the denatured trappings of urban society, however, one might also discover nostalgic longings for the popular traditions of the English rural past. Like the fairs, processions and other crowd spectacles of the city, the masquerade revivified the festive life of earlier centuries in a new capitalistic and modern form.[10]

The first important public masquerades in London were those organised by Heidegger in 1717 at the Haymarket Theatre.[11] (Heidegger, who makes a memorable appearance in *The Dunciad*, also produced the first Handel operas in England.) The new venture was an instant scandal – and an instant success. In the 1720s and 1730s, Heidegger's 'Midnight Masquerades' drew between seven and eight hundred people a week. Tickets were sold at White's coffee-house and the Haymarket itself, and no one entered the theatre without ticket and disguise. The event, which began at nine or ten, frequently lasted until early the next morning. In Swift's 'The Progress of Marriage' (1721–2) an errant wife returns from a masquerade: 'At five the footmen make a din, / Her ladyship is just come in'.[12] Heidegger continued to hold masquerades at the Haymarket until his death in 1749.

The occasion had its pretensions to exclusivity: George II and the Prince of Wales are both reputed to have attended public masquerades.[13] But its real appeal lay in its heterogeneous and carnival-like atmosphere. It drew on all social ranks equally, and permitted high and low to mingle in a single 'promiscuous' round. 'All state and ceremony are laid aside', wrote one witness in the *Weekly Journal* (25 January 1724), 'since the *Peer* and the *Apprentice*, the *Punk* and the *Duchess* are, for so long a time, upon an equal Foot'. Costume reinscribed the theme of class confusion. As Christopher Pitt wrote in *On the Masquerades* (1727):

> Valets adorned with coronets appear,
> Lacquies of state and footmen with a star,
> Sailors of quality with judges mix,–
> And chimney-sweepers drive their coach-and six.[14]

Not all observers were pleased with the masquerade's 'strange Medley' of persons. 'It is possible', wrote Mary Singleton in *The Old Maid*, 'the confused mixture of different ranks and conditions, which is unavoidable at a masquerade, may well be agreeable to the dregs of the people, who are fond, even at every price, of gaining admittance into a place where they may insult their superiors with impunity'.[15]

Given the liberating anonymity of the scene, collective behaviour was unrestrained. Drinking, dancing, gaming and intrigue flourished, ordinary decorum was overturned, and a spirit of saturnalia reigned. Not surprisingly, the masquerade quickly came under attack from moralists and divines. A host of anti-masquerade satires and pamphlets were published in the 1720s and continued to appear into the 1780s. Civil authorities made periodic attempts to suppress masquerades, particularly during times of social unrest, but these efforts were never very successful. For most of the century the masquerade retained a raffish and seductive hold on the public imagination. Large masquerades were held at Ranelagh Gardens and Marylebone in the 1740s and 1750s, and again at Carlisle House in Soho Square, the Pantheon and Almack's in the 1760s and 1770s. *Town and Country Magazine* for May 1770 reported a masquerade at the Pantheon attended by 'near two thousand persons'. Only after the French Revolution did the masquerade lose something of its subversive appeal, though occasional masquerades continued to be held in London well into the nineteenth century.[16]

Though public in nature, the masquerade had the reputation – and *frisson* – of an underground phenomenon. From the start it was felt to epitomise the clandestine sexual life of the city. This 'libidinous Assembly', wrote Addison on the *Spectator*, was perfectly contrived for the 'Advancement of Cuckoldom', being nothing more than a scene of 'Assignations and Intrigues'.[17] In his satiric *Masquerade Ticket* of 1727, Hogarth highlighted the erotic nature of the event by depicting Haymarket masqueraders cavorting beneath statues of Venus and Priapus and two large 'Lecherometers' – fanciful devices for measuring sexual excitement. Masquerade debauchery was a popular theme in eighteenth-century fiction. In the novels of Defoe, Fielding, Richardson and Smollett, the masquerade was a conventional setting for seduction and adultery. Other writers regularly linked it with scenarios of defloration, rape and perversion.[18] 'To carry on an Intrigue with an Air of Secrecy' or 'debauch a Citizen's Wife', exclaimed a character in Benjamin Griffin's *The Masquerade* (1717), 'what Contrivance in the World so proper as a Masquerade?'[19] The anonymous writer of the *Short Remarks upon the Original and Pernicious Consequences of Masquerades* of 1721 was less sanguine: the masquerade, he wrote, was nothing more than a '*Congress to an unclean end*'.[20]

Underlying such complaints was a sense of the moral scandal implicit in costume itself. 'The being in disguise', wrote the author of *Guardian* 142, 'takes away the usual checks and restraints of modesty; and consequently the beaux do not blush to talk wantonly, nor the belles to listen; the one as greedily sucks in the poison, as the other industriously infuses it'.[21] Travesty eroticised the world. Not only was one freed of one's inhibitions, one might also experience, hypothetically at least, a new body and its pleasures. The exchange of garments was also an exchange of desires. The result was a flight from the 'natural' – from all that was culturally preordained – into new realms of voluptuous disorder.

By all accounts, the masquerade was indeed a scene of unusual erotic stimulation. Many disguises, first of all, had an undeniably fetishistic power. Masks were considered notorious aphrodisiacs, associated with prostitutes (as in Hogarth's *Harlot's Progress*) and the perverse heightening of passion. 'A Woman mask'd', Wycherley's uncouth Pinchwife had observed in *The Country-Wife* (1675), 'is like a cover'd Dish, gives a man a curiosity, and appetite, when, it may be, uncover'd 'twould turn his stomack'.[22] But the mask also released its wearer from ordinary moral controls. Women, it was felt, were particularly freed from constraint. 'The mask secures the Ladies from Detraction, and encourages a Liberty, the Guilt of which their Blushes would betray when barefac'd, till by Degrees they are innur'd to that which is out of their Vertue to restrain'.[23] Combined with the mysterious black domino, the mask remained for the century the veritable icon of transgressive desire.

But costumes themselves were also highly suggestive and provided a rich symbolic lexicon of libidinous possibility. Granted, not every disguise of the century was meant to titillate; almost all masquerades had their requisite Turks and conjurers, Harlequins and shepherdesses, hussars and Pierrots, orange-girls and Punches. Eighteenth-century masquerade costumes were sometimes merely playful, exotic or picturesque. Casanova

himself appeared as a relatively innocuous Pierrot at an Italian masquerade.[24] But given the premium on voyeurism and self-display, visual scandal held a special place. Where else, indeed, might one find 'a *Nobleman* [dressed] like a *Cynder-Wench*', or 'a *Lady of Quality* in *Dutch Trowsers*, and a *Woman of the Town* in a *Ruff* and *Farthingale?*'.[25]

Transvestite costume was perhaps the most common offence against decorum. Women strutted in jack-boots and breeches, while men primped in furbelows and flounces. Horace Walpole describes passing 'for a good mask' as an old woman at a masquerade in 1742. Other male masqueraders disguised themselves as witches, bawds, nursery-maids and shepherdesses.[26] At a Richmond masquerade, *Gentleman's Magazine* reported in April, 1776, 'a gentleman appeared in woman's clothes with a head-dress four feet high, composed of greens and garden stuff, and crowned with tufts of endive nicely blanched'. 'The force of the ridicule', the account continued, 'was felt by some of the ladies'. At Almack's in 1773, one man appeared as a 'procuress' and another as 'Mother Cole', the matronly bawd in Cleland's *Memoirs of a Woman of Pleasure*.[27] Female masqueraders in turn metamorphosed into hussars, sailors, cardinals or Mozartian boys. The Duchess of Bolton, Elizabeth Inchbald and Judith Milbanke, among others, appeared in male costumes at masquerades at one time or another during the century.[28] In Griffin's *The Masquerade*, the heroine attends as 'a kind of Hermaphroditical Mixture; half Man, half Woman; a Coat, Wig, Hat, and Feather, with all the Ornaments requisite'. Costumes representing the 'Amazonian' goddess Diana (popular throughout the century) were likewise androgynous in nature.[29] The anti-masquerade writers, not surprisingly, found cross-dressing a palpable sign of masquerade depravity. The author of the *Short Remarks* complained that the confounding of garments had ever 'been used by Wantons, to favour their lascivious Designs'. This 'artifice of the old Serpent,' he wrote, was clearly intended to 'regale and heighten the Temptation'. Eighteenth-century masqueraders may not, indeed, have been oblivious to such imperatives. Judith Milbanke, who appeared along with her sister as 'two smart Beaux' in 1778, complacently observed that she had made by far 'the prettiest Fellow of the two',[30] and the scandalous Harriette Wilson, recollecting a

[*Facing*] Engraving of a Pantheon masquerade by Charles White, 1773 (courtesy Trustees of the British Museum)

masquerade at which she and a female friend dressed as an 'Italian or Austrian peasant-boy and girl', carefully recorded in her memoirs the various risqué comments they received from bystanders.[31]

But other costume types were also designed to inflame. The *parodia sacra*, or ecclesiastical parody, offered an opportunity to play upon themes of celibacy and forbidden desire. A classic vestige of carnival tradition, ecclesiastical disguise featured prominently in contemporary costume catalogues such as Thomas Jeffery's *Dresses of Different Nations* (1757) and remained fashionable throughout the century. Wayward nuns and priests, perversely amorous 'Devotees', and licentious Capuchins are a staple in contemporary masquerade stories and illustrations. 'I will be a Prude, a religious Prude', exclaims the flirtatious Lady Frances in Charles Johnson's *The Masquerade* (1719), 'I will appear in all the gloomy inaccessible Charms of a young Devotee; there is something in this Character so sweet and forbidden'.[32] By a predictable symbolic inversion, prostitutes were thought particularly likely to assume pious vestments. A writer in the *Weekly Journal* (25 January 1724) described meeting a pretty nun at a masquerade who 'rapt out an Oath' and made it known 'that she was of the Sisterhood, and belonged to a certain Convent, of which Mother N[eedham], is Lady *Abbess*'. In Henry Robert Morland's painting *The Fair Nun Unmasked* (1769), a simpering mock-*religieuse* is shown removing her mask and suggestively exposing the jewelled crucifix on her bosom.

Still other disguises were profane from the start. Miss Chudleigh, later the Duchess of Kingston, shocked onlookers by appearing at the Jubilee masquerade in 1749 as a bare-breasted Iphigenia – 'so naked,' Mrs Montagu remarked, 'that the high priest might easily inspect the entrails of the victim'.[33] Several semi-pornographic prints commemorated her exploit. In 1755 the writer of *The Connoisseur* for 6 February described a gallant who went to a masked 'Frolick' with 'no breeches under his domino'. In 1768 Miss Pelham appeared at a masquerade as a 'blackamoor' with her legs exposed to the thighs,[34] and in 1770 a man went to one of Mrs Cornelys's masquerades in Soho Square as Adam, in a flesh-coloured silk body stocking complete with 'an apron of fig leaves worked in it, fitting the body to the utmost nicety'. The result, according to *Gentleman's Magazine*, was a certain 'unavoidable indelicacy'.[35]

This paradoxical connection between masquerading and nakedness, it is worth noting, was a joke that recurred in various forms throughout the century.

[*Facing*] Elizabeth Chudleigh as a bare-breasted Iphigenia at the Jubilee Masquerade, 1749 (courtesy Trustees of the British Museum)

Popular wisdom held that there was a causal relation between masquerading and (subsequent) states of undress: those who 'dressed up' for the masquerade would undoubtedly bare themselves later – when they retired to brothels or bagnios to consummate their secret liaisons. Such a sequence is implicit in Plate 5 of Hogarth's *Marriage à la Mode,* in which an adulterous wife and her lover have retreated to a bagnio for sex after a masquerade. At other times, less logically, the masquerade itself was associated with images of naked excess. In *Guardian* 142 (24 August 1713), Steele linked an attack on masquerades ('the devil first addressed himself to Eve in a mask') with a parody of the 'Evites', an imaginary cult of fashionable women who wore only fig-leaves. In 1755 Miss Chudleigh's scandalous appearance as Iphigenia prompted a satiric scheme for a 'Naked Masquerade'. At this 'alfresco' event, described in *The Connoisseur* (1 May 1755), female masqueraders were to disport themselves as '*Water-Nymphs* and *Graces*', and male masqueraders in 'the half-brutal forms of *Satyres, Pans, Fauns,* and *Centaurs*'. 'The *Pantheon of the Heathen Gods, Ovid's Metamorphoses,* and *Titian's Prints*', the author argued, would supply 'a sufficient variety of undrest characters'. In the resulting orgy, bucks might run mad with their mistresses 'like the Priests and Priestesses of *Bacchus* celebrating the *Bacchanalian* mysteries'.

To what extent was the Dionysian promise in masquerade spectacle fulfilled? Certainly, if all masquerades were disreputable, some were less reputable than others. Acts of outright sexual intercourse (if they occurred at all) took place, one suspects, only at the most clandestine and subfusc affairs, and certainly not at events like Heidegger's 'Midnight Masquerade' or Mrs Cornely's public subscription balls. The sexual subculture, for instance, had its own more or less unbuttoned versions of the masquerade. In her scandalous memoirs of 1797, the courtesan Margaret Leeson described a private masquerade at which a couple performed love feats 'buff to buff', and, later, another masquerade given by 'Moll Hall' which degenerated into an orgy.[36] The author of the piece on the 'Naked Masquerade' noted in passing that he modelled his entertainment on an actual event that had taken place the year before at Pimlico 'among the lowest of the people'. The participants, he observed, had been sent to Bridewell, but 'the same act, which at the *Green Lamps* or *Pimlico* appears low and criminal, may be extremely polite and commendable in the *Haymarket* or at *Ranelagh*'. Similarly, in one of the numerous popular histories of Jonathan Wild, there is a description of a secret homosexual masquerade party attended by Wild, which featured a group of 'He-

Whores', 'rigg'd in Gowns, Petticoats, Head cloths, fine lac'd Shoes, Furbelow Scarves, and Masks', all 'tickling and feeling each other, as if they were a mixture of wanton Males and Females'. This licentious gathering has been identified as the notorious 'Sodomitish Academy' run by 'Mother Clap' in Field Lane, Holborn.[37]

The public masquerade was nominally more restrained, in that the shift into overt sexual behaviour was seldom possible. This is not to say, however, that the masquerade's bacchanalian reputation was undeserved. The occasion was indisputably a catalyst for certain kinds of behaviour, and functioned throughout the century – along with brothels, bagnios and the London piazzas and parks – as an acknowledged public setting in which illicit sexual contacts might be made. Of couse, evidence regarding actual behaviour at masquerades must be primarily circumstantial; the scandal associated with the occasion meant that few participants recorded incriminating escapades directly. Often one must rely on journalistic accounts, literary descriptions and the sometimes exaggerated comments of the masquerade's detractors. Still, eighteenth-century observers agreed (and common-sense confirms) that the masquerade was indeed a 'Country of Liberty' – a realm where transgressive liaisons were easily formed, precisely because they might remain anonymous.[38]

The Haymarket masquerade had its quota of prostitutes, first of all, owing in part to its location in the heart of London's prostitution district. Disguise permitted the prostitute, like the sharper, to ply her precarious trade in relative safety. The 'Sisterhood of Drury' appear frequently in masquerade accounts throughout the century. On the night of a recent ball, wrote an observer in the *Weekly Journal* (25 January, 1724), 'all about the Hundreds of *Drury*, there was not a *Fille de Joie* to be had that Night, for Love nor Money, being all engaged at the Masquerade; and several Men of Pleasure receiv'd Favours from Ladies who were too modest to shew their Faces, and many of them still feel the Effects of the amorous Flame which they received from the unknown Fairs'. The author of *A Seasonable Apology for Mr. H———g—r*, one of many anti-masquerade satires from the 1720s ironically dedicated his work to the infamous bawd Mother Needham, whose many minions, he observed, exploited the 'Mask of artificial Maidenhead' in addition to the ordinary mask of disguise.[39] In Addison's satire in *Guardian* 154, a nun makes an assignation with a 'heathen god' at a masquerade, and then agrees to meet him nearby in 'the Little Piazza in Covent-garden', the famous haunt of London's 'trading dames'.

Few eighteenth-century commentators acknowledged the economic necessity which drove prostitutes to masquerades; the popular theme of the whore-in-disguise was used merely to underwrite the moral assault on the event itself. Yet, amid a conventional attack in *The Masquerade* ('Thus Fortune sends the gamesters luck, Venus her votary a —'), Fielding offered the following unintentionally sympathetic vignette:

> Below stairs hungry whores are picking
> The bones of wild-fowl, and of chicken;
> And into pockets some convey
> Provisions for another day.

The lines may serve as a stark reminder that prostitutes constituted, after all, the most wretchedly exploited underclass in eighteenth-century London, and that some were undoubtedly driven to the masquerade out of more than simple concupiscence.

It was not just the 'Punk', however, who found a special range at masquerades. Women in general assumed unprecedented liberties. The misogynist view of the age, of course, was that any woman who attended a masquerade did so, like the harlot, in order to seek unlawful sexual pleasure. The taboo against unescorted women and girls going to masquerades remained in force throughout the century.[40] It mattered little whether a woman was a virgin or not; any woman, it was assumed, fell into sexual danger at masquerades. In a salacious story in the *Weekly Journal* (8 February 1724) entitled 'The Balls, a Tale,' a wayward young woman persuades her mother to let her go to a masquerade.

> Virgins to Midnight Masques would go,
> And not a Mother durst say, No;
> She pass'd for unpolite and rude,
> And Miss would cry, *Mamma's a Prude*.

Needless to say, she quickly gives up her maidenhood to a sly domino named Roger. A few weeks later the same newspaper offered the following maxim: 'Fishes are caught with Hooks, Birds are ensnar'd with Nets, but Virgins with Masquerades'.[41] In turn, in older women the masquerade was thought to prompt adulterous longings. The occasion was perfect for cuckoldry, wrote Addison, because 'the Women either come by themselves or are introduced by Friends, who are obliged to quit them upon their first Entrance'.[42] Lady Bellaston, who seduces Tom Jones at the Haymarket while disguised as the 'Queen of the Fairies', is a stereotypical eighteenth-century version of the older female masquerade libertine. In the satirical pamphlet *A Seasonable Apology for Mr. H———g—r* (1724), the comical 'Countess of Clingfast' and her 'Committee of Matrons' likewise relieve themselves of frigidity, green-sickness and 'obstructions' by attending masquerades.

We need not mimic the pervasive misogyny of contemporary moralists (or the relentlessly anti-sexual ideology they endorsed) to recognise the element of truth in their animadversions. The critics were right to link masquerading with female sexual emancipation; the masquerade indeed provided eighteenth-century women with an unusual sense of erotic freedom. Disguise obviated a host of cultural proscriptions and taboos. A woman in masquerade might approach strangers, initiate conversation, touch and embrace those whom she did not know, speak coarsely – in short, violate all the cherished imperatives of ordinary feminine sexual decorum. Of course, only the boldest might openly acknowledge such pleasures. 'I love a masquerade', wrote the brazen Harriette Wilson, 'because a female can never enjoy the same liberty anywhere else'.[43] In an account of a Pantheon masquerade in 1773, *Lady's Magazine* offered similar sentiments, purportedly through the voice of an anonymous female participant: 'Indeed a masquerade is one of the most entertaining diversions that ever was imported; you may hear and see, and do every thing in the world, without the least reserve – and liberty, liberty, my dear, you know, is the very joy of my heart'.[44]

Most important, masquerading granted women the essential masculine privilege of erotic object-choice. 'It is delightful to me', Wilson wrote, only half-facetiously, 'to be able to wander about in a crowd, making my observations, and conversing with whomsoever I please, without being liable to be stared at or remarked upon, and to speak to whom I please, and run away from them the moment I have discovered their stupidity'.[45] Elsewhere in her memoir, she described meeting several lovers at masquerades. It would going too far, perhaps, to call the masquerade a feminist counterpart to the brothel; eighteenth-century culture, unremittingly patriarchal in structure, was never so Utopian in its sexual arrangements. Nonetheless, the masquerade offered contemporary women a subversive – if temporary – simulacrum of sexual autonomy. Besides obvious demi-mondaine figures like Wilson and Margaret Leeson, such distinguished women as Mary Wortley Montagu, Fanny Burney and Elizabeth Inchbald acknowledged a fondness of masquerade privileges.[46] But unknown women too, one may assume, experienced unprecedented sensual release in the comic displacements of the night.

Likewise, homosexuals may have found a similar latitude at public masquerades. So much seems clear, at least, from contemporary attacks on the masquerade, which frequently called attention to 'unnatural' liaisons struck up there. The sensational *Short Remarks upon the Original and Pernicious Consequences of Masquerades*, for example, was in large part a barely-concealed assault on homosexual practices at the masquerade. Masquerade transvestism, charged its author, had led its proponents towards 'Excesses, which otherwise they durst scarce have thought of' and was making the nation a veritable '*Sodom* for Lewdness'. Citing infamous cross-dressers and bisexuals of antiquity – Sporus, Caligula, Heliogabalus and so forth – he warned that such men had been 'branded in History as Monsters of Nature, the Scum, and Scandal, and Shame of Mankind'. Modern masqueraders merely imitated the vice-ridden 'Corybantes' and 'dancing priests' of the past; the pagan '*Festum Kalendarium*', scene of travesty, perversion and blasphemy, was 'the black Original we transcribe in our Masquerades'.

Fielding adopted a somewhat less dire tone in *The Masquerade*, but likewise condemned the masquerade as a world of enveloping sexual chaos, in which any kind of wrongful connection was possible. Complaining of the effeminate men ('little apish butterflies') everywhere to be seen at the masquerade, the poet's Muse cries:

> And if the breed been't quickly mended;
> Your empire shortly will be ended:
> Breeches our brawny thighs shall grace,
> (Another Amazonian race.)
> For when men women turn – why then
> May women not be chang'd to men?

That Fielding connected transvestism with active homosexuality is obvious from his later anti-lesbian satire, *The Female Husband* (1746). This semi-prurient work (based on an actual case tried by Fielding's cousin) described how a woman named Mary Hamilton disguised herself as a man and tricked several women into marriage precisely in order to satisfy 'unnatural' carnal urges.[47] As if to illustrate Fielding's vision of ensuing sexual disorder, a suggestive satiric engraving from the first half of the century, 'The Masquerade Dance', depicted an all-male group of masqueraders performing a wild hornpipe to the music of a piping devil.

Yet the presence of homosexuals at masquerades can be deduced in other ways too. The Haymarket, as I have mentioned, was near to Covent

Garden and Spring Gardens, both important sites for male as well as female prostitution. Along with molly-clubs and similar underground sexual establishments, masquerade rooms featured in the clandestine erotic topography of the new male homosexual subculture that was gradually coming into being in eighteenth-century London.[48] Even in supposedly 'decent' or non-pornographic accounts, the masquerade is an acknowledged setting for acts of real or ostensible homoerotic flirtation. At a masquerade described in *Guardian* 154, for example, the male narrator, disguised as Lucifer, is accosted by a 'Presbyterian Parson' who calls him a 'pretty fellow' and offers to meet him in Spring Gardens. Later in the same piece, the narrator finds himself strangely attracted to an 'Indian King' who, admittedly, turns out to be a woman in disguise. Similar errors are recorded elsewhere. According to her biographer, Mrs Inchbald, who appeared as a man at a masquerade in the 1780s, unwittingly 'captivated the affections' of her own sex as a result.[49] The *Weekly Journal* in 1724 had an account of a man who went to the Haymarket dressed as a female Quaker and was mistakenly almost 'ravished' there by a young male domino.[50] And, in a particularly lascivious episode in Smollett's *Peregrine Pickle* (1751), a character dressed in women's clothes at a masquerade is forced, 'in consequence of the Champaign he had so liberally swallowed that afternoon', to micturate in front of a group of fascinated male masqueraders. He is subsequently accosted by a Frenchman who compliments him on his 'happy pisse' and fondles him, through the Frenchman later denies knowing his true sex.[51]

But eighteenth-century pornographic writing, as one might expect, confirms the presence of outright same-sex solicitation at masquerades. In Cleland's *Memoirs of a Woman of Pleasure* (1749), Fanny Hill's fellow prostitute Emily, disguised as a boy, is approached by a 'handsome domino' at a public masquerade. His courtship, she finds, is 'dash'd with a certain oddity', but she attributes this to the 'humour' of her disguise and not to any misunderstanding about her sex. His intentions are clearly homosexual, however; he has taken her for a 'smock-fac'd boy', tries to sodomise her in a nearby bagnio and, in a moment of lubricious crisis, must be redirected 'down the right road'. While clearly obscene in design, the episode also points towards the underlying sociological reality; that Cleland (himself reputed to be a 'sodomite' by several contemporaries) took for granted the association between the masquerade and homosexual seduction here, as with other realistic details in the novel, reflects more than mere pornographic convenience.[52]

For those hedged round by the implicit and explicit taboos of eighteenth-century sexual morality, therefore, the masquerade offered unprecedented pleasures and opportunities. Borrowing a term from the sociologist, we might call it a 'backstage' area in eighteenth-century urban life – a setting in which ordinarily proscribed impulses might safely be indulged.[53] The irony was that to go 'backstage' was also to go 'on stage'; to adopt a new self, to play a new role, through the hallucinatory derangements of costume. Throughout the century, the masquerade mediated in a paradoxical fashion between public and private spheres. Behind the mask, one preserved the essential moral and psychological privileges of privacy, while participating at the same time in the spontaneous exchanges of the group. Disguise was the crucial means towards such mediation – the gesture which at once licensed collective exchange and infused the occasion with its secretive, compelling aura.

Yet, to identify the masquerade as a privileged space for the morally unconventional does not entirely explain its powerful hold on eighteenth-century English culture. I have argued that some people may have self-consciously sought its freedoms – prostitutes, libertines, feminists, the sexual avant-garde. The masquerade had much to do, certainly, with the subterranean liberalisation of erotic life in eighteenth-century London,[54] but in speaking of a 'culture of travesty' I have made large claims, admittedly, for something that remained in one sense a local phenomenon. Thousands attended masquerades during the century, but what of those who never ventured to the Haymarket, Ranelagh or Soho Square? How did the carnivalesque exploits of an urban minority impinge upon the imaginative life of society as a whole?

We cannot underestimate the power that the idea of the 'Midnight Masquerade' held in eighteenth-century discourse. Indeed, we might speak of the masquerade as one of the defining *topoi* of eighteenth-century cultural rhetoric. The numerous literary and artistic transformations of the masquerade were at least as significant, in some sense, as the institution itself. Whether or not they attended, the majority of English people knew about the masquerades. As witnessed by a host of novels, stories, poems, pamphlets, squibs and engravings, the event remained a subject of fascination throughout the century.[55]

And, in a way, masquerade liberty was as much a common imaginative property – part of the fantasy-life of the age – as it was the privilege of the masquerade crowd. The appeal of the mask, as we have seen, was that it permitted an escape from self; internalised moral and psychological constraints disappeared – for how could one be held responsible when one was not oneself? The logic of ordinary moral agency was suspended; whatever one did, whatever ensued, might be attributed to 'someone else' or assimilated to the supposedly innocent realm of 'accidents'. Yet similar psychological fictions operated in the masquerade fantasies of the century. In stories of masquerade seduction and adultery, the timid reader might safely identify with an 'other' – seducer or victim, adulterer or adulteress – without risk, obviously, to his or her consciously-held scruples. Heavy didacticism added a comfortable (if spurious) protective moral layering to these powerfully charged sexual narratives. Like the related genre of the criminal biography, the masquerade tale typically gratified prurient or subversive interests while parading as 'instructive' commentary. And just as the criminal biography, with its implicit glorification of the miscreant, reflected a growing popular revolt against traditional religious values (or so John Richetti has argued in *Popular Fiction before Richardson*), so the sensational masquerade tale may have articulated a new subliminal collective hostility toward age-old sexual prohibitions and taboos.[56]

One might go so far as to say that masquerade fantasy operated as a conceptual tool – a symbolic mechanism through which suppressed forms of behaviour found representation. Virtually any form of perverse or proscribed sexual contact might be depicted in masquerade literature, so long as it was made to seem unintentional – an accidental function of the chaos and anonymity of the scene. The 'mistake' was the crucial covering fiction. Innocent men thus couple unwittingly with prostitutes in a host of masquerade stories: in *Spectator* No. 8, for example, an unfortunate Templar mistakes 'a *Cloud* for a *Juno*' and discovers his *faux pas* too late. In still other accounts, virginal young women and loyal wives are ruined as a result of tragic masquerade errors –usually when they confuse a rapist with a fiancé or husband. In a sensational tale by Eliza Haywood in *The Female Spectator* (1746), the heroine Erminia allows herself to be escorted home from the masquerade by a man she takes to be her fiancé and is forcibly undone by him. In an 'Affecting Masquerade Adventure' from 1754, a similar fate awaits Matilda, who is seduced after a masquerade by a mysterious domino she believes to be her husband.[57]

Other fanciful consummations were even more lurid. I have already mentioned cases of accidental homosexuality at the masquerade; accidental incest was another popular motif. The writer of the *Short Remarks* described an unfortunate gentleman who 'debauch'd his own Daughter' by mistake at a masquerade and died of horror at the discovery. In the play

The Masquerade; or, The Devil's Nursery (1732), a 'Virtuous Wife' is 'an Incestuous Mother made' after another tragic masquerade mix-up.[58] 'By thee,' the author of *A Seasonable Apology for Mr. H—g—r* wrote of the masquerade, 'Sons aspire to the Wombs from whence they sprung; and Daughters wantonly embrace the Loyns that begot them'.

While typically presented as proofs of the masquerade's diabolical nature, these narratives of accidental union also provided readers with a new and highly specific grammar of the illicit. In adumbrating their shocking tales of unwitting prostitution, adultery, homosexuality and incest, masquerade writers also gave unprecedented centrality to previously unmentionable desires – all the myriad taboo forms, in short, of non-marital, non-procreative sexuality. Their scenarios covertly dramatised new modes of intimacy, enacted outside the traditional framing institutions of marriage and the law. Like the mask, the fiction of accident was in the end, one suspects, nothing more than an enabling device, the psychological means by which subversive sexual themes found utterance. Concealed in the popular moralistic inventory of 'accidental' masquerade attachments was an unprecedented imagery of transgressive pleasures.

The destabilising power of the masquerade was expressed as much in its representations as in its own intrinsic disorders. We cannot separate the real and the fictive masquerade, for both were a part, ultimately, of a larger imaginative experiment in violation. Jean Starobinski has written that the most profound discovery of the eighteenth century was its 'invention of liberty' – the intense evocation, at least in fantasy, of the freedom of the individual.[59] This is not to discount Theodore Tarczylo's argument elsewhere in this volume; Enlightenment *philosophes* did not in practice automatically extend the concept of freedom into the realm of Eros, nor may we consider eighteenth-century society anywhere in Europe as sexually permissive in the modern sense. But one may still speak of the general liberalising and individualistic tendency in eighteenth-century thought. (In England, the intellectual history of feminism from Astell to Wollstonecraft lends power to such a generalisation.) In the realm of sexual ideology, the movement toward individualism manifested itself variously – in a growing resistance to traditional moral authority, in self-conscious attempts to redefine the controlling institutions of marriage and the family, in the various calls for the emancipation of women, and, increasingly, in the new and controversial perception of sexual freedom as one of the privileges of civilisation. For sexual radicals such as the Marquis de Sade, erotic individualism culminated, quite predictably, in an assault on the bastion of heterosexuality itself.

Western culture over the past two centuries has largely internalised (if not always officially sanctioned) this historic idealisation of sexual freedom. In the twentieth century, the unconstrained nature of desire – and the need of human beings to pursue diverse objects of gratification – has become a psychological if not a political common-place. We need not be orthodox Freudians to accept the idea of the polymorphousness of the modern subject, for whom, in theory at least, all avenues of sexual pleasure stand open. Dryden's verse, 'Love variously doth various minds inspire', has been echoed most recently by Michel Foucault, who argues that through its relentless 'eroticization of the body', modern Western culture has animated new objects of desire and defined forms of erotic subjectivity unknown to our forebears.[60]

Yet it is impossible to separate these important intellectual developments, finally, from the 'structures of everyday life' that gave rise to them. The great theme of sexual liberty inevitably germinated in the fertile ground of eighteenth-century social practice. The real function of the masquerade may ultimately have been a heuristic one. Even while it posed as frivolity, the masquerade was also a living catalyst for reflection – a mechanism for conceptualising, as it were, the Protean future of desire. Its 'studied Devices of Pageantry and Disguise', as Benjamin Griffin called them in 1717, were also rehearsals for future transgression: theatrical experiments in the carnivalisation of sexual life itself. To its voluptuous confusions, we owe – at least in part – our modern (perhaps sentimental) image of the boundlessness, freedom and incorrigibility of Eros.

The masquerade introduced a new moral irony into sexual relations. Masquerade travesty was a mark of the profane; the inversion of sacred categories. Yet, once acknowledged, the urge toward desacralisation spread outwards into society at large. In the culture of travesty, an historic new self-consciousness invaded the silent pleasure-world of the body. The flight from the 'natural' had begun; the modern challenge to traditional moral and psychic structures was inaugurated. To be sure, the eighteenth-century poet of masquerade railed against the 'lewd joys' of the fantastic scene,

> Where sexes blend in one confus'd intrigue,
> Where the girls ravish and the men grow big,. . .
> Nor credit what the idle world has said
> Of lawyers forc'd, and judges brought-to-bed,
> Or that to belles their brothers breathe their vows. . .[61]

Yet even as he turned, sardonically, from the 'enormities' of the occasion, he preserved them, in the shape of an anthology – which was also a blueprint – for a universal masquerade.

Notes

1 Henry Fielding, 'An Essay on the Knowledge of the Characters of Men', in *Miscellanies*, ed. Henry Knight Miller, Oxford, Clarendon Press, 1972, I, p. 155; Owen Sedgewick, *The Universal Masquerade: or, The World Turn'd Inside Out*, London, 1742; Samuel Johnson, *The Rambler*, No. 75, 4 December 1750, in *British Essayists*, ed. Alexander Chalmers, Boston, 1856, XVII, p. 92; Oliver Goldsmith, *Works*, ed. Peter Cunningham, New York, G. P. Putnam's, 1908, I, p. 153.
2 On Boswell's impersonations, see Max Byrd, *London Transformed: Images of the City in the Eighteenth Century*, New Haven, Yale University Press, 1978, pp. 95–7.
3 Henry Fielding, *The Masquerade*, London, 1728, reprinted in *The Female Husband and Other Writings*, ed. Claude E. Jones, English Reprints Series, Liverpool, Liverpool University Press, 1960; Joseph Addison, *The Spectator*, No. 14, 16 March 1711. All citations from the *Spectator* are drawn from the Oxford edition, Donald F. Bond, ed., Oxford, Clarendon Press, 1965, 5 vols.
4 Michel Foucault, Introduction, *Herculine Barbin*, trans. Richard McDougall, New York, Pantheon, 1980, p. xvii.
5 *Universal Spectator*, 14 December 1728.
6 E. C. Cawte, *Ritual Animal Disguise*, Cambridge, D. S. Brewer, 1978, Ch. 3, esp. pp. 71 and 86.
7 On popular entertainments in the English Renaissance, see C. L. Barber, *Shakespeare's Festive Comedy: A Study of Dramatic Form and its Relation to Social Custom*, Princeton, N.J., Princeton University Press, 1959, and Michael D. Bristol, *Carnival and Theatre: Plebeian Culture and the Structure of Authority in Renaissance England*, London, Methuen, 1985. For a description of masquerading at the court of Charles II, see Gilbert Burnet, *History of His Own Times*, ed. Thomas Burnet, London, 1818, I, p. 292. Further anecdotal information on Restoration masquerades can be found in William Connor Sydney, *Social Life in England from the Restoration to the Revolution*, New York, Macmillan, 1892, pp. 367–72.
8 Peter Burke, *Popular Culture in Early Modern Europe*, New York, Harper and Row, 1978, p. 249. See also Joseph Spence, *Letters from the Grand Tour*, ed. Slava Klima, Montreal, McGill-Queens University Press, 1975, p. 95.
9 See, for example, the letter condemning 'mock Carnivals at Ranelagh-house' in *Gentleman's Magazine*, May 1750.
10 On the commercialisation of popular entertainment in eighteenth-century England, see Burke, *Popular Culture*, pp. 248–9, and J. H. Plumb's essay 'Commercialization and Society' in *The Birth of a Consumer Society: The Commercialization of Eighteenth-Century England*, London, Europa, 1982, pp. 265–85.

11 See G. F. R. Barker's biographical essay, 'John James Heidegger', *Dictionary of National Biography*. Public masquerades had in fact been established a few years earlier in London: there were advertisements for public masquerades at Lambeth-Wells, Spring Gardens, and elsewhere in *The Spectator* as early as 1711 (see Bond's note in the Oxford edition, I, p. 36). Heidegger's Haymarket balls later in the decade, however, attracted by far the most public attention.
12 Jonathan Swift, *The Complete Poems*, ed. Pat Rogers, New Haven, Yale University Press, 1983, p. 245.
13 See 'Heidegger', *DNB*, and J. Ireland and John Nichols, *Hogarth's Complete Works*, Edinburgh, 1883, pp. 229–30.
14 Christopher Pitt, 'On the Masquerades', *Poems and Translations*, London, 1727, reprinted in Samuel Johnson, ed., *Poets of Great Britain*, London, 1807, XLVII, pp. 19–21.
15 Mary Singleton [Frances Brooke], *The Old Maid*, No. 11, 24 January 1756.
16 Pierce Egan depicts a Regency masquerade in *Life in London*, London, 1821, Book II, Ch. 3. Byron attended a masquerade at Burlington House in 1814. See Leslie A. Marchand, *Byron: A Portrait*, Chicago, University of Chicago Press, 1970, p. 171.
17 Addison, *Spectator*, No. 8, 9 March 1711.
18 Suggestive masquerade scenes occur in Defoe's *Roxana*, 1724; Mary Davys' *The Accomplished Rake; or, The Modern Fine Gentleman*, 1727; Richardson's *Pamela*, Part 2, 1741; Cleland's *Memoirs of a Woman of Pleasure*, 1749; Fielding's *Amelia*, 1751; Smollett's *Adventures of Peregrine Pickle*, 1751, and a host of minor works of the period. A typically melodramatic shorter tale is the 'Affecting Masquerade Adventure', published in *Gentleman's Magazine*, December 1754.
19 Benjamin Griffin, *The Masquerade; or, An Evening's Intrigue*, London, 1717.
20 *The Conduct of the Stage Consider'd, with Short Remarks upon the Original and Pernicious Consequences of Masquerades*, London, 1721. I refer to this work elsewhere as the *Short Remarks*.
21 Richard Steele, *The Guardian*, No. 142, 24 August 1713, in *British Essayists*, Vol. XV. All further citations from *The Guardian* are from this edition.
22 William Wycherley, *The Country-Wife* (III, i), *The Complete Plays of William Wycherley*, ed. Gerald Weales, New York, Norton, 1966, p. 293.
23 *Weekly Journal*, 19 April 1718.
24 See *The Memoirs of Casanova*, trans. Arthur Machen, New York, G. P. Putnam's, 1959, IV, p. 557. On the history of masquerade costume, see Aileen Ribeiro, *The Dress Worn at Masquerades in England, 1730 to 1790, and its Relation to Fancy Dress in Portraiture*, New York, Garland, 1984, and my recent study, *Masquerade and Civilization: The Carnivalesque in Eighteenth-Century English Culture and Fiction*, Stanford, Stanford University Press, 1986, Ch. 2.
25 Griffin, *The Masquerade*, I, i.
26 See Horace Walpole's letter to Mann, 3 March 1742, in *Horace Walpole's Correspondence*, ed. W. S. Lewis, et al., New Haven, Yale University Press, I (17), 359. *Connoisseur*, 1 May 1755, described 'one gentleman above six foot high, who came to the Masquerade drest like a child in a white frock and leading-strings, attended by another gentleman of a very low stature, who

officiated as his nurse'. The 'two great Girls, one in a white frock, with her doll' described in *Gentleman's Magazine*, February 1771, were also undoubtedly female impersonators.

27 *Lady's Magazine*, February 1773.
28 At a magnificent masquerade given by her husband in 1769, the Duchess of Bolton appeared first in 'a Man's Black Domino', then, later in the evening, as a Persian princess. See *The Diaries of a Duchess: Extracts from the Diaries of the First Duchess of Northumberland (1716-1776)*, ed. James Greig, London, Hodder & Stoughton, 1926, p. 91. Elizabeth Inchbald, who had appeared as Bellario on the London stage, went to a masquerade in male dress in 1781. See James Boaden, *Memoirs of Mrs. Inchbald*, London, 1833, I, pp. 140-1. On Judith Milbanke's male impersonation, see *The Noels and the Milbankes, Their Letters for Twenty-Five Years*, ed. Malcolm Elwin, London, Macdonald, 1967, p. 93. For other cases of eighteenth-century female cross-dressing, see Diane Dugaw, 'Balladry's Female Warriors: Women, Warfare, and Disguise in the Eighteenth Century', *Eighteenth-Century Life*, IX, n.s. 2, 1985, pp. 1-20.
29 Miss Milner, the heroine of Inchbald's *A Simple Story*, 1791, is described by another character as wearing 'mens cloaths' when she appears as the goddess Diana at a masquerade in that novel. Ribeiro comments on the features of the Diana costume in *The Dress Worn at Masquerades*, pp. 261-4.
30 *The Noels and the Milbankes*, p. 93.
31 Harriette Wilson, *The Memoirs of Harriette Wilson Written by Herself*, London, The Navarre Society, 1924, II, pp. 607-11.
32 Charles Johnson, *The Masquerade: A Comedy*, London, 1719, II, ii.
33 E. J. Climenson, ed., *Elizabeth Montagu, The Queen of the Blue-Stockings*, London, John Murray, 1906, I, p. 264. One of the many satiric engravings commemorating Miss Chudleigh's exploit is the plate entitled 'Miss Chudley in the Actual Dress as she appear'd in ye character of Iphigenia at ye Jubilee Ball or Masquerade at Ranelagh', British Museum, Print Room no. 3031.
34 Ribeiro, *Dress Worn at Masquerades*, p. 32.
35 *Gentleman's Magazine*, March 1770.
36 Margaret Leeson, *Memoirs of Margaret Leeson, Written by Herself*, Dublin, 1797, III, pp. 4-10.
37 *Select Trials for Murders, Robberies, Rapes, Sodomy, Coining, Frauds, and Other Offences at the Sessions-House in the Old Bailey*, London, 1742, II, pp. 257-8. Gerald Howson comments on Margaret Clap in *Thief-Taker General: The Rise and Fall of Jonathan Wild*, London, Hutchinson, 1970, pp. 63-4.
38 James Ralph, *The Touchstone: or, a guide to all the reigning diversions*, London, 1728, p. 191.
39 *A Seasonable Apology for Mr. H——g—r*, London, 1724.
40 See, for example, Eliza Haywood's warnings in *The Female Spectator*, 3rd edition, London, 1750, I, pp. 32-3. In a letter to Lady Bradshaigh, 17 August, 1752, Samuel Richardson complained that 'the sex is generally running into licentiousness; when home is found to be the place that is most irksome to them; when Ranelaghs, Vauxhalls, Marybones, assemblies . . . and a rabble of such-like amusements, carry them out of all domestic duty and usefulness into infinite riot and expense'. See *Correspondence*, ed. A. Barbauld, London, 1806, VI, 25.

41 *Weekly Journal*, 18 April 1724.
42 Addison, *Spectator* 8.
43 Wilson, *Memoirs*, II, p. 616.
44 *Lady's Magazine*, February 1773.
45 Wilson, *Memoirs*, II, p. 616.
46 Lady Mary Wortley Montagu wrote that the Venetian custom of going about in masks led to 'a universal liberty that is certainly one of the greatest *agremens* in life'. She likewise believed that the amorous freedom of Turkish women was due to the 'perpetual masquerade' of the veil. See Robert Halsband, *The Life of Lady Mary Wortley Montagu*, Oxford, Clarendon Press, 1956, pp. 71 and 185. For Fanny Burney's description of a 1770 masquerade, see *The Early Diary of Frances Burney 1768–1778*, ed. A. R. Ellis, London, 1889, I, pp. 64–5. Boaden describes Inchbald's early love of 'frolics' in the *Memoirs*, I, pp. 140–1. Inchbald herself spoke nostalgically of masquerades and other 'exploded fashions' in her preface to Cowley's *Belle's Stratagem* in the *British Theatre* series, London, 1808, XIX, pp. 4–5.
47 Henry Fielding, *The Female Husband*, London, 1746, reprinted in *The Female Husband and Other Writings*, ed. Claude E. Jones, Liverpool, Liverpool University Press, 1960. On the historical and rhetorical dimensions of Fielding's pamphlet, see my essay, 'Matters Not Fit to be Mentioned: Fielding's *The Female Husband*, *ELH*, 49, 1982, pp. 602–22.
48 See Randolph Trumbach, 'London's Sodomites: Homosexual Behavior and Western Culture in the Eighteenth Century', *Journal of Social History*, II, 1977, pp. 1–33. On the eighteenth-century molly club, see Alan Bray, *Homosexuality in Renaissance England*, London, Gay Men's Press, 1982, pp. 81-114.
49 Boaden, *Memoirs of Mrs. Inchbald*, I, p. 140.
50 *Weekly Journal*, 18 April 1724.
51 Tobias Smollett, *The Adventures of Peregrine Pickle*, ed. James L. Clifford, rev. Paul-Gabriel Boucé, Oxford, Oxford University Press, 1983, pp. 244–5.
52 John Cleland, *Memoirs of a Woman of Pleasure*, ed. Peter Sabor, Oxford, Oxford University Press, 1985, pp. 154–6. On Cleland's own rumoured homosexuality, see Sabor's introduction, p. xiii.
53 On the concept of the 'backstage' area, see Erving Goffman, *The Presentation of Self in Everyday Life*, Garden City, N.Y., Anchor Books, 1959, pp. 112–20.
54 Trumbach discusses the emergence of sexual subcultures in eighteenth-century London in 'London's Sodomites', p. 23. See also Lawrence Stone's comments on the 'relaxed' nature of sexual attitudes in mid-eighteenth-century London in *The Family, Sex and Marriage in England 1500–1800*, New York, Harper & Row, 1977, pp. 332–5. One may dispute, of course, the extent of this tolerance; the punishments for sodomy become progressively harsher in England over the course of the century. Yet the intensifying official attack on homosexuality also suggests its growing prominence as a subcultural phenomenon.
55 On the role of the masquerade topos in eighteenth-century popular culture, see my recent essay 'The Carnivalization of Eighteenth-Century English Narrative', *PMLA*, 99, 1984, pp. 903–16.

56 John Richetti, *Popular Fiction Before Richardson: Narrative Patterns 1700–1739*, Oxford, Clarendon Press, 1969, p. 59.
57 *Gentleman's Magazine*, December 1754.
58 *The Masquerade: or, The Devil's Nursery*, Dublin, 1732.
59 Jean Starobinski, *The Invention of Liberty*, trans. Bernard C. Swift, Geneva, Albert Skira, 1964.
60 See *The History of Sexuality: An Introduction*, trans. Robert Hurley, New York, Pantheon, 1978, for Foucault's most influential statement on the post-Enlightenment proliferation of 'discourses' on sexuality. To be sure, Foucault is sometimes contradictory on the subject of whether the new descriptions of sexuality entailed new practices: in the 'Preface to Transgression' in *Language, Counter-Memory, Practice: Selected Essays and Interviews*, ed. and trans. Donald F. Bouchard, Ithaca, Cornell University Press, 1977, Foucault denies that the eighteenth century proffered 'any new content for our age-old acts' (p. 30). However, in a posthumously published interview, Foucault speaks of the modern 'eroticization of the body' as a concrete expansion of the 'possibilities of pleasure'. See Bob Gallagher and Alexander Wilson, 'Michel Foucault – An Interview: Sex, Power, and the Politics of Identity', *The Advocate*, 7 August 1984, p. 27.
61 Christopher Pitt, 'On the Masquerades', lines 51–5.

7

Vulnerability and the age of female consent: legal innovation and its effect on prosecutions for rape in eighteenth-century London[1]

ANTONY E. SIMPSON

The law of rape, as this developed in eighteenth-century England, did not then (and has not since) attract much attention from social and legal historians. This is despite the fact that it was the legal interpretations of this place and time which determined the enduring substance of the law in this area, as this applies in Anglo-American jurisdictions.

Even those few historical accounts which address this crime have downplayed the revolutionary legal changes which occurred in the eighteenth century. Susan Edwards, for example, begins her study of the development of the rape law in 1800 on the assumption that, since scarcely any legislation strictly relevant to the prosecution of rape had been enacted in the preceding three centuries, this law had not changed during this time.[2] The only study of this offence I have encountered which directly addresses Anglo-American society in the eighteenth century is not well-informed about the law in this area.[3]

In a sense, Edwards' position is correct – but it is also misleading: there *was* no legislation affecting rape enacted in the eighteenth century. However, this does not mean that the rape law did not develop. The many and dramatic legal changes which undoubtedly occurred in this area of law in the eighteenth century were achieved through case-law, and not through statute. Varying interpretations of general legal standards greatly affecting the outcomes of rape prosecutions were applied in this period. These concerned the competency of witnesses, the level of force applied and resistance offered, and the precise intent of the aggressor.

However, the greatest difficulty in the prosecuting of rape came to lie in the existence of various, and competing, legal definitions as to what constituted the fact of carnal knowledge. Between the 1770s and the 1820s at least, these definitions generally became tougher, and therefore more favourable to the defence, and the fact of carnal knowledge harder to prove in court.

It would, however, be wrong to characterise this period as one in which the emergence of uniformly tighter standards of legal proof became the major impediment to prosecutions of this nature. The fact was that confusion rather than toughness came to characterise the law of rape in England in this period. The major problem faced by the victim in initiating a prosecution was that she would have little idea of which particular definition of carnal knowledge was to be applied in her case.[4]

Although all legal developments in this area occurred through case-law, the most dramatic of them had its origin in statute. As is shown below, it was a combination of careless legislation and conservative and poorly thought-out application of it, which together brought about the effective reduction of the age of female consent from twelve years to ten.

Rape, defined as the unlawful carnal knowledge of a woman by force and against her will, was traditionally a capital crime from early Anglo-Saxon times.[5] Under the Normans, this punishment was 'mitigated' to castration and loss of the eyes and, two centuries later, the offence was reduced to the status of misdemeanour by the First Statute of Westminster.[6] This legal innovation was apparently not notably successful, 'this lenity being productive of the most terrible consequences',[7] and some ten years later, the crime was redefined as a capital felony by the Second Statute of Westminster.[8]

This premodern legislation cannot necessarily be associated with a greater concern for the crime of rape and its punishment: it has been shown that not one prosecution was carried out under the First Statute during the first forty-five years of its existence.[9] The earlier penalty of castration and blinding may well also have been an empty threat. It was not taken very seriously by at least one thirteenth-century judge who habitually joked about its theoretical severity when entertaining his friends.[10]

Between the thirteenth century and the commencement of Victoria's reign, some statutory modification of the law of rape did occur. However, the principles of the two Statutes of Westminster were preserved intact throughout this period, even though they were fundamentally confused and created a legacy of difficulty which was not satisfactorily dealt with until well into the Victorian period.

The First Statute quite clearly made it an offence to have carnal knowledge of 'any wife or maiden of full age' without her consent, or 'any maiden within age' whether with or without consent. No ambiguity existed within this piece of legislation as to what constituted the age of consent: it was 'agreed on all hands to be twelve' and corresponded to the minimum age at which a woman could legally be married.[11]

It was important to note that acceptance of twelve as the age in point was not arbitrary, nor was it based on logic or consensus. Twelve was the stipulated age in canon law which, in this and other instances, strongly influenced common law, and was also supported in another source which in its turn had a profound effect on English ecclesiastical law – the Talmud.[12]

The Second Statute, which transformed a misdemeanour into a felony, appears to have been a faulty item of legislation in that it ignored the issue of sexual acts involving children below the age of discretion, where the question of consent did not apply.[13] As the Second Statute was considered as amending rather than repealing the earlier, the legal situation remained that the violation of a girl below the age of twelve continued to be classed as a misdemeanour, if achieved with her consent. If the act took place without her consent, it became a capital offence under the Second Statute, as in cases where victims were of discretionary age. The apparent shortcomings of this statute are more understandable if it is accepted that its primary objective was the punishment, not of rapists but of those convicted of abduction – an offence which included marrying a minor without her parents' consent. This fact accounts for the focus of the Act on females of marriageable age (that is to say, of twelve years and over) and its seeming lack of concern for violation of those below this age.[14] Abduction became a capital offence in its own right in 1557 and was reduced to a single felony in 1820.[15]

Some of the problems occasioned by the faulty language of the 1285 Act surfaced in a court case heard before the the Court of Queen's Bench in 1571, when one W. D. was indicted for the rape of a seven-year old. Although there was little doubt as to the fact of the matter, this gentleman was acquitted owing to the chance of having been indicted under the wrong statute: he was charged under the 1285 Act, which required evidence of force, regardless of the age of his victim. His acquittal presumably reflected his having achieved his goal through persuasion rather than violence.[16]

The error committed by the court was simply in charging W. D. with an inappropriate offence. If he had been charged under the First Statute of Westminster he would, all other things being equal, have been convicted. However, it appears to have been the defects in the law, rather than in this particular circumstance of its inefficient administration, which attracted attention at the time. The realisation brought about by this case, that a man in W. D.'s situation could only be successfully prosecuted for a misdemeanour, carrying a maximum penalty of two years' imprisonment plus a fine, was a direct influence on an Act passed five years later and specifically intended to protect female children from sexual abuse.[17]

There is a possibility that a contributing factor in W. D.'s aquittal was a belief that rape of a child below nine was impossible, and therefore no offence in law.[18] If this is so, the problem was subsequently resolved as this argument was never accepted in the Old Bailey at any point in the eighteenth century. I have not found any evidence of it ever being offered, but John H. Langbein cites a 1678 Old Bailey case in which it was used by the jury, against the direction of the judge, to justify the acquittal of Stephen Arrowsmith, accused of raping an eight-year-old.[19]

The first effect of the 1576 Act was to reinforce the strength of the punishment for rape by disqualifying those convicted of this crime, either as principals or accessories to the fact (later known as principals in the second degree) from claiming benefit of clergy, and thereby becoming liable to conviction for a 'single', or non-capital, felony only.[20] However, the second and more important consequence was to change the violation of female children from a misdemeanour into a capital felony. In doing so, it took the significant step of redefining the age at which consent became an issue in cases of felony from twelve to ten.

There are a number of points of interest about this item of legislation. In the first place, it did not incorporate this type of sexual abuse within the law of rape, but actually created a new legal offence: unlawful and carnal knowledge of children. This division of the rape law into two separate and distinct categories, depending on the age of the victim and the need to prove force, persisted in nineteenth-century legislation.[21]

In and of itself, this innovation is perhaps little more than an historical curiosity. However, this separation of the law protecting those defined as adults and children asumes rather more significance when the effect of the 1576 law in isolating a group of children in a particular age-group is considered.

The principal contribution of the Elizabethan statute was to lower the effective age of consent to ten. In cases of violation, or attempted violation, of girls below this age, the question of consent therefore did not arise. This redefinition of the age of consent was an important development: the First Statute of Westminster, it will be remembered, stated this age to be twelve and, in doing so, had the backing of common law which held this to be the recognised age at which girls could exercise theoretical discretion in decisions to marry or to engage in sexual activity.

Again, the 1576 statute must be seen as amending, rather than replacing, the earlier legislation. Violation of girls under age of ten, regardless of the issue of consent, became a capital felony, but only the First Statute continued to provide protection for female children between the ages of ten and twelve. Carnal knowledge of girls in this age-group, if obtained with their consent, continued to be a misdemeanour.

The Elizabethan statute can be seen as the last significant piece of legislation on this topic until the late nineteenth century. Other legislation was enacted, but merely reiterated and codified principles already established.[22] In fact, misdemeanour prosecutions under the First Statute were something of a dead letter in the eighteenth century and beyond, and charges of this kind were almost never brought. In all the records I have examined,[23] there is only one case of such a prosecution being instituted: John Osborne was tried for raping Susanna Talbot, a girl under ten, and 'having carnal knowledge of her knowing her to be under twelve'.

Although he had confessed to the fact and appeared to have infected the girl with venereal disease, he was acquitted owing to the failure of the prosecution to supply acceptable proof of the child's date of birth.[24] The only other similar prosecution I have traced occurred in 1840, under the Victorian statute. In this, a man was convicted of assaulting a girl between the ages of ten and twelve with intent to rape her, even though she was a consenting party.

The Twelve Judges overturned the verdict, not because the legal principle involved had been interpreted incorrectly, but because the form of the indictment should not have used the term 'assault'. The charge should have been 'attempting to commit a statutable offence'.[25]

To all intents and purposes, the common-law notion that the age of consent for a girl was twelve was displaced by the 1576 enactment which placed the age of sexual discretion two years below that which a girl could legally marry.

This doctrine persisted throughout much of the nineteenth century. The age of consent was raised to thirteen in 1875, and to sixteen by the Criminal Law Amendment Act ten years later.[26] The 1576 statute had compounded the obscurity of the law by reinforcing the legal coexistence of *two* separate ages of consent. In doing so, it had created a complicated, but by no means impenetrable, legal situation which was for some reason never properly appreciated by jurists at any point in the period.

There has been much published discussion of the factors surrounding the raising of the age of consent in the Victorian period.[27] However, no attention has hitherto been paid to the change in this age which occurred in the previous century.[28]

By accepting without reservation the changes embodied in the Elizabethan statute, and by ignoring the clear legal fact that carnal knowledge of a girl between the ages of ten and twelve was at least an indictable misdemeanour, the courts effectively evaded a statutory obligation and imposed their own definition of ten as the age of female consent. This had an unsound basis in statute and in common law. The dramatic nature of this legal innovation is underscored by the fact that, throughout the period of study, no doubt whatsoever existed as to the age of *male* discretion. It was then, and is now, clearly understood to be fourteen.

Failure of judges and attorneys to appreciate the complexity of the law in this field appears to have been almost universal. The following speech made by a prosecution attorney to a jury, and left uncorrected by the judge, is a fair statement of how the law on this point was understood at the time. The fact that it was incorrect reflects the likelihood that this area of the law had never attracted sophisticated analysis by jurists: '[T]he age of consent is extended by an Act no farther than the age of ten – this unfortunate object is eleven, one year beyond the age in the Act; therefore the question of consent will be material for you to consider in the present case'.[29]

To all intents and purposes, then, the eighteenth and early nineteenth century legal systems accepted the revision of the common law implicit in the 1576 Act. A few legal authorities of the period appeared to entertain doubts about the ability of the Elizabethan statute to affect the common-law age of consent in this way. Hale felt that carnal knowledge of a girl between the ages of ten and twelve constituted rape no matter what the circumstances, and cited as his authority the fact that it was the First Statute of Westminster and that alone which specifically referred to this age-group. Since this statute placed the age of discretion at twelve, he argued, subsequent legislation, which did not really address this particular problem, must be considered to follow this statute on this point.[30]

Blackstone's view was less assured. Whilst accepting the authority of Hale's position, he noted that, logic apart, 'the law has in general been held only to extend to infants under *ten*'.[31] All other authorities, from at least the mid-eighteenth century on, appear to have followed Blackstone in accepting the innovation of the 1576 statute in effectively lowering the age of female consent with little or no qualification.

In criminal courts in London and in the provinces, this position was accepted without reservation. In no case, in the Old Bailey at least, was the ten-year rule challenged, and in only one instance (see above) was there acceptance of the fact that what would now be called statutory rape of a child between ten and twelve was, at the very least, an indictable misdemeanour. As Table 1 shows, rape prosecutions were associated with a high rate of acquittal throughout the period.[32] Failure to charge defendants with a misdemeanour of which they could be convicted, rather than with a felony of which they usually could not, must have greatly damaged the chances of the prosecution in those cases in which the victim was between ten and twelve.

Why then did judges, prosecutors and their attorneys fail to take advantage of a law which permitted a defendant charged with raping a child between ten and twelve to be convicted without evidence regarding victim consent, or lack of it, being introduced? The answer probably lies in a combination of ignorance and indifference. Jurists may simply have been unaware of the provisions of the law regarding the protection of victims in the ten-to-twelve age-group. This area of the law was not well covered in legal texts of the time and, when it was, the analysis included was often misleading and obscure. In their avoidance of definitive statements on this point, these texts helped to perpetuate flawed conceptions of the law of rape.

The haphazard manner in which the law was interpreted and applied suggests a confused, rather than a purposive, approach to the prosecution of this type of offence, but it was one which placed concern for the defendant over concern for the victim. This was apparent in all aspects of this field of law, and it is just not true that 'Whilst the statutory provisions relating to rape have evolved to protect women, procedural rules have evolved with the protection of the (male) defendant in mind'.[33]

Interpretations of statute law and legal rules alike reflected a continued and growing concern for malicious rape prosecutions. This concern of course reflected a particular view of sexuality and the relations between the sexes. However, as will be shown, it was encouraged by a cumbersome legal inheritance and by the position occupied by the criminal courts in the settlement of disputes.

A serious legal impediment to the successful prosecution of accused rapists was purely historical in origin and concerned the fact that these defendants could not generally be tried on multiple charges. A court could

Table 1 Prosecutions for rape in the Old Bailey, 1730–1830

1 Years	2 Rape prosecutions	3 Guilty (No.)	4 Guilty (%)	5 No. Executed	6 % of guilty executed	7 Victims under 10	8 % of total	9 Guilty no.	10 Guilty (%)
1730–34	12	2	17	1	50	4	33	1	25
1735–39	20	7	35	6	86	4	24	0	0
1740–44	12	2	17	2	100	6	50	0	0
1745–49	15	3	20	0	0	4	27	1	25
1750–54	18	1	6	0	0	8	44	1	13
1755–59	12	0	0	0	0	4	33	0	0
1760–64	8	3	38	0	0	2	25	0	0
1765–69	15	4	27	3	75	6	40	1	17
1770–74	28	5	18	1	20	2	7	0	0
1775–79	24	3	13	3	100	5	21	1	20
1780–84	8	1	13	0	0	0	0	0	0
1785–89	13	0	0	0	0	2	15	0	0
1790–94	10	2	20	1	50	1	10	1	100
1795–99	8	3	38	4	100	1	13	1	100
1800–04	4	1	25	1	100	2	50	1	50
1805–09	13	3	23	2	67	2	15	0	0
1810–14	14	1	7	0	0	0	0	0	0
1815–19	13	3	23	2	67	1	8	1	100
1820–24	14	2	14	0	0	0	0	0	0
1825–29	24	5	21	2	40	3	60	1	33
1830	9	0	0	0	0	0	0	0	0
Total	294	51	17	28	55	57	19	10	18

Notes

Columns 1 to 4 present the numbers of capital prosecutions for rape in the periods designated, numbers of guilty verdicts, and conviction rates.

Columns 5 and 6 present the numbers executed in each period and the execution rates, as percentages of those found guilty of this crime.

Columns 7 to 10 present numbers of prosecutions in those cases where victims were under ten years of age, the percentaged these represent of all rape prosecutions, and the conviction rates in this category.

VULNERABILITY AND THE AGE OF FEMALE CONSENT

Table 2 Prosecutions for assault with intent to commit rape in the Old Bailey, 1740–1830, and in the City of London Quarter-Sessions, 1740–1830

1 Year	2 AICR prosecutions	3 Guilty No.	4 Guilty (%)
[1730–34]	0	0	0
[1735–39]	2	1	50
1740–44	2	0	0
1745–49	2	1	50
1750–54	4	3	75
1755–59	4	1	25
1760–64	6	1	17
1765–69	6	5	83
1770–74	4	2	50
1775–79	6	4	67
1780–84	1	0	0
1785–89	6	4	67
1790–94	2	1	50
1795–99	7	1	14
1800–04	6	2	33
1805–09	5	2	40
1810–14	4	0	0
1815–19	4	4	100
1820–24	3	2	67
1825–29	6	3	50
1830	1	1	100
Court totals:			
LOB	4	2	50
MOB	0	0	0
LQS	77	36	47
Grand Totals	81	38	47

Notes

Columns 1 to 4 present numbers of misdeameanour prosecutions for attempted rape in the courts studied, numbers of guilty verdicts, and conviction rates in each period designated.
Years marked in square brackets denote prosecutions in the Old Bailey only.

The abbreviations LOC, MOB and LQS refer to cases heard in the Old Bailey London side, the Old Bailey Middlesex side, and the City of London Quarter Sessions respectively.

Sources: Tables 1 and 2 are based on the records of the Old Bailey, between 1730 and 1830, and the City of London Quarter Sessions, between 1740 and 1830.
These records include:
The Old Bailey Proceedings, 1730 to 1830.
Corporation of London Sessions *Minute Books*, January 1740 to October 1767; December 1768 to January 1785. Corporation of London Record Office [hereafter CLRO] SM 107–34; 135–50.

Corporation of London Sessions Minute Books (Gaol Delivery, Oyer and Terminer), February 1785 to December 1830. CLRO SMG 1–11.
Corporation of London Sessions Minute Books (Peace), February 1785 to December 1830. CLRO SMP 1–9.
Data on execution rates have been drawn from contemporary newspaper accounts, and from the following work, which was based on court records destroyed by enemy action in the Second World War: Woolrych, Humphry W. *The History and Present Results of the Present Capital Punishments in England: To Which are Added, Full Tables of Convictions, Executions, Etc.*, London, Saunders and Benning, 1832.

try the rape defendant on either a felony or a misdemeanour charge, but not on both in the same trial. This position had its support in the rule that those accused of felonies, unlike those accused of treason or misdemeanours, had, in theory at least, *no* right to be defended by counsel. Trials for felonies and other types of indictable offence could not therefore be combined, as the rules under which they were tried were different.[34]

This impediment was not so severe in the early part of the period studied. It did not become embedded in the law until 1787.[35] However, the felony/misdemeanour rule was applied quite rigorously in the Old Bailey from the middle of the century on. No accused rapist was ever tried for both rape and its attempt at the same time in this court after the 1740s.[36]

As accused rapists could not be tried on multiple charges, because of these technical difficulties, victims, and the lawyers and magistrates who advised them, had to choose the offence to be taken to court. In terms of the problem involving victims in the ten-to-twelve age-group, prosecutors and grand juries may well have felt more comfortable in charging a man with a felony which was well-documented in the law, rather than with a misdemeanour which, in the eighteenth-century legal opinion, was rather obscure. The root of this problem therefore centred on the unusual legal relationship between the formal charges on which a person accused of sexual attack could be indicted and tried.

Under the rules of double jeopardy which prevailed at the time, a defendant acquitted on a capital charge *could* subsequently be tried for the same fact, if the subsequent charge was non-capital. Those acquitted of rape could be, and sometimes were, tried for the misdemeanour of assault with intent to commit rape. However, this was a rare phenomenon: of the 294 capital cases of this nature heard in the Old Bailey over the period studied, forty originated in the City of London. Only two of these forty cases resulted in convictions. Of the thirty-eight acquittals, only six were followed by trials for the related misdemeanour and only one resulted in a conviction.[37]

The apparent unwillingness of the authorities or the victims to pursue an unsuccessful capital prosecution with a lesser charge cannot rightfully be attributed to a lack of interest in seeing miscreants brought to their just deserts. The reason why so few acquitted rapists were subsequently tried on misdemeanour counts was that the crimes of rape and its attempt were so defined in law as to be mutually exclusive.

A successful prosecution for rape required that force, penetration and/or emission (the rules varied over the period studied) be proven. Successful prosecution of the attempt required that it be shown that the full fact of carnal knowledge had *not* been achieved. An unsuccessful rape prosecution in which a serious effort had been made to prove the full fact could not therefore be profitably followed by a misdemeanour trial for the attempt.[38]

There is no doubt that many misdemeanour prosecutions were undertaken when the crime was rape itself. This was recognised in newspaper accounts of the time which, as a matter of routine, referred to prosecutions for attempts as 'rapes'.[39] Many victims, and the magistrates to whom they brought their complaints, may well have preferred to press a charge which, not being capital, might not deter a jury from convicting. As a comparison of Tables 1 and 2 shows, the conviction rate for attempted rape was considerably higher than that for rape itself.

Given the above, one can understand why few unsuccessful rape prosecutions were followed by prosecutions for the misdemeanour. However, it is less easy to understand why capital acquittals were *never* followed by prosecutions on lesser charges under the First Statute of Westminster, in those cases where the victim was above ten, but under twelve. In such prosecutions, proof of lack of consent would, of course, have been unnecessary. Proof of carnal knowledge alone would have substantiated a misdemeanour conviction.

It should not be thought that rape cases involving children were a rarity in the London courts. Table 1 shows that about one-fifth of all cases of capital rape involved children below the age of ten. If it had been possible to tabulate the number below the age of twelve, it is certain that this proportion would have been very much higher. Furthermore, there is every indication that this proportion is an understatement of victims in this age-group: after about 1790, most reports of such cases in the *Old Bailey Proceedings* give no details of the offence, and often do not give even the name of the victim. It is likely that many cases after this date represented instances of child molestation, even though they were not reported as such.

This opinion is strengthened by the fact that if the numbers of rape prosecutions for the years 1730 through 1789 only are taken into account, the proportion of child victims rises to twenty-five per cent.

This tentative finding is further supported by the pattern of cases of assault with intent to commit rape heard in the City of London Quarter Sessions and reported in Table 2. Data on these were drawn from the Sessions *Minute-Books* which, unlike the *Old Bailey Proceedings*, usually do show whether or not the victim was under ten. Of the entire seventy-seven cases of this nature heard in this court, thirty-four of the victims – almost half – were under ten. Child molestation must be accepted as an important characteristic of rape cases in this century.

This fact is all the more interesting in that child abuse seems to have been primarily a Metropolitan phenomenon. Most of the available statistics of rape prosecutions undertaken on the provincial circuits in the period do not include cases of child abuse – either because these rarely occurred, or perhaps because they were incorporated in tabulations of other cases of rape.

Two of the nine circuit courts, Norfolk and the Western, however, did break their figures down according to whether the victim was above or below the age of ten. In the former, two capital convictions out of sixteen (thirteen per cent) involved children, and in the latter, four out of twenty-eight (fourteen per cent).[40] These figures suggest that, unlike the Metropolis, rape cases in the provinces did not represent the consequences of the same apparent obsession with young children.

Certainly the 'defloration mania' of the English, or rather the residents of the Metropolis, during the eighteenth and nineteenth centuries has been well-publicised. Fanny Hill had her problems with the ill-favoured Mr. Crofts, who perceived at least a temporary cure for his impotence in the taking of her virginity.[41] The art of reconstituting lost maidenheads was well-known in London from at least the mid-seventeenth century.[42]

It has been suggested that interest in paedophilic sex accelerated during the nineteenth century and reached its peak just before 1900.[43] The prevalence of brothels catering to customers with this taste is well-documented throughout the period and represented a familiar aspect of the business of prostitution.[44]

Explanations for the increasing popularity of this perversion have not so far been forthcoming, and no-one has yet improved upon Iwan Bloch's essentially Anglophobic attribution of English interest in the spoliation of innocence to innate racial beastliness.[45]

VULNERABILITY AND THE AGE OF FEMALE CONSENT

A more likely, if not more interesting, explanation concerns the close relationship between the prevalence of venereal disease and the popularity of sex with children. A 'defloration mania' there was. Its peculiar existence in the Metropolis is, however, better explained by the great prevalence of VD in Britain's capital than by the secret desires of its inhabitants. A possible key to the riddle is contained in a comment made by a London newspaper following the indictment of a clergyman for molesting a number of young children:

> Those slayers of the human race, called *Quacks*, and other *infernal wretches*, propagate a notion among the ignorant, that if such a horrid act is committed on a child, that the person indisposed will entirely be freed from the disorder. And the writer is certain, from such *inhuman advice*, that many persons of *weak understandings* have been tempted to a crime which their nature shudders at; so that there is every reason to think, that many unfortunate people have committed so melancholy an act, who, in other respects, were honest, industrious people and good members of society.[46]

It should be noted that the above statement was not issued by the defence, but by an independent source, and the culprit in question, the Reverend Benjamin Russen, was not of the urban low life, but was a man of education and substance, and a minister of the Established Church.

Moreover, the belief appears in context other than the court-room to suggest that abuse of children in this way was common. The report of the Lock Hospital for the six-year period ending in 1746 noted that more than fifty children had been treated for VD in this period. This situation was ascribed to: 'a received opinion among the lower people, both male and female, that if they have commerce with a sound person, they will get rid of the disease.'[47]

The belief was a prevalent one and it is, therefore, not surprising that it was commonly presented as a defence by those accused of attacking little girls and who had been caught dead to rights.[48] What is perhaps surprising is that, throughout the century studied, the fact of this belief was accepted by the courts and by medical experts, not in extenuation of the crime, but as a persuasive means of comprehending it. In the Moody case, an apothecary giving evidence said 'he was sorry to declare he had seen many instance(s), in his practice, of children being injured from the age of four years by men who foolishly and wickedly thought by that means to remedy themselves'.

This popular notion was referred to as a genuine, if mistaken, belief by judges in the cases of Davenport and Scott. Adherence to it was widespread throughout the Georgian period at least. Its prevalence was used to explain the actions of James Booty, aged fifteen, who raped five or six children, all under seven, before his eventual conviction and execution at Tyburn in

1722.[49] The belief was alive and well in the reign of George IV and the judge in the Beauchamp case, heard in 1826, referred to it as 'an absurd but mischievous error that prevails amongst ignorant persons'.

Furthermore, the belief was reflected in the circumstances surrounding the cases reaching the courts. Of the fifty-seven rapes of little girls identified as having reached the Old Bailey, fifty-five of them include sufficient data to enable a determination to be made on whether the transmission of venereal disease was a factor in the proof or discovery of the crime. In most cases, thirty-two out of the fifty-five, this was so, and the typical scenario was of the rape of a child being discovered by her mother, who observed the symptoms of disease in her daughter. The prevalence of desperate men willing to act upon this traditional belief in how their infection might be cured was phenomenal.

There are, of course, many difficulties inherent in the use of prosecution rates for crimes of this nature as indicators of the incidence of the proscribed behaviour itself. This is certainly true today, with levels of unreported rapes being variously estimated at between double and one hundred times the reported rate.[50] Reliable estimates of the incidence of child rape are at least as hard to come by, although there are suggestions that this is a crime even less likely to be reported than the rape of an adult woman.[51] Official statistics in the setting studied here are even less valuable as indicators of criminal activity of this sort, and some of the reasons for this were doubtless similar to those in operation today.

In eighteenth-century London, cases of child molestation resulting in infection in the victims may well have been more likely to reach the courts because they were less easily hidden from parents, neighbours and the authorities. One can assume that then, as now, this kind of crime only reaches the light of day when parents and other responsible adults are compelled to recognise it. This scenario might help to explain the apparently differential rates of child rape in London and the provinces: outside of London, where VD appears to have been less prevalent, such cases were perhaps less likely to reach the attention of the authorities. This would produce lower *recorded* rates of child rape outside London, but might disguise actual rates not very different from those in the Metropolis.

Such reasoning undoubtedly saps the strength of the thesis presented here. However, if we can accept the existence of tremendously varied estimates of this crime in the late twentieth century, we can surely not expect more clarity from the eighteenth century in this regard. This crime is furtive and secretive, in its perpetration and in its reception by friends and relatives of the victim. Discussion of a possibly higher unreported rate in the provinces is interesting, but ultimately barren.

The fact remains that in those cases of rape and its attempt which reached the London criminal courts, children under ten were shown to be prime targets of the rapist's attentions. This finding is dramatic when it is considered that most victims were of modest social class, whose families had to assume the difficulties and costs of these prosecutions. This circumstance must reflect an even higher proportion of crimes discovered and *not* brought to the attention of the authorities than is encountered in the present day. Prosecution rates should here be regarded as *indicators*, but not *measures*, of a very prevalent urban crime.

It cannot be assumed that defendants who used the VD myth in their defences necessarily believed in it. Some may have used it in a deliberate effort to make their actions understandable to those in judgement over them. Others may have used it to make their actions comprehensible to themselves. Nonetheless, the myth could not have been invoked in this way unless it was understood at some level by society at large. Acceptance of this conclusion is sufficient to support a view of the myth as a powerful influence on sexual expression in Georgian London.

We should not denigrate the strength of folk beliefs which then served in place of an informed body of medical knowledge. Scientific notions about the nature of physiology and disease were then rudimentary and, as P.-G. Boucé has shown, often barely distinguishable from fantasy and myth.[52] Old wives' tales relating to the physiology of sex persisted long after the eighteenth century, and many authors have referred to the famous debate conducted within the columns of the *British Medical Journal* in 1878 over whether the touch of a menstruating woman could spoil a ham.[53]

We should be especially careful of discounting the power and persistence of the particular belief at issue here. There is ample evidence that a number of subcultures in the United States in the twentieth century have held strongly to some version of the view that sexual congress, forced or otherwise, with an immature female constitutes the only sure cure for a man with VD.[54] Such views represent but one instance of the pervasive folkloric theme of the curing of disease by its transference through touch.

In any case, one would not have to subscribe to the belief to follow its dictates. Men fortunate enough to be uninfected would wish to stay that way, and the younger one's sexual partner, the less the chances of infection. This was, of course, realised at the time. The anonymous author of *Satan's Harvest Home* remarked on the great numbers of child prostitutes ('Where the Devil do all these B—s come from?') and answered his own question by pointing up the desire of 'gallants' to avoid disease.[55]

The effects of the belief and of the prevalence of disease cannot therefore be trivialised. It reflected the fact that venereal disease was prevalent in London, although perhaps not in the rest of the country, and was incurable. Unfortunately, there are no data indicating how widespread VD was in Britain outside London.[56] However, almost all the accounts I have come across seem to portray the problem as a London phenomenon, and those that do describe its existence outside the capital refer to it only in garrison towns.[57]

It is significant in this context that in the nineteenth century, when VD began to be considered as a *national* problem, interest in child brothels seems to have accelerated.[58] It is also revealing that no interest was taken in regulating prostitution until attention was drawn in the mid-nineteenth century to the prevalence of infection among soldiers in military bases in the provinces.[59] William Acton's discussion of prostitution, written in 1869 and the most comprehensive treatment of the subject in its day, does pay attention to the problem of spreading VD. However, all the statistical data and discussion of this particular aspect of it that he includes make reference only to the Metropolis and to the military.[60]

The strong implication of the available evidence is that venereal infection was not a problem in the civilian population outside London before the middle of the nineteenth century. If this is so, then the differential between the proportions of rape cases involving children in London and in the provinces is explained as a combined function of the power of folk-belief and the exigencies of the London situation.

The primitive belief in this supposed cure for venereal infection was one born and sustained no doubt by desperation in a world in which its onset presaged a life of discomfort and misery,[61] and a succession of alternative cures which only served to further undermine the health, and possibly shorten the life.[62]

One could, of course, argue that this belief acted as a convenient rationale for those who sought children solely for their own perverted gratification. It is now believed that paedophilia is associated with male feelings of inadequacy, shame and guilt,[63] and it has been suggested that such feelings existed in abundance in the eighteenth and early nineteenth centuries.[64] However, if this were so, one would not expect the crime to have been generally limited to the confines of the Metropolis.

London was the venereal, as well as the administrative, capital of the country. The unusual prevalence of child molestation in this city reflected, to a large extent, the distracted efforts of infected males to cure themselves at someone else's expense.

Reactions of the populace to crimes of this nature were typically violent. In Westminster in 1826, Denis Doolan was mobbed on leaving the court after being convicted of the attempted rape of two sisters, aged four and six. 'The officers . . . had some difficulty in saving him from being torn to pieces by the women'.[65] Sixty years earlier, Dugal Paterson, in the pillory for abusing his own daughter, was given a similarly rough time. At the end of the ordeal, he was dragged from the coach brought to carry him away, and hauled to a pump where the crowd 'pumped him till he was almost dead'.[66]

In a world in which humanitarian attitudes toward children were increasingly appreciated, this widespread abuse of little girls provided an eloquent statement of continued male willingness to take advantage of the vulnerability of childhood.

I have argued elsewhere that relations between men and women, at least those of the working classes, in the eighteenth-century urban setting, were to a great extent shaped by structural forces. The population shift to the Metropolis was a consequence of the enclosure movement and was, for those so affected, closely associated with downward social mobility. One result of this, I aver, was the emergence of a unique, urban working-class male culture, which served to compensate its adherents for loss of status brought about by their move to the city.

The principal characteristic of this culture was a strong 'masculinity ethos', which celebrated the manly attributes of independence, toughness and aggression.[67] Such an ethos undoubtedly encouraged male denigration of women and of those men who did not, or could not, live up to this class-based definition of what constituted the proper style for a man. However, the ethos certainly did not countenance sexual molestation of children. Child abuse went quite against values which extolled patriarchy and the benevolent application of power and strength.

The prevalence of child molestation in this and later periods did not therefore flourish in a permissive social environment. Its root cause, as noted, lay in the widespread nature of venereal disease, and folk-belief as to its cure. However, male willingness to act on such belief, if not condoned by popular values, was encouraged by ease of access to child victims.

There is no evidence that those rape victims who brought their cases to court, and who were usually of the lower social strata, were typically abused by those far above them on a social scale.[68] On the other hand, women and girls domestic service can be shown to have been especially vulnerable in this way.

As the results of an analysis of all 294 cases of rape and eighty-one attempted rape heard in the Old Bailey and the City of London Quarter Sessions over a one-hundred-year period show, routine victimisation of female servants in this way was a matter of fact. In ninety-one of the 372 cases, it is possible to determine the occupation of the victim, and in sixty-one instances (sixty-seven per cent of those about whom this information is available) the victim was a domestic servant. This finding must be accepted with some reservation. L. L. Robson's analysis of women convicts transported to Australia in the years following 1787 has shown that the designation 'domestic servant' was applied quite loosely, and was frequently assumed by women who were not employed in this line of work when arrested, if they ever had been.[69] It could well have been so applied to women who brought cases to court.

However, when the circumstances of these cases of sexual assault are examined, it becomes clear that women and girls in service of some description constituted the bulk of the victims. Of 189 valid cases, thirty-five involved allegations of abuse of servants by masters, eight by workmates, and thirty-five by other members of the household, excluding members of victims' own immediate families. Together these accounted for seventy-eight, or forty-one per cent, of the 189 cases.

Vulnerability of female servants, many of whom were children, to sexual abuse in the work-place was therefore an established fact. Women in this position were under attack in more ways than one. The small size of households in London at this time meant that the numbers of servants in them was generally restricted to one or two.[70] Female domestics were therefore denied the peer support and protective structures available to their contemporaries in the large aristocratic households which were then the rule in many other parts of the country.

They were vulnerable because of their situation and because of their sex. Sexual exploitation of them by their masters was taken for granted.[71] In rural areas the strong possibility of victimisation of this kind was recognized as an occupational hazard for young servant-girls bound for the capital.[72]

They were also possibly subject to other forms of physical abuse, and were largely excluded from the family life of the households in which they worked because of a widespread suspicion of servants as harbingers of crime.[73] The powerlessness and vulnerability of the female servant was widely recognised. Moll Flanders, who understood such things from personal experience, knew exactly what she was doing when she decided to remove her maid from London before discharging her.[74] The unemployed female domestic in

London was commonly thought to be the main contributor to the ranks of prostitution.

Children, including child domestics, must have been especially vulnerable to attack within the households in which they lived and worked. This susceptibility extended to attack from within the victim's own family. Little protection against incestuous attack was given by the courts.

Sexuality within the family, for example, did not attract much attention from the law. Incest was not uncommon in cases of rape and attempted rape heard in the Old Bailey.[75] Incest was not, however, an offence in English criminal law at this time. It was, in fact, not made so until 1908, and ten years of serious lobbying were required to get a prohibition against it on the statute books.

Concern for it, when it came, has been variously attributed to intensified interest in the family as a social unit,[76] and to the policy of social purity organisations to use the enactment of an anti-incest statute primarily as a political statement of their own strength.[77]

It is generally thought that eighteenth-century society saw the progressive development of affective relations within the family, and of more protective attitudes towards children.[78] If so, this development was insufficient to counter the selfish needs of many men. Some understanding has been obtained here of the motivation of child molesters at this time, although it is less easy to see why developments within the criminal law were so obstructive of the prosecution of this sort of behaviour.

However, the very functional explanation of child sexual abuse given here, although, one hopes, persuasive, does not perhaps tell the full story. Considerable differences in cultural values separate the eighteenth century from the nineteenth, when the 'defloration mania' reached its full bloom. A comparison between the pornography of the 1700s and that of the following century suggests that sexual obsessions of the later period included an unparalleled strain of cruelty.

Eighteenth-century pornography is characterised by its bawdiness and vulgarity.[79] There is nothing in this century which compares in pure nastiness to that Victorian underground classic, the *Experimental Lecture* of 'Colonel Spanker'. The macabre double-play in Spanker's name in the French translation of this work – the only edition I have been able to locate – is indicative of the anti-female violence which is the compelling focus of this narrative.[80]

However, any social factors acting to encourage men, or rather men of a certain stamp, to exploit and abuse the powerless were undoubtedly supported into the nineteenth century by escalating fear of venereal disease and continuing popular belief as to the nature of its cure. Perverted practice was given as much justification as it could ever have been.

What is particularly interesting here is the failure of the criminal law to offer adequate protection to those eligible for victimisation in this scenario.

Developments in the eighteenth-century law of evidence tended, on the whole, towards greater judicial discretion concerning the age at which a witness could be accepted. The net effect of this was sometimes to allow the testimony of infants who, in an earlier period, would have been disqualified on the grounds of age alone. Nonetheless, there is a certain irony here: judges continued to exercise discretion over whether to admit the testimony of those below the age of twelve.[81]

An era which preserved this principle was also one which had effectively – through policy and not through law, as has been shown – lowered the age of consent to ten. Thus was created the anomalous position of a ten- or eleven-year old who was considered old enough to exercise discretion in sexual matters, but too young to marry and possibly too young to understand the meaning of a sworn oath. It is hard to consider this as a logical advance over an earlier age which at least considered the age of understanding in all matters to be one, and defined this as twelve.

Sexual abuse of children flourished in eighteenth-century London because of an unfortunate coincidence of female vulnerability and perceived male need. The failure of the courts of this time to preserve the ancient common-law rights of female children does not indicate much concern for childhood or its protection. This fact stands strongly against opinion which views this period as one in which childhood became defined as a status demanding care and protection.

Notes

1 Research for this study was supported by a grant from the Social Science Research Council, New York.
2 *Female Sexuality and the Law; A Study of Constructs of Female Sexuality as they Inform Statute and Legal Procedure*, Oxford, Martin Robertson, 1981.
3 Barbara S. Lindemann, '"To ravish and carnally know": Rape in eighteenth-century Massachusetts', *Signs: Journal of Women in Culture and Society*, X, 1984, pp. 63–82.
4 For a detailed analysis of the development of all aspects of the rape law, and the pattern of its prosecution in London between 1730 and 1830, see Simpson, *Masculinity and Control: The Prosecution of Sex Offences in Eighteenth-Century London*, Ph.D. dissertation, New York, New York University, 1984, pp. 114–311.

5   This and the following discussion of the law in pre-modern times is based on a number of standard historical sources, including Sir Edward Coke, *The Second Part of the Laws of England, Containing the Exposition of Many Ancient and Other Statutes*, London, 1797, 3 Vols, and Vol 1, pp. 180–1 Vol. 2, pp. 432–6; and Edward H. East, A *Treatise of the Pleas of the Crown*, London, J. Butterworth, 1803, 2 vols, Vol. 1, pp. 434–49.
6   3 Ed. I c. 13 (1275).
7   Sir William Blackstone, *Commentaries on the Laws of England*, Oxford, Clarendon Press, 1765–9, 4 Vols, Vol. 4, p. 212.
8   13 Ed.I c. 34 (1285).
9   Gilbert Geis, 'Lord Hale, witches and rape', *British Journal of Law and Society*, V, 1978, pp. 26–44.
10 J. M. Kaye, 'The making of English criminal law: (1) The beginnings – a general survey of criminal law and justice down to 1500', *Criminal Law Review*, IX, 1977, pp. 4–13.
11 East, A *Treatise of the Pleas of the Crown*, 2:434.
12 Gershon Melber, *Rape and Other Sexual Offences in the Hebrew Laws and in the English Law*, Unpublished L1.D dissertation, Jerusalem, Hebrew University, 1960, pp. iii–xii.
13 'It is provided, that if a man do ravish a woman, married maid, or other, where she did not consent neither before nor after, he shall have judgment of life and of member', East, A *Treatise of the Pleas of the Crown*, 2:435.
14 J. B. Post, 'Ravishment of women and the Statutes of Westminster', in J. H. Baker, ed. *Legal Records and the Historian. Papers Presented to the Cambridge History Conference, 7–10 July, 1975, and in Lincoln's Inn Old Hall on 3 July, 1974*, London, Royal Historical Society, 1978, pp. 150–60.
15 4 and 5 Philip and Mary, c.8, ss. 2 and 3, 1 Geo.IV, c.115; *The Times* 12 April 1826 and 15 May 1827; P. R. Glazebrook, 'The making of English criminal law: (3) The reign of Mary Tudor', *Criminal Law Review*, IX, 1977, pp. 582–97.
16 Mortimer Levine, 'A more than ordinary case of rape, 13 and 14 Elizabeth I', *American Journal of Legal History*, VII, 1963, pp. 159–64.
17 18 Eliz. I, c.7, 1576.
18 Levine, 'A More than Ordinary Case of Rape', p. 163.
19 The judge refused to accept their reasoning and their verdict and, on his further instruction, the jury returned a second verdict – this time of guilty. 'The criminal trial before the lawyers', *University of Chicago Law Review*, XLV, 1978, pp. 263–316, at p. 293.
20 Accessories continued to be liable to the same punishment as principals from this time on. But, as with other legal rules in the eighteenth century, this policy was not always followed. Two men convicted as accessories to a rape in 1773 were sentenced merely to be burnt in the hand and imprisoned for one year; R. v Lennard, Graves and Guy, Old Bailey, *Annual Register*, XVI, part 1:120.
21 The distinction was maintained in 9 Geo.IV, c.31, 1828, and 4 and 5 Vict., c.56, 1841.
22 This legislation includes 9 Geo.IV, c.31, 1828, and 1 Vict., c.85, 1837.
23 These include all sources documenting indictments and prosecutions for rape and its attempt heard in the Old Bailey between 1730 and 1830, and the City of

London Quarter Sessions between 1740 and 1830. See Tables 1 and 2.
24 *Old Bailey Proceedings*, (hereafter cited as *OBP*), sessions ending 12 December 1748 (Case No. 106).
25 See: R. v Martin, in: William Moody, *Crown Cases Reserved for Consideration; And Decided by the Judges of England. From the Year 1824, to the Year 1837*, London, Saunders and Benning, 1837–44, 2 Vols, 2:123–4.
26 See Fraser Harrison, *The Dark Angel; Aspects of Victorian Sexuality*, London, Sheldon Press, 1977, pp. 71–2 and 276.
27 For example, Ann Stafford's account of the campaigns waged by W. T. Stead and others in the 1880s to raise the age of consent to sixteen takes existing interpretations of this age as historically unproblematic; *The Age of Consent*, London, Hodder and Stoughton, 1964.
28 The outstanding historical discussion of this subject, despite its title, focuses upon social attitudes toward rape prosecutions, and ignores this and many other peculiarities in the development of the law; Edwards, *Female Sexuality and the Law*.
29 R. v Scott, *OBP* sessions beginning 14 September 1796 (469). Scott was convicted on the capital charge.
30 Sir Matthew Hale, *Historia Placitorum Coronae. The History of the Pleas of the Crown*, new ed. by Sollom Emlyn and George Wilson, London, T. Payne and others, 1800, 2 vols. 1:631.
31 Blackstone, *Commentaries*, 4:212.
32 The conviction rate for accused rapists in the Old Bailey between 1730 and 1830 was 17 per cent. For accused burglars and robbers, it was 56 and 25 per cent respectively; Simpson, *Masculinity*, pp. 842–8.
33 Edwards, *Female Sexuality and the Law*, p. 49.
34 This situation was remedied in 1836, when accused felons were granted the same rights as other accused persons by statute; 7 Will.IV & 1 Vict., c.85; *Annual Register*, LXXVIII, 1836, Part 1:162–67.
35 R. v Harmwood, Winchester Assizes, Spring 1787, in William O. Russell, *A Treatise on Crimes and Misdemeanours*, 3rd ed., by Charles S. Greaves, London, Saunders and Benning, 1843, 3 vols, 1:681.
36 John Thompson was the last person so tried. He was tried, and acquitted, of the rape, attempted rape, and murder of Mary Grayling, aged nine, *OBP* sessions beginning 15 January 1742 (21).
37 R. v Jenkins, *OBP* 20 September 1825 (1484); Corporation of London Sessions *Minute-Book [Peace]* November 1825.
38 James Griffith was acquitted of the attempt at Surrey Assizes in 1825, after the judge so directed the jury, 'the misdemeanour merging in the capital offence', in Russell, *A Treatise*, 1:681.
39 For example, at Kingston Assizes, William Fielder, who was obviously convicted of the misdemeanour, was sentenced to one year 'for ravishing his master's daughter'; *Morning Post*, 10 April 1777.
40 Statistics on prosecutions heard in the assizes during the late 1700s and early 1800s are included in: Great Britain, House of Commons, Select Committee on Criminal Laws, *Report. . .*, London, 1819.
41 John Cleland, *Fanny Hill; Memoirs of a Woman of Pleasure*, London, Granada, 1964 (orig. 1749), pp. 25–31.

42 Roger Thompson, *Unfit for Modest Ears; A Study of Pornographic, Obscene and Bawdy Works Written or Published in England in the Second Half of the Seventeenth Century*, London, Macmillan, 1979, p. 73.
43 Iwan Bloch, *Ethnological and Cultural Studies of the Sex Life in England. . .*, New York, Falstaff Press, 1934, pp. 139–44.
44 One brothel of this kind was described as being especially well-known and, in 1830, had been in existence for twenty-five years; Michael Ryan, *Prostitution in London, With a Comparative View of that of Paris and New York. . .*, London, John Bennett, 1839, p. 141.
45 He describes it with some glee as due to 'the general coarseness, brutality and grossness of the Englishman in his sexual expression'; *Ethnological and Cultural Studies*, p. 141.
46 *Morning Chronicle*, 1 August 1777.
47 Quoted by Edward J. Bristow, *Vice and Vigilance; Purity Movements in Britain Since 1700*, Dublin, Gill and Macmillan, 1977, p. 60. This statement raises the interesting possibility that young boys could be abused in this way by infected women. I have not encountered confirmation of this in any of the primary materials used in my own research. See, however Note 48.
48 R. v Moody, *London Evening-Post* 8–10 August 1780; R. v Davenport, OBP sessions beginning 17 February 1796 (191); R. v Scott, OBP sessions beginning 14 September 1796 (469); R. v Beauchamp, Westminster Quarter Sessions, *The Times* 30 October 1826.
49 *Lives of the Most Remarkable Criminals Who Have Been Condemned and Executed for Murder, Highway Robberies, Housebreaking, Street Robberies, Coining, or Other Offences; From the Year 1720 to the Year 1735. Collected from Original Papers and Authentic Memoirs*, London, Reeves and Turner, 1873, 2 Vols, 1:111–13. This fairly detailed account of this case which shows sympathy for the culprit. Young Booty is portrayed as a *naïf* motivated by desperation rather than malice. There are interesting, but inconclusive, hints that he may have been put in his predicament by an infected servant-girl acting in a deliberate fashion. See Note 47.
50 All these estimates 'share one trait: they are based on no evidence. They were pulled from the air or from the respondant's gut reaction'; Thomas W. McCahill, Linda C. Meyer, and Arthur M. Fischman, *The Aftermath of Rape*. Lexington, MA, Lexington Books, 1979, p. 83.
51 Reasons cited for this, over and above those cited to explain general reluctance to report rape, include the tendency of children to keep their victimisation secret, and the desire of parents to protect their child from further harassment, or to protect an offender who was a family member or a friend; Sedelle Katz and Mary Anne Mazur, *Understanding the Rape Victim; A Synthesis of Research Findings*, New York, John Wiley, 1979, especially pp. 45–7 and 185–91.
52 'Some Sexual Beliefs and Myths in Eighteenth-Century Britain', in Paul-Gabriel Boucé, ed., *Sexuality in Eighteenth-Century Britain*, Manchester, Manchester University Press, 1982, pp. 28–46.
53 See, for example, Harrison, *op. cit.*, p. 57.
54 See Wayland D. Hand, *Magical Medicine; The Folkloric Component of Medicine in the Folk Belief, Custom and Ritual of the Peoples of Europe and America*, Berkeley, University of California Press, 1980, pp. 18–19 and 309–10. For politicised

references during the immigration debates of this period to the prevalence of the belief among non-Anglo-Saxon groups, see Allan M. Brandt, *No Magic Bullet; A Social History of Venereal Disease in the United States Since 1880*, New York, Oxford University Press, 1985, pp. 20–21.

55 He admitted that in doing so they 'destroy, it is true, a great deal of Beauty by only browsing upon the Buds'; *Satan's Harvest Home: Or the Present State of Whorecraft, Adultery, Fornication, Procuring, Pimping, Sodomy, and the Game at Flatts, and Other SATANIC WORKS, Daily Propagated in this Good Protestant Kingdom*, London, 1749, pp. 1–2.

56 Lawrence Stone's discussion assumes it to have been a nation-wide problem, but all of the evidence he cites refers to the Metropolis; *The Family, Sex and Marriage in England, 1500–1800*, abridged ed., New York, Harper Colophon, 1979, pp. 340–81.

57 For example, *London Evening-Post* 25–28 September 1779 includes an allegation that one quarter of the troops stationed in a Kent town were infected. The only account I have found that discusses its prevalence among civilian propulations outside London refers to Scotland; Ebenezer Gilchrist, *An Account of a Very Infectious Distemper Prevailing in Many Places*, Edinburgh, John Balfour, 1770.

58 Edward Shorter suggests that venereal disease existed 'at the margins of society' until about 1850; *A History of Women's Bodies*, New York, Basic Books, 1982, p. 264.

59 Judith R. Walkowitz, *Prostitution and Victorian Society; Women, Class and the State*, Cambridge, Cambridge University Press, 1980; Paul McHugh, *Prostitution and Victorian Social Reform*, New York, St Martin's Press, 1980.

60 *Prostitution*, 2nd ed., Introduction by Peter Fryer, New York, Praeger, 1969 (orig. 1869), pp. 77–83.

61 Laurence Sterne provides a moving, and not at all self-pitying, personal account of what it was like to suffer from this sort of ailment in his *Journal to Eliza*, London, J. M. Dent, 1960 (orig. 1775).

62 Frédéric Buret, *Syphilis in the Middle Ages and in Modern Times*, translated by A. H. Ohmann-Dumesnil, Philadelphia, F. A. Davis, 1895; Walkowitz, *Prostitution*, pp. 52–65.

63 Anthony Storr, *Sexual Deviation*, Baltimore, Penguin, 1964, pp. 100–8.

64 The outstanding analysis in this area attempts to relate changes in child-rearing practices to changes in male perception of gender roles. See Gordon Rattray Taylor, *The Angel Makers; A Study in the Psychological Origins of Historical Change, 1750-1850*, Rev. ed., London, Secker and Warburg, 1973.

65 *The Times*, 14 December 1826.

66 *St. James's Chronicle; or, British Evening-Post* 3–5 April 1766.

67 This thesis is developed fully in Simpson, *Masculinity*.

68 Of the 141 cases of rape and attempted rape in the courts studied in which defendant occupation is given, fifteen were 'gentlemen', eighteen were domestic servants, and fifteen were other servants. The remainder pursued a variety of occupations of the lower and 'middling' classes.

69 *The Convict Settlers of Australia; An Enquiry into the Origin and Character of the Convicts Transported to New South Wales and Van Diemen's Land 1787–1852*, Melbourne, Melbourne University Press, 1965, pp. 74–85. Robson notes that

'Almost all female convicts were listed as domestic servants of one sort of another', p. 84.
70 D. V. Glass, 'Socio-economic status and occupations in the City of London at the end of the seventeenth century', in A. E. J. Hollaender and William Kellaway, eds., *Studies in London History Presented to Philip Edmund Jones*, London, Hodder and Stoughton, 1969, pp. 373–89, Richard Wall, 'The age at leaving home', *Journal of Family History*, III, 1978, pp. 181–202.
71 One contemporary view of the prevalence of this phenomenon was that: '(i)n no age, in no country, in no city, in the whole world, is this fashionable, but atrocious crime (be)come so notoriously common as among us'; *Morning Post*, 24 November 1777. The findings of A. L. Beier suggest that this was so in London a century and more earlier; 'Social problems in Elizabethan London', *Journal of Interdisciplinary History*, IX, 1978, pp. 203–21.
72 The following verse was traditionally addressed to young West Countrywomen about to make this journey: 'Now Hussey a Month's Wages or a Month's Warning; And Bed to your Master every Morning', *Satan's Harvest Home*, p. 4.
73 The increasing isolation and vulnerability of the domestic servant in eighteenth-century London, and the redefinition of this line of work as a female occupation, are documented in: J. Jean Hecht, *The Domestic Servant Class in Eighteenth Century England*, London, Routledge and Kegan Paul, 1956, and E. S. Turner, *What the Butler Saw; Two Hundred and Fifty Years of the Servant Problem*, London, Michael Joseph, 1962.
74 Daniel Defoe, *The Fortunes and Misfortunes of Moll Flanders*, New York, Airmont Publishing, 1969 (orig. 1722), p. 134.
75 Of the 189 cases in which the relationship between defendant and victim is given, ten involved sexual abuse by a member of the victim's own family. A further thirty-five involved abuse by a member of the victim's household.
76 Anthony S. Wohl, 'Sex and the single room: Incest among the Victorian working classes', in Anthony S. Wohl, ed., *The Victorian Family; Structure and Stresses*, New York, St Martin's Press, 1978, pp. 197–216.
77 Victor Bailey and Sheila Blackburn, 'The Punishment of Incest Act of 1908: A case study of law creation', *Criminal Law Review*, XI, 1979, pp. 708–18.
78 Philippe Ariès, *Centuries of Childhood; A Social History of Family Life*, translated by Robert Baldick, New York, Vintage Books, 1962, and Stone, *Family, Sex, and Marriage*.
79 A representative example of this is John Wilkes' *Essay on Women, and Other Pieces. . .*, London, J. Hotten, 1871 (orig. 1763).
80 'Le Colonel cinglant', *Conférence experimentale*, Amsterdam, Auguste Brancart, 1886. (Imprint reads: 'Londres: Société des Bibliophiles Cosmopolites, 1880'.)
81 See Hale, *Historia Placitorum Coronae*, 1:633–4.

8

A touch of danger:
The man-midwife as sexual predator

ROY PORTER

Medicine was traditionally the least prestigious of the learned professions. Its endemic failure in the fight against disease and death was there for all to see. It was tainted through and through by its *Doppelgänger*, charlatans and quacks, and by the shop-counter mentality of its poor relation, the apothecaries' trade. Moreover, in a culture whose religion inculated belief in the corruptions of the flesh, medicine suffered from guilt by association: disgust at vile bodies, their stench and decay, rubbed off onto the profession itself. As a result, to the cynical, such branches of medicine as surgery seemed little better than butchery, just as new areas of medical specialisation, such as venereology, appeared implicated in the vices responsible for the disease.[1] Priests ministered to the cure of souls, but the faculty dealt in lower, perishable things. As Coleridge was to put it: 'Doctors are *shallow* animals; having always employed their minds about Body and Gut, they imagine that in the whole system of things there is nothing but Gut and Body'.[2] Little wonder, then, that moralists, looking back to the Golden Age, emphasised that it was only the corruptions of civilisation which had brought physic into being at all. Medicine itself was a mark of degeneracy.[3]

And so the medical profession was constantly liable to the lash, lampooned from the Jacobean stage and Molière up to the satires of the Augustans.[4] A popular genre of publications, rasping and ribald, with titles such as *Medicina Flagellata* (1722), set out to give the profession a taste of its own medicine, pronouncing: 'physician, heal thyself'.[5] The burden of the attack was almost timeless. Collectively, the profession was monopolistic, individually physicians were pompous asses, spouting obscure mumbo-jumbo in dead tongues, long on theory, short on knowledge.[6] Growing fat off human misery, they had a stake in sickness. Indifferent to suffering, they indulged in absurd speculative wrangling (in the eighteenth century, two doctors actually slew each other in a duel over rival hypotheses of fever).[7] Yet all that their theorising achieved was to expose their own asininity. After all, when in the 1720s the peasant woman, Mary Tofts, claimed to give birth to litters of rabbits, it was eminent London practitioners, such as Nathaniel St André, who credulously supported her in her imposture.[8] In short, public suspicion of the medical profession ran deep. 'I have swallowed the weight of an Apothecary in Medicine', complained Elizabeth Mongagu, 'and what I am better for it, except more patient and less credulous, I know not'.[9] Proverbial wisdom summed up the public's verdict on what Hogarth dubbed 'the company of undertakers': 'a physician is more dangerous than the disease'; 'a young physician fattens the churchyard'; 'one doctor makes work for another'.

Much of this abuse was ancestral: it had been the gripes of Cato and Plutarch in Rome.[10] Yet a newer line became more prominent in post-Restoration times, a growing suspicion of the practitioner as a corrupter of morals, as a threat to female modesty, even as a libertine. Now, the links between sexual reproduction and the medical profession were of course deep, not least because one consequence of Christianity's distrust of the flesh was that it had fallen to medicine's lot to provide the main discourse in which sexuality could legitimately be discussed.[11] Partly because Christianity did not provide an *ars amatoria*, it was medical or pseudo-medical writers who set out a *scientia sexualis*. From the Naples physician Giovanni Sinibaldi's *Geneanthropeiae* of 1642 (abbreviated in English in 1658 as *Rare Verities. The Cabinet of Venus unlocked*), through to Dr Nicolas Venette's best-selling *Tableau de l'amour conjugal* (1684), translated into English as *The Mysteries of Conjugal Love Reveal'd* (1703), and a host of comparable eighteenth-century volumes, it was medical writers who spelt out the mechanics of copulation and offered remedies for sexual defects and diseases. Moreover, it was they who also provided vindications of sexual pleasure as an activity healthy both for the individual and (as James Graham was to insist) for society in general.[12] As Dr Erasmus Darwin put it, 'animal attraction' was the purest source of human felicity; 'the cordial drop in the otherwise vapid cup of life'.

Darwin's *Temple of Nature* (1803) was a paean to the 'Deities of Sexual Love'.[13]

In contrast to the increasingly repressive tone of medical sexology in the nineteenth century, associated most notoriously in England with Dr William Acton,[14] writers during the Enlightenment typically struck a hedonic pose,[15] not least James Graham, who set up his headquarters at the 'Temple of Hymen' at the Adelphi in the Strand. Graham lectured to fashionable crowds about the invigorating properties of happy sexuality. Among other techniques for stimulating eroticism, Graham advocated the use of pornography. People should have 'their passions aroused and excited by the sight of rich, warm or what are called lascivious prints, statues and paintings'. Similarly, when wives had failed to get pregnant 'in the ordinary course of things,' he recommended 'celebrating the rites of Venus in a variety of ways'. He also hired out his 'celestial bed' to barren couples at £50 a night. Its properties (tapping, claimed Graham, universal electromagnetic energies) would restore potency and fertility.[16] Graham was undoubtedly popular for a time, at least with outré circles in the metropolis. But the suspicion he drew down upon himself – he was widely condemned as a charlatan, or even a madman, and magistrates barred him from lecturing in various provincial towns – shows that dabbling in matters sexual was at best a mixed blessing for doctors' public standing.[17]

This was particularly so as pornography often gave itself a veneer of respectability by passing itself off as medical science. Catchpenny 'anatomical' works pruriently describing the genitalia, parading sexual freaks, or describing practices such as flagellation, were put out in increasing quantities in the eighteenth century by unscrupulous publishers such as Edmund Curll under the guise of medical education.[18] Yet it is not easy in many cases to draw hard-and-fast lines between 'legitimate' medical works and mere pornography. Texts such as *Onania*, the best-selling blast against masturbation, hover ambivalently between reform and titillation,[19] and practitioners such as Venette and the surgeon, John Marten, spiced their writings on generation and venereal diseases with bawdy anecdotes.[20]

Thus doctors were readily associated in the public mind with carnal knowledge. But from the Restoration onwards, the sexual ambiguities of the very practice of medicine came to the fore. Bawdy prints, poems and tales increasingly explored the undertones of medicine as a comprehensive double entendre or euphemism for sexual activity, or presented medicine as a mask for lechery. One Restoration collection of bawdy tales, *Sportive Wit*, contains a drollery called 'A Close Stool and a Chamber Pot Chuse out a Doctor', in which, as Roger Thompson notes, the basic premise is that medical practitioners are interested in one piece of female anatomy only. The same collection contains another item, 'A Colledge of Doctors', which shows the fellows of the College poking their Clyster pipes in the wrong hole, and indulges in endless double meanings over taking pulses, making injections, and the like.[21] This equation between medicine and the art of lechery became a staple of bawdy. Take, for instance, John Ellis's anonymous poem, *The Surprize*.[22] Its doggerel unfolds the story of a maid awaiting her apothecary who is coming to administer an enema. Instead, her admirer, Timante, steals into her chamber and assumes 'the apothecary's duty':

> Up stairs Timante gently came
> (One well acquainted with the Dame)
> And finding all the passage free
> While none perceiv'd him, in bolts he.
>
> Of beauty what a sudden Blaze
> Strikes our Spectator with Amaze
> As double-topt Parnassus shows
> When cover'd with new fall'n Snows,
> He spy'd an Engine on a Chair,
> Which he, good Man, with harmless Mind
> Took up, and guess'd the Use design'd,
> Resolv'd the Task himself would dare he
> And so he did, and play'd the Part.

To some degree, this identification of doctors with sexual licence may have been prompted by the unsavoury reputations of certain practitioners. Samuel Pepys, for instance, waxed righteously indignant in noting that Dr Alexander Frazier, Charles II's principal physician, was 'so great with my Lady Castlemaine and Stewart at court in helping to slip their calves when there is occasion'.[23] Early in the eighteenth century, two leading London physicians, Dr John Woodward and Dr Richard Mead, hardly raised the tone of the profession when they met in a duel (supposedly Mead disarmed Woodward and generously exclaimed 'Take your life', to which Woodward responded, 'Anything but your physic').[24] Yet both were to become notorious for sexual improprieties. Woodward was, in any case, a butt of satire for his grotesque vanity, pomposity and disputatiousness.[25] Moreover, anti-Woodward satires abound with innuendoes about his supposed homosexuality (a 'great Lover of Boys') or transsexuality. Of one patient, it was alleged, Woodward 'attacked him behind, and made an Evacuation in his Body'.[26] Mead, for his part, though a highly successful society figure (no man lived more in 'the broad sunshine of life', according to Samuel Johnson),[27] grew notorious as an old lecher. William Stukeley noted his 'decrepit amours', and the Reverend Edmund Pyle managed simultaneously to accuse and exculpate him by remarking that the President of the Royal Society, Martin Folkes, was the 'most foolishly and beastly vicious in the wenching way of any body I ever heard of, – a good deal beyond Dr Mead'.[28] Mead's dirty deeds were first brought before the public in a pamphlet, *The Cornutor of Seventy-Five. Being a genuine Narrative of the Life, Adventures, and Amours of Don Ricardo Honeywater, Fellow of the Royal College of Physicians at Madrid, Salamanca, and Toledo; and President of the Academy of Sciences in Lapland*,[29] which alleged that Mead liked to be whipped by his mistress, but, still proving impotent, contented himself with 'combing her red locks'. He was then of course immortalised in the guise of Dr Kunastrokius in *Tristram Shandy*:[30] 'I own I never could envy Didius in these kinds of fancies of his: – But every man to his own taste. – Did not Dr Kunastrokius, that great man, at his leisure hours, take the greatest delight imaginable in combing of asses' tails, and plucking the dead hairs out with his teeth, though he had tweezers always in his pocket?'

Yet it would be a mistake to attribute this growing sexual suspicion of the medical profession wholly to individual notoriety. Unease about the physician's potential for sexual insinuation and exploitation ran deeper, grounded in developments and tensions integral to medicine itself. In the broadest sense, what was at issue was the question of medicine's domain, and the rules of ethics and etiquette governing medical practice. What special privileges and prerogatives – if any – did the physician possess, by virtue of his healing office, which would dissolve taboos and override the protective layers of privacy and decency surrounding patients in their normal social intercourse? The patient was simultaneously a moral self, integral and inviolable, yet also a diseased body needing treatment. How could both these imperatives be satisfied? Were there zones of the body too secret, too delicate, too charged with meaning, to be stripped bare and exposed to the physician's inspection, his hand, eye or mind?[31]

It is not easy to tell what public opinion thought physicians might with propriety do at the bedside. Early formulations of medical ethics, such as Dr John Gregory's *Observations on the Duties and Offices of a Physician* (1770) and Thomas Percival's *Medical Ethics* (1803) are almost silent as to the proper limits of medical intrusiveness (being a liberally-educated gentleman, the physician should possess an instinctive tact in such matters).[32] Nor are the introductory clinical lectures delivered by eighteenth-century professors, such as William Cullen at Edinburgh, any more illuminating as to the balance of intrusion and privacy governing a doctor's history-taking, or his right to inspect patients' bodies.[33] Potentially, much could be discovered about actual practice by systematic research into doctors' case notes and the patients' response as revealed by their letters and diaries, but such work has hardly begun.[34]

And, in any case, inquiries into medical etiquette would make sense only in the context of an assured grasp of that fascinating yet protean subject, propriety itself, as it governed the presentation of the self in everyday social life. Pioneering researches on the private and the public, on psychological space, and on the changing terrain of rude and refined behaviour have been conducted by Richard Sennett, Norbert Elias, Erving Goffman and others.[35] Yet most of our knowledge remains less about practice than about prescription. In actual cases we remain woefully ignorant of the subtle dialectics between behaviour and norms. Which parts of the body might properly be put on public display? Which bodily functions was it normal, and which taboo, to perform in public or even speak of? Obviously current practice modulated over the course of time: Pepys caught Lady Sandwich 'doing something upon the pot' in a public room in the 1660s. Would that have happened a century later?[36] When such shifts occur, how do we explain such modification in the 'done thing' or interpret the enigmatic play of what Sterne termed 'delicacy' and 'concupiscence', the double-edged values of concealing and revealing?[37]

Of course, there can be no clear-cut answers to these questions, since norms differed between the sexes (the double standard) and from class to class – indeed they served as ways of defining group against group. Propriety was context-dependent and subject to the mode. Fashion, convention, morality and tradition clearly tugged in different directions, witness the tussles Samuel Pepys had as to whether his wife, Elizabeth, should wear heavy cosmetics (Pepys disapproved) or a vizard (Pepys approved).[38] Such questions of the psycho-sociology of decency formed a leitmotif in the writings of Bernard Mandeville – perhaps significantly a medical practitioner. Particularly in *The Virgin Unmask'd*, he challenged conventional wisdom on female decency. In a dialogue opening with a dispute between Antonia, a young lady, and her aunt Lucinda over the young lady's décolletage ('I don't invent the fashions,' the niece claims),

Mandeville has the aunt explain that 'modesty' is actually artful titillation: concealment tantalises. Mandeville thus acknowledges the Enlightenment belief in the relativism of morals and *moeurs*.[39]

Norms and practices thus involved complex codes. In eighteenth-century circles, a lady might with propriety reveal her bosom but not her ankle. Partners might make love in close proximity to servants, for menials were 'invisible'. A fashionable lady might properly receive morning callers *en déshabillé* in her chamber, conversing with them while she performed her toilette, and thereby revealing to them parts of her person it would have been indecent to display in any other context. Such advertisement of the play of permission and transgression produced the sort of sexual *frisson* so powerful throughout the century.

Against this backdrop, what may seem remarkable to us is how far the physician was expected to keep his distance. In the routine clinical encounters of the seventeenth or eighteenth century, anything more than the most perfunctory and formal physical contact – as for example that involved in pulse-taking – was extremely unusual between doctor and patient. The physician would of course scan the visible symptoms of sickness, but these generally involved features of the body – eye colour, facial complexion – exposed to public view in any case. There is no indication that it was normal for patients to remove clothing and expose 'private' parts of their person to ocular inspection, still less that physicians undertook physical examination using their hands.[40]

What might be taken as 'reticence' was not primarily for decency's sake. It was first and foremost because traditional medicine had little expectation that scrutiny of the body in general, or palpation of its surfaces, would yield valuable diagnostic information. Sickness was fundamentally seen as 'constitutional'. In such cases the appropriate course of action for the physician was to 'take a history', asking the patient for an account of his 'complaint' and probing into details of life habits, diet, personal crises, etc, to build up a view of the distemper as an expression of the patient's life-history.[41]

Indeed, the eighteenth-century physician may have encroached upon the intimacies of his patient less than his predecessors, in that the practices of urine and faeces gazing, so prominent earlier, had fallen out of fashion.[42] True, various pioneers, such as Auenbrugger, were advocating extension of physical methods such as palpation and auscultation, and of course, from the early nineteenth century onwards, a battery of new diagnostic technology became available, starting with the stethoscope.

Yet the signs are that the English medical profession itself took up these aids rather haltingly and, as Reiser had stressed, they met considerable opposition from their patients, who found their space being invaded. Not till the present century did the mark of the good general practitioner, in the public mind, become his willingness to give a good overall physical examination.[43]

Hence, if the traditional physician kept his distance, it was for sound medical reasons, not primarily out of 'delicacy', and yet such practice set the norms for what 'decent' medical practice was. That is a very important fact, for it explains why those modes of healing which *did* involve or invite boundary-breaking between physician and patient – above all, physical contact – proved so disturbing. Some index of their wholly exceptional nature is given by the special healing practice of the royal touch, the residual thaumaturgical power claimed by the royal lines of England and France, particularly for the cure of scrofula. The implication of the fact that *kings* could cure by touch was that no-one else might.[44] Once royalty ceased the healing touch – the practice was abandoned by the Hanoverians – that power passed, so to speak, not of course to the medical regulars who were sceptical of such claims, but to popular practices and 'fringe' practitioners. Eighteenth-century mothers pressed the limbs of their sick infants against the corpses of executed felons at the gallows, there being a superstitious dialectic between life and death, crime and health.[45] Meanwhile, various laymen made names for themselves by performing healing by their charismatic touch. Most famous in the late Stuart period was the Irishman, Valentine Greatrakes ('the Stroker'), whose healing ministries, first in Ireland and later in England, aroused much animosity amongst the medical profession and scientists alike. Physicians typically tried to scotch the suggestion that Greatrakes possessed preternatural powers.[46] In his *Levamen infirmi* (1700), Dr David Irish made short work of such claims to healing at a stroke:[47]

> Of late what a Noise have *Hornsuckers and seventh Sun Stroakers* made in the world: the one pretends, by Sucking, to quell the *violent pain*, while the other, by Stroaking, Monarch like, triumphs (if you will believe him) over the Kings-Evil;
>
> 'Tis true; some Diseases are curable by the Touch of Remedies, as Physicians, who can only Skilfully apply them, well know; but to cure without the Application of Remedies, is contrary to Nature;

Irish emphatically denied the power of healing by 'touch': '*for then every Man* would cure by touching. Besides, all diseases are cured by taking away the Causes; but neither the Sucker, nor Stroaker, pretend to this'.

In the late seventeenth century, Greatrakes' claim to heal by touch did not widely alert sexual suspicions. A century later, by contrast, the activities of Franz Anton Mesmer, the pioneer 'hypnotist', stirred up a sexual hornets' nest. Mesmer never claimed any preternatural powers, insisting he operated solely as a medium for a natural superfine fluid called animal magnetism, which possessed profound health-giving capacities when allowed to flow freely through the body. Moreover, in time, he found that he could exercise his healing abilities without physical contact. Even so, the supercharged emotional atmosphere of his 'séances', which typically involved mainly female patients who fell into ecstatic states and lost their self-possession, seemed to spell sexual danger, and one of the grounds on which a secret section of the Report of 1784, commissioned by Louis XVI to investigate Mesmerism, argued for its suppression, was it tendency to sexual licence.[48] Throughout nineteenth-century France, hypnotism was always easy prey to be discredited on the grounds that it opened the floodgates to the debauching of wives and daughters.[49]

Though in Georgian England the Mesmeric movement was smaller, equivalent dangers were noted.[50] Mesmerism invited the collapse of normal restraint. Critics grew apoplectic about mesmeric 'suggestion', hinting at the slippery slope from 'touching' to 'touching up', and the ambivalence of the Mesmeric art of 'making passes'. The anonymous author of *A letter to a physician in the country on animal magnetism* thus reported his experiences (real or fictitious) of being healed at the hands of the Mesmeric doctor's assistant, a 'singularly gifted damsel', who:

> Supported herself by leaning on me one hand, while she employed the other in feeling, and wandering lightly, with no unpleasant friction, over the region of the thorax: occasionally straying down the sternum, towards the ensiform-cartilage, and short ribs; and then at times insensibly creeping along the abdomen, in a direction to the os-pubis; which, as my sensations of every kind are naturally rather acute, produced nearly the complicated, and semi-painful effect of tickling. Not willing, however, to interrupt her interesting researches, I bore her tantalizing touches with determined resignation.

He could, he concluded, hardly resist the 'meltings', 'intuitive vibrations', 'fatal fascinations' and 'ecstatic deliriums' of the 'crisis'.[51]

This shift from the relative erotic innocuousness of Greatrakes' stroking to the dynamite of Mesmeric activities (paralleled in their *frisson* by James Graham's contemporary experiments in sexual rejuvenation)[52] suggests how powerfully sensibilities towards the body had shifted over the intervening century. A greater premium was now placed on physical privacy, and the new cult of sensibility had heightened perceptions of the delicate nuances of body sensation and nervous response. In such an atmosphere, the body easily became wholly identified with sexuality. Blushing, the pounding heart, the racing pulse, the trembling hand, the tearful cheek – all became eloquent in a sign language of refined, suppressed sexual expression.[53] Thus, at the mainly comic level, in *Tristram Shandy* almost all mentions of the operations of body and mind become sexual *double entendres*,[54] while, in the more refined atmosphere of *A Sentimental Journey*, Sterne was to explore the feverish sensibilities of this displaced yet universal sexuality: '. . . Trust me, my dear Eugenius, I should have said "there are worse occupations in this world than feeling a woman's pulse. . ."'[55]

It is, of course, no accident that the supercharged feeling of the narrative culminates in the final establishment of physical contact:

> But the fille de chambre hearing there were words between us, and fearing that hostilities would ensue in course, had crept silently out of her closet; and it being totally dark, had stolen so close to our beds, that she had got herself into the narrow passage which separated them, and had advanced so far up as to be in a line betwixt her mistress and me: . . . So that when I stretched out my hand, I caught hold of the fille de chambre's. . .[56]

The ambiguity of Sterne's aposiopesis – of what did his hero's hand catch hold? – was playful. It became a topic of deadly earnest, however, in the hue and cry called up over another form of 'laying on' of hands – the relatively new and deeply controversial art of man-midwifery. Of course medical men had 'laid'[57] women (the common term for delivering babies) long before the eighteenth century.[58] Traditional childbirth was normally a women-only rite, but when a delivery supervised by a midwife went wrong, a surgeon was summoned who, with the aid of surgical instruments, would draw the baby (generally dead) out of the womb. There are signs, however, of the emergence of a small number of specialist male practitioners before the close of the seventeenth century, Percival Willughby being a famous instance.[59]

Yet it was not until the eighteenth century that the man-midwife became socially conspicuous, both numerically and, more so, as a perplexing figure in the public mind and an anomaly in the medical profession.[60] When, for example, Joseph Reed referred to David Garrick as 'the greatest theatrical Man midwife that ever assisted at the labours of the Stage', the conceit was self-conscious, almost jokingly grotesque.[61] For, as essayists and print-makers never tired of emphasising, there was something inherently 'amphibious', as a contradiction in terms, about even the very name of the 'man-midwife' (surely explaining why Sterne's Dr Slop wished to be known by the more genteel appellation of *accoucheur*).[62]

Old-style medical history saluted the rise of the male obstetrician as marking real progress in child delivery. Supposedly possessing greater anatomical expertise than the traditional Mother Midnight, and armed with his new forceps, the man-midwife represented a leap forward in safety. This interpretation has been challenged by feminist historians, who have seen the change as a double-step back. On the one hand, it endangered mother and child alike, for the man-midwife was (it is alleged) unsympathetic, in a hurry, out to dazzle, wildly over-interventionist and trigger happy with his dangerous and unnecessary instruments, the forceps. The traditional midwife, by contrast, had let Dame Nature take her course. On the other hand, the elbowing out of women from obstetric practice meant that, in yet another sector of public life, women were becoming reduced to dependent status. All of this amounts, according to Mary Daly, to a 'gynaecological crusade to shorten women's lives'.[63]

This is not the place to adjudicate the issue, though if indeed the man-midwife did prove so disastrous to life and limb, the question of why male operators became the practitioners of choice for women becomes highly intriguing.[64] I wish rather to focus upon the contemporary controversy surrounding the new practitioner. Numerous midwives went into print deploring the erosion of their profession and the rise of the male accoucheur. In the writings of Sarah Stone, Elizabeth Nihell, Mary Stephen, Martha Mears and others, there is a standard litany of arguments.[65] Experience, history and tradition all lay on the side of the female practitioner. Men's claim that only their skills could safely deliver infants was contradicted by centuries of safe deliveries by midwives. If anatomical expertise were vital, that was an argument not for supplanting midwives but for educating them. And, in any case, instruments were very rarely needed; their excessive use by men constituted more of a threat than a safeguard to women's health.

These arguments obviously cut some ice, but they did not perhaps express the deepest sources of suspicion against the male operator, viz the perception of him as a sexual infiltrator, a violator of female modesty.

For most of the eighteenth century, and well into the nineteenth, a series of books and pamphlets by *male* authors thundered out abuse against man-midwifery, casting it as a little better than a cover for adultery. The case was made early in Frank Nicholls' anonymous *The Petition of the Unborn Babes to the Censors of the Royal College of Physicians*, where he depicted a kind of Hogarthian Man-midwives' Progress. They are allowed, he said, 'to treat our wives in such a manner, as frequently ends in their destruction, and to have such intercourse with our women, as easily shifts itself into indecency, from indecency into obscenity, and from obscenity into debauchery'.[66]

The indictment was further elaborated. The gravest offence, according to Philip Thicknesse's *Man-Midwifery Analysed* (1764), was the manual manipulation of women's private parts which influential midwives such as William Smellie had urged as integral to their allegedly superior techniques of diagnosis and delivery.[67] For Thicknesse, just to quote such authors was enough to condemn them. How could indecencies – indeed quasi-pornography – such as this be justified?

> Dr. Smellie in his 'Treatise on Midwifery', page 91, speaking of the parts of generation in women, observes that 'The Clitoris, with its Praeputium, is found between the Labia on the middle and fore part of the Pubis; and from the lower part of the Clitoris, the Nymphae rising, spreads outwards and downwards to the sides of the Os Externum, forming a kind of Sulcus or furrow, called the Fossa magna, or Navicularis, for the direction of the Penis in coition, or of the Finger in touching, into the Vagina'.[68]

Smellie was apparently suggesting, *Candide*-like, that female anatomy had been designed to suit the convenience of the man-midwife's finger. Smellie might pretend, argued Thicknesse, that digitation helped ascertain the foetal position and guide its expulsion. Yet women had been performing deliveries successfully ever since the Egyptians, and 'little did the poor Egyptian ladies think, that it would be three thousand years, before Doctor Smellie would be born, and the art of *touching* . . . be brought to perfection'.[69] What needed to be done, could perfectly well be done by women: 'There is not any thing necessary in midwifery, but what a woman can learn, and execute, with more propriety, and with as much safety as men. Instruments are always injurious, often dangerous, and scarce ever necessary. The world was peopled much better, before the mungrel name of man midwives was known; they were imported here from France . . .'[70]

So why the resort to male operators? Obviously something sinister was afoot, indeed the whole business was a smokescreen, hiding the designs both of these 'touching gentry'[71] and of lickorish ladies. Thicknesse conjured up the typical scenario of the man-midwife's insinuation into the home, indeed the breast, of a fashionable lady:

> Upon my arrival, if her husband happens to be present, he must retire; for I know too well, the pain that he must feel, on hearing even the first necessary question. Therefore nothing but an affected, stiff air, a grave face peeping out of a profound wig and my hand kept warm in my muff, must transpire, till the husband is gone out of the room; and from that instant; the dressing-room becomes sacred to me and my patient. I then proceed to ask such questions, with an air of gravity and importance, that must confound a woman of modesty beyond imagination: upon perceiving her embarrassment, I get up, take her by the hand, and tell her how very unlike her conduct is to my lady Lucy Like It, whom I have just left; that her ladyship thought she was with child, but that I could perceive no circle round her nipples, nor by the touch had I any reason to believe she was breeding: This reconciles my new patient; she hears, and wonders at Lady Lucy's conduct; but believing it no more than is common, and that the Doctor has a licence to take, and she to grant these liberties, she acquiesces. I then proceed to examine her breasts, nipples, &c. by which I am soon able to discover what further liberties I may proceed to, under the sanction of my great wig, and my grave face; and if once admitted to the touch, all difficulties for five or six months after, are removed: my patient and I understand one another; secrecy is the work; my character, and her honour seal it.[72]

As this passage suggests, what agitated Thicknesse was less the designs of individual accoucheurs than the temptations intrinsic to the very operation of a male practitioner touching a women's sexual organs. How could it not inflame the passions? 'If men-midwives under these circumstances stand unmoved, they are part of the human species I am a stranger to!'[73]

Thicknesse did not want to let man-midwives off the hook: 'I . . . look on them, as I should on the Emperor of Morocco, or the Bashaw of Tangier, going to his seraglio'.[74] Yet in the last resort the target of his wrath has less these 'touching gentry' than the woman who patronised them. It was a commonplace of censures against medicine that fine ladies loved to have physicians dancing attendance, and basked in the flattery which fashionable practitioners were eager to pay them.[75] For Thicknesse, ladies' relations with men-midwives encouraged this frailty to rise to the pitch of vice and crime. Rather as today in popular Freudian interpretations of female rape fantasies,[76] Thicknesse regarded female resort to Man-midwives as a device for enjoying forbidden pleasures with impunity, for indulging in adultery without having to accept responsibility for it. Man-midwifery thus spelt an act of violation, but the person violated was less the wife than the husband. And yet the husband simply got what he deserved, for he who hired a man-midwife was little better than a pander. Thicknesse could only 'look on the husband who consents to it, with contempt and indignation'.[77] And if the husbands were wittols, the wives were bawds:

> I would as soon send my wife to visit a Covent-Garden hostess, as be familiar with these male midwife Trumpeters. . . Lard, Madam, who is your doctor? says one: well, I'll never have a woman, my doctor is the sweetest man! so gentle, so humane, so patient! and then he is so safe: with a thousand such fine things of the Doctor, that the Trumpeter soon makes half the circle in love with her dear doctor, before they have even seen him, and determine to consult him the next morning.[78]

Similar arguments are developed in other works fulminating against the man-midwife. As the onslaught grew standardised, it is not worth analysing each.[79] One further instance alone may serve as typical: *Thoughts on the times* by Francis Foster (1779).[80] For Foster, the basic fact about childbirth was that labour was 'Nature's work'.[81] Women were nature's midwives, and male practitioners were not as 'safe' as women.[82] Their services should be necessary only in the extremely exceptional case (for Foster, not even a knowledge of anatomy was needed for nine hundred and ninety-nine births out of a thousand: if it had been, primitive societies would have died out long ago).[83] Man-midwifery was, therefore, totally redundant (a *surgeon* could perform the exceptional operation).

Worse than redundant, it was an evil, for through its practice women were 'actually polluted' and 'violated', as any glance at the pages of an obstetrics manual would confirm.[84] Like Thicknesse, Foster too quoted Smellie's *Treatise on Mid-wifery*, Vol. I, p. 261:

> This os externum (Entrance to the Vagina) must be gradually opened by introducing the Fingers one after another, in form of a Cone, after they have lubricated with Pomatum, moving and turning them in a semi-circular Motion, as they are PUSHED UP. If the Head is so low down that the HAND cannot be introduced HIGH UP in this Form, let the Parts be dilated by the Fingers turned in the Direction of the Coccyx, &c. &c. &c. . . . Must not this unnatural Friction inflame, and excoriate Parts of Exquisite Sensibility . . .and render the Distention afterwards, apt to occasion an Inflamation?[85]

Such digitation – 'perhaps for hours'[86] – recommended by 'horn books' could not help but produce sexual frenzy in both parties: '. . .A Man-Midwife is not a piece of wood: The *Doctor* does not divest himself of the *Man*'.[87]

'It is possible,' Foster went on, 'for a Man in health, to range over a pretty Woman thus and not be inflamed almost to Madness?! . . .Shut up with her, where he knows that no Person dare intrude . . . First, taking one Liberty then another . . .'[88] And if the man-midwife rises to 'madness', his patient falls into a 'delirium'.[89] It might all masquerade as medicine, but 'Does it obliterate the idea in her Breast – does it obliterate the Idea in his that she is a women . . . and that he is, a man? Can it remove those natural Sensations, to which it is no more in our Power to be insensible, than to add to our Height?'[90]

Who was to blame? Obviously the man-midwife was himself a sinister figure and, like Thicknesse, Foster had no sympathy for the husband: 'If any other man were to be caught, taking such Liberties, the Husband would deem it sufficient Grounds for a separation – Doctor's Commons &c!'[91] And yet ultimately the guilty party was the wife, 'setting all decency at defiance'; 'it is but lately that our women became so depraved'.[92] Foster painted a lurid picture of purportedly respectable matrons queuing up to receive the sexual services of this gigolo of a man-midwife. 'A particular friend of mine,' he wrote,

> (who is a good deal in Company with a man-midwife of great practice) happened to be at a Doctor's House, one Evening, when no less than six Women of Fashion came in Chairs during the Course of it . . . to be informed whether they had sustained any Injury by a Fright occasioned by a high wind. The ladies were attended, one by one, in the Doctor's examining Room.[93]

What were such women but scandalous hypocrites?

> And strange Inconsistency! there are Ladies who submit to all these scandalous Exposures, with surprizing Effrontery whose modesty, notwithstanding, would, I make no Doubt, be quite shocked, if, on getting off their Horse, or out of their Carriage, their petticoats stuck, and discovered their knee or . . . What a Farce! They would pretend to be ashamed to show their legs – and yet feel no Shame of showing their •••••••!!![94]

Thanks to such hypocrisies, the man-midwife usurped the husband. The accoucheur ingratiated himself rather like the 'confessor'[95] in Popish countries, until 'he is seated in the Husband's throne – his sacred rights are infringed'.[96] Foster concluded with a call to men to expel this usurper: 'We owe it to ourselves – we owe it to our lives – to our children . . . and – we owe it to our Country'.[97]

Thus the rise of the man-midwife was portrayed as a social catastrophe, not so much because the practitioners in question were especially blackguardly – they were but men! – but because the practice removed the bodyguard of propriety so vital to protect the weaker vessel. Blame is heaped upon the women much more than upon the man-midwives. Indeed, in one such work, the man-midwife is specifically portrayed as the women's dupe and victim. *The Man Midwife Unmasqu'd* (1738) versifies what is allegedly a true case, in which a pregnant women applies to a man-midwife for an examination:

> She wanted some money
> 'Tis true, and some . . .,
> She fail'd of the first,
> But the latter had Luck in.[98]

She offers him temptation. He falls for it and tells her:

> . . . I'll do what I can,
> And may venture to say, you will find me a Man:
> A Man both of Judgement and Skill I do mean,
> By Judgement and Skill I my Credit maintain:

> But then in each Point you must follow Direction,
> And as your Case lies, must admit of Inspection.
> To give Demonstration that he did respect Her,
> He kneel'd down before her, and then did Inspect Her.

But, *post coitum*, she plays the wronged women, demands money and, when he refuses, brings the doctor to court on a rape charge. The court acquits him.

What are we to make of these anti-man-midwife tracts?[99] For one thing, they throw into relief the controversy currently raging over the rise of male obstetricians during the eighteenth century. Feminist historians characterise it as yet another chapter in the patriarchal subordination of women.[100] This may be so. Yet it seemed not a triumph but a threat to a substantial section of male opinion who evidently regarded it as a chapter in the emergence of female licence, and an insidious challenge to male authority.

It is obviously pointless to ask how far these lurid accounts of digitating man-midwives ('the touching gentry') and lecherous ladies mirrored truth, or were just mere phantoms of the misogynistic imagination; pathetic tokens of male insecurity. Neither gentlewomen nor obstetricians are likely to have recorded their conquests in their diaries.[101] Polemicists referred in rhetorical terms to supposedly notorious cases of man-midwives and their patients being caught red-handed. Thicknesse wrote, 'That some of these Touching Gentry have been prosecuted, and severely punished for their lustful attempts, in touching their patients, is a notorious truth; that hundreds of them get off, and that many succeed, cannot be doubted'.[102] And Foster asked: '. . . have not too many Midwife Doctors been detected in crim. con. with their favourite Ladies, to render Argument on this Head necessary?'[103] But, in default of names, we are left in the dark. Only one case hit the headlines, in which a man-midwife, Dr Morley, seduced a patient, Mrs Biker, and was brought to court and forced to pay compensation.[104]

Yet if our evidence of man-midwives actually caught red-handed is slight, we can document another service that man-midwives did perform for their female clients; one which, once it came to light, would have aroused hardly less suspicion amongst male opinion. For it is clear that man-midwives were colluding in the delivery and subsequent concealment of illegitimate babies.[105] Early in the nineteenth century, William Wadd recalled the following story about William Hunter, by contemporary agreement easily the most respectable and eminent male practitioner:

> During the American war, he was consulted by the daughter of a peer, who confessed herself pregnant, and requested his assistance: he advised her to retire for a time to the house of some confidential friend; she said that it was impossible, as her father would not suffer her to be absent from him a single day. Some of the servants were, therefore, let into the secret, and the Doctor made his arrangement with the Treasurer of the Foundling Hospital for the reception of the child, for which he was to pay £100. – The lady was desired to weigh well if she could bear pain, without alarming the family by her cries; she said "Yes," – and she kept her word. At the usual period, she was delivered, not of one child only, but of twins. The Doctor bearing the two children, was conducted by a French servant through the kitchen and left to ascend the area steps into the street. Luckily the lady's-maid recollected that the door of the area might perhaps be locked, and she followed the doctor just in time to prevent his being detained at the gate. He deposited the children at the Foundling Hospital, and paid for each £100. The father of the children was a Colonel of the army, who went with his regiment to America, and died there. The mother afterwards married a person of her own rank.[106]

As the transcripts of testimony at divorce trials disclose, Hunter was also active in helping society ladies to conceal the fruits of adulterous liaisons. For example, Hunter had acted as obstetrician to the Duchess of Grafton.[107] When she later became pregnant by Lord Ossory, she made clandestine advances to Hunter through the good offices of the surgeon, Robert Adair, to secure his services.[108] No names were mentioned, but Hunter deduced her identity. Hunter was sworn to the strictest secrecy.[109] As her term came on, the duchess retired to Combe, near Kingston in Surrey. Going into labour, she summoned Hunter.[110] He arrived shortly after the baby was born and confirmed its and the mother's good health.[111] His duty was then to take the baby back with him to his London house without arousing suspicions.[112] There he had already fixed up a suitable wet-nurse, for whom he had found appropriate lodgings at Piccadilly. Hunter had agreed to take responsibility for the infant's health and for ensuring that the wet-nurse received regular payments.[113] On the journey down to Surrey, Hunter had observed strict secrecy, travelling with the blinds down and keeping their exact destination from the coachman. Hunter gave the two postilions 'half-a-crown each, and said, that if he found it was not known where they had been, they should have half-a-crown more each'.[114]

Hunter performed similar services for Lady Bolingbroke, when she became pregnant by Topham Beauclerk.[115] Hunter was familiar with her because he had earlier delivered her children by Lord Bolingbroke.[116] Once again, cloak-and-dagger operations were used. As he put it at her subsequent divorce trial: 'every means were made use of to keep her being brought to bed a secret'.[117] The secrecy was enjoined upon him from the very first. As Hunter testified:

> Some time in or about the month of January, or February last, the deponent received a note from Lady Bolingbroke, wherein she desired that he would come to her in the evening, she wanted to speak with him; that he conceived from the contents of the said note, that it was upon some secret business . . . that he accordingly went on the same evening, when it was dark, to Lady Bolingbroke's house, at the upper end of Charles Street, Berkley [sic] Square; that upon that night, or some other, when he visited Lady Bolingbroke, upon his knocking at the door and asking for Lady Bolingbroke, the footman asked him his name, but the deponent refused telling him; but ordered the said servant to tell his lady that a gentleman wanted to speak to her, and he accordingly carried up such a message, and soon afterwards Lady Bolingbroke's woman came down, and shewed the deponent into a little back room up stairs, where, in a very little

time, Lady Bolingbroke came to him, and then appeared to the deponent to be very much flurried, and almost fainting; insomuch that the deponent looked upon her to be under some great misfortune.[118]

All his visits were under cover of darkness, and he

> always went on foot though it rained, that his own servants might not know he was going there; and the said Lady Bolingbroke, still to preserve the secret, told the deponent, that when he wrote, or she should write to him upon her illness, that they should make use of a feigned name in such letters, lest any of them should by accident be lost.[119]

Hunter visited her several times during pregnancy, was present to deliver her child, and sent her packages of medicine.[120]

We do not have Hunter's reflections on his role in all this. At the Grafton divorce trial, he recalled saying to the duchess's maid: 'Mrs. Tyson, use no names while I am here, as I desire to know nothing of this case, but circumstances of health:'[121] and there is no reason to doubt that one of his motives was his duty as a doctor to safeguard life. Yet his feelings are likely to have been rather more complex. For one thing, Hunter, an ambitious Scot who immensely loved hobnobbing in High Society, may well have enjoyed the vicarious power these escapades conferred. Unmarried himself, he may have felt scant sympathy for the wronged husbands. And, not least, Hunter probably leapt at the liberal rewards he reaped from these affairs, being a great advocate of the 'happiness of riches'.[122]

Yet, ultimately, Hunter's own personal motives are irrelevant. What may be significant is that in him and others of his ilk, society ladies in distress found able confederates and compliant accomplices in their liaisons, and that Hunter showed no signs of moral qualms despite the irregular behaviour they forced upon him. Whether or not there was truth in the allegations made by Thicknesse and others of sexual goings-on between fine ladies and man-midwives, well might the rise of the man-midwife have left husbands feeling dubious about the part they were prepared to play in helping to conceal the fruits of adultery. The enduring role of the doctor as the ambivalent ally of wives in their manoeuvres against their spouses had obviously begun.

Notes

1 See F. Bottomley, *The Body in Western Christendom*, London, 1979. The

close ties between certain doctors and body-snatchers would form a concrete instance.
2 E. L. Griggs (ed.), *Collected letters* of *Samuel Taylor Coleridge*, 1, Oxford, 1956, p. 256. Coleridge to Charles Lloyd, Sr., 14 November 1796.
3 Cf. W. Buchan, *Domestic Medicine*, London, 1772, p. xxiv.
4 See for instance H. Silvette, *The Doctor on the Stage. Medicine and Medical Men in Seventeenth Century England*, Knoxville, 1967; M. Nicolson and G. S. Rousseau, *'This Long Disease My Life': Alexander Pope and the Sciences*, Princeton, 1968.
5 [Anon.] *Medicina Flagellata*, London, 1722; Gregory Glyster [pseud.], *A Dose for the Doctor*, London, 1789.
6 C. Probyn, 'Swift and the Physicians: Aspects of Satire and Status', *Medical History*, xviii, 1974, pp. 242–56, and Roy Porter, 'The language of quackery in England, 1660–1800', pp. 73–103 in Peter Burke and Roy Porter (eds.), *The Social History of Language* Cambridge, 1987, pp. 73–103.
7 See *Essays in the Bilious Fever: Containing the Different Opinions of those Eminent physicians John Williams and Parker Bennet of Jamaica which was the Cause of a Duel and Terminated in the Death of Both*, London, 1752.
8 See G. S. Rousseau, *Tobias Smollett. Essays of Two Decades*, Edinburgh, 1982, pp. 165f.
9 Quoted in Roy Porter, 'The patient's view: doing medical history from below', *Theory and Society*, xiv, 1985, pp. 175–98 on p. 189.
10 See Vivian Nutton, 'Murders and miracles: lay attitudes towards medicine in classical antiquity', in Roy Porter (ed.), *Patients and Practitioners: lay perceptions of medicine in pre-industrial society*, Cambridge, 1985, pp. 23–53.
11 For general perspectives, see M. Foucault, *A History of Sexuality*, Vol. 1, Introduction, London, 1978.
12 See R. Thompson, *Unfit for Modest Ears*, London, 1979, pp. 171f; Roy Porter, 'The Sexual Politics of James Graham', *British Journal for Eighteenth Century Studies*, v, 1982, pp. 199–206, and P.-G. Boucé, 'Aspects of sexual tolerance and intolerance in eighteenth-century England', *The British Journal for Eighteenth-Century Studies*, iii, 1980, pp. 173–89.
13 Quoted in Roy Porter, 'Mixed feelings: the Enlightenment and sexuality in eighteenth century England', in P.-G. Boucé (ed.), *Sexuality in eighteenth-century Britain*, Manchester, 1982, pp. 1–27. For Erasmus Darwin's views see D. King-Hele, *The essential writings of Erasmus Darwin*, London, 1968, Chs. 5 and 6.
14 See F. J. Barker-Benfield, *The horrors of the half-known life*, New York, 1976, and A. McLaren, 'The pleasures of procreation', in W. F. Bynum and Roy Porter (eds.), *William Hunter and the eighteenth century medical world*, Cambridge, 1985, pp. 323–420.
15 See Roy Porter, 'Medicina e Sessualita', *Prometeo*, iii, 1985, pp. 6–25.
16 Porter, 'Mixed Feelings'.
17 Roy Porter, 'Sex and the singular man: the seminal ideas of James Graham', *Studies on Voltaire and the Eighteenth Century*, ccxxviii, 1984, pp. 3–24.
18 See P. Pinkus, *Grub Street*, London, 1968; R. Straus, *The Unspeakable Curll*, New York, 1970; David Foxon, *Libertine Literature in England, 1660–1745*,

New York, 1966, and Peter Wagner, *Eros Revived: erotica of the Enlightenment in England and America*, London, 1987.
19 See Peter Wagner, 'The veil of science and morality: some pornographic aspects of the *Onania*', *The British Journal for Eighteenth-Century Studies*, iv, 1983, pp. 179–84; George S. Rousseau, 'Nymphomania, Bienville and the rise of erotic sensibility', in P.-G. Boucé (ed.), *Sexuality in Eighteenth Century Britain*, Manchester, 1982, pp. 95–120. With several of Bernard Mandeville's works, it is an open question how far they were serious or designed to titillate; see, for example, his anonymous *A Modest Defence of Public Stews: or, an Essay upon Whoring as it is now practis'd in these Kingdoms. Written by a Layman*, London, 1724.
20 N. Venette, *Le Tableau de l'amour conjugal*, Amsterdam, 1687; John Marten, *Gonosologium Novum*, London, 1709, and the attacks on Marten by John Spinke: *Venus's Botcher*, London, 1709, and *Quackery Unmask'd*, London, 1709.
21 See Roger Thompson, *Unfit for Modest Ears*, pp. 158f.
22 [E. J.], *The Surprize or the Gentleman turn'd Apothecary. A Tale Written Originally in French prose; afterwards Translated into Latin: and from thence now Versified in Hudibrastics*, London: printed and sold by the Booksellers of London and Westminster, 1739.
23 R. Latham and W. Matthews (eds.), *The Diary of Samuel Pepys*, 11 vols, London, 1970–83, V: 275.
24 See J. Levine, *Dr. Woodward's Shield*, Berkeley, 1977, pp. 9, 17.
25 Roy Porter, 'John Woodward, a droll sort of philosopher', *Geological Magazine*, cxvi, 1979, pp. 395–417.
26 See *The Life and Adventures of Don Bilioso de L'Estomac*, London, 1719, pp. 16–17, and for his ambiguous gender, *An Account of the Sickness and Death of Dr Woodward*, London, 1719, p. 8: readers will wish to know 'of what sex he dyed'.
27 See A. Zuckerman, 'Dr Richard Mead (1673–1754): A biographical study', Ph.D., University of Illinois, 1965, pp. 220f.
28 *Memoirs of a Royal Chaplain, 1729–1763: The Correspondence of Edmund Pyle, D. D. chaplain in Ordinary to George II, with Samuel Kerrich D. D., Vicar of Dersingham, Rector of Wolferton, and Rector of West Newton*, ed. by Albert Hartshorne, London, 1905, p. 330.
29 *The Cornutor of Seventy-Five. Being a genuine Narrative of the Life, Adventures, and Amours, of Don Ricardo Honeywater, Fellow of the Royal College of Physicians at Madrid, Salamanca, and Toledo; and President of the Academy of Sciences in Lapland. Containing, amongst many other diverting particulars, his Intrigue with Dona Maria W—s, of Via Vinculosa, anglice, Fetter-Lane, in the City of Madrid*, London, n.d. Mead was defended in *Don Ricardo Honeywater Vindicated. In a Letter to Doctor Salguod, Physician in Ordinary to His Royal Highness the Prince of Asturia's Household, and Man-midwife: The reputed Author of a Scurrilous Pamphlet, Entitled, The Cornutor of Seventy-five*, London, 1748. See especially pp. 28f.
30 C. Ricks (ed.), *Laurence Sterne: Tristram Shandy*, Harmondsworth, 1970, p. 43. Sterne explained himself thus in a letter: 'I do him first of all honour –

speak of Kunastrokius as a great man – (be he who he will) and then most distantly hint at a droll foible in his character – and that not first reported (to the few who can ever understand the hint) by me – but known before by every chamber-maid and footman within the bills of mortality': *Letters of Laurence Sterne*, ed. Lewis P. Curtis, Oxford, 1935, p. 89.

31 It is not appropriate to explore the deeper issues here, involving fundamental conceptions of the embodied self, of mind/body relations, religious notions of resurrection, legal questions about ownership of the body, emotive issues such as dissection, and so forth. See B. Turner, *The Body and Society*, London, 1984.

32 Both merely mouth a few generalities about the need for physicians to respect decencies.

33 I thank Dr C. Lawrence, of the Wellcome Institute for the History of Medicine, for this information.

34 A start has been made in J. Lane, 'The doctor scolds me: the diaries and correspondence of patients in eighteenth-century England', in Roy Porter (ed.), *Patients and Practitioners*, pp. 207–47. But her article contains little material directly relevant to this issue. She does however point out that eighteenth-century physicians were often badly wrong with their diagnoses, and were perceived to be wrong. This suggests some failure of close doctor/patient contact or communication.

35 N. Elias, *The Civilising Process*, Oxford, 1983; R. Sennett, *The Fall of Public Man*, Cambridge, 1976, and, more generally, E. Goffman, *The Presentation of Self in Everyday Life*, Harmondsworth, 1969. More closely focused for present purposes is Fenella Childs, 'Prescriptions for Manners in eighteenth century Courtesy Literature', D. Phil., Oxford 1984.

36 Lawrence Stone, *The Family, Sex and Marriage in England 1500–1800*, D. Phil., London, 1977, p. 150. Stone has a useful discussion of shifting boundaries of what was sexually permissible.

37 For prudery, see P. Fryer, *Mrs. Grundy: studies in English prudery*, London, 1963; M. Jaeger, *Before Victoria*, London, 1956, and E. Trudgill, *Madonnas and magdalens*, London, 1966.

38 R. Latham and W. Matthews (eds.), *The Diary of Samuel Pepys*, London, 1970, ii, pp. 101–3. See R. Porter, 'Making Faces: Physiognomy and Fashion in Eighteenth Century England', *Etudes anglais*, xxxviii, 1985, pp. 385–96.

39 B. Mandeville, *The Virgin Unmask'd*, London, 1709, esp. pp. 1–4, 'A Discourse Upon Nakedness and Dress', and L. G. Crocker, *An Age of Crisis: man and world in eighteenth century thought*, Baltimore, 1963.

40 See R. L. Engle and B. J. Davis, 'Medical Diagnosis, Present, Past and Future', *Archives of Internal Medicine*, cxii, 1963, pp. 512–43, and I. Galdston, 'Diagnosis in historical perspective', *Bulletin of the History of Medicine*, ix, 1941, pp. 367–84. S. Reiser comments in *Medicine and the Reign of Technology*, Cambridge, 1978, p. 7: 'The failure of doctors to examine the body in the presence of internal disease, and the reluctance of patients to allow it, were common in the early nineteenth century'.

41 See, for discussion, W. F. Bynum, 'Health, disease and medical care' in G. S. Rousseau and Roy Porter (eds.), *The Ferment of Knowledge*, Cambridge, 1980, pp. 211–54.

42 For uroscopy, see the references in Roy Porter, 'I think ye both quacks: The Controversy between Dr Theodore Myersbach and Dr John Coakley Lettsom', in W. F. Bynum and Roy Porter (eds.), *Medical Fringe and Medical Orthodoxy*, London, 1986, pp. 56–78.
43 See M. Foucault, *The Birth of the Clinic*, London, 1972; J. S. Reiser, *Medicine and the Reign of Technology*, Cambridge, 1978, and C. Lawrence, 'Incommunicable knowledge: science, technology and the clinical art in Britain, 1850–1914', *Journal of Contemporary History*, xx, 1985, pp. 503–30.
44 M. Bloch, *The Royal Touch*, London, 1973, and R. Crawfurd, *The King's Evil*, Oxford, 1911.
45 See P. Linebaugh, 'The Tyburn Riot against the surgeons', in D. Hay, P. Linebaugh, E. P. Thompson (eds.), *Albion's Fatal Tree*, London, 1975, pp. 65–118.
46 See N. Steneck, 'Greatrakes the Stroker: the interpretations of historians', *Isis*, lxxiii, 1982, pp. 159–85, and A. Brian Laver, 'Miracles no wonder! The mesmeric phenomenon and organic cures of Valentine Greatrakes', *Journal of the History of Medicine*, xxxiii, 1978, pp. 35–44.
47 D. Irish, *Levamen Infirmi*, London, 1700, p. 37.
48 For mesmerism, see R. Darnton, *Mesmerism and the end of the Enlightenment in France*, Cambridge, Mass. 1968, and V. Buranelli, *The Wizard from Vienna: Franz Mesmer and the origins of hypnotism*, London, 1976.
49 R. Harris, 'Murder under hypnosis', in W. F. Bynum, Roy Porter and Michael Shepherd (eds.), *The Anatomy of Madness*. 2 vols, London, 1985, ii, pp. 197–241.
50 The early history of English mesmerism awaits study. For contemporary accounts and attacks see J. Martin, *Animal Magnetism examined*, London, 1790, and [anon.], *The mysteries of animal magnetism displayed* (n. p., 1789). See also Roy Porter, '"Under the Influence": Mesmerism in 18th century England', *History Today*, 1985, pp. 22–9; Jonathan Miller, 'Mesmerism', *The Listener*, 22 November 1973, pp. 685–90.
51 [Anon.], *A letter to a physician in the country on animal magnetism*, London, for J. Debrett, 1786, p. 31.
52 Roy Porter, 'Sex and the singular man'.
53 Illuminating here is J. Hagstrum, *Sex and sensibility*, London, 1980. For blushing, see C. Ricks, *Keats and Embarrassment*, Oxford, 1984.
54 Jacques Berthoud, 'Shandeism and sexuality' in V. Grosvenor-Myer (ed.), *Laurence Sterne: Riddles and Mysteries*, London, 1984, pp. 24–38.
55 L. Sterne, *A Sentimental Journey through France and Italy*, ed. G. Petrie, Harmondsworth, 1967, p. 75.
56 *Ibid.*, p. 148.
57 The language of 'laying' is of course full of *double entendre*.
58 See Irving S. Cutter and Henry R. Viets, *A Short History of Midwifery*, Philadelphia, W. B. Saunders, 1964; James Hobson Aveling, *English Midwives: Their History and prospects*, London, J. and A. Churchill, 1872, reprint London, Hugh K. Elliott, 1967, and Herbert Ritchie Spencer, *The History of British Midwifery 1650 to 1800*, London, John Bale Sons and Danielson, 1927, reprinted New York, AMS Press, 1978.

59 See P. Willughby, *Observations in Midwifery*, Warwick, 1863, and A. Wilson, 'Participant versus patient: seventeenth century childhood from the mother's point of view', in Porter (ed.), *Patients and Practitioners*, pp. 129–44.
60 See J. Donnison, *Midwives and Medical Men*, New York, 1977, and Edward Shorter, *A History of Women's Bodies*, Harmondsworth, 1980.
61 Quoted in D. M. Little and G. M. Kahrl, *The Letters of David Garrick*, 3 vols, Oxford, 1963, ii, p. 544. The date was 1766.
62 For the use of terms such as 'mungrel' and 'amphibious', see P. Thicknesse, *Man Midwifery Analysed*, London, 1764, p. 18. Compare [F. Foster], *Thoughts for the Times*, London, 1779: 'The very Name, demonstrates that their office is unnatural. Man-Midwife is a contradiction in Terms! – It is a manifest Absurdity! – What can be more ridiculous? – It implies a Thing that is neither a "man" nor a "Man-Midwife", must consequently be a Monster in Nature!!!'
63 See B. B. Schnorrenberg, 'Is childbirth any place for a woman? The decline of midwifery in eighteenth century England', *Studies in Eighteenth Century Culture*, x, 1981, pp. 393-408; J. Donnison, *Midwives and Medical Men*, London, 1977; Margaret Connor Versluysen, 'Midwives, medical men and "poor women labouring of child"; lying-in hospitals in eighteenth century London', in H. Roberts (ed.), *Women, Health and Reproduction*, London, 1981, p. 18–49. For a counterblast, see E. Shorter, *A History of Women's Bodies*, New York, 1982. For the quotation, see Mary Daly, *Gynaecology*, London, 1979, p. 260.
64 For one element in the debate, see D. N. Harley, 'Ignorant midwives – a persistent stereotype', *Bulletin of the Society for the Social History of Medicine*, xxviii, 1981, pp. 6–9; Adrian Wilson, 'Ignorant Midwives, a rejoinder', *ibid.*, xxxii, 1983, pp. 46–9, and Bernice Boss and Jeffrey Boss, 'Ignorant midwives, a further rejoinder', *ibid.*, xxxiii, 1983, p. 71.
65 Sarah Stone, *A Complete Practice of Midwifery*, London, 1737; Elizabeth Nihell, *A Treatise on the Art of Midwifery*, London, 1766, and Martha Mears, *The Pupil of Nature*, London, 1797.
66 Frank Nicholls, *The Petition of the Unborn Babes to the Censors of the Royal College of Physicians of London*, London, 1751, p. 6. Cf. B. This, *La Requête des Enfants à Naitre*, Paris, 1982.
67 P. Thicknesse, *Man Midwifery Analysed*, London, 1764. For Thicknesse, see P. Gosse, *Dr. Viper*, London, 1952.
68 Quoted in Thicknesse, *Man Midwifery Analysed*, p. 26. He is quoting William Smellie, *A Treatise on the Theory and Practice of Midwifery*, 3 vols, London, 1752–64, I, p. 91. For Smellie, see R. W. Johnston, *William Smellie*, Edinburgh, 1952. Thicknesse remarks apropos of Smellie (p. 6): 'The modest Doctor, in his first chapter, shews plainly that touching is an essential part of the practice of Midwifery; and that, in his opinion, those parts of a women were formed by nature, not only for the direction of the Penis in coition, but for the direction of the Doctor's finger in touching'.
69 Thicknesse, *Man Midwifery Analysed*, p. 17.
70 *Ibid.*, p. 22.
71 *Ibid.*, p. 15. 'Touch' was of course slang for sexual intercourse. As a technical

medical term, it was almost exclusively reserved for gynaecological examination. Thicknesse explained the function of touching thus (p. 8): 'to see if any emotion arise in the touched lady's breast, that the Doctor may take advantage of'.

72 Ibid., p. 9.
73 Ibid., p. 10.
74 Ibid., p. 21.
75 See B. Mandeville, *A Treatise of the Hypochondriack and Hysterick Passions*, London, 1711 and *Medicina Flagellata*, London, 1722, p. 25.
76 For discussion, see John Forrester, 'Rape, Seduction and psychoanalysis', in Sylvana Tomaselli and Roy Porter (eds.), *Rape*, Oxford, 1986, pp. 57–83.
77 Thicknesse, *Man-Midwifery Analysed*, p. 22. Important here of course was the contemporary witchhunt against masturbation. See J. Stengers and A. Van Neck, *Histoire d'une grande peur. La masturbation*, Brussels, 1984.
78 Thicknesse, *Man-Midwifery Analysed*, p. 24.
79 Thus see also *The Danger and Immodesty of The Present Too General Custom of Unnecessarily Employing Men-Midwives*, London, 1772, and John Blunt [pseud.], *Man-Midwifery Dissected, or the Obstetric Family Operator*, London, 1793.
80 [F. Foster],*Thoughts on the Times*, 2nd ed., London, 1779. This book also denounced many other features of the indulgence and licence permitted to women, not least fashionable education.
81 Ibid., p. 93.
82 Ibid., p. 84.
83 Ibid., p. 86. 'There cannot be a greater Error than that the knowledge of Anatomy is necessary for any Cases, but that unhappy one in many thousands'.
84 Ibid., p. 89.
85 Ibid., p. 122. The Smellie quotation comes from his *Treatise on the Theory and Practice of Midwifery*, 3 vols, London, 1752–64, I, p. 261.
86 Ibid., p. 122.
87 Ibid., p. 120.
88 Ibid., p. 189.
89 Ibid., p. 193.
90 Ibid., p. 161.
91 Ibid., p. 178.
92 Ibid., p. 94.
93 Ibid., p. 165. Other sources suggested that women expected man-midwives to offer sexual titillation. 'Gregory Glyster' said the obstetrician must be ready with a fund of 'fashionable recitals of *seduction, rapes, fornication, and adultery*': *A Dose for the Doctor*, London, 1789, p. 27.
94 Ibid., p. 160.
95 Ibid., p. 172.
96 Ibid., p. 173.
97 Ibid., p. 200. For a similar attack on 'pusillanimous' husbands who fail to defend their wives from accoucheurs who indulge in 'sly touches', see J. Blunt [pseud.], *Man Midwifery Dissected*, London, 1793, p. xv.

98 *The Man Midwife Unmasqu'd*, London, 1738. This is complemented by *The Lady's Decoy and the Man Midwife's Defence*, London, 1738. It claims to depict the real story of a Dr. D, but I have not been able to discover his identity.
99 These, it should be noted, continued into the nineteenth century. See [Anon.], *Observation on the Impropriety of Men being employed in the Business of Midwifery*, London, 1827; M. Adams, *Man-Midwifery Exposed*, London, 1830; John Stevens, *Man-Midwifery Exposed*, London 1849; W, Talley, *He, or Man-Midwifery*, London, 1863, [Anon.], *The Accoucheuse and the Accoucheur*, London, 1864.
100 See D. Ehrenreich and D. English, *Witches, Midwives and Nurses*, Old Westbury, N.Y., 1973.
101 Adrian Wilson, 'William Hunter and the varieties of man mid-wifery', in W. F. Bynum and Roy Porter (eds.), *William Hunter and the Eighteenth Century Medical World*, Cambridge, 1985, pp. 343–70, and E. Shorter, 'The Management of normal deliveries and the generation of William Hunter' in *ibid.*, pp. 371–84.
102 Thicknesse, *Man Midwifery Analysed*, p. 15.
103 [F. Foster], *Thoughts on the Times*, p. 120.
104 [F. Forster], *Thoughts on the Times*, p. 29. For a similar case see J. Mck. Adair, *Essays on Fashionable Diseases*, London, 1709, p. 257.
105 Traditionally, of course, male authors had accused female midwives of performing socially corrosive services such as trading in abortifacients. See A. MacLaren, *Reproductive Rituals*, London, 1984, pp. 89ff, and *Trials for Adultery*, iii, London, 1797, pp. 4–5.
106 W. Wadd, *Mems., Maxims and Memoirs*, London, 1827, p. 283. For contemporary testimony of Hunter's respectability, see, for example, *The Danger and Immodesty of the present too General Custom of unnecessarily Employing Men-Midwives*, London, 1772, 1, and [F. Foster], *Thoughts on the Times*, p. 152. For Hunter, see Samuel Foart Simmons, *The Life and Writings of the Late Dr. William Hunter*, London, 1783. This has been reissued, together with John Hunter's marginal notes and an important reassessment by C. H. Brock, in *William Hunter 1718–1783*, Glasgow, 1983; R. Hingston Fox, *William Hunter, Anatomist, Physician, Obstetrician, with Notices of his Friends*, London, 1901; Sir Charles Illingworth, *The Story of William Hunter*, New York, 1946, and G. C. Peachey, *Memoir of William and John Hunter*, Plymouth, 1924.
107 See *Trials for Adultery, or the History of Divorces*, I, London, 1779, pp. 8ff.
108 *Ibid.*, pp. 10, and 139.
109 *Ibid.*, pp. 12, and 102.
110 *Ibid.*, p. 12.
111 *Ibid.*, p. 13.
112 *Ibid.*, p. 148.
113 *Ibid.*, pp. 143, and 184.
114 *Ibid.*, pp. 149, and 102.
115 *Trials for Adultery*, I, London, 1779.
116 *Ibid.*, p. 71.

117 Ibid., p. 76.
118 Ibid., p. 72.
119 Ibid., p. 74.
120 Ibid., p. 113.
121 *Trials for Adultery*, IV, London, 1780, p. 144.
122 See C. H. Brock, 'The happiness of riches', in W. F. Bynum and Roy Porter (eds.), *William Hunter and the Eighteenth Century Medical World*, Cambridge, 1985, pp. 35–56, and Roy Porter, 'William Hunter: a surgeon and a gentleman' in *ibid.*, pp. 7–34.

Part 3
Sex at the margins

9

'Passing women'
– A study of gender boundaries in the eighteenth century

LYNNE FRIEDLI

'The putative center welcomes selective inhabitants of the margin in order better to exclude the margin. And it is the center that offers the official explanation; or, the center is defined and reproduced by the explanation that it can express . . .' (Gayatri Spivak)[1]

Although the phenomenon of 'passing women' or women who dressed as men is by no means specific to the eighteenth century, what is apparent from the late seventeenth century is a number of texts which indicate a growing interest in female transvestites.[2] By passing women, I refer to women who attempted to live, work or marry as men during some time in their lives. This practice is quite distinct from theatrical cross-dressing, which was common until the middle of the century, and the cross-dressing that was a feature of a number of clubs for men throughout the period. It is not clear to what extent cross-dressing among women also involved sexually transgressive practices, although the two were seen to go together in the case of men.[3] Transvestism allows access to experiences that are defined as accessible to one gender only – a notable feature of the Molly Clubs was participation in traditionally female rituals.[4] Women who cross-dressed generally gained the higher social and economic status associated with being male. They had access to occupations that were limited to men, notably in the military field. In addition, dressed as men they enjoyed greater mobility and employment prospects, with better pay, and faced less possibility of sexual attack, with the opportunity to pursue traditional courtship patterns with members of their own sex.[5] While both men and women spoke of the pleasures of cross-dressing, men (apart from prostitutes) had nothing to gain materially from the adoption of femininity and it remained largely a social practice.

References to women who dressed as men feature most commonly as anecdotes in newspapers and periodicals, less frequently in medical 'case histories' and occasionally in court records. The latter of course reveal only those women who were prosecuted and, as yet, no case has come to light of a woman being prosecuted unless she married, or attempted to do so. Lord Hardwicke's Marriage Act (1754) may have made such marriages more difficult, or prosecution more likely. *The Fleet Registers* give three examples of women marrying each other, with no record of any action being taken against them.[6] Whereas men who were prosecuted in relation to homoerotic practices were charged with sodomy, a specifically sexual offence, women who married were charged with fraud. Sexual relations between women rarely attracted the attention of the courts, and neither women who merely dressed as men, nor those who married, were the focus of public disapproval in the way that Molly Clubs and effeminate men were.[7]

In the absence of quantitative documentary evidence in the form of court records, acts of parliament or parish registers, accounts of passing women have remained largely anecdotal, in the form that itself became so popular during the eighteenth centry. Little attempt has been made to relate it to medical and epistemological debates about the nature of sexual difference.[8] I intend, therefore, to place this study of an apparently minor idiosyncrasy in the context of three areas: a) shifting notions of what constituted masculinity and femininity; b) medical interest in hermaphrodites as an example of the importance attached to defining precisely gender boundaries, and c) texts which function as part of a pornographic genre that uses transgression to invite pleasure, and by transcending the limit of acceptable behaviour, define those limits.

By the end of the eighteenth century, the dominant identity for woman was that of wife and mother. That this marks a specific shift in the meaning of 'woman as sign' is perhaps most clear in the importance attached to childhood, and the special status it achieved during the period.[9] Of course, women were seen as wives and mothers before the eighteenth century. What is new is an understanding of these roles as constituting a specific status or profession – in and of themselves. Mothering is broken down into constituent parts – feeding, clothing, diet, exercise, education – each of which becomes an area of endless scrutiny. Concern with population and child mortality, as well as the enormous influence of Locke's notion of the *tabula rasa*, meant that the environment of the child was seen as crucial. Ultimately all women must be educated to become mothers who contribute positively to the health and good habits of their children. The ideal of the love match, the companionate marriage, can be seen as providing an environment considered favourable to the development of the mother role and the nurturing of children. Positive images of marriage in the eighteenth century contrast strongly with the unpopularity of this institution in polite and radical culture in the seventeenth century.[10]

Through a range of images in visual art, literature, medical texts, didactic tracts and legislative reform, whatever is thought to interfere with adequate mothering, from arranged marriages, to apprenticeship patterns, is called into question. The movement that sees the midwife made accountable to the medical man also calls upon the father to supervise more closely the way in which his children are reared, to 'know what is done in the darkest recesses of his house'.[11]

The idea of the chaste wife, caring for her children at home and restraining, through her modulating influence, the excesses of her husband, could only ever be a fiction for the majority of the population. What is significant, however, is the power this image achieves, drawing as it does on nature and the natural, and its dominance in didactic discourse. A range of texts on child-care, wet-nursing, infanticide, illegitimacy, prostitution, health and education come to define the rights and duties of the wife and mother in such a way as largely to preclude any consideration of women except in relation to these roles.[12] While it would be inaccurate to suggest that women were seen as 'not sexual', opposing images of sexuality as good and evil are reconciled in the maternal figure.[13] Within the family the spontaneous and potentially disruptive aspects of female sexuality are contained, while woman's qualities as nurturer can be realised to greatest effect. The symbolism invested in the body of the mother is that of nature as harmonious, benevolent and well-ordered. Like the landscaped garden (nature contained), the woman suckling her child points to the importance of contradictory definitions of nature in this period. 'Nature unschool'd' is contrasted with constant references to nature to define the normal.[14]

While the role of mother could be used to curb the excesses of decorative and sexual femininity, it also emphasised a close relationship between women and qualities seen as nurturing. The corresponding role of father, above all in its supervisory capacity, promoted a version of masculinity wholly compatible with the entrepreneurial spirit of an ascendant middle class. In precisely the period when women's opportunities for gainful employment were undergoing erosion, an image of femininity involving qualities incompatible with competing on the market-place gained currency. What is crucial here, in terms of debates about women, is the extent to which the function of mothering, and the qualities associated with it, become the mainstay of the late eighteenth and early nineteenth century feminist debate.[15] In Mary Wollstonecraft's *Vindication of the Rights of Woman* (1792), the problems of sexual expression for women are displaced by the special status of the mother and sexuality is sublimated in maternal fulfilment. The middle-class man is persuaded that a predominant emphasis on the sexual side of marriage is, like the pleasures of the seraglio, an aristocratic decadence, which he is invited to denounce in favour of the chaste wife who will best educate his children.[16] In Wollstonecraft's fiction, suffering is perpetually connected to inadequate mothering.[17] The arguments expressed in *Vindication* were not, as has been widely suggested, seen as wholly unacceptable, but on the contrary were quite in line with current ideas on the education of women, and were already being practised with success in charity schools.[18]

The significance attached to the role of mother had a number of important implication in relation to the adoption or rejection of a feminine identity.[19] Firstly, it provided a very specific definition of what a woman was and, secondly, it opened up the 'feminine' as an object of medical enquiry. The accounts of passing women that follow, therefore, occurred in a context where the role of women was a prominent subject of debate, while the discussion of hermaphrodites gives some indication of the role of the nascent medical profession in this area.

That passing women were prosecuted for fraud suggests that the major issue was deception and the consequent usurpation of rights and privileges, rather than sexual deviance in itself.[20] In this period, deception becomes important notably in the areas of religion and medicine, and takes on a special meaning in relation to women because of the connection between *appearance* and sexual attraction and gendered associations in the opposition between knowledge and superstition. The metaphors that inform medical descriptions of women's bodies suggest that women are constitutionally more susceptible to influence; more credulous. As such, they are more likely to fall prey to the excesses of religious enthusiasm or the harmful effects of quackery, and women figure prominently in both areas.[21] Women, then, are easily deceived but also more capable of deception. They use deceptive practices, primarily in relation to their appearance, to heighten their sexual attractiveness – the cosmetic rituals satirised by Swift and Pope.[22] The attacks of writers like Defoe and Cobbett on 'empty accomplishments' are a criticism of women who value their sexual identity and allow it to take precedence over preparation for the duties of motherhood.

Men were also satirised in this period for excessive 'foppery', culminating in the caricatures of the 'macaroni' during the 1770s.[23] There is, however, an important distinction to be made between attacking men for not being masculine enough, and attacking women for being too feminine: both critiques serve to confirm the value of being male. Not only must the distinction between masculinity and femininity be preserved, but what constitutes the masculine is defined through ridicule of the feminine. Deception is seen to erase hierarchies essential to the health and stability of society. Masquerade allowed men of questionable pedigree to appear in high society; in *High Life Below Stairs* (1772) a maid is easily transformed into a mistress.[24] By the 1790s, the extravagance of male attire was replaced by skirtless coats, cropped heads and the accessory of the heavy stick. Georgiana Hill suggests that such unencumbered dress implied readiness for action, its plainness a foil for the beauty of the female in clinging décolleté.[25]

The deception of passing women encompasses an *implied* rejection of the maternal role and appropriation of the sexual role of the male. The texts that follow give some indication of the most common variations of cross-dressing: the woman who married and was prosecuted, the actress who cross-dressed with impunity, and the female soldier who received an honourable discharge on discovery of her sex. The final case of Chevalier D'Eon is a rare example of a man who lived as a woman.

The Female Husband (1746) by Henry Fielding is a reworking or fictional account of the case of Mary Hamilton, who was convicted of fraud in Taunton, Somerset, for posing as a man and subsequently marrying one Mary Price.[26] According to the court records, she left home at fourteen, dressed in her brother's clothes and, having served an apprenticeship, set up as a quack doctor under the name of Charles Hamilton. On 16 July 1746 she married Mary Price and on 18 September 1746 was arrested after her wife declared publicly that Charles was not a man but a woman. The court records say: 'after their marriage they lay together several nights and that the said pretended Charles Hamilton who had married her aforesaid entered her body several times, which made this woman believe at first that the said Hamilton was a real man'.[27]

Whether Mary Price was in fact unaware that Charles was a woman is impossible to say, given that once she decided to end the marriage it was in her own interests to convince the court that she was innocent. A letter from the presiding magistrate, asking for advice on the case notes: 'The Gen'll of the Corporation of Glaston as well as the principal inhabitants, are desirous that the woman imposter who was sometime since committed, sho'd be punished in the severest manner the Quarter Sessions can'.[28]

Mary Hamilton was publicly whipped in four market towns and imprisoned for six months. The case was reported in three newspapers and later in the *Gentleman's Magazine*. The following, from the *Bath Journal* catches the typical tone: 'There are great numbers of people flock to see her in Bridewell, to whom she sells a great deal of her quackery; and appears very bold and impudent. She seems very gay, with Perriwig, Ruffles and Breeches; and it is publicly talked that she has deceived several of the fair sex by marrying them'.[29]

The *Gentleman's Magazine* called her 'an uncommon, notorious cheat' and neither court records nor press reports give any indication that her deception was perceived as a sexual crime.[30] However, it is on the sexual aspects of the trial that Fielding chooses to focus. In his account, Hamilton marries on three occasions, each time successfully deceiving her wife by means of 'something of too vile wicked and scandalous nature'. It is by boasting about her marital experiences that the innocent Mary Price causes doubts to be raised about her husband, and her mother to cry out, 'O Child, there is no such thing in human nature'.[31]

At first appearance, the text incorporates a number of familiar themes: the contagious nature of vice, corruption of innocence and the absolute sanctity of male and female roles – 'that propense inclination which is for very wise purposes implanted in the one sex for the other'.[32] While every reference to the nature of the relationship between the two women is prefaced by a refusal to speak – 'which decency forbids me even to mention' – the function of the text is to delineate a female sexuality that is unlimited in its excesses, 'monstrous, unnatural, diabolical, vicious'. As such, *The Female Husband* has much in common with the genre of pornographic fiction that was becoming increasingly popular in this period.[33] Like *Fanny Hill* (1746), Mary Hamilton is initiated by another woman who was 'no novice in impurity, which as she confessed, she had learnt and often practiced at Bristol with her methodistical sisters'.[34] The pleasures of surveillance through the 'peepholes' in Cleland's classic are matched by the pleasures of the imagination evoked by Fielding. The secrecy of his text invites the reader to speculate endlessly on 'transactions not fit to be mentioned' and must imply that, far from being surprising, such examples of 'unnatural lusts' will be very familiar to readers.[35]

In comparison with the two texts that follow, Fielding's account can be seen to preclude a reading that constitutes gender roles as a site of struggle; 'unnatural lusts' function not to make problematic concepts of 'natural' sexual expression, but to excite the reader. The innocence of the wife prevents any suggestion of a consensual union, while the image of the methodist seductress relies on the currency of contemporary satires on the ludicrous excesses of religious enthusiasm.[36]

The autobiography of Charlotte Charke (1710–60) is ostensibly an elaborate apology aimed at a reconciliation between the author and her father, written when she was on the point of starvation. Possibly with this in mind, she characterises her adoption of male attire as the result of an event of absolute secrecy which 'concerns no mortal now living but myself'.[37] Charlotte Charke worked variously as a strolling actress playing men's parts, a grocer, a clerk, a pastry cook, a hog merchant, a man-servant and a writer. After a year of marriage at an age when she had 'no more distinguishing sense than a kitten', she gave birth to a daughter, decided to leave her husband and subsequently adopted men's clothing off-stage on a fairly regular basis. Her role as an actress seems to have protected her from prosecution, although she was imprisoned several times for debts.

The main interest of the narrative lies in her ability to explore a number of roles normally reserved for men, in a manner which oscillates between a caricature of herself and of the mystique with which gendered roles are invested: 'I was indeed of the opinion of Leander in *The Mock Doctor* that a few physical hard words would be necessary to establish my reputation; and accordingly had gathered up a many fragments as served to confound their senses and bring 'em into a high opinion of my skill in the medicinal science'; 'Making seeds and plants the general subject of my discourse, was the true characteristic of the Gardener; as, at other times, a Halter and horse-cloth brought into the house and awkwardly thrown down on a chair, were emblems of my stable profession'; 'The rise and fall of sugars was my constant topick', and 'I was entirely lost in forgetfulness of my real Self'.[38] The text provides a reading that suggests that the world is indeed a stage, where gendered roles have no meaning outside the costume, accessories and acting ability that constitute them. What limits the actress are the conventions of her audience: when her identity as Mr Brown is exposed, she loses her job as a clerk; when her child is ill she remarks: 'The people's compassion was moved, 'tis true; but as I happened not to be known to them, it drew them into astonishment, to see the figure of a young gentleman so extravagently grieved for the loss of a child'.[39]

Charlotte Charke never manages to reconcile her 'natural propensity to a Hat and Wig, in which at the age of four years, I made a very considerable figure' with the secret behind her persistent adoption of male attire.[40] It is this that subverts a closed reading; a satisfactory reconciliation of cause and effect in the form of an 'official' explanation for her behaviour. Like a number of other women writers, she exposes, both in her description of her own marriage and that of her daughter's, the contradictions of the duty of obedience to 'an inconsiderable fool'. In addition, her avid exploration of every role save that of wife might be read as a search for confirmation of her subjectivity, culminating in her intention to appear in 'The Catalogue of Authors'.[41] Charlotte Charke's autobiography is unusual in the extent to which she challenges a public/private division that is fundamental to the ordering of male/female roles. This is not merely because a woman who writes for publication necessarily enters the public arena, but because she speaks *from* the area of the 'public' in her various occupations.[42] The 'personal' or 'private' is largely silent, like the shadowy figure of her companion, Mrs Brown, slipping quietly in and out of the text. Recently, Pat Rogers has argued that 'what is missing in 18th century accounts . . . is a sense of the discovery of a new self through disguise.[43] On the contrary, adopting 'male' occupations enables Charke to forget her 'feminine' self in moments of autonomy. As the *Gentleman's Magazine* commented, 'diffidence and timidity do not appear to have been Charlotte's foibles, nor indeed any other that distinguish the sex'.[44] Again, it is the perceptions of her audience that challenge her sense of self, as when a neighbouring woman persuades Charlotte's mother that a gun is an unsuitable accessory for a daughter. The text in fact provides an unusual example in this period of a woman whose sense of self is defined primarily in relation not to her familial status (wife, mother, spinster, daughter) but to her occupational status. On her début in the theatre, she says: 'My name was in Capitals on this second attempt; and I dare aver, that the perusal of it from one end of the Town to the other, for the first week, was my most immediate and constant business'.[45]

Charlotte Charke explores the theme of male cross-dressing in her novel *The History of Henry Dumont* (1756). Typically, she makes her effeminate man a foreigner, either French or Italian, and then subjects him to violent abuse and attack from both the public and her hero, Mr Dumont: 'My behaviour could not in any degree give the smallest hope to the unnatural passion of such a detestable brute. I therefore think it incumbent on me to make an example of the villain', and 'The history of this affair in a few minutes got wind, sufficient to blow a whole mob together. And when the male-madam was permitted to decamp as he was . . . they snatched him from his supporters and very handsomely ducked him in the fish pond'.[46]

Instances of men who cross-dress to attract other men are rare in eighteenth-century novels and the addition of this episode, which is incidental to the plot, is perhaps significant, given the author's own behaviour. She leaves no record of any erotic inclination towards woman, and declines to persist in her disguise when a young woman falls in love with her and has hopes of marriage. Possibly she identified, or wished to identify herself, as strongly masculine and her hero's violent response to effeminacy represented a working-out of her ambivalent relationship to symbols of femininity.

The Female Review: or, Memoirs of an American Young Lady (1797), written by Herman Mann, is a justification of the enlistment of Deborah Sampson as a soldier during the American War of Independence (which he refers to as the civil war).[47] Women who dressed as men to become soldiers or sailors form by far the most common and most publicised of the recorded incidents of cross-dressing. Women like Hannah Snell fired the public imagination and female soldiers were both celebrated and reviled in popular ballads.[48] The high status of qualities associated with a military career gave women who showed them an increased value as 'honorary men', and served to validate qualities seen as masculine. As Brantome observes: "tis much better for a woman to be masculine and a very amazon and lewd after this fashion, than for a man to be feminine . . . for the more manlike she is the braver she is'.[49]

In the biography of Hannah Snell (1750), her bravery is used to comment upon the prevalence of effeminacy and its extremes among men and women. Snell's 'decent men's apparel (is) an incontestable proof of her aversion to the present fashionable hoop'.[50] Her courage marks an implicit criticism of defective masculinity and entitles her to male privilege: 'she boldly commenced a man – at least in her dress – and no doubt she had a right to do so, since she had the real soul of a man in her breast'.[51]

Mann says of Sampson, 'but her aspect is rather masculine and serene, than effeminate and sillily jocose'.[52] The 'exceptional' women merely reinforced the distance between the roles of men and women normally, and the adoption of masculinity in *clearly defined circumstances* can be seen to confirm the value of being male. The effeminate man cannot enjoy the same status because to be female is necessarily to be despised.[53] This is particularly significant in a period when women's highest status is that of mother – the one area of the feminine that the man is believed unable to adopt.

Herman Mann compares enlisting as a soldier, an unnatural act in a woman, with *civil* war, an unnatural event in society. This metaphor evokes powerfully the disturbing nature of conflict where one would expect harmony and coherence. Civil war is seen to represent the collapse of natural bonds of authority and is, like the French Revolution, a pervasive symbol of chaos, leading to a succession of unnatural events. The fact that familial metaphors predominated in colonial discourse reinforced the sense of a natural bond between Britain and America, while also allowing justification of the American War of Independence in terms of the child resisting the tyranny of the parent. As the area of rebellion most acceptable in the child is in the choice of marriage partner, it is interesting that Mann shows Sampson to be fighting for liberty and the protection of her chastity: 'and we may excuse even a female for taking arms in defence of all that is dear and lovely', 'Females! this effusion was from the veins of your tender sex, in quest of the LIBERTY, you now so serenely possess', and '. . . and that many of her own sex were either ravished or deluded to the sacrifice of their chastity, which she had been taught to revere, even as dear as life itself'.[54]

Because the narrative includes 'quotes' from the heroine, the text provides a plural reading. The voice of Deborah Sampson challenges the restrictions of the female sphere, 'a prison where I must drag out the remainder of my existence in ignorance', while the narrator constantly asserts that 'she has not the least wish to usurp the prerogatives of our sex'.[55] It is by no means clear that Deborah Sampson enlisted for patriotic reasons and, as the author notes, her departure coincided with her mother's suggestion that she accept a local suitor. After eighteen months as a common soldier, her gender was discovered and she received an honourable discharge in November 1783. She is said to have remained in men's clothing, although she married a man in the following year. It is at this point that the narrative is devoted to the question of her relationships with women:

> Had she been capacitated and inclined to prey, like a vulture, on the innocence of her sex, vice might have hurried vice, and taste have created appetition. Thus, she would have been less entitled to the clemency of the public. For individual crimes bring on public nuisances and calamities. And debauchery is one of the first. But, incapacity, which seldom begets desire, must render her in this respect, unimpeachable.[56]

Having established that Deborah Sampson is innocent of attempting to use her disguise sexually, Mann draws a moral from his exceptional heroine that is applicable to *all* women: 'Thus, Females, whilst you see the avidity of a maid in her teens confronting dangers and made a veteran example in war, you need only half the assiduity in your proper, domestic sphere, to render your charms completely irresistible'.[57]

The heroic status of female soldiers like Hannah Snell was possible because they were seen as exceptional. The problem of cross-dressing here seems to hinge firstly on whether or not it was seen as linked to sexual deviance, and secondly on whether it appeared to be moving from individual, marginal status to a more general and hence more central practice. In the climate of instability and reaction to events in France and the apparent collapse of order, a correspondent to the *Gentleman's Magazine* writes: 'A more unpleasant sight can scarcely be seen than that of a woman imitating the dress of our sex; and it is infinitely worse when they so far forget themselves as to imitate that of a soldier . . . . the acquiescence of the ladies in masculine vices, as it is more general, is also of worse consequence to the State'.[58]

The case of Chevalier D'Eon (1728–1810) attracted a great deal of attention in England, so much so that 'eonism' became the psychiatric term for men who adopted female dress. The Chevalier came to England in 1752 in connection with preliminary talks leading to the Treaty of Versailles. He first attracted attention owing to a number of alleged plots to return him forcibly to France. The Chevalier gained sympathetic press coverage and the issue was couched in terms that reflected on the freedom of England and the justice of her laws. Some time during the 1760s, the Chevalier began to appear publicly in women's clothes. The story was circulated that he had been brought up as a boy and for political reasons had only now been able to appear in his true gender. There is some question as to why the Chevalier adopted female dress and it may be, as Bullough asserts, that he did so unwillingly, on the order of Louis XVI.[59] Nevertheless, he kept newspaper cuttings of even the smallest reference to cross-dressing, hermaphrodites and related issues, which seems to indicate that the subject was not only topical, but of particular interest to him.[60] My main concern here, however, is with public reaction to the case of the Chevalier and its coverage in the press.

The appearance of Chevalier as a woman led to a flurry of speculation as to his true gender. *The Morning Post* declared two hundred thousand pounds to be at stake, and the debate raged as to whether he was 'either a man, an hermaphrodite or any other animal'.[61] The *Public Ledger* asked, 'why cannot the Chevalier at once declare, whether he is man, or woman, or whether of the doubtful gender?' (26 August 1776). Legal disputes over gambling on this issue culminated in the case of Hayes v. Jaques, heard by the Court of the King's Bench in July 1777. At the trial, two doctors testified that the Chevalier was a woman; one said that he had treated her for 'women's disorders' and the other that she had made suggestions of an amorous nature to him. The court ruled that he was a woman and the Chevalier signed an affidavit swearing that he had no interest in the bets taken out on the question.[62] In spite of the court's ruling, interest in the Chevalier continued.[63] *The Morning Heald and Daily Advertiser* (1785) wrote an article stating that he had always been a woman and concluding: 'the visitation of M. D'Eon to this country in the attire of the feminine, it is hoped will operate so forcibly as to induce such ladies who have usurped a right of wearing breeches, to leave them off'.[64]

In 1783, the *Daily Advertiser* declared General Washington to be a female in an article referring to both the Chevalier and Hannah Snell.[65] Between 1794 and 1796, the Chevalier fenced publicly in women's clothes and drew large crowds at Bath, Brighton, Oxford and Worcester. In spite of the *Public Ledger's* characterisation of him as an 'impertinent French female', press coverage was generally favourable. The Chevalier was seen as a woman who had been forced to adopt the disguise of a man but had now gone back to his proper sex. The fact that he had been noted for his reticence with women when in breeches added to the feeling that he could not be a man, while overall his status as an aristocrat afforded him some protection. In the issue of the *Gentleman's Magazine* reporting on his court case, another news item appeared about a woman convicted at Guildhall, Westminster, for wearing men's clothes and marrying three women. She was sentenced to stand pillory and serve six months in jail.[66]

When the Chevalier died in 1810, he was discovered to be a man and his body was examined. He was declared indisputably male, but: 'the throat was by no means a man's; the shoulders were square, the breast remarkably full, the arms, hands and fingers those of a stout female; the hips very small and the legs and feet corresponding with the arms'.[67]

Prior to eighteenth-century enshrinement of the problem in medical discourse, the existence of hermaphrodites appears to have been of little concern.[68] The legal aspect is addressed by Coke on Littleton: 'Every heire is either a male, or female, or an hermaphrodite, that is both male and female. And an hermaphrodite shall be heir, either as male or female, according to that kind of the sexe which does prevail'.

Issue in law depended on having a human shape: 'Persons deformed, having human shape, idiots, madmen, lepers, deafe, dumbe, blinde, minors and all other reasonable creatures, have power to purchase and retaine lands or tenements'.[69]

The medical debate about whether or not hermaphrodites existed, which began in the middle decades of the period, can be seen in the context of an enormous interest in monsters, monstrous births and other strange natural phenomena. What was at issue was the elasticity of nature, how to define her boundaries, and whether monsters were 'original' or created by 'accident'. In *Philosophical Transactions* of the Royal Society (1740), an article on monsters addresses this problem: 'The business is to find some plausible reasons about the origins of monsters . . . if we endeavour to push our knowledge so far, we find ourselves surrounded with clouds, we grope in the dark and it is very difficult, if not impossible, to catch nature in the fact'.[70]

In their study of attitudes to monsters in the sixteenth and seventeenth centuries, Park and Daston argue that there is a shift from the view of monsters as prodigies or wonders (a view that continued to inform popular culture) to monsters as examples of medical pathology.[71] The abnormal becomes interesting for what it can teach about the normal – monsters are both defined *by*, and used *to* define more precisely, the normal. Park and Daston suggest that artifice or 'fakes' emerge as a new causal category. Interest in the strange and monstrous, therefore, constitutes not an opening-up, but a closure. The singular has meaning only as a specimen of the general.[72] In addition, as is clear in the medicalisation of hermaphrodites, the objects of medical study are denied subjectivity in that they can only speak from their place within the discourse of pathology.[73]

The 1741 and 1783 editions of Chambers *Cyclopaedia* note the dispute as to the existence of hermaphrodites and quote Dr Quincy as saying it is a result of 'lascivious frictions'. However, the entry concludes: 'But we have an authentic account in the history of the Royal Academy of Sciences, of a real hermaphrodite: which may put the point out of question'.[74]

The question is taken up by the Royal Society on three occasions around 1740, and in 1750 the case of Michel-Ann Drouart aroused considerable interest when she was exhibited as an example of hermaphroditism to the medical profession.[75] In 1771 William Cadogan declared in an article in the *Gazetteer and New Daily Advertiser* that he had seen many examples of such cases.[76]

In 1741, James Parsons published his *A Mechanical and Critical Enquiry*, in which he sets out to establish firstly that hermaphrodites do not exist, and secondly that belief in them has been due solely to midwives and doctors mistaking a large clitoris for a penis:

> 'How few there were, who (from the obscurity of the clitoris in females in a natural state), knew that any such part existed. It is not therefore much to be wondered at, that at the first sight of a large clitoris divers odd conjectures should arise, and supply the fancy of those unskilled in due knowledge of the part, with matter sufficient for the erection of a new doctrine.[77]

Parsons is concerned to counteract 'superstitious mysteries' and 'occult causes' and his language is characteristic in its appeal to men of science to follow only nature and reason in their pursuit of knowledge. His account of the persecution and cruelty faced by hermaphrodites is drawn from classical sources and serves to distance the reader from the relatively uncontentious position of the hermaphrodite in seventeenth and eighteenth-century society. The 'monster', capable of inspiring fear and wonder, is reduced to the status of 'poor woman', suffering from what Parsons terms 'macroclitorideus'. His interest in this disorder is shared by James, who in his *Dictionary* (1743-5), in a lengthy section on 'tribades', returns repeatedly to the size of the clitoris which is: 'so shamefully large as to protuberate without the lips of the pudenda', 'so preternaturally large as to prove a monstrous deformity', and 'of enormous bigness . . . of so extraordinary a size as to resemble a penis'.[78]

'Macroclitorideus' is said to hinder coitus and both James and Parsons decribe how in certain countries, 'that useless part is removed'.[79] This is an interesting remark as it was well known that the clitoris was essential to female sexual pleasure.[80] What is apparent is that emphasis on the size of the clitoris provided a metaphor for confronting the excess of female sexuality, which found its most threatening expression in the appropriation of the male role – 'women's abuse of them with each other'.[81] The fear and fascination with which European society encountered the apparently unlimited sexuality of the female 'other' in African and Oriental culture finds its counterpart in descriptions of sexual aberrations closer to home.[82] This fear is neutralised through the techniques of surgical intervention – James's description of how a surgeon should perform clitoridectomy provides reassuring symbol of the medical profession's capacity to curb nature's intemperance.

In 1750, George Arnaud published his *Dissertation on Hermaphrodites*, undertaking to classify the different types precisely and inviting the public to submit details and pictures of any cases they knew of.[83] He divides hermaphrodites into imperfect (male and female) and perfect. An hermaphrodite is male when the penis is perfect but the vagina not large enough to admit a penis, although still allowing a monthly discharge of blood. An hermaphrodite is female when all the female reproductive parts are present, and the clitoris is free, like a penis, but not perforated for urination. The perfect hermaphrodite exhibits the full parts of generation of both sexes.

Arnaud sees careful classification as crucial, firstly because legal disputes regarding gender are referred to physicians, and secondly because of the importance of reproduction:

> As it is possibly on the relation of physicians and surgeons that divines and lawyers determine on the species to which those should keep, to whom nature has given faculties so opposite, either for administering the sacraments or doing them justice in civil and criminal affairs: 'tis in these cases that surgeons ought to be perfectly informed in the structure and relation of these parts which constitute hermaphrodites; and that they ought to give a good deal of attention to the nature of the secretions peculiar to those organs, without which they would be guilty of very great mistakes, by forbidding those parts which possibly might be the fittest for generation. . . .[84]

The True History and Adventures of Catherine Vizzani (1755) is interesting because it is ostensibly translated by a doctor, who attempts to find a physiological explanation for her abnormal behaviour.[85] The case concerns an Italian woman who dressed as a man and was shot while trying to elope with the niece of a minister. The author states that he dissected the body, removing the parts of generation, but found nothing unusual. The English translator criticises him for not suggesting the causes of her behaviour: 'It should seem that this irregular and violent inclination . . .

must either proceed from some error in nature or from some disorder or perversion in the imagination'.[86]

Whether the abnormal was natural or not natural is clearly still in question. Arnaud says of nature: 'she has exhibited irregular, vicious and unseemly conformations of parts,' while Parsons asserts:

> 'if there was not so absolute a law with respect to the being of only one sex in one body, we might then indeed expect to find every day many preposterous digressions from our present standard'.[87]

The French case of Anne Grand-Jean is interesting because, although she was diagnosed as an hermaphrodite, she was ordered to adopt female clothing, confirming the tendency to regard hermaphrodites as deformed women. In *Reflexions sur les Hermaphrodites relativement à Anne Grand-Jean* (1765), the author acknowledges the existence of hermaphrodites, but argues that, because the clitoris resembles the penis, it is not difficult to imagine how women have been taken for men and deceived innocent women. He argues that correct identification of gender is crucial because the greatest crime is to use each sex as you please, one day a woman, one day a man. In this respect he suggests that it isn't merely genitals that determine sex, but the whole body. Again, he mentions removal of enlarged clitorises in Ethiopia and the Orient, and describes the operation as simple and not dangerous.[88]

Concern with hermaphrodites may be seen as part of what Foucault calls the attempt to 'decipher the true sex'.[89] The cases of Anne Grand-Jean and Catherine Vizzani suggest a medical context where abnormal behaviour must be rationalised in terms of pathology. What is apparent is that the increasing range of disorders to which the female body and feminine sexuality are susceptible cannot, ultimately, be explained solely in relation to the 'organical parts of woman'. Bienville, in *Nymphomania* (1775), sees an enlarged clitoris as a symptom, not the cause, of a disorder that, like the workings of the womb itself, is veiled in darkness. Like hermaphrodites, afflicted women are filled with a strong desire to conceal their disease, requiring the 'piercing and enquiring eye of the experienced practitioner to discover the problem'.[90] Speculation about the disorders of the imagination marks out the terrain for the passage from dissection of the genitals to dissection of the mind in nineteenth-century psychiatry.

The medical profession concerned itself with defining the limits of the natural and, in the main, looked for explanations of gender difference in the body. The courts were concerned with deception; the attempt to usurp the prerogatives of masculinity. Where it was clear that a woman who dressed as a man had a valid explanation, her rebellion could be reconciled when the special circumstances were revealed and she resumed her true sex.

The ease with which so many women passed as men suggests that standards of masculinity may not have been very high. With half of the population under sixteen, a large proportion of men in the community would have been beardless youths, with high pitched voices: an important factor, for women enlisting as new recruits were likely to be young. The increasing condemnation of effeminacy may thus point to an unease with such fluid boundaries in a society which was confronting the apparent erosion of many other social, political and geographical distinctions. Such an analysis would shift emphasis from understanding the construction of effeminacy as a symbol of attacks on social decadence, to evidence of a more general epistemological concern with clear-cut categorisation. The fact that passing women, even when they were involved in sexually transgressive practices, were not the object of severe punitive measures raises a number of theoretical problems about the operation and exercise of power in relation to 'masculinity' and 'femininity'. With the consolidation of the family as the space of feminine influence and the sphere of the woman, this structure itself serves to place effecive limits on the extent of transcendence of gender roles, above all for the woman who has no identity outside her familial status, in precisely the period when the concept of the 'individual' assumes such significance. To the extent that this family unit depends on male authority, in its symbolism as a microcosm of society, deviance by the man must be punished from outside, while individual fathers and husbands punish the transgressions of wives and daughters.

It might be argued that 'woman' is invented as a social category from around the end of the seventeeth century. Far from emerging after centuries of neglect to receive attention in philosophical, medical and legal discourse, these discourses constitute 'woman' and define a subject which will henceforth be referred to as the 'woman question'. The feminist debate was part of this movement, while passing women and hermaphrodites were of concern precisely because they made problematic the definition of gender. Ultimately, however, the power of 'mother' as symbol and identity marked out the area of primary intervention in the exercise of power in relation to femininity. It never became necessary to pass legislation with regard to erotic practices between women; they continued to move between the fluctuating boundaries of medical and pornographic discourse, where they flourish still.

Notes

1 Gayatri Spivak 'Explanation and culture: marginalia', *Humanities in Society*, 2 Summer 1979, p. 206. I should like to acknowledge my debt to Peter Hulme and Ludmilla Jordanova for their personal support and comments on an early draft. Special thanks to Pat Reynolds, to whom this chapter is dedicated. Part of this work was read to the Femininst History Conference, London, July 1985 and appeared in *Trouble and Strife. A Radical Feminist Journal*, Issue 6 Summer 1985.

2 The term 'passing' dates back to the 1920s, when it was used to refer to Black Americans 'passing' as white. It is used here to identify the practices of women 'passing' as men, and to distinguish it from other forms of cross-dressing. The *Oxford English Dictionary* dates the word 'transvestite' back to 1652, when it referred to women who dressed as men: 'How often did shee please her fancy with the imagination of transvesting herself, and by the help of a man's disguise deceiving the eyes of those that watched her deportment?' Marion Jones, 'Transvestite playing', *The Revels History of Drama 1660–1750*, Vol. 5, London, 1976, discusses the popularity of women playing men's roles in this period and suggests that the predominantly male audiences found women in breeches titillating.

3 Edward Ward, *History of London Clubs*, (1709), London, 1756, 'There are a particular gang of sodomitical wretches in this town, who call themselves Mollies, and are so far degenerated from all masculine deportment or manly exercises, that they rather fancy themselves women, imitating all the little vanities that custom has reconciled to the female sex, affecting to speak, walk, tattle, courtesy, cry, scold, and to mimick all manner of effeminacy', p. 265. Ward is the earliest example of the use of 'Molly' for sodomite. Molly was previously a generic term for girl, shifting to a contemptuous reference, occasionally to prostitutes. During the eighteenth century, it came to refer specifically to an effeminate man. OED cites 'a miss Molly, an effeminate fellow, a sodomite', 1785; See also Iwan Bloch, *Sexual Life in England*, London, 1958; Alan Bray, *Homosexuality in Renaissance England*, London, 1982; and Anthony E. Simpson, *Masculinity and Control: The Prosecution of Sex Offences in 18th Century London*, New York, 1984, discusses effeminacy and the emergence of a 'homosexual type' in the context of an ethos of masculinity among lower-class men.

4 Ward, 1756, describes 'mollies' participating in ritual childbirth and marriage ceremonies. While Ward is concerned with sensationalism and cannot be considered a reliable witness, he is an important example of the nascent construction of the 'effeminate type', who was to come under increasing attack, as both archetypal sodomite and symbol of social decline. On the latter, see John Brown, *An Estimate of the Manners and Principles of the Times*, London, 1757, 2 vols. Although, as Bray 1982 argues, the childbirth story is unsubstantiated by other evidence, witnesses in contemporary sodomy trials frequently refer to marriages: 'There is a bed in that middle room, for the use of the company when they have a mind to go there in couples and be married; and for that reason they call that room, The Chappel (sic)'. *Select Trials at the*

Sessions House in the Old Bailey for Murder, Robberies, Rapes, Sodomy, Coining, Frauds, Bigamy and Other Offences, London, 1742, trial of George Whitle.

5 From a sample of 34 women who cross-dressed between 1700 and 1800, sixteen were soldiers, sailors or pirates, five were convicted of offences related to same-sex marriage, four were discovered in the course of prosecution for other offences, e.g. petty larceny, five simply lived as single men, following various professions, were discovered and not prosecuted, three believed themselves to be hermaphrodites and one cross-dressed to escape prison. See Dorothy George, *London Life in the 18th Century*, London, 1925, on declining employment opportunities for lower-class women , and also K. D. M. Snell, *Annals of the Labouring Poor: Social Change in Agrarian England 1660–1900*, Cambridge, 1985.

6 Lord Hardwicke's Marriage Act made the punishment for performing a marriage outside a church, without a licence or publication of banns, fourteen years' transportation; John Southerden Burn (ed.), *The Fleet Registers*, London, 1883.

7 Simpson, 1984, from his analysis of court records in London between 1730 and 1830 notes a marked increase in the severity of punishments for offences related to sodomy. He suggests a degree of popular harrassment of homosexual men and argues, 'dislike of mollies was a principal manifestation of contempt for the effeminate male . . .', p. 785. An exception of a slightly later date is the case of Woods and Pirie v. Helen Cumming Gordon (1811). The case concerns two women who brought a libel suit against Dame Gordon after her public statement regarding their sleeping together 'indecently' forced them to close their school. The women won the case, but the trial provides an interesting discussion of perceptions of female sexuality in this period. In the testimony of the council for the defence, a lengthy list of literary sources is cited as evidence of erotic practices between women and Lord Glenlee notes, 'I have very little doubt that in all ages and countries, women have enjoyed this mode of pleasure seeking', Lillian Faderman, *Scotch Verdict*, New York, 1983 p. 87. An interesting comparison with the English record can be found in the German trial of Catherina Linck and Catherina Muhlhahn, which resulted in the execution of Linck for sodomy in 1721, 'A lesbian execution in Germany, 1721. The trial records', trans. Brigitte Erickson, *Journal of Homosexuality*, Vol. 6, Nos. 1/2 Fall/Winter 1980/1981, pp. 27–40.

8 See Jonathan Katz, *Gay American History. Lesbians and Gay Men in the U.S.A.*, New York, 1978, for an account of passing women in America 1782–1920, and Lillian Faderman, *Surpassing the Love of Men. Romantic Friendships & Love Between Women from the Renaissance to the Present*, London 1981. Faderman's work is problematic in its desire to provide a lesbian genealogy, often at the cost of historical accuracy. Above all, she fails to distinguish adequately who is speaking, where and from which positions of power or resistance, as she moves indiscriminately from court record to novel, from diary to pornographic handbook. In *Scotch Verdict* she fails to distinguish clearly between Fielding's sixpenny pamphlet and the court case of Mary Hamilton, stating incorrectly both that Fielding was the judge, and that the accused was found guilty of homosexual behaviour.

9 The term 'woman as sign' comes out of an understanding of the category 'woman' as the repository of a range of meanings, a symbol in discourse. What I am arguing here is that these meanings are historically specific; from around the early eighteenth century, the symbol 'woman' incorporates new ideas about the significance of the mother, ideas which are crucial to an understanding of shifts in the meaning of gender-loaded categories: man/woman, town/country, culture/nature, mind/body, reason/feeling. For a discussion of these categories in an Enlightenment context, see L. J. Jordanova, 'Natural facts: a historical perspective on science and sexuality', in Carol MacCormack & Marilyn Strathern (eds.), *Nature, Culture and Gender*, Cambridge, 1980, pp. 42–69. For an historical overview in relation to the development of science, see Carolyn Merchant *The Death of Nature. Women, Ecology and the Scientific Revolution*, London, 1982. There is an extensive literature on the growth of the idea of childhood as a period of special development in the eighteenth century: P. Ariès, *Centuries of Childhood*, Harmondsworth, 1973; J.-L. Flandrin, *Families in Former Times*, Cambridge, 1979; I. Pinchbeck and M. Hewitt, *Children in English Society*, Vols. 1 and 2, London, 1969, 1973. See also W. Cadogan, *An Essay Upon Nursing and the Management of Children, from their Birth to Three Years of Age*, London, 1748.

10 Cadogan 1748; W. Buchan, *Domestic Medicine: or, a Treatise on the Prevention and Cure of Diseases by Regimen and Simple Medicines*, 1772, London; Christopher Hill *The World Turned Upside Down*, Harmondsworth, 1972 on anti-marriage attitudes of some seventeenth-century religious sects; Carol Duncan, 'Happy Mothers and Other New Ideas in French Art', *Art Bulletin* 55, 1973, pp. 570–83 discusses the popularity of 'natural' images of the family in eighteenth-century painting.

11 S. Tissot, *An Essay on Onanism or a Treatise Upon the Disorders produced by Masturbation*, Dublin, 1760; 'On changes in childbirth practices', J. Donnison (ed.), *Midwives and Medical Men*, London, 1977.

12 Daniel Defoe, *The Family Instructor*, London, 1715; Cadogan 1748, and Buchan 1772.

13 Jane Sharp, *The Compleat Midwife's Companion: or, the Art of Midwifery Improv'd*, London, 1725, 4th ed., is one of many authors who discuss female sexual pleasure in this period. See also *The Pleasures of Conjugal Love Explain'd In An Essay Concerning Human Generation*, London, 1740 (a translation of N. Venette's *Tableau de l'amour Conjugal*, 1688, and Norah Smith 'Sexual Mores in the 18th Century: Robert Wallace's "Of Venery"', *Journal of the History of Ideas*, xxxix 1978 pp. 419–33.

14 Discussion of Enlightenment ideas about nature in MacCormack and Strathern, 1980.

15 See Gina Luria, *The Feminist Controversy in England 1788–1810*, New York, 1974, for a collection of works in facsimile. Earlier female apologists saw marriage as the mainstay of women's subordinate status in society and tended to favour celibacy. See Mary Astell *A Serious Proposal to the Ladies*, London, 1694; Lady Mary Chudleigh, *The Ladies Defence*, London, 1701. Margaret Cavendish (1623–73) argues that women do not benefit by having children 'for though it be the part of every good wife to desire children to keep alive the

memory of their husband's name and family by posterity, yet a woman has no such reason to desire children for her own sake', cited in Joan Goulianous (ed.), *By a Woman Writt. Literature from Six Centuries by and about Women*, Baltimore, 1974, p. 65.

16 Mary Wollstonecraft, *Vindication of the Rights of Woman*, 1792, Harmondsworth, 1978, 'The father of a family will not then weaken his constitution and debase his sentiments by visiting the harlot, nor forget, in obeying the call of appetite, the purpose for which it was implented. And the mother will not neglect her children to practise the arts of coquetry, when sense and modesty secure her the friendship of her husband' (p.89). Resistence to sexual exploitation in the form of calls for chastity in marriage or women's right to sexual abstinence in marriage becomes a notable feature of feminist debates in the nineteenth and early twentieth centuries.

17 Wollstonecraft celebrates friendship and places predominant emphasis on the companionate marriage. Sexual passion or romantic love is seen as transitory and is placed in direct contrast with the fulfillment offered by motherhood. Crucially, this is also the area in which the 'private' gains public validity and she bases her central argument for an improvement in women's education on the fact of their roles as mothers. In *The Wrongs of Woman: or, Maria. A Fragment*, 1798, pp. 82, the heroine's feeling of fragmentation of self is resolved through her sense of identity as a mother as she writes to her child. See also the description of Mary's mother in *Mary A Fiction*, 1788, pp. 1ff. Both are reprinted in *Mary and The Wrongs of Woman*, J. Kinsley & G. Kelly (eds.), Oxford, 1980.

18 Catherine Cappe, *Observations on Charity Schools, Female Friendly Societies and other subjects connected with the views of the Ladies Committee*, York, 1805.

19 The extent of the dominance of mother as symbol (above all in relation to women's sexual identity) is nowhere clearer than in the ferocity with which Sade attacks her. As Angela Carter, *The Sadeian Woman*, New York, 1978, has shown, Sade strips nature of morality, demystifies the sacred role of mother and severs any necessary link between sexuality and reproduction. Sade is threatening precisely because he shows that nature is not maternal, but is governed only by the pursuit of pleasure. The self-denial of the mother, her virtue, is exposed as hypocrisy, and is experienced by the daughter Justine as a constraint on her own sexual pleasure.

20 Fraud and the related areas of forgery, impersonation and copyright became the focus of increasing concern in law from the end of the seventeenth century. The first attempt to pass a law for the prevention of frauds and perjuries was in 1673, and an act was passed in 1677. It was concerned mainly with wills, land ownership, deeds of transfer etc. and the necessity for written evidence to validate such transactions. The act was also intended to facilitate creditors' recourse to law in the case of unpaid debts. In 1709 copyright was established in the name of the author, and in 1721 impersonation (formerly a misdemeanour), with intent to defraud, was made a felony without benefit of clergy. W. Blackstone, *Commentaries on the Laws of England*, London, 1765–9; J. S. Cockburn, *Crime in England 1550 – 1800*, London, 1977; Isabel Rivers (ed.), *Books and their Readers in 18th Century England*, Leicester, 1982. What is

at issue here is not only a concern with property, ownership and authority, but a need to establish, with increasing precision, the parameters of the factual. Concern with the problem of evidence is aimed at counteracting any discrepancy between appearance and truth. The need to define precisely what constitutes valid evidence is fundamental to Enlightenment epistemology, notably in the areas of religion, natural history, philosophy and law.

21 The dominant areas of popular non-conformist practice lay in prophecy, preaching and the curative techniques of physical and spiritual healing, as well as exorcism. On women and religious dissent, J. F. C. Harrison, *The Second Coming: Popular Millenarianism 1780–1850*, London, 1979; Barbara Taylor, *Eve and the New Jerusalem: Socialism and Feminism in the 19th Century*, London, 1983, contains some eighteenth-century material.

22 Alexander Pope, 'The Rape of the Lock', 1714, *The Poems of Alexander Pope*, John Butt (ed.), London, 1965, and Jonathan Swift, *A Beautiful Young Nymph Going to Bed*, London, 1734.

23 See examples of caricature of the 'macaroni' and men's effeminate fashions in G. Paston, *Social Caricature in the 18th Century*, London, 1905. See also Aileen Ribeiro, 'The Macaronis', *History Today*, July 1978, pp. 463–8; *The Dress Worn At Masquerades in England 1730–1790 and its relation to Fancy Dress in Portraiture*, London, 1984, and D. Kunzle, *Fashion and Fetishism: a Social History of the corset, tight lacing and other forms of body sculpture in the West*, London, 1982.

24 A reproduction of this appears in Paston, 1905, p. 128.

25 See Georgiana Hill, *History of English Dress*, Vol. 2, London, 1893. The theme of the deceptive appearance of women and its relation to sexual deviance come together in a cutting satire, W. King, *The Toast. An Heroic Poem in Four books*, London, 1736, where the central character, Myra, is transformed into a hermaphrodite:
   Not a counterfeit belle cou'd their prying escape
   Who had made a new face, or had mended her shape. . .
   Yet the Dames who pollute their own sex they lik'd worse
   And the tribads were all set aside with a curse.

26 See Henry Fielding, *The Female Husband*, 1746; Liverpool, 1960, reprinted with more extravagant detail as *The Surprising Adventures of a Female Husband*, London, 1813. See also S. Baker, 'Henry Fielding's The Female Husband: Fact and Fiction', *PMLA*, 74, 1959, p. 213–24, and T. Castle, 'Matters not fit to be mentioned: Fielding's *The Female Husband*', *ELH*, 49, 1982, p. 602–22.

27 Somerset Quarter Sessions, 13 September 1746.

28 Quarter Sessions Records 9 September 1746. Letter from Thomas Hughes to Henry Gould. Gould was Henry Fielding's cousin.

29 *Bath Journal*, 22 September 1746.

30 *The Gentleman's Magazine* 28 November 1746. Notices also appeared in *Daily Advertiser* 7 November 1746, and *St James Evening Post*, 8 November 1746.

31 Fielding, p. 48.

32 Fielding, p. 30.

33 David Foxon, *Libertine Literature in England 1660-1745*, New Hyde Park, 1965, and R. Thompson, *Unfit for Modest Ears*, London, 1980.

34 Fielding, p. 31, and John Cleland, *Fanny Hill: Memoirs of a Woman of Pleasure*, 1749, London, 1964.
35 'Sapphic interludes' were in fact very common in both erotica and 'medical' texts, although the extent of the readership of such works is impossible to determine. See Cleland, 1749; *The Covent Garden Magazine*, January – August 1774; Denis Diderot, *The Nun*, 1796, Harmondsworth, 1982, trans. L. Tancock; H. G. R. Mirabeau, *Histoire secrete de la cour de Berlin*, Paris, 1789; R. James, *A Medicinal Dictionary*, London, 1743–5, 3 vols, and J. Quincy, *Lexicon Physico-Medicon*, 1719, London, 1794 11th edition.
36 See, for example, Hogarth's engraving, *Credulity, Superstition and Fanaticism: A Medley*, 1762.
37 Charlotte Charke, *A Narrative of the Life of Mrs. Charlotte Charke written by herself*, 1755; London, 1929, p. 216.
38 Charke, pp. 33ff.
39 Charke, p. 83.
40 Charke, p. 213.
41 It is out of an understanding of subjectivity as constructed in language in relation to sexual difference that psychoanalytic debates about women and language have arisen. Aspects of this debate appear in E. Marks and I. de Courtivion, *New French Feminisms: An Anthology*, Sussex, 1982. In Lacanian theory, the subject is split in its constitution through language; the 'I' can only perceive itself through the reflected image of others' perceptions of it. As Lacan argues, this split subjectivity takes on a double meaning for women: that the woman should be inscribed in an order of exchange of which she is the object, is what makes for the fundamentally conflictual, and I would say, insoluble, character of her position: the symbolic order literally submits her, it transcends her . . . There is for her something insurmountable, something unacceptable, in the fact of being placed as an object in a symbolic order to which, at the same time, she is subjected as much as the man'. This is cited in J. Mitchell and J. Rose (eds.), *Feminine Sexuality. Jacques Lacan and the école freudienne*, London and Basingstoke, 1982, p. 45. See also Deborah Cameron, *Feminism and Linguistic Theory*, London and Basingstoke, 1985.
42 Dale Spender, *Man Made Language*, London, 1982, Ch. 7 on women and writing for publication. It is perhaps significant that in those genres where women have predominated – autobiography, epistolary fiction and the novel – conflict is personalised, tending to displace any sense of general or collective protest.
43 Pat Rogers, 'The Breeches Part', in P.-G. Boucé (ed.), *Sexuality in 18th Century Britain*, Manchester, p. 254. 'Forgetfulness' as a metaphor for an ambiguous relationship to gender identity is a feature of several other ostensible autobiographies of passing women. See *The Life and Adventures of Mrs. Christian Davis commonly called Mother Ross, by her own mouth*, London, 1740, and *The Life and Surprising Adventures of Mary Ann Talbot in the name of John Taylor, related by herself*, London, 1809.
44 *Gentleman's Magazine*, November 1755. Charlotte Charke's life was serialised in *Gentleman's Magazine* from September to December 1755.
45 Charke, p. 50. Patricia Meyer Spacks, *Imagining a Self. Autobiography and*

Novel in 18th Century England, London, 1976, suggests that the crucial relationship through which Charke defines herself is filial (p. 74). It seems to me, rather, that Charke's appeal to her father is almost certainly a strategy to gain financial assistance. The autobiography itself is a last ditch attempt to make money when all else has failed. The 'dutiful daughter apologies' could be read as a convention in the same tradition as preface eulogies – which in Charke's case, she dedicates to herself.

46 Charlotte Charke, *The History of Henry Dumont*, London, 1756, p. 60 and 66–7.
47 Herman Mann, *The Female Review: or, Memoirs of an American Young Lady by a citizen of Massachussetts*, Dedham, 1797; Boston, 1866, ed. J. A. Vinton, New York, 1974.
48 C. M. Simpson, *The British Broadside Ballad and its Music*, New Jersey, 1966. *Gentleman's Magazine*, July 1750, celebrates the career of Hannah Snell (1723–92) and features a portrait of her on the cover. Hannah Snell enlisted in 1743 after the desertion of her husband and the death of her child. At some time after 1749 she took to the stage, and, according to the *Gentleman's Magazine*, gave public accounts of her heroic exploits. Snell's status thus depended on the fact that she was exceptional and had reasons for enlisting that could easily be rationalised:

Hannah in breeks behav'd so well
That none her softer sex could tell . . .
Her fortitude to no man's second
To woman's honour must be reckon'd.

See also *The Female Soldier or; The Surprising Adventures of Hannah Snell*, London, 1750.

49 Brantôme (Pierre de Bourdeille), *The Lives of Gallant Ladies*, 1665, London, 1969, p. 115.
50 *The Female Soldier*, 1750, p. 128.
51 *The Female Soldier*, 1750, p. 65.
52 Mann, p. 163.
53 The idealisation of the 'sentimental' man, whose refined sentiment is a mark of his capacity for genius, does not challenge this. The heightened sensibility and imagination that distinguished an intellectual élite (the poetic melancholy that characterised a literary genre from Thomas Gray to Coleridge), the cultural pursuits that enabled men to advance civilisation, in women constituted a failure to fulfil their maternal role. This is clear in medical discussions of hysteria and melancholy (hypochondria), which are marked by the same symptoms only diversified by the difference of sex; 'in women therefore this malady is called hysteric passion; in men, hypochondriac melancholy', John Leake, *Medical Instructions towards the Prevention and Cure of Chronic Diseases Peculiar to Women*, London, 1781, p. 253. See also Andrew Wilson, *Medical Researches: Being an Enquiry into the Nature and Origin of Hysterics*, London, 1777. On melancholy, see George Cheyne, *The English Malady*, London, 1733, and *The Natural Method of Cureing*, London, 1742. While melancholy achieves a certain status, hysteria above all interferes with

women's capacity to mother.
54 Mann, pp. 141 and 173–4.
55 Mann, p. 257.
56 Mann, p. 248.
57 Mann, p. 188.
58 *Gentleman's Magazine*, January 1795. Events in France during the aftermath of the Revolution raised a number of questions about the position of women on both sides of the channel. Although notions of women's moral power generally saw exercise of that power only in terms of the family sphere, in her analysis of the 'cahiers de doléance' presented to the Estates General in 1789, Ruth Graham finds, 'according to these pamphlets, women's moral ascendency over men, a gift of nature, entitled them to political rights'. 'Rousseau's Sexism Revolutionised' in *Women in the 18th Century and other Essays*, P. Fritz & R. Morton (eds.), Toronto, 1976, p. 131. The widespread mobilisation of women and the impact of the clubs they opened called into question women's participation in the *public* sphere. In 1793, all women's clubs were closed down by order. In the report of the Committee of General Security on this decision, the adoption of men's clothes by revolutionary women was strongly condemned and was seen in the same context as women's participation in public government. Darline, Gay, Levy et. al. (eds.), *Women in Revolutionary Paris 1789–1795*, London, 1979.
59 Vern L. Bullough, *Sexual Variance in Society and History*, New York, 1976.
60 *Des Parties des Gazettes Anglaises et Etrangères que j'ai pu recueiller*, Vol. 1, 1763–1775, Vol. 2, 1771–1785, in the *D'Eon Collection*, Brotherton Library, Leeds.
61 *The Morning Post* 26 August 1776. See also *The Westminster Gazette or, Constitutional*, 21 September 1776.
62 Chevalier D'Eon Manuscripts, *D'Eon Collection*. See also E. A. Vizatelly, *The Life and Adventures of Charles D'Eon de Beaumont otherwise known as Mademoiselle la Chevalière D'Eon 1728–1810*, London, 1895. This biography is illustrated by an eighteenth-century print of a midwife, half man, half woman, which appeared in *Man-Midwifery Dissected*, London, 1793, and was used to satirise male midwives, with particular reference to their opportunities to take sexual advantage of their patients.
63 In 1768, the Chevalier had joined the Lodge of Immortality as a freemason. Although the Lodge broke up in 1771, the acceptance of the Chevalier was used to satirise freemasonry. In the engraving, *The Discovery or Female Freemason* (1771), the Chevalier appears dressed as a woman, flanked by two pictures - one of Mary Tofr, a women widely believed to have given birth to rabbits in 1726, and one of the bottle conjuror, an imposter of 1749 who drew large crowds by advertising that he would creep into a quart-size bottle.
64 *The Morning Herald and Daily Advertiser*, 26 November 1785.
65 *Daily Advertiser* 25 January 1783.
66 *Gentleman's Magazine*, July 1777. The woman concerned was Ann Marrow, whose behaviour so incensed the crowd that she was blinded by the pillory. Such antagonism suggests that women who lacked the heroic appeal of a soldier were vulnerable to public hostility. The more favourable treatment of

Constantine Boone, convicted of both bigamy and fraudulent marriage in 1719, may relate either to a greater tolerance in an earlier period, or to her status as a 'monster', as she was exhibited as an hermaphrodite at Southwark Fair. *The Newgate Calendar*, London, 1796.
67 Captain J. Buchan Telfer, *The Strange Career of Chevalier d'Eon de Beaumont*, n.d., c. 1830.
68 The hermaphrodite was an important symbol in the alchemical and hermetical tradition, representing the unity of the male/female principle. While the 'new science' of the seventeenth century drew centrally on this tradition, it ultimately retained the experimental philosophy of Bacon and Newton's empirical method, while negating all associations of magic, astrology, alchemy and mysticism. See Frances Yates *Giordano Bruno and the Hermetic Tradition*, London, 1964; Merchant, 1982; B. Easlea, *Witchhunting, Magic and the New Philosophy*, Sussex, 1980, and the bibliographical introduction of M. C. Jacob, *The Radical Enlightenment. Pantheists, Freemasons & Republicans*, London, 1981.
69 Edward Coke, *A Commentarie upon Littleton*, London, 1628, Section IL.I.C.I.
70 *Philosophical Transactions for the Year 1732–1744*, ed. J. Martin, London, No. 456, January 1740.
71 Katharine Park and Lorraine J. Daston, 'Unnatural Conceptions: The Study of Monsters in Sixteenth and Seventeenth Century France and England', *Past and Present* No. 92, August 1981, p. 20–54.
72 Bakhtin makes a related point in his study of the grotesque. Mikhail Bakhtin, *Rabelais and his World*, trans. Helene Iswolsky, Massachussetts, 1968. He argues that from the seventeenth century there is a move towards a rejection of the ambivalence of the grotesque, in a search for singular meanings. While it is true that the grotesque was revived in the romantic period, as Bakhtin suggests, the genre had lost its carnivalesque character. For example, 'In Romantic grotesque, madness acquires a sombre, tragic aspect of individual isolation'. (p.39).
73 See Michel Foucault, *Herculine Barbin. Being the Recently Discovered Memoirs of a 19th Century Hermaphrodite*, Sussex, 1980.
74 Ephraim Chambers, *Cyclopaedia: or, a Universal Dictionary of Arts and Sciences*, London, 1741, 1783. Chambers also points to the importance of deciding on one sex and then sticking to it.
75 J. J. L. Hoin, *Nouvelle Description de l'hermaphrodite Drouart tel qu'on le voit à Dijon en Aout 1761*, Paris, 1761.
76 *Gazetteer and New Daily Advertiser*, 30 May 1771. See also the work of Maupertuis on monsters, which he used in *Système de la Nature*, 1757, to reject preformation theories of generation. This work and others are discussed in E. B. Gasking, *On Generation*, Baltimore, 1966, pp. 70ff.
77 James Parsons, *A Mechanical and Critical Enquiry into the Nature of Hermaphrodites*, London, 1741 p. 9.
78 R. James, *A Medicinal Dictionary*, London, 1743–5, 'Tribades'.
79 Parsons, p. 11.
80 See Note 13. Sharp, 1725, says 'This Clitoris will stand and fall as the Yard doth, and makes Women lustful and take delight in Copulation; and were it

not for this they would have no desire nor delight, nor would they ever conceive'. (p. 36).
81 Parsons, p. 10.
82 E. Said, *Orientalism*, London, 1980.
83 G. Arnaud de Ronsil, 'A Dissertation on Hermaphrodites' in Jordan de Pelerin (ed.), *A Treatise on Venereal Maladies*, London, 1750, p. 425–82.
84 Arnaud, p. 448. This may be compared with T. Browne, *Pseudodoxia Epidemica*, London, 1669, 5th edition, commenting on the enforcement of one sex only: 'whereby, endeavouring to prevent incontinency, they unawares enjoined perpetual chastity; for being executive in both parts, and confined to one, they restrained a natural power and ordained a partial virginity.' (p.157).
85 G. P. S. Bianchi, *An Historical and Physical Dissertation on the Case of Catherine Vizzani, containing the adventures of a young woman who for eight years posed in the habit of a man . . . with some curious and anatomical remarks on the nature and existence of the hymen . . . to which are added certain needful remarks by the English editor*, London, 1751. The English translator is John Cleland.
86 Bianchi, p. 53.
87 Parsons, p. 7.
88 *Reflexions sur les Hermaphrodites, relativement à Anne Grand-Jean, qualifiée telle dans un Mémoire de M. Vermeil*, Lyons, 1765 n.p. This case is also mentioned in a letter from David Garrick to George Coleman (27 January 1765). He says that the annulment of Grand-Jean's marriage and forcing her to adopt female clothing are thought unjust in Paris. David M. Little and George M. Kahrl (eds.), *The Letters of David Garrick*, Vol. 2, London, 1963.
89 Michel Foucault, 1980, p.viii, See also Colin Gordon (ed.), *Power/Knowledge. Selected Interviews and Other Writings 1972–1977*, Sussex, 1980.
90 M. D. T. Bienville, *Nymphomania or A Dissertation Concerning the Furor Uterinus*, London, 1775, trans. E. Sloane Wilmot, p. 64. See also G. S. Rousseau, 'Nymphomania, Bienville and the rise of erotic sensibility', in Boucé, 1982, pp. 95–119.

10

Sex and Shamanism in the eighteenth century[1]

GLORIA FLAHERTY

There were many revolutions during the eighteenth century. The scientific one has remained one of the most difficult to grasp in its entirety. The quantitative investigation of nature, methodologically associated with Sir Isaac Newton, did, indeed, proceed to clarify many phenomena. It also caused a simultaneous rise in professionalism in fields like medicine,[2] which then brought about the diminution of folk-healing, midwifery and other nurturing and curing skills that were not yet explicable by rational means.[3] All such developments took place with great opposition and relentless questioning. Leading minds, among them Johann Wolfgang von Goethe, staunchly rejected Newtonianism and any other forms of scientific determinism in favour of the holistic, organic approaches so often associated throughout history with the wise women.[4] Others, who also admired hermetic thinkers like Paracelsus and considered alchemy the source of pharmacology as well as chemistry, liked to think of the adage that yesterday's superstitions might just turn out to be tomorrow's scientific data.

Still others followed generations of philosophers in concentrating on the mysterious relationship of the mind to the body. They had read not only Herodotus and Hippocrates, but they were thoroughly familiar with Greek philosophy and mythology as well. Consequently, they had some awareness of hypnotic gazes, auto-suggestion, magnetism and incubative sleep. Their reactions to the plethora of contemporary European cases of possession and exorcism, sensitives, quakers, convulsives and psychic mediums under-scored the need for paying some kind of scientific attention to the occult, or what had replaced witchcraft and eventually became known as the night-side of nature. The social and anthropological as well as psychological ramifications of such matters attracted the interest of still others opposed to a strictly mathematical interpretation of the world.

The ammunition for this on-going scientific revolution was supplied throughout the Enlightenment and well into the nineteenth century by researchers in various fields. Much of what was done in medicine, anatomy, psychology, pharmacology, ethnography and anthropology related in one way or another to the scores of reports by those who ventured forth to investigate firsthand the frigid Arctic areas, the expanses of the Americas, the wilds of Siberia, the deserts of the Middle East, the torrid zones of Africa, the distant plains of Australia and the ever-changing landscapes of India. What most of them sent back consisted of much more than facts and measurements spiced with titillating references to the exotic. Since their training and background in medicine or the incipient social sciences had involved them in the controversy of mechanistic versus organic approaches, they strove to observe not only the observable and measurable but also, more importantly, the hidden reaches of human existence and the universal inclination, as one writer put it, 'übernatürliche Weise, das erklären zu wollen, was der Verstand nicht zu fassen vermag' ('to want to explain as supernatural whatever human reason is not capable of grasping').[5] Again and again, they encountered the phenomenon that had already in the eighteenth century come to be known as Shamanism.

While some hopelessly ethnocentric European explorers continued to debunk Shamanism as the puerile hocus pocus of ineducable aborigines, an increasing number felt compelled to study it because of its uncanny power over the imagination and its inexplicable efficacy. Many disbelievers even gained great respect for it after having been cured or helped by native healers. During the Enlightenment – two or more centuries before Carlos Castaneda decided to apprentice himself to the Yaqui sorcerer Don Juan Matu – European explorers were probing the knowledge of wise natives in order to expand the parameters of their science. They attended shamanic séances, examined costumes and musical instruments, interviewed practitioners, scrutinised participants, experimented with mind-altering substances, collected artefacts whenever possible, and asked many questions about ecstatic visions, ascensionism and bilocation.

Attempting to relate the unknown to the known, they mentioned similarities to what they had learned about European mythology, literature and history during their earlier readings in the humanities.

One configuration of topics that comes up again and again like a leitmotif in eighteenth- and early nineteenth-century writings on Shamanism has to do with sexuality and gender differences. All over the world, satisfaction of the sex drive seemed to be considered a matter of nature, like any other bodily function. Sexual activity was recognised as being conducted quite openly and without the kinds of restraints and restriction known in Europe. While some peoples were reported to condone incest of any kind, others forbade only parental incest, and still others allowed for none.[6] There were even numerous amusing stories of earlier Christian missionaries so embarrassed by the totally naked post-pubescent females who came to welcome them that they barricaded themselves in their living quarters, lest they succumb to the temptations of the flesh. In one instance, at least, the native men were recorded as wondering, 'What, are these prophets not men like us? Why do they not accept these girls? How could a man possibly pass them by? Why do they do us such an affront?'[7]

Such stories and observations, along with subsequent attempts at explaining them, reveal much about the Enlightenment and its ability to allow for sexuality as a means for perceiving or coming to terms with the secrets of nature, the superhuman, the awesome, or religious mystery.[8] The twentieth-century interpreters, who disagree among themselves as to whether sex is of primary or secondary importance within what they conceive as the pristine model of archaic Shamanism, interestingly enough base many of their claims on reports from the very epoch they so often disavow as inhibiting genuine scientific progress about such subjects, namely, the Enlightenment.[9]

The object of this paper, is not to explain how twentieth-century shamanistic research has been informed by, and still depends on, data gathered during the so-called Enlightenment. It is, rather, to show what those investigations turned up about a single configuration of topics that nowadays has happened to become even more significant for scholarly inquiry.

In the eighteenth century, the origin of the shaman was usually reported as being shrouded in mystery. Many observers were told that shamans originated from a seed, or sperm, or semen, or some component of a divine male body that impregnated some human female in one way or another.

At death, the shamanic seed, or whatever, returned to the gods in the great beyond, where, after a proscribed number of reincarnations, it remained permanently.

From its earliest years on earth, it clearly revealed a distinct predisposition for the shamanic calling. The child was usually pathologically sensitive, susceptible to bleeding from the nose and mouth, given to epileptic or other kinds of seizures, or sexually under- or over-endowed.[10] In many societies, the attribution of gender was reported to depend on the willingness and ability of children to imitate parental sex acts, which were performed frequently, unabashedly and openly. And parents themselves were brought up to observe carefully the activities of children as regards such matters. If a male child had no desire to do such sexual imitation, or if he regularly did so *per posteriora*, as it was called, his parents then dressed him in feminine garb and subsequently reared him as a female. Any such behaviour was generally interpreted as indicative of a strong predisposition for the shamanic calling.[11]

Many societies looked for that predisposition in either male or female children. A very well-experienced voyager provided one of the best summations in a book published in 1793 for popular consumption:

> Die Zauberer sind bei diesen Völkern von beidenei Geschlechte; doch mit dem Unterschiede, dass die männlichen Zauberer sich notwendig bequemen müssen, die Kleidung der Weiber zu tragen, und dass sie nie heurathen dörfen, obgleich die Zauberinnen wohl heurathen können. Sie werden schon von der zartesten Kindheit an zu diesem Geschäfte bestimmt. Es werden vorzüglich dazu weibische und weichliche Kinder erwählet, oder solche, welche die fallende Sucht, den Sankt Veits Tanz und andere krampfhafte Zufälle haben; indem man glaubt, dass solche schon leibhaftig von den bösen Geistern besessen, und in den krampfhaften Zufällen so verstellt and hingerissen werden. Man kleidet diese Kinder schon frühzeitig in weibliche Kleider, und giebt ihnen die Trommel und Kürbisklapper zum Spielzeuge. Wenn sie erwachsen sind, lernen sie die Kunst zu Zaubern von anderen berühmten Zauberern.[12]
>
> (The sorcerers among these people are of both sexes; however, with the difference that the male sorcerers must necessarily accommodate themselves to wearing the clothing of women, and that they may never marry, although the sorceresses, to be sure, can marry. They are destined to this business from the most tender age of childhood. Chosen for it, above all, are delicate and effeminate children, or those who have epilepsy, St Vitus dance, and other convulsive seizures; in that one believes that such children are already incarnately possessed by the evil spirits and are so transposed and transported during their convulsive seizures. One dresses these children already very early on

in female garb, and one gives them the tambourine and gourd-rattle as toys. When they are grown, they learn the art of sorcery from other famous sorcerers.)

One European analyst thought that early deviance from the heterosexual norm had to be related to hermaphroditism, a subject of increasing interest to eighteenth-century medical researchers, among them the famous Albrecht von Haller. Another analyst attributed such behaviour to an 'Uebermas von Pituita, oder von wässerigter schleimigter Feuchtigkeit'. (excess of mucus, or of aqueous phlegmatic humours').[13] He also thought that it must run in families, since the office of shaman was so often inherited the world over: 'diese Personen und Familien sind es vorzüglich, die unter den Mongolischen Völkern zu den vermeynthlichen Zauberern oder den in America sogenannten Jongleurs, in Africa zu Fetischirern oder Ganga's, und in Siberien zu Schamanen erkohren werden'.[14] ('these individuals and families are particularly the ones who are selected among the Mongolian peoples to become the would-be jugglers, in Africa, the fetish-wielders or gangas, and in Siberia, the shamans'.) Many European writers pitied those children who, they thought, were doomed from infancy, whether they succeeded in becoming shamans or died trying.[15]

Preparing for initiation into the mysteries was again and again reported to be long and arduous. As soon as the youngster exhibited the tribally acknowledged signs, he was given over to an older shaman with whom he then went to reside, purportedly for purposes of instruction.[16] According to some explorers, those older shamans often read the signs in the behaviour of certain exceptionally good-looking male children with normal organs, so as to be able to claim them as 'adoptive sons'.[17] In such cases, the rewards were great for all concerned, including the son, who was not only regularly outfitted in new clothing and painted 'fancifully' by his new 'father', but also indoctrinated into the mysterious ceremonies and thereby provided with a livelihood.[18] Many travellers to the Middle East wrote of the willingness of parents to sell their young sons into sexual servitude, whether of a religious or secular nature.[19]

While many Europeans were deeply troubled about depriving such children of their human rights as well as their biological sex, they nevertheless went on to make their reports and analyses according to the current state of scholarly methodology. In addition to being subjected to a variety of pederastic acts, they reported, the shamanic proselyte had to endure a wide range of psychological as well as physical terrors. Once he reached puberty, he was forced to fast for days on end, to ingest hallucinogenics in increasing doses, to smoke certain substances, to anaesthetise his skin, to swallow purgatives and vomatives, to engage in physical activity to the brink of complete exhaustion, and so on.

The relationship of drugs to sex and ecstasy had long been of great interest to European physicians. Jean de Nynauld, for example, had written in 1615 that varying amounts of belladonna, aconite and opium mixed together so as to produce unguents could, when rubbed into the skin, suspend all feelings of pain and induce the kind of deep sleep that produced sensations of transport as well as visions of the most unrestrained sexual activity. Despite their purported diabolical origins, he considered their properties most worthy of medical attention,[20] and so did others, who learned from reports of the witch-trials and from the *Malleus Maleficarum* that flying and sexual intercourse in public with many partners, accompanied by music and dancing, were always part of the witches' sabbaths.[21]

Those who followed in the eighteenth century continued to concentrate on the ways and means of affecting the mind through the body. The physician Jerome Gaub openly wrote that he wished to obtain the concoctions used by the wise women, that is, the shamankas, in order to 'fall into a profound stupor, invariably accompanied by the same vision of having been transported after a long aerial journey into a distant place, where they intermingle, cohabit, and dance with others of their ilk, all of this being so firmly impressed on their fancy that no argument after they awake can convince them that it was an empty dream'.[22]

Eighteenth-century analysts were especially concerned about learning how sexuality could be made to wield the mind and even conquer rationality. Some explorers revealed their amazement that the assassins, who were not only reputed to be scientifically knowledgeable but also noted for being 'infatué de la magie', were so unquestioningly obedient to their leaders. The Middle-Eastern gardens of sexual delights – repeatedly mentioned in European literature – at least since Marco Polo, who happened to be one of the first Westerners to witness a shamanic séance in the Orient and describe it soberly – were then brought up, as was the use of hashish.[23] The stories of hashish-induced sexual arousal contained in the *Tales from the Thousand and One Nights*, which had become available in the major European languages by the late eighteenth century, only served to confirm such matters.

On the other hand, some eighteenth-century analysts sought explanations for the effects on the mind of sustained sexual abstinence, celibacy, virginity, chastity or generally-controlled sexuality. While one wrote of tobacco as a means of 'deadening the fires of concupisence and the revolts of the flesh',[24] another wrote about what he had heard of superhuman powers originating in sexual self-discipline and strict behaviour, that is, living extremely abstemiously. The latter also described the ways that were used to reconcile any and all illicit sexual activities: 'Das Blutziehen, namentlich aus den Ohren und Lippen, der Zunge und den Geschlechtstheilen, welches durch Magueystacheln oder Rohrstücken geschah, die man durch Haut and Fleisch stiess, wurde von den jungen Priestern besonders weit getrieben, and hatte die Bedeutung einer Busse and Peinigung an dem Körpertheil mit welchem gesündigt worden war oder welcher einer solchen Ascetik am meisten zu bedürfen schien'.[25] ('Drawing blood, namely out of the ears and lips, the tongue and the sexual organs, which happened with maguey thorns or pieces of reeds, which were pushed through skin and flesh, was done to particular extremes by the young priests, and had the meaning of an atonement and torture of that part of the body which had sinned or which appeared to need such asceticism the most'.)

Some Brazilian tribes were reported to require sexual abstinence of their shaman and to employ only female virgins to perform the purification rituals in preparation for the séance: 'Before entering, he must have abstained from his wife for nine days; and as he enters he has to be washed by a virgin girl. Once he is in the chamber of mysteries, the people withdraw. He then lies prone on the prepared bed. He makes a thousand grimaces and invokes the spirit'.[26] Equal esteem for the magnificent magic of the virgin was found among the Indians of North America: 'They attribute to virginity and chastity certain particular qualities and virtues, and it is certain that, if continence appears to them an essential condition for gaining success, as their superstition suggests to them, they will guard it with scrupulous care and not dare to violate it the least bit in the world for fear that their fasts and everything that they could do besides would be rendered useless by this non-observance'.[27]

Observers of shamanic séances submitted so many descriptions that innumerable kinds of analyses resulted. The sexual aspects of the preparations, the music, the chanting, the dancing, the trance, the convulsions, the writhing and the ecstatic visions were rarely overlooked. Often there were comparisons to the orgies of Graeco-Roman antiquity. Joseph François Lafitau wrote of American hermaphrodites or sufferers of the Scythian disease, American companions of Diana, vestal virgins, Bacchantes, and others who consorted with spirits. He viewed what he knew about the American orgy as a primordial means of coming closer to the divine power of the universe.[28] He surmised that such sexual behaviour on so wide a scale was somehow necessary to maintain the integrity and unity of the particular society.[29] With no hesitation, Lafitau even tackled the sensitive subject of lycanthropy, acknowledging its existence since the very beginning of time and explaining it as a separation of the soul from the body that allowed for the kind of physical transformation whereby the subject comported himself as a raging, ravaging, sexually insatiable animal.[30]

Those werewolves who stalked, captured, conquered and killed their prey often consumed it. Although Europeans generally had great difficulty coming to terms with cannibalism – especially after the numerous incidents reported during the relatively recent period of starvation in the Baltic areas – there were those who insisted that it had ritualistic significance among many non-European peoples. A report about Sumatra explained that human flesh was not eaten there in order to satisfy hunger, but rather to attract the attention of the gods. Continuing in the same manner, its author described the preparation of the carcasses, which were not devoured entirely raw. After rubbing them with lemon and salt, they 'rösten sie ein wenig über einem Feuer, das zu dem Zweck bereitet wird, und verzehren die Bissen mit einem wilden Enthusiasmus'.[31] ('roast them for some time over a fire that has been prepared for that purpose and consume the morsels with a wild enthusiasm').

The ancients had long been blamed for transmitting orgiastic rituals to northern Europe. Paul Einhorn's *Historica Lettica* (1649), for example, bemoaned the lascivious songs and dances that always seemed to accompany them, if not form their core. He likened contemporary Christianity to a fragile veneer over deeply entrenched pagan beliefs, for even during the most holy celebration of Advent and Christmas, there was 'ein schandloss abscheulich Fest, mit tantzen, springen, singen und grawsahmen Geschrey, auch fressen und sauffen gehalten, da sie denn von einem Hause zum andern, mit solchem grawsahmen und üppigen Wesen gegangen, und also dieselbe nacht zugebracht. Dieses schandlose Fest, haben sie, ohn Zweifel vorzeiten von den alten abgöttischen Heyden als den Griechen und andern empfangen'.[32] ('held an abominably loathsome party, with dancing, hopping, singing, and gruesome clamour, in addition to gourmandising and drinking, whereby they then went from one house to the next in such a dreadful and voluptuous condition and spent the night there. This vile celebration they received without doubt in earlier times from the ancient idolatrous heathens like the Greeks and others'.) Reports from Siberia supported the seventeenth-century idea that possession by pagan spirits could overwhelm superficially Christianised people, stimulating them to fornicate even on high holidays like Easter.[33]

References to music and dance recur throughout all the writings on Shamanism as indispensable components of the rituals. James Burney, son of the renowned musicologist, emphasised their importance while describing how the natives of the Pacific Northwest received Captain James Cook.[34] Discussing the 'wolf or shaman's dance' as a kind of dramatic performance, he brought the idea of the performing arts together with those of mind-altering substances, total sexual abandon and tribal ritual.

Other analyses of the shamanic séance were coloured by eighteenth-century European standards of morality, or they revealed superficial understanding of primitivism, sexuality and magic. The Indians of North America, according to one, 'reden viel von Entzückungen und Visionen einiger Landsleute, die für todt sind gehalten worden, die aber nachher wieder aufgelebt sind, und ihre Geschichten erzählt haben, welche dahin abzwecken, die Ausübung der Tugend und moralischen Pflichten angelegentlich zu machen'.[35] ('talk much about ecstasies and visions of some of their compatriots, who have been considered dead, but who thereafter have come alive again and told their stories, which aim at making earnest the practice of virtue and moral duties'). Another emphasised the dissoluteness of African prophetesses: eyes wide open, these women, with their indisputably remarkable knowledge about medicinal plants, began to move more and more violently until foaming profusely at the mouth. The convulsions they suffered were so severe that their bodies were forced into superhuman positions defying all belief. Then, suddenly, 'Ist die Verzückung vorüber, so legt sich das Weib gemeiniglich auf den Rücken und macht sehr unanständige Bewegungen'.[36] ('when the ecstasy has passed, the women lays herself down, usually on her back, and makes very indecent motions'). Polynesian enthusiasm, which allegedly involved the literal entry of the god into the medium, was interpreted as an excuse for general promiscuity, whether prostitution or adultery or whatever.[37]

The enormous sex drive of shamans was often related to their purported personal fecundity as well as their power to assist or increase the fertility of their adherents. The Yakuts told about the daughters of a certain chieftain who led his people into a new land so as to escape more powerful invaders.

Among the refugees was a youth of great strength and skill whose influence increased to such a degree that he finally admitted his powers over nature and declared himself to be a shaman. He refused the chieftain's natural daughter in favour of the adopted one, with whom he then had twelve sons.[38]

There were other nations that believed mighty shamans could cause pregnancy merely by casting a spell or bestowing an object like a fish or a bird. Even different kinds of cases of male pregnancy were reported from places like Greenland, where the shamans applied their supernatural powers to aid in the delivery of what usually was said to be a seal or a walrus. Actually, that was already recognised in the eighteenth century as one of the ways of curing men of otherwise inexplicable abdominal pains.[39] Shamans cured lovesickness among the American Indians by using the powers, 'selbst aus der Ferne, Verliebten Gegenliebe zu schaffen'.[40] ('to produce even from the distance lovers for those in love').

So great was the sexual capacity of Tahitian shamans that they were said to demand the wives of fellow tribesmen as more than occasional, non-ritualistic partners in sex: 'Zuweilen verlangen ihre Zauberer von ihnen, dass sie ihr Weib nach den Wäldern schicken, um sich dem Ersten dem Besten daselbst Preis zu geben; allein einiger Frauen Sittsamkeit und Ehrgefühl hindert sie in solchen Fällen zu gehorchen'.[41] ('sometimes their sorcerers demand of them that they send their wives into the woods, in order to abandon themselves to the first and best of them; however, the morality and honour of some women hinder their obedience in such cases').

The male organ, along with the fluids it emitted, was a common motif in most native mythologies known to the eighteenth century. Some thereby described the process of shamanic death and regeneration. In one example, a white bear grabs the shaman's toe and drags him out into the water, whereupon a walrus bites into his organ and eats it, him, and the bear. As soon as all the bones are thrown back onto the ground, the shaman's soul re-enters his body and he comes alive again.[42] Another example has to do with the creator of the world, a certain Kutka, and his wife, Chachy, whose magical, shamanka-like powers protect him, at least, whenever she desires to do so. The people who regarded them as supreme deities told many stories about them: 'Besonders beschreiben sie Kutka als den grössten Unfläther und Sodomiten, der alles zu stupriren versuchet. Sie erzehlen dass er einsmals Seemuscheln stupriret, und weil sich diese zugeschlossen, dadurch um das genitale gekommen seye, welches nach diesem Chachy von ohngefehr in einer gekochten Muschel-Schaale gefunden, und ihrem Manne wieder angeheilet'.[43] ('Especially they describe Kutka as the greatest lewd beast and sodomite, who tries to rape everything. They tell that he once violated sea mussels and because these closed themselves, he thereby lost his male genitals, which after a while were located by Chachy in a cooked clamshell and healed back onto her husband'.)

The fluids from the shaman's sexual organs and body were also reported to have great ritualistic importance. He supplied his urine not only for healing, but also for sanctifying. One explorer described a copulation ceremony by writing, 'Sobald der Hottentottenpriester in den Kreis der Männer kommt und an den Bräutigam herantritt, spricht er zu ihm einige Worte und spritzt ihn mit seinem Urin von oben bis unten nass; dasselbe tut er auch mit der Braut, sobald er zu dieser in den Kreis der Frauen tritt.'[44] (As soon as the Hottentot priest enters the circle of the men and approaches the bridegroom, he utters a few words to him and sprays him wet with his urine from top to bottom; the same thing he does with the bride as soon as he steps towards her in the circle of the women'.) The shaman repeated the procedure two more times before giving the couple his blessing and wishing them a strong, healthy son within the year. When those sons eventually reached puberty, their rites of passage included a similar spraying with shamanic urine.

The shaman's semen was reported to be equally important among other peoples. In some areas of the world, barren women were made to engage in variegated sexual activity with a shaman so as to become fertile. Because his semen was believed to promote good health and stimulate growth, it was, among other things, generously applied to sickly male babies. Some peoples even believed it was the means whereby his magic could be transferred through pederastic acts in which the young adept served as the passive partner.[45] Generally, the shamanic powers were considered to be so great that nothing could resist them except, perhaps, the excrement or menstrual blood of a virgin.[46]

The shaman also played a major role in various ceremonies marking sexual maturation. Although female virginity was highly honoured, it was not considered absolutely pure until it was consecrated, which meant that pubescent girls in North and South America as well as in Europe and elsewhere had to suffer defloration by the man who wielded the greatest power, that is, the shaman or the sovereign, who claimed to know how to control nature and neutralise its impurities.[47] The 'first-night right' remained a common complaint in some areas of eighteenth-century Europe, finding its most wonderful artistic treatment in Wolfgang Amadeus Mozart's *Le Nozze di Figaro*, which was based on the play by Pierre de Beaumarchais.

The puberty rites of young males were generally recognised as separating them once and for all from their mothers and all the womanly influences they had constantly been subjected to since birth. The physical torments they endured were designed to test their faith as well as their self-confidence, courage and strength. Practically every nation had procedures to establish bonds between the candidate and the local male society whose members stood as role-models. Male games, including 'ball-play', dance, martial arts and the chase, were intended, as one analyst wrote, 'to influence the passions of the young men present' and to develop manly ambitions. A result could be 'sometimes lascivious interludes'.[48] Candidates were usually expected to perform as the active partner in homosexual acts, the recorded purpose being that not only experience but potency and strength would thereby be gained.

The Hottentots were reported as going so far as to require the surgical removal of the left testicle in full public view – the left side, like the night, being commonly associated with women among primitive peoples. Their ceremony, described in a publication of 1719, began with the mature man forcing the young candidate to lie down on the earth and spread his limbs apart, so that they could be fastened to stakes. Two mature men then knelt on his arms and feet so that the candidate could not move, while another positioned himself across his chest so that the candidate could neither move nor see what was about to happen. In the meantime, a sheep had been fetched and ceremoniously butchered in order to provide the still warm fat that the shaman mixed together with pulverised medicinal herbs. He then formed the mixture in a ball and inserted it into the open wound before he sewed it together with a bone needle threaded with animal sinew. When the stitches were removed, the shaman 'schmiert ihn mit Nierenfett ein und benässt ihn über den ganzen Leib mit seinem Urin, gleichsam als "letzte Ölung," welche ihm zu guter Letzt gegeben wird',[49] ('rubs him with suet and wets him across the whole body with his urine, as though it were 'extreme unction, given him as the last good stroke',). While the candidate crawled away in abject pain, the men began their feast of roasted mutton. The women, who continued to remain separate, only got the drippings, but they were not denied hemp leaves to smoke.

This eighteenth-century reporter rejected as erroneous all interpretations of the ceremony that he had heard of, claiming that it just had to be 'ein

Stück ihres Gottesdienstes' ('a part of their divine service') whereby the boy gained recognition from his father and the other men as one of them. Thereafter he could no longer tolerate being called a molly-coddle or sissy, for that would be a terrible insult to his newly acquired manhood. And, furthermore, he would be guaranteed total support from the male society, 'wenn er nun aus Bosheit oder im Zorn seine Mutter schlägt und dabei sagt, er stehe nicht mehr unter ihrer Zucht'.[50] ('whenever he now, whether out of malice or in rage, hits his mother and thereby says he is no longer subject to her discipline'.).

Mothers were more often than not blamed for adversely influencing the self-identity and gender of their male children. The desire to make them over into their own image was reported to be so strong in some women that many peoples had even established legitimate means for its realisation. In the West Indies, for example, the sixth son born to a woman with no daughters was reared as a female and remained permanently among the segregated women, doing female work and engaging in sex only with unmarried men.[51] Mothers elsewhere were viewed as being simply over-protective of their sons. One explorer wrote rather sympathetically from the European point of view: 'The women seem very fond of their offspring; dreading the effects of war, and the dangers of the chase; some of them bring up their males in a very effeminate manner, and are happy to see them taken by the chiefs, to gratify their unnatural desires. Such youths are dressed like women, and taught all their domestic duties'.[51]

Although mature men might have accepted ritualistic pederasty and themselves engaged in sex with other men, they were usually reported as being against the transvestitism imposed on their progeny by the women. Fathers were often described as doing whatever they could to wrest their sons from the clutches of the females in order to secure them their male identity.[53] They were not, however, always very successful.

The eighteenth century knew the 'women men' to be ubiquitous among the Polar peoples, the Asians, the Indians of the Americas, and the various inhabitants of the Russian Empire. According to a very recent study, the Spanish Conquistadores had already encountered massive numbers of such transvestites in the sixteenth century, categorised them as pagan sodomites and, on authority of the Inquisition, sought to exterminate them.[54] The Russians called the 'women men' *tschupans,* while the Canadians used the word *bardaches.*[55] They were biological males socialised to perform as females. Consequently, they were classified and treated as the latter. As to be expected, the early writers who analysed and interpreted travel accounts recalled Herodotus and likened such transvestites to the 'women men' of the Scythians and all the other extremely fierce warriors, like the Celts and the Germans.[56]

Sometimes the 'women men' were shamans, but not always. Among polygamous peoples they were highly prized as wives, for they were supposedly stronger than the women because they were neither subject to menstruation nor to annual pregnancy.[57] A later evaluation of a report about the inhabitants of the Aleutian archipelago gave confirmation to this: 'Cet Auteur confirme ce que d'autre voyageurs avaient rapporté sur le vice contre nature qui règne malheureusement depuis un tems immémorial dans cet archipel. De beaux garcons y sont élevés et habillés comme des filles; on leur fait apprendre des ouvrages de femmes, et ensuite ils sont exactement regardés comme des concubines'.[58] ('This author confirms that which some other voyagers have reported about the vice against nature which unfortunately has reigned since time immemorial on that archipelago. Good-looking boys are reared and dressed as females; they are made to learn women's work, and subsequently they are regarded exactly as concubines'.)

Sometimes Christianised monogamous men cohabited with 'women men' or tried to make them their legal spouses. Although none of the eighteenth-century documents consulted for this paper mentioned their ingesting any substances which might possibly have affected their hormonal balance, many of the 'women men' became such complete transsexuals that it was virtually impossible for anyone to distinguish them from females. One explorer acknowledged that by describing an incident: 'As proof how easily this mistake may be made, it once happened, that a toyon brought one of these unnatural beings to church to be married to him, and the ceremony was nearly finished, when an interpreter, who came in by chance, put a stop to the proceedings, by making known to the priest, that the couple he was joining in wedlock were both males'. Another explorer wrote: 'so completely are they unsexed from their manhood, that had they not been pointed out to me, I should not have known them but as women. I add with some satisfaction, that the encouragement of this abomination is almost solely confined to the chiefs'.[59]

Those in the eighteenth century who strove to grasp the meaning of shamanism were, needless to say, products of their own times. They could not help but think historically, or in terms of development and progress. The many accounts they read seemed to indicate that the phenomenon manifested itself at different times in different ways among different peoples in different areas of the globe. They struggled to describe it and came up with words meaning archaic, classical, decadent, underground, modified, Christianised, and so on. Despite the plethora of seemingly contradictory information, many of them were, indeed, able to recognise some very basic similarities that seemed to point to a common denominator.

The status of women, for one, was generally described as being appalling. Their living quarters were often segregated, they were excluded from all religious services, they were treated as chattels that could be traded for animals or objects, and they were subjected to polygamous situations. As one explorer saw fit to sum up:

'Bey allen schamanischen Heiden wird das weibliche Geschlecht für weit geringer, als das männliche und des Dienstes der Wollust, Kinderzeugens und häuslicher Verrichtungen wegen vorhanden angesehen und ihm daher verächtlich und hart begegnet. Man gesteht ihm die Rechte der Menschheit in einem geringen Grade zu und hält es von den Göttern verworfen überhaupt für unrein und zur Zeit der monatlichen Veränderung oder im Wochenbette für verbannet und Menschen und Vieh, gefährlich'.[60]

('Among all the shamanistic heathens, the female sex is viewed as being much inferior to the male sex and only present in order to perform the services of lust, childbearing and housekeeping. She is treated contemptuously and harshly. One grants her human rights only to the most minimal degree and considers her totally rejected by the gods as impure, and, during her monthly menstruation or when pregnant, ostracised as dangerous for human beings and animals alike.).

Despite such hardships and privations, that writer had often heard that many of those women managed to live to be eighty years of age.[61] Many peoples were reputed even to lack respect for Mother Earth. Some believed she had had to be banished from heaven because she so willingly let herself be seduced.[62] Others preferred to think, 'Zu allerunterst in der Erde wohnt ein grosses schlimmes Weib'.[63] ('At the very bottom of the earth there dwells a big bad female'.)

Strange paradoxes turned up again and again. Women who died in childbirth, for example, were often revered as holy and able to transfer mysterious powers. In eighteenth-century Mexico, 'man begrub sie im Tempel einer bestimmten Göttin und glaubte dass ihre Seele nicht in die Unterwelt, sondern nach Westen ins Haus der Sonne eingehe; ihr Haar und ihre Finger galten als Talisman für den Krieger, ihr linker Vorderarm als Zaubermittel um Menschen in einen todtenähnlichen Schlaf zu versenken, daher die Leiche stets Gefahr lief dieser Theile beraubt zu werden'.[64] ('one buried her in the temple of a particular goddess and believed that her soul did not go to the underworld but to the house of the sun in the west; her hair and her fingers counted as talismans for warriors, her left forearm as a magic means that could induce the kind of deep sleep that was like death, consequently such a corpse was always in danger of being robbed of these parts').

In many places, the female was considered a kind of vehicle of the divine spirit of the universe. Those who believed in the transmigration of souls often held views like the following: 'Die Seele geht aber nicht auf Thiere Über, sondern auf Menschen, und zwar gewöhnlich auf Verwandte weiblichen Geschlechtes'.[65] ('The soul does not pass over into animals, but rather into human beings, and, indeed, usually into relatives of the female sex'.) Some people thought that the divine entered the female during thunder-storms, when the lightning flashed downwards.[66] Her supernatural connections were evident in her menstrual cycle as well, since it seemed to follow the waxing and waning of the moon. She seemed to be born with her own magic, that is, privy to the mystery of birth and fecundity as well as longevity.[67]

If all that were true, the thinkers of the European Enlightenment reasoned, then women must at one time have had much more control over her own existence and that of her children than she presently had. Long before Johann Jakob Bachofen – who just happened to be an avid reader of eighteenth-century travel accounts – formulated his theories of mother right, first-hand observers, like Lafitau, were recalling their Herodotus and writing about matrilineal descent and matriarchal powers among peoples very much alive in the world of the eighteenth century.[68] They had already suspected that sex was the common denominator in Shamanism. Male transvestite shamans, they thought, had to be imitating shamankas so as to co-opt their boundless magic, and their fellow tribesmen accepted that because it served to keep that female magic under male control.

Notes

1 I gratefully acknowledge that this research was partially supported by Bryn Mawr College Committee on Faculty Awards and Grants with an award from the Hardenberg-Clark Fund.
2 Michel Foucault, *The Birth of the Clinic: An Archaeology of Medical Perception*, tr. A. M. Sheridan Smith, reprint New York, 1973, pp. 20, 31 and 46.

3 Barbara Ehrenreich and Deirdre English, *Witches, Midwives, and Nurses: A History of Women Healers*, New York, 1973, pp. 13–16 and Marta Weigle, *Spiders and Spinsters: Women and Mythology*, Albuquerque, 1982, pp. 62–5.
4 Evelyn Fox Keller, *Reflections on Gender and Science*, New Haven and London, 1985, Ch. 3, esp. pp. 56–61; Jeanne Achterberg, *Imagery in Healing: Shamanism and Modern Medicine*, Boston and London, 1985, pp. 15–16 and 61–3, and Lester S. King, *The Philosophy of Medicine: The Early Eighteenth Century*, Cambridge, Mass. and London, 1978, pp. 12, 18, 37 and 58.
5 Heinrich Johann Holmberg, *Ethnographische Skizzen über die Völker des Russischen Amerika*, 2 parts, reprint Helsingfors, 1855 and 1862, I, p. 68.
6 Jean-Baptiste Labat, *Nouveau voyage aux Isles de l'Amérique*, den Haag, 1724, reprint Paris, 1931, pp. 117-24. For additional references, see Werner Krauss, *Zur Anthropologie des 18. Jahrhunderts*, Munich and Vienna, 1979, p. 129.
7 As quoted in English from Claude d'Abbeville by John Hemming, *Red Gold: The Conquest of the Brazilian Indians, 1500–1760*, Cambridge, Mass., 1978, p. 210.
8 Benjamin Walker, *Sex and the Supernatural: Sexuality in Religion and Magic*, New York, Evanston, San Francisco and London, 1973, pp. 14–19. John Atkins, *Sex in Literature*, vol. 4, *High Noon: The Seventeenth and Eighteenth Centuries*, London and New York, 1982, pp. 96, 256, 262, and 274–7, and Reay Tannahill, *Sex in History*, New York, 1980, pp. 341–2.
9 Mircea Eliade, for example, disputed Leo Sternberg's hypothesis of the sexual origins of shamanism, *Shamanism: Archaic Techniques of Ecstasy*, tr. Willard R. Trask, Bollingen Series LXXVI, Princeton, 1974, pp. 73–4. Arne Runeberg, *Witches, Demons and Fertility Magic: Analysis of Their Significance and Mutual Relations in West European Folk Religion*, Helsinfors, 1946, reprint 1979, p. iii, evidences a strong feeling against the 'Enlightenment'. Such negative feelings also coloured the otherwise valuable work by Gisela Bleibtreu-Ehrenberg, *Tabu Homosexualität: Die Geschichte eines Vorurteils*, Frankfurt a.M., 1978, p. 88; *Mannbarkeitstriten, Zur institutionellen Päderastie bei Papuas und Melanesiern*, Frankfurt a.M., Berlin and Vienna, 1980, pp. 12–13 and 16, and *Der Weibmann, Kultischer Geschlechtswechsel im Schamanismus: Eine Studie zur Transvestition und Transsexualität bei Naturvölkern*, Frankfurt a.M., 1984, pp. 63 and 70. In a similar vein is Wilhelm E. Mühlmann, *Die Metamorphose der Frau: Weiblicher Schamanismus und Dichtung*, 2nd rev. ed., Berlin, 1984, p. 18.
10 Johann Gottlieb Georgi, *Bemerkungen einer Reise im Russischen Reich*, 2 vols., St Petersburg, 1775, I, p. 280.
11 Georg Wilhelm Steller, *Beschreibung von dem Lande Kamtschatka*, Frankfurt and Leipzig, 1774, reprint, Quellen und Forschungen zur Geschichte der Geographie und Reise, Vol. 10, ed. Hanno Beck, Stuttgart, 1974, pp. 289 and 350–1, and Thomas Falkner, *Beschreibung von Patagonien und den angrenzenden Theilen von Südamerika*, Gotha, 1775, p. 114.
12 Johann Reinhold Forster, *Karakter, Sitten und Religion einiger merkwürdigen Völker*, Halle, 1793, pp. 79–80.
13 Christoph Meiners, 'Ueber die sympathetische Reizbarkeit, und einige daraus zu erklärende Erscheinungen in den schwachen Völkern', *Göttingisches Historisches Magazin*, Vol. 2, Hannover, 1788, p. 48.

14 ibid.
15 Urey Lisiansky, A Voyage Round the World in the Years 1803, 4, 5, & 6, London, 1814, p. 207.
16 Joseph François Lafitau, Moeurs des sauvages Amériquains, comparées aux moeurs des premiers temps, 2 vols., Paris, 1724, I, pp. 344–5. Henceforth, I shall cite the recent and generally available English translation, Customs of The American Indians Compared with The Customs of Primitive Times, tr. and ed., William N. Fenton and Elizabeth L. Moore, The Publications of the Champlain Society, 2 vols., Toronto, 1974 and 1977, I, pp. 221–2. Compare Christoph Mieners, 'Ueber die Mysterien der Alten, besonders über die Eleusinischen Geheimnisse', Vermischte Philosophische Schriften, 3 vols., Leipzig, 1775–6, III, p. 175.
17 As summarised in Gustav Klemm, Allgemeine Cultur-Geschichte der Menschheit, 10 vols., Leipzig, 1843–52, II, pp. 170–1, and III, p. 123.
18 Maximilian Prinz zu Wied, Reise in das Innere Nord-America in den Jahren 1832 bis 1834, 2 vols. and illustrated vol., Coblenz 1839 and 1841, reprint Munich, 1970, II, p. 166.
19 Johann Ludwig Burckhardt, Reisen in Arabien, enthaltend eine Beschreibung derjenigen Gebiete in Hedjaz, welche die Mohammedaner für heilig achten, Weimar, 1830, reprint Stuttgart, 1963, p. 294.
20 Jean de Nynauld, De la lycanthropie, transformation, et extase des sorciers, Paris, 1615, pp. 24–26, 68 and 108.
21 Runeberg, pp. 227–9, and Michael J. Harner, 'The Role of Hallucinogenic Plants in European Witchcraft', Hallucinogens and Shamanism, ed. Michael J. Harner, London, Oxford, and New York, 1973, reprint 1981, pp. 129–30.
22 L. J. Rather, Mind and Body in Eighteenth Century Medicine, A Study Based on Jerome Gaub's De regimine mentis, Berkeley and Los Angeles, 1965, p. 113.
23 Joseph Deguignes, Histoire générale des Huns, des Turcs, des Mogols, et des autres Tartares occidentaux, &c. avant et depuis Jesus-Christ jusqu'à present, 5 vols., Paris, 1756–8, III, pp. 221–2.
24 Lafitau, Customs, II, p. 83.
25 Theodor Waitz, Anthropologie der Naturvölker, 6 pts, Leipzig, 1859–72, IV, pp. 152–3. John Lee Maddox, The Medicine Man: A Sociological Study of the Character and Evolution of Shamanism, New York, 1923, reprint 1977, p. 47, contended that natives 'learned, therefore, unwittingly and no doubt accidentally, that the phenomena of the religious life are to a large extent based on sexual life'.
26 As quoted in English from André Thevet by Hemming, p. 60.
27 Lafitau, Customs, I, p. 218. Compare Robert Eisler, Man into Wolf, an Anthropological Interpretation of Sadism, Masochism, and Lycanthropy, London, 1948, reprint Santa Barbara, 1978, p. 19. One cannot help but think of François-René de Chateaubriand and his enormously successful Atala (1801) with its medicine men, priests, gourd rattles, manitous and the great significance of virginity among the Indians.
28 Lafitau, Customs, I, p. 155. Compare the German translation, Johann Friedrich Schröter, Allgemeine Geschichte der Länder und Völker von America, 2 vols., Halle, 1752–3, I, pp. 88–9.

29 Lafitau, *Customs*, I, p. 155.
30 *Ibid.*, p. 371.
31 'Nachrichten von Sumatra', *Beiträge zur Völker- und Länderkunde*, J. R. Forster and M. C. Sprengel (eds.), Leipzig, 1781–3, p. 300.
32 Paul Einhorn, *Ueber die religiösen Vorstellungen der alten Völker in Liv- und Ehstland: Drei Schriften*, Riga, 1857, reprint Hannover, 1968, p. 19. Compare his *Reformatio Gentis Letticae*, 1636, *ibid.*, pp. 56–8.
33 *Das Leben des Protopopen Avvakum*, tr. Gerhard Hildebrandt, Göttingen, 1965, p. 87,
34 Erna Gunther, *Indian Life on the Northwest Coast of North America As Seen by the Early Explorers and Fur Traders during the Last Decades of the Eighteenth Century*, Chicago and London, 1975, p. 44.
35 Gottfried Erich Rosenthal, *Neue anti-Pandora oder angenehme und nützliche Unterhaltungen über Lebensart, Sitten, Gebräuche und natürliche Beschaffenheit verschiedener Völker und Länder, auch über Gegenstände der Naturlehre, Geschichte und Technologie*, 2 vols., Erfurt, 1795–6, I, p. 311.
36 Klemm, III, p. 369.
37 Waitz, VI, p. 383.
38 Martin Sauer, *An Account of a Geographical and Astronomical Expedition to the Northern Parts of Russia*, London, 1802, pp. 109–10.
39 Paul Egede, *Nachrichten von Grönland, Aus einem Tagebuche, gefüht von 1721 bis 1788*, Copenhagen, 1790, p. 94.
40 Waitz, III, p. 212.
41 Forster, p. 73.
42 Egede, p. 79.
43 Steller, p. 263.
44 Peter Kolb, *Caput Bonae Spei Hodiernum, Lebensbeschreibung der Hottentotten*, Nuremberg, 1719, reprint, Schriften der Volkshochschule der Stadt Marktredwitz, XXII, Marktredwitz, 1975, p. 40.
45 Lafitau, *Customs*, I, pp. 221–2; Georgi, *Bemerkung*, I, p. 280, and Jan Cornelius de Pauw, as cited in Krauss, p. 128. See also the various publications of Bleibtreu-Ehrenberg.
46 Johannes Scheffer, *Lappland Das ist: Neue und wahrhafftige Beschreibung von Lappland und dessen Einwohnern*, Frankfurt a.M. and Leipzig, 1675, pp. 162–3.
47 Waitz, I, p. 457, a footnote not only provides eighteenth-century bibliography but also discusses abuses. In a very interesting review of Terence J. Gorman's *Hamann on Language and Religion*, Oxford Theological Monographs, Oxford and New York, 1981, published in the *German Quarterly*, Vol. 57, No. 3, Summer 1984, p. 470, James C. O'Flaherty astutely points out the biblical connections as well as the sexual overtones of 'Spermaloge', a word used by Hamann, the Magus of the North, to describe himself.
48 William Bartram, *Travels through North and South Carolina, Georgia, East and West Florida, the Cherokee Country, the Extensive Territories of the Muscogulges or Creek Confederacy, and the Country of the Chactaws*, Philadelphia, 1791, reprint London, 1792, pp. 368–9.
49 Kolb, pp. 22–3.
50 *Ibid.*, p. 25.

51 Waitz, IV, p. 376.
52 Sauer, p. 176.
53 Maximilian, II, p. 133.
54 Bleibtreu-Ehrenberg, *Mannweib*, pp. 104–5, 134–5 and 181, pointed out that Ruth Benedict appropriated the word in her discussion of the Zunis for *Patterns of Culture* (1934). Bleibtreu-Ehrenberg then explained that the word derived neither from the French nor from the Amerindian languages. According to her, it was related to the Persian *barah* (male prostitute) and the Arabian *bardag* (double sex). Neither she nor Benedict attempted to explain how or why the word was so commonly used in the closing decades of the eighteenth century.
55 Steller, p. 289, and Maximilian, II, p. 132.
56 Klemm, VIII, p. 12. Eliade relegated sexuality to a secondary aspect of Shamanism, yet he nevertheless gave it much attention. See, for example, *Shamanism*, pp. 257–8 and 351-2.
57 Maximilian, II, pp. 132–3 and Waitz, IV, p. 243. Compare also Alfred Robinson, *Life in California*, New York, 1846, reprint New York, 1969, pp. 283–4.
58 Charles de Rechberg, *Les Peuples de la Russie, ou Description des Moeurs, Usages et Costumes des Diverses Nationes de L'Empire de Russie*, 2 vols., Paris, 1812–13), II, sig. 2 recto.
59 Lisiansky, p. 199.
60 Johann Gottlieb Georgi, *Beschreibung aller Nationen des Russischen Reichs, ihrer Lebensart, Religion, Gebräuche, Wohnungen, Kleidungen und Übrigen Merkwürdigkeiten*, 4 pts., St Petersburg, 1776–80, III, p. 376.
61 *Ibid.*, IV, p. 412.
62 Lafitau, *Customs*, I, p. 82.
63 Egede, p. 103.
64 Waitz, IV, p. 133.
65 Holmberg, p. 65.
66 Steller, pp. 278–9.
67 Maximilian, II, pp. 269–70.
68 Joseph Campbell, 'Introduction', *Myth, Religion, and Mother Right: Selected Writings of J. J. Bachofen*, tr. Ralph Mannheim, Bollingen Series LXXXIV, Princeton, 1967, p. xxxiii. In *The Masks of God: Primitive Mythology*, 1959, Campbell had already acknowledged, 'It is, in fact, most remarkable how many primitive hunting races have the legend of a still more primitive age than their own, in which the women were the sole possessors of the magical art' (p. 314).

Index

abdomen, 215
abduction, 183
Aborigines, 262
abortion, 92
abstinence, 35
abuse, sexual, self and verbal, 74, 78, 183, 192, 193, 197, 198, 200, 207, 216, 242, 250
accoucheurs, 216, 218
Acton, William, 196, 208
Adair, Robert, 223
Addison, J., 4, 157, 160, 168
adolescent sexuality, 29
Adorno, T., 6
adultery, 11, 39, 161, 166, 171, 217, 219, 269
adultress, 73, 94, 173
aesthetics, 11, 44, 96, 106, 115, 127, 131, 133
Africa, 248, 262
Akenside, M., 7
alchemy, 269
America, 88, 136, 137, 141, 222, 242, 243, 262, 271
    North, 63, 267
    United States, 195
American Indians, 270, 272
Anacreon, 121
anal intercourse, 74
anatomy, 217, 219
Ancillon, Charles, 56
André, Nathaniel St, 215
androgyny, 141, 163
'animal attraction', 207
animal magnetism, 63, 214
animals and sex, 158, 206, 245, 268, 272, 275, 281
anthropologist, 104, 134, 138, 141
    sexual, 10
anthropology, 102, 136, 138, 262
anti-Christian views, 69, 74, 133
anti-clericalism, 2, 81, 83, 86, 87, 88, 91, 107 108, 110, 115, 117, 118, 122, 129, 130, 133, 135
anti-feminism, 99, 140
anti-Oedipus, 13
anti-onanist, 22, 23, 27, 30, 31, 37, 40
antidote, 87
aphrodisiacs, 63
Apollinaire, Guillaume, 28

INDEX

apothecaries, 207, 209
Arbuthnot, Dr John, 58
archaeology, 78, 89, 91, 101, 102, 103, 119, 122, 138, 140
Arianism, 117
Ariès, P., 6
aristocracy, 127, 129, 131, 158
Aristotelian tradition, 89
Aristotle, 90
    Masterpiece, 8, 48, 88, 93
    Compleat Experienc'd Midwife, 87
    De Generatione et Corruptione, 88
Armstrong, John, 49, 50
Arnauld, George, 248, 249
Arnold, Matthew, 136
Arrowsmith, Stephen, 184
art, 42, 116, 134, 236
    artist's mind, 8
    Hogarth prints, 8
    nudes, 9
art history, 113
artificial insemination, 60
artists
    Boucher, 9, 26
    Cozens, 109
    documentary eye/visual puns, 9
    Fragonard, 26
    Greuze, 26
    Hogarth, 9
    Watteau, 26
asceticism, 34
Ashbee, H. S., 52
assaults, 185, 190
Astell, Mary, 183
Astle, Thomas, 121
Asylum, Lock, 79, 80
Athens, 11
attorneys, 194, 187
Auenbrugger, 212
Augustans, 206
Augustinian tradition, 89, 90 *see also* St Augustine
aura, 172

auscultation, 212
Australia, 198, 262
Austria, 6

babies, 215, 222
Bablot, Louis-Nicolas, 92
baccantes, 118
Bacchus, 166
bachelors, 72, 120, 123, 127, 131
Bachofen, Johann Jakob, 284
bagnios, 77, 166, 167, 171
Balsamo, Guiseppe, alias Count Cagliostro, 63
banishment, 31
Banks, Sir Joseph, 106, 122, 126, 127
barbarism, 40, 109
Barker-Benfield, H., 3
bastards, 79
Bath, 63
Bavaria, 6
bawdy, 10, 48, 55, 58, 60, 61, 63, 70, 71, 79, 80, 163, 167, 199, 208, 209, 219
Baxter, Andrew, 121
beastliness, 200
beasts, 93, 94
Beauclerk, Topham, 231
beauty, 246
beaux, 161, 163
Beckford, William, 108, 109, 141
bedchamber, 70, 77, 81
beliefs, sexual, 86, 87, 92, 96, 133, 193, 195, 200, 206, 268
belladonna, 266
Bellaston, Lady, 168
belles, 161, 175
Bellet, Isaac, 91, 91, 94
belly, 93
Bentham, Jeremy, 2
bestiality, 29, 36, 39, 40, 94
Bienville, N., 249
bigotry, 90, 102
birth, 185, 207, 240, 246, 272, 273

INDEX

birthmarks, 89, 93
birth-rate, 32, 33
bisexuals, 59, 74, 119, 139, 141, 170
Blackstone, W., 196
blasphemy, 170
Bloch, Iwan, 121, 200
Blondel, James Augustus, 89, 96, 94
blood, 90, 91, 94, 256, 275
blood-spitting, 91
blushing, 50, 215
boarding-school, 71
body, 38, 64, 74, 86, 90, 93, 96, 98, 132, 134, 161, 164, 175, 206, 210–12, 236–9, 246, 248, 249, 263–8, 272
Boileau, Jacques, 50
Bolingbroke, Lady, 223, 224
Bolingbroke, Lord, 223
Bolton, Duchess of, 163
Bon Ton magazine, 51, 59
Booty, James, 193
bosom, 49, 93, 164, 211
Boswell, James, 5, 6, 7, 9, 11, 111, 121, 157
botany, 60
Boucher, 26
    nude images, 9
bourgeoisie, 28, 31, 34, 41
Bowdler, Dr, 9
Brantome, 242
breasts, 86–8, 164, 217–19, 246
Britain, 87, 141, 192, 195, 243
British Medical Journal, 195
British Museum, 117
brothels, 3, 51, 71–3, 157, 164–70, 192–3, 196
buggery, 3, 51
Bulgaria, 53
Bullough, V., 245
Burney, Fanny, 169
Burney, James, 269
Byron, Lord, 133, 141

Cadogan, William, 247
Caligula, 170
cannibalism, 268
Canning, George, 130
caricatures, 239–41
carnal acts, 38, 41, 96–7, 132, 171
carnal knowledge, 182–6, 190–2, 208
carnivals, 158–60, 163, 173, 175
Carter, Angela, 9
Casanova, 2, 9, 27, 163
Castaneda, Carlos, 262
Castlemaine, Lady, 209
castrati, 57
castration, 56–7, 183
Cato, 207
Catullus, 122
'celestial bed', 208
celibacy, 32, 36–8, 163, 268
Celts, 274
censorship, 7
ceremony, 269–75
Ceres, 127
Chamfort, 33, 39
Charke, Charlotte, 12, 157, 240, 241
charlatans, 47, 60, 206, 208
Charles II, 14, 158, 208
chastity, 2, 34, 36, 39–40, 41, 244, 267
chemistry, 261
child, sex and the, 79–80, 183–200, 263
child abuse, *see* child, sex and the
childbirth, 10, 87–99, 215–23
child-care, 236
childhood, 6, 196–200, 234–6, 265
child molestation, *see* child, sex and the
China, 11, 116
    patriarchal, 11
Christian morality, 69–70
Christian strictness, 38
    dechristianisation, 31, 102–3, 107, 115, 119, 122, 133–4, 137, 207

INDEX

Christianity, 74–5, 102, 110, 117, 133, 262, 269, 275
Church, Christian, 34–41, 139–40, 193
clandestine sex, 160–71, 223–4
Clarissa Harlowe, 4, 9
Clark, J. C. D., 6
Cleland, J., 71–82, 163, 171, 239
    and homosexuality, 3
clergy, 31–3, 184
clitoridectomy, 247
clitoris, 217, 247, 248, 249
clubs, 52, 131
    molly-clubs, 171, 235
Cobbett, W., 238
coital positions, 37, 69
coition, 6, 55, 89, 93, 97–8, 208, 218, 270–1
Coleridge, S. T., 132, 206
Combe, Dr Charles, 121
Comfort, Alex, 63
conception, 59–61, 88–99
    'false conception', 87–8, 91–3
concubines, 33, 275
confession, 64, 185
congenital malformation, 93–4
conjurers, 161
consent, 99, 181–92, 200, 218
Consistory Court, 74
consummation, 173
contagion, 91
continence, 87, 111, 116, 136, 159
contraception, 34–6
convictions (criminal), 183–93
Cook, Captain James, 269
copulation, *see* coition
Cornelys, Theresa, 159
corruption, 47, 73, 132, 156, 206, 247
    sexually currupt countries, 53
    corrupters, medical practitioners as, 207
Corsica, 32
costume, 157–66, 171–2, 240–1, 262

courts
    criminal, 181–93, 223, 235, 238–9, 245, 249
    royal, 158
Cozens, Alexander, 109
Cozens, John Robert, 109–11, 127, 132
cravings, 87, 91, 106
Crébillon, 26
crime and criminality, 29–31, 75, 80, 181–200 *see also* rape
criminal biography, 173
criminal courts, *see* courts, criminal
criminal law, 200
Criminal Law Amendment Act, 185
criminal obscenity, 123
Crocker, Lester, 3
cross-dressing, 74, 163, 170, 234–46
    en travestie, 11 *see also* Transvestite
cruelty, 199
cuckold, 82
    cuckolddom, 160
    cuckoldry, 168
Cullen, William, 211
Culpeper, Nicholas, 87
cures, 40, 192, 262, 270
    touching cures, 213–15
    for venereal disease, 193–7
Curll, Edmund, 47, 51, 56, 58, 208
Cust, Lionel, 120
Cyclopses, 94
cylinder, 52, 53 *see also* dildo

Daly, Mary, 216
Damer, Judith, 125
Darwin, Dr Erasmus, 1, 60, 207–8
daughters, 79, 173, 194, 205, 214, 241, 250, 269–70, 273
death, 59, 109, 130, 265, 270, 275–6
debauchees, 3, 39
debauchery, 57, 123, 160, 173, 217
decadence, 3, 123, 250
decency, 74, 211–13, 220, 239

INDEX

deception, 237–40, 249
defloration, 161, 271
  'defloration mania', 193, 199
Defoe, Daniel, 160, 173, 238
deformities, 91–9, 246–9
degeneration, 39, 206
delicacy, 211
deliriums, 214, 220
delivery, *see* childbirth
demography, historical, 30–2
demon, 105, 134
d'Eon, Chevalier, 157, 238, 243–6
deportation, 31
Descartes, R., 12, 90
desire, 62, 102, 127, 142, 161, 175, 176, 193
  repression of sexual, 27, 31, 33, 34
destitution, 33, 75
deviance, 28–31, 237, 244, 250
  moral, 32
devil, 166, 174
d'Holbach, 2
Diderot, D., 2, 11, 26, 34, 39, 40
dildo, 53–5
Dilettanti, Society of, 106 ff.
Dionysiacs, 118
disguises, *see* cross-dressing, masquerade
dissection, 248
divorce, 223–4
doctors, 31, 34–40, 46–50, 206 ff.
  The Mock Doctor, 240
domestic service, *see* servants
domesticity, 4, 15, 244, 273
domino, male, 171, 173
Don Giovanni, 3
Doolan, Denis, 205
Dover, 139
dreams, 90–1, 98, 266
Drouart, Michel-Ann, 247
drunkenness, 80, 82
Dryden, John, 175
Duc de Richelieu, 27

Duten, Louis, 117
dwarfs, *see* deformities

Eagleton, Terry, 9
eccentricities, 87
ecstasy, 269
Edinburgh, 211
education, of women, 236–8
Edwards, Susan, 181
effeminacy, 250
Egyptians, 217
Einhorn, Paul, 268
ejaculation, 36, 98
electric, body, 98
Elias, Norbert, 211
Ellis, John, 209
embryology, 91
embryos, 61–3
Empedocles, 88
enema, 209
enigmas, 159 *see also* masquerade
Eros, 174, 175
'eros minoritaire', 13
erotic writings, 14, 69 ff., 112–13, 160–1, 171–4, 215, 242, 249
erotica, 54–7, 64
eroticism, 2, 26, 72, 174, 208
  auto-eroticism, 37,
  'oral eroticism', 14
Ethiopia, 249
ethnography, 262
eugenics, 96
eunuchs, 56–9
Eve, 166
evil, 3, 35, 97
execution, 193
exoticism, 10–12, 112, 161, 261–3

Faderman, Lilian, 13
family, 4, 69, 71, 77–8, 87, 174, 197–9, 250
Fanny Hill, 3, 9, 69 ff.

INDEX

fantasy, 3–5, 72, 82, 87–8, 89, 98, 172, 195, 219
Far East, 116
Farington, B., 121, 130, 131
father, 94, 139, 250
fecundation, 91
fecundity, 38, 61–2, 277
Female Spectator, The, 173
femininity, 235 ff., 263–5
feminism, 82, 174, 221, 237, 250
fertility rites, 116
festivals, 158
fetishistic, 75
fever, 215
Ficino, Marsilio, 88
Fielding, Henry, 12, 54, 75, 156, 157, 160, 168, 170, 246, 247, 248
flagellation, 50, 51, 52, 216
Flaherty, Gloria, 10
Flandrin, Jean-Louis, 30, 31
flattery, 226
flesh, 86, 92, 214, 215, 271, 275, 276
flirtation, 171
flogging, 51, 52
foetus, 61, 86, 88, 90, 93, 98, 99
folklore, 7, 14
fop, 157
'foppery', 246
forceps, 224
fornication, 57, 73
Foster, Francis, 227, 228, 230
Foucault, Michel, 2, 5, 64, 140, 157, 175
Foundling Hospital, 79, 230
Fragonard, 26 see also artists
France, 14, 26, 29, 31, 32, 48, 53, 61, 86, 96, 117, 141, 221, 225, 252
Frazer, Sir James G., 137
Frazier, Dr Alexander, 217
freaks, 56, 86ff. 95, 98, 99, 216
freedom, 28, 32, 33–5, 41, 75, 96, 108, 140, 161, 172, 174
freemasons, 13

French, 30, 59, 72, 131, 207, 230, 250, 253, 257
  hygienists, 92
  ladies, 63
  libertine novels, 75
French Revolution, 8, 28, 42, 64, 128, 136, 141, 160, 251
Freud, S., 2, 28, 29, 41, 137
Freudian, 2, 3, 37, 175, 226
friendship, 13, 106, 111
frigidity, 169
frivolity, 175
Funnell, Peter, 106, 107, 119

Galen, 88
Garrick, David, 223
Gaub, Jerome, 274
Gay, Peter, 6
'gay science', 133
gender, 75, 158, 242, 243, 245, 248, 252, 253, 256, 257, 258, 271, 272, 281
  female, 73
  gender-based division, 4
  revolution, 69
  roles, 15, 75
  stereotype, 8
generation, 256
Geneva, 63
genitalia, 12, 48, 49, 128, 216, 257
Gentleman's Magazine, 51, 98, 163, 164, 247, 249, 252
George II, 159
George IV, 121, 202
Germany, 56, 63
germination, 61
gesture, 172
Gibbon, E., 121
gigolo, 228
God, 35, 95
goddess, 125, 163, 283, 289
gods, 134, 138, 139, 158, 167, 272,

INDEX

277, 283
Godwin, William, 3
Goethe, 7, 261
Goffman, Erving, 211
Goldsmith, O., 131, 157
Gordon, Thomas, 122
Gore, Charles, 110 ff.
Grafton, Duchess of, 223–4
Graham, James, 63, 208, 214
Grand-Jean, Anne, 249
Grand Tour, 108 f.
Gray, Thomas, 7, 110, 125 f.
Greatrakes, Valentine, 213 f.
Greece, 108–9, 111, 113, 115, 133–4, 136, 138, 261, 268
Gregory, Dr John, 210
Greville, Charles, 120
Griffin, Benjamin, 161, 163, 175
grotesque, 105, 134 f., 208, 216
Grub Street, 51 f., 74, 121 f.
Grundyism, 14
Guildhall, 80
guilt, 72, 109, 161, 196, 207
gynaecological literature, 10 *see also* sexual advice literature

Hackert, Philip, 111
Haller, Albrecht, 265
Hamilton, Charles, 238
Hamilton, Emma, 9
Hamilton, Mary, 12, 171, 238 ff.
Hamilton, Sir William, 101 ff.
d'Hancarville, Baron, 101 ff.
Handel, G., 159
harlequins, 163
harlots, *see* prostitution
Harrison, Jane, 137
hashish, 267
Haskell, Francis, 112, 114, 116
Hathaway, Richard, 60
Haymarket, 158 ff.
Haywood, Eliza, 174
healing, 210 ff., 216 f.

health, 87, 96, 193, 212, 216, 220 f.
heathens, 268, 274
Hecquet, 35
hedonism, 133, 139
Heidegger, John James, 159ff., 166
Heliogabalus, 170
Henry VIII, 158
Herdt, Gilbert, 139
hermaphrodite, 12, 51, 57, 59, 148, 163, 234 f., 244 ff., 263, 267
Herodotus, 261, 273 ff.,
heroes, 72, 86, 214, 242
heroine, 71 f., 163, 173, 243
Heron, Robert, 134
heterosexuality, 141, 174, 267
Hill, Fanny *see* Fanny Hill
Hill, Georgiana, 238
Hill, Sir John, 60 ff.
Hippocrates, 88, 261
Hogarth, William, 59, 74, 80, 82, 161, 164, 208, 217
Holland, Lady, 132
Holroyd (Lord Sheffield), 121
homoeroticism, 101 ff., 170, 234
homosexuality, 3, 39, 41, 55 ff., 74 f., 101 ff., 157 f., 167 ff., 209, 272
  punishment of, 30, 35,
  subcultures, 12, 28
homosociality, 101 ff.
honour, 42, 218
Hope, Thomas, 13
hormones, 275
hospitals, 82, 192
Hotel-Dieu, 86
Hotten, J. C., 52
Hottentots, 272
Hugues, Pierre François, 107, 112
humours, 90, 264
Hunter, William, 222 f.
husbands, 4, 73, 77, 82, 94, 96, 131, 171, 174, 217 ff., 237 ff., 250
hymen, 49, 96 ff., 207
hypnotism, 213, 261

INDEX

iconography, 94, 102
idiots, 245
illegitimate births, 30 f., 223, 237
illness, *see* health, venereal disease
imagination, 12, 86 ff., 136, 160, 218, 221, 240, 243, 248, 263
impersonation, 74, 158 ff.
impotence, 33–4, 194
impregnation, 38, 271
incest, 30–1, 173, 198 f., 262
Inchbald, Elizabeth, 163, 169
indecent behaviour, 30, 215 f.
India, 116 f., 263
infanticide, 236
infidelities, 3
Inglis-Jones, Elizabeth, 107
initiation, 265 f.
instruments, 217
intercourse, sexual, 60, 94 f., 173, 215
Irish, Dr David, 213

James, R., 247
Jeffery, Thomas, 164
Jenkins, Thomas, 113
Jews, 103
Johnson, Charles, 164
Johnson, Samuel, 3, 73, 157, 209
Jonathan Wild, 156, 166
Juvenal, 123

Keightley, Thomas, 136
Keuls, Eva, 139, 140
King, Lester S., 88
Kingsley, Charles, 136
Kingston, Duchess of, 166
Kinsey Report, 29
Knight, Richard Payne, 13, 101 ff.
Kolle, Oswalt, 63
Kotzwara, Franz, 52

labia, 217
Lady's Magazine, 169
Lafitau, Joseph François, 266 ff.

Lamettrie, 2
Langbein, John H., 184
La nouvelle Héloïse, 3
law, 14 f., 51 f., 76, 181 f., 249
Lawrence, Sir Thomas, 131
lechery, 208
Leeson, Margaret, 164, 169
legislative reform, 235
Lennox, Charlotte, 156
Lesage, Georges-Louis, 52
lesbian, 53 ff., 74
   history, 13
Lewis, Wilmarth, 127
libertarianism, 1 f., 15, 41, 141
libertinism, 2, 69 ff., 123, 141, 158, 169, 208
libido, 3, 161
Lincoln, Lord, 127 f.
Linnaeus, C., 1, 60
Lock Hospital, 79–80, 193
Locke, J., 236
London, 50 ff., 156 ff., 181 ff.
London Tradesman, The, 79
Lord Hardwick's Marriage Act (1754), 235
Louis XVI, 214, 244
love, 2, 6, 13, 46 ff., 71, 206, 242
   connubial, 96
   love letters, 127
   physical, 28
   venus, 52
Lovelace, 9
love-making, 96, 212
love-sickness, 270
Lucifer, 171
lust, 7, 51, 53, 97, 220, 239, 274
lycanthropy, 268

Macfarland, Thomas, 132
MacHeath, 9
macrocephalous, 94
madness, 28, 41, 220, 245
Magdalen Hospital, 82

INDEX

magic, 14, 34 f., 63, 158, 268 ff.
magistrates, 190, 238
magnetism, 261
maidenheads, 192 f.
Malcolm, James Peller, 104
Malebranche, 87 ff.
malformation, *see* deformity
malnutrition, 90
Malone, Edmund, 101
Mandeville, Bernard, 211
manhood, 140, 273
man-midwives, 14, 206 ff.
Mann, Hermann, 241 f.
manuals, sex, 86 ff., 215 ff.
Marcus, Steven, 138
Marivaux, 26
marriage, 38 f., 53 ff., 110 ff., 182, 185, 200, 231, 234–6, 263
    statistics, 22, 23, 24, 31 f.
    secret, 34 f.
Marten, John, 47 f., 92, 207
Marx, Karl, 28, 29, 34
masculinity, 74 f., 196 f., 234 f., 248–50
Mason, William, 125 f.
masquerade, 11, 156 ff.
masturbation, 2, 10, 31 ff., 64, 207
Mathias, T. J., 122 f.
Maty, Paul Henry, 117
Maubray, John, 94
Mayer, Hans, 13
Mead, Dr Richard, 209
Mears, Martha, 217
medical profession, 206 ff., 236, 248
Meibomius, John Henry, 51
melancholy, 14, 97, 192
menarche, 82
menstruation, 96 f., 195, 274
menstrual blood, 87, 272
menstrual cycle, 276
mercury, 47
Mesmer, Franz Anton, 63, 213 *see also* animal magnetism

Messman, Frank, 106 f.
microscope, 92
midwifery, 86 f., 217 f., 234 f., 261
Milbanke, Judith, 163
Miller, Philip, 60
Miller, Vincent, 61
minors, 181 ff.
missionaries, 263
Mitter, Partha, 116
modesty, 210 f.
molestation, *see* rape
Molière, 207
Moll Flanders, 9, 156, 198
Monro, Dr Thomas, 109
monsters, 88 f., 170, 246 f.
    Frankenstein, 10
    sexual, 58 f., 87
Montagu, Ashley, 104, 137 f.
Montagu, Elizabeth, 164, 207
Montagu, Mary Wortley, 169
Montesquieu, 27
Morland, Henry Robert, 164
Morley, Dr, 222
mother, 139, 168, 193 f., 223 f., 271 f.
motherhood, 87 ff., 234 ff.
Mother Midnight, 216
Murray, Sir Gilbert, 137
mythology, 27, 42, 86 ff., 111, 132 f., 195, 261 f.

Naples, 109 f.
nature, 35 f., 61, 94, 128 f., 137f., 157 f., 247–8, 262 f.
Neo-Hellenism, 112, 116
Neo-Lucretianism, 130
nervous system, 3
    nervous centres, 38
Neumann, Eric, 139
neurosis, 4
Newton, Sir Isaac, 261 f.
Nicholls, Frank, 217
Nietzsche, F. 133
Nihell, Elizabeth, 216

INDEX

nudity, 38, 93
nutrition, 61
nymphae, 217
nymphomania 2, 10, 12, 249

obesity, 36
obscenity, 47, 104, 123, 216
obstetrician, male, 14, 38, 215 ff.
obstetrics, 87, 90 f., 215 ff.
occult, 246
offences, sexual 182 ff., 234 f.
Old Bailey, 184 ff.
opium, 266
Orford, Lord, 131
organs, sexual, 38, 94 f., 219, 247, 270
orientalism, 11, 116 f., 248, 266
Osborne, John, 185
Ossory, Lord, 223
Ovid, 105

paedophilia, 195
paganism, 101 ff., 268 ff.
pain, 49, 62, 79, 215, 223, 265
palpation, 212 f.
Pamela, 4, 8
Pantheon, 160, 164, 169
Paré, Ambroise, 48 f., 89 f.
Parr, Dr Samuel, 133
Parsons, James, 246 f.
Passerano, Count Radicati di, 104
'passing women', 234
paternity, 88
Paterson, Dugal, 205
patients, 208 ff.
patriarchal,
    Christianity, 11, 169, 222
    sexuality, 11
Paulson, Ronald, 8 f.
Pechey, John, 92
pederasty, 271
penetration, 37, 192
penis, 60, 127 f., 217, 246 f.
Pepys, S., 6, 211

Percival, Thomas, 210
perversions, 38, 52, 54, 75, 102, 161, 173, 192, 248
Peter the Great, 109
Petronius, 123
phallus, 101 ff.
pharmacology, 262
physical examination, 212 ff.
physicians, *see* doctors
physiology, 195
pica, 87, 92, 97, 98
pierrots, 161
Pinkerton, John, 134
Pine, Robert Edge, 109
Pitt, Christopher, 159
pleasure, 1, 34 f., 51, 63, 69 f., 82, 140, 160 ff., 208, 218, 237, 241, 248
Pliny, 88
Plutarch, 207
politics, sexual, 105 f.
pollution,
    involuntary, 36
    nocturnal, 36
    voluntary, 36, 40
Polynesians, 11, 270
Pope, Alexander, 57, 95, 130, 238
pornography, 51 f., 101, 113, 164, 170 f., 207–8, 215, 234 f.
Portland, Duke of, 121
potency, 208, 271
poverty, 28
power and sexual relations, 82, 157, 172, 196, 212 f., 267
predator, 14, 206
pregnancy, 91 ff., 269
prejudice, 34, 62
Priapism, 12
Priapus, 101 ff.
Price, Mary, 238 f.
Prince, Uvedale, 128
priesthood, 30, 38, 63, 266 ff.
Priestley, Joseph, 130

INDEX

Prince de Ligne, 27
prints, pornographic, 14, 207ff., 153, 158
procreation, 2, 38, 40, 60, 75, 86, 92f., 174
promiscuity, 56, 102, 158, 261
prosecution, *see* criminal courts
prostitutes, 2, 9 f., 31, 71 f., 160 f., 196, 235, 270
prudery, 116 f., 164, 168
psychology, 12, 64, 95, 159, 172 f., 247, 262, 265
puberty, 49, 271 f.
punishment, 31, 41, 182 f.
Pyle, Revd Edmund, 210

quackery, 46 f., 192, 206, 236 f.
Quakers, 171
Quillet, Claude, 49, 96

Raleigh, Sir Walter, 117
Rambler's Magazine, 57
Ranelagh, 159 f., 166, 172
rape, 15, 29, 31, 161, 181 ff., 219, 221
Raphael, 132
rapists, 15, 174, 190 ff.
Reed, Joseph, 215
Reformation, 2
    Counter-reformation, 2
Regnault, 94
Reiser, Stanley, 213
religion, pagan, 113 f., 265 f.
repression, 41, 108, 109, 141
    in society, 27 ff.
    of sexuality,
reproduction, sexual, 34 f., 207
Restoration, 105, 141
Richardson, Samuel, 4, 7, 160
Richetti, John, 173
ridottos, 159
ritual, 102 ff., 158, 234, 238, 266 ff.
    initiation, 11
Robson, L. L., 198

Rochester, Earl of, 141, 158
Rococo,
    civilisation, 5
Rogers, Pat, 241
Rogers, Samuel, 133
roles,
    lesbian, 75
romance, 11, 69 f., 134 *see also* love
Rome, 207
Rousseau, J. J., 3 f., 26, 34, 39, 41, 129
Rowe, Nicholas, 96
Royal College of Physicians, 89, 217
Royal Society, 60, 208, 247
Russen, Revd Benjamin, 193

Sade, Marquis de, 3, 9, 27, 42, 174
Said, Edward, 10
St. Augustine, 89, 95
    Augustinian tradition, 90
St Jerome, 89
Sampson, Deborah, 243 f.
Sandwich, Lady, 212
satire, 54, 58, 88, 161, 167 f., 206 f., 238
    satirical cartoons, 51, 54
savages, 11
Scaliger, 105, 134
scandal, 163, 164, 170
science, 246 f., 261 f.
    applied to sex, 46, 61, 88 f., 111, 137, 195, 207
    scientists, 214, 240
Scythians, 273
'seances', 214, 262, 268
Sedgwick, Owen, 156
seduction, 10, 76 f., 160, 173
self-display, 161 f.
semen, 3, 37, 60, 61, 96, 140, 271 f.
Sennett, Richard, 211
sensuality, 2, 5, 39, 57, 132, 158, 168f.
servants, 12, 39, 42, 61, 71, 76 ff., 140, 198, 212, 223, 240

INDEX

sex,
    hostility to, 39
    interpretations of, 5
    kinky, 52
    lust and sin, 8
    satisfaction, 28
sexologists,
    Masters and Johnson, 38
sexology, 2, 13, 37, 57, 207
sexual aberrations, 247
    abstinence, 267
    abuse, 196 f.
    advice literature, 48 f.
    Aristotle's *Masterpiece*, *Onania*, 7
    Aristotle's *Masterpiece* and Venette's *Tableau de l'amour conjugal*, 48
    aids, 52
    attitudes, 6, 16
    attraction, 237 f.
    custom, 119
    danger, 168, 212
    decorum, 168
    defamation, 75
    desires, 30, 64
    deviance, 236, 244
    disorder, 170
    education, 40
    emancipation, 168
    enlightenment, 3, 129, 140, 141
    fantasies, 64
    fertility, 125
    freaks, 207
    freedom, 28, 174
    identity, 238
    imitation, 265
    licence, 208, 214
    perversity, 54
    radicals, 174
    subculture, 164
    therapy, 62
Shamanism, 261 ff.
shame, 72, 171, 196, 220

Shelley, Mary, 10
Simpson, Anthony, 5, 15
sin,
    buggery, 2,
    lust and sex, 9, 54, 58, 95, 98
Sinibaldi, Giovanni Benedetto, 89, 207
Slop, Dr, 215
smallpox, 91
Smellie, William, 215 f.
Smollett, Tobias, 87, 160, 171
Snell, Hannah, 242
Society for the Reformation of Manners, 74
Society of Dilettanti, *see* Dilettanti, Society of,
sodomite, 2, 7, 28, 50, 72, 106 ff., 169f., 235, 273
'Spanker, Colonel', 199
Spence, Joseph, 127
Spinke, John, 47
spinsters, 241
spirits, 90, 99, 266 f.
spouses, 38, 223, 224, 275 *see also* wife
Starobinski, Jean, 140, 174
Stephen, Mary, 215
sterility, 39
Sterne, Laurence, 15, 98, 210, 215
stethoscope, 212
Stone, Lawrence, 6, 105
Stone, Sarah, 214
Streetser, Thomas, 61
stroking, 213, 272 *see also* Greatrakes, Valentine
Stukeley, William, 210
Stumpf, Claudia, 110
suckling, 237
suicide, 139
Swift, Dean Jonathan, 94, 238
Symonds, John Addington, 132

taboos, 10, 46, 60, 63, 104 f., 136, 139, 167 f.

INDEX

Tahiti, 3
Tahitians, 10 f., 269 f.
Talbot, Susanna, 185
Talmud, 183
testicles, 272
theology, 133
Thicknesse, Philip, 215 ff.
Thirlwall, Connop, 136
Thompson, Roger 208
Thurlow, Edward, 121
Tissot, sexual literature, 93
Tofts, Mary, 61, 90, 207
Toland, John, 143
Tom Jones, 9, 168
touch, 168, 206 ff.
Townley, Charles, 101ff.
Tracy, Destutt de, 128f.
transsexuals, 59
  transsexuality, 209, 274
transvestism, 156 ff., 234 ff., 273 see also cross dressing
travestie, see cross dressing
Tristram Shandy 10, 11, 97, 99, 134, 210, 215
Turner, Daniel, 89 ff.
Turner, Frank, 136
Tyburn, 194

umbilical cord, 91
urban, 31, 156 f., 172, 192 f.
Ussel, J. van, 30, 41
Utopian, 169

vagina, 218 ff., 247
Vanbutchell, Martin, 63
vanity, 42, 87
venereal disease, 47, 51, 80, 82, 92, 185, 192 ff., 207
venerology, 206
Venette, Nicolas, 12, 36, 48, 92, 207
  Tableau de l'amour conjugal, 7, 48, 92, 206
Venus, 52, 160, 168, 208

vices, 206, 218, 241, 244, 274
victimisation, 199
victims, 41, 99, 181 ff.
Victorians, 136 f., 182 f., 198, 199
violence, 37, 61, 91, 183 f., 198
virginity, 49, 61, 168, 169, 211, 267, 271
virility, 38
visions, 263
Vizzani, Catherine, 248, 249
Voltaire, 26
voyeurism, 27, 163

Wadd, William, 222
Walkowitz, Judith, 15
Walpole, Horace, 105 ff., 158, 163
Ward, Ned, 51
Washington, General, 244
Watteau, 26, 74
wedlock, 274, see also marriage
Weimar, 110
Welch, Saunders, 72, 74
Westall, Richard, 132
wet-nursing, 78
whipping, 52, 81, 208, 209, 239
whores, see prostitution
wife, 2, 41, 53, 72, 77 f., 114, 132, 158 f., 164, 174, 182, 211, 212, 218, 219, 222, 236 f., 249, 265, 270, 273, 274
  Victorian, 4
Wilbraham, Roger, 120
Wilde, Oscar, 132
Wilkes, John, 11, 111, 122 f., 141
Williams, Charles Hanbury, 128
Willis, Thomas, 90
Willughby, Percival, 215
Wilson, Harriette, 164, 169
Winckelmann, 113 f.
witchcraft,
  trials, 28, 262, 266
Wollstonecraft, Mary, 174, 237
womb, 48, 62, 87, 97 f., 174, 215, 248

INDEX

Woodward, Dr John, 209
Wordsworth, William, 132
wounds, 91
Wright, Thomas, 136

Yahoos, 94

Zodiac, 97
Zoffany, J, 114 f.
zoophile, 41